Unlocking the Mysteries of Cataloging

Unlocking the Mysteries of Cataloging

A Workbook of Examples

Elizabeth Haynes and Joanna F. Fountain

Foreword by Michael Gorman

Westport, Connecticut • London

Library of Congress Cataloging-in-Publication Data

Haynes, Elizabeth (Dorothy Elizabeth)
Unlocking the mysteries of cataloging : a workbook of examples / Elizabeth Haynes and Joanna F. Fountain ; foreword by Michael Gorman.
p. cm.
Includes bibliographical references and indexes.
ISBN 1-59158-008-0 (alk. paper)
1. Cataloging—Specimens. 2. Cataloging—Problems, exercises, etc. 3. Anglo-American cataloguing rules—Problems, exercises, etc. 4. MARC formats—Problems, exercises, etc. I. Fountain, Joanna F. II. Title.
Z693.3.S65H39 2005
025.3—dc22 2005009198

British Library Cataloguing in Publication Data is available.

Library of Congress Catalog Card Number: 2005009198
ISBN: 1-59158-008-0

First published in 2005

Libraries Unlimited, 88 Post Road West, Westport, CT 06881
A Member of the Greenwood Publishing Group, Inc.
www.lu.com

Printed in the United States of America

The paper used in this book complies with the Permanent Paper Standard issued by the National Information Standards Organization (Z39.48–1984).

10 9 8 7 6 5 4 3 2 1

Dedication

This work is dedicated to all our students, past and future, who have asked prodding questions and helped us to focus on the needs of the learner as well as of the ultimate catalog user, and to our families and colleagues, who have encouraged us throughout the process of taking our ideas all the way to a finished product.

Elizabeth Haynes Hattiesburg, Mississippi	Joanna F. Fountain Austin, Texas

Contents

Foreword

One of the great sadnesses of modern library education is the de-emphasis of cataloguing (I prefer the *AACR2* spelling) as a central element of what every librarian should know and essential training in how to think like a librarian. It is a shocking fact that it is possible to graduate from some American Library Association–accredited Library and Information Service (LIS) schools with a master's in library science (or equivalent) without ever having taken a course in cataloguing. I am therefore delighted to welcome this valuable work, which can be used at many levels and in many ways to increase the quantum of knowledge about this most important of library topics.

This workbook has an allied Web site, which is a good example of useful symbiosis between print and digital technology—a good deed in a naughty world. The examples are drawn from all the categories of material dealt with by Part I of *AACR2* and present all relevant information from the appropriate chief source of information. They are accompanied by the relevant *AACR2* rule numbers and questions and instructions, all of which focus the students' attention on the rules they need to produce a complete and accurate bibliographic record. Because the examples are arranged in an increasing order of difficulty, a student can work at her or his own pace. The associated Web site contains full bibliographic and MARC (MAchine Readable Cataloging) records for each example, which are password protected for instructors. I believe the workbook and Web site will provide a flexible tool for teaching and learning, both for classroom and Web-enhanced asynchronous instruction and for self-study. It should appeal to LIS teachers and students in cataloguing courses, to cataloguing teachers as a supplementary tool in their own teaching, and to cataloguers to use a supplement to their codes and manuals of practice. I commend Drs. Fountain and Haynes on the concept and execution of this valuable tool and commend its use to all engaged in learning about and practicing cataloguing—the central art of librarianship.

Michael Gorman
Dean of Library Services
California State University, Fresno
Editor, AACR2 *(1978 and 1988 revision)*
Author, The Concise AACR2

Introduction

When we were in graduate school studying to be librarians, there was no such thing as *Anglo-American Cataloguing Rules*, and MAchine Readable Cataloguing (MARC) was only something that the Library of Congress was using—nothing we'd ever need to know much about. Subject headings all came from one's local authority file, which was maintained on cards, and "classification" was almost entirely synonymous with Dewey.

But there *were* rules and a format. There *were* authority files. Items were classified—largely by subject—and there was a growing interest in adding nonprint materials to library collections. It was all there, and we learned what there was to learn at that time. That knowledge has carried us through to the present, when we have international sets of rules, standards, authority files, and electronic tools to help with the creation of catalogs that anyone in the world with access to the Internet can use to find an item in a library!

We have chosen as examples for cataloging practice real books, recordings, objects, maps, and so forth. Most of these items—or other similar ones—may be found readily for examination or further experience. It is our intent to give at least one or two examples of a wide variety of types of materials that are currently to be found in libraries. The only major format that we did not include is serials. We selected items from public, school, academic, and special libraries and have arranged at least the book examples in some order of difficulty, from our perspective as teachers. The nonbook examples are arranged in format groups after all the books, with only some degree of order of ease. Probably the most challenging examples involve the same title in a variety of versions and formats—such as the Mother Goose and Lord of the Rings titles. Teachers will find such groups of particular use, because they serve to highlight differences in treatment from one medium or version to another.

It will be most helpful in using this book if the user has access to a combination of print and electronic resources, including access to the Internet via the World Wide Web. At the end of this introduction you will find a basic list of resources, to which you will want to add as you discover others that help you in your learning, practice, and teaching.

You will find it useful to go to the Book Companion Web site that supplements this book: <http://www.lu.com/workbook>. There you will be able to see more details, enlarge the views of what is necessarily tiny for reproduction here and enjoy seeing the color and layout of the sources needed for cataloging and teaching. The companion Web site includes a special password protected section for instructors who adopt the workbook for a course. You may get a password when you review or adopt the workbook. For more information, email <workbook@lu.com>.

You should know that there are some things we did not try to do. First, this is not a textbook, although we hope it will be useful as a companion to the existing textbooks in the field. To identify successfully the content of any cataloging record, you will need access to a copy (print or electronic) of the publication *Anglo-American Cataloging Rules*, 2nd revised edition (*AACR2r*). We used the Rules current as of the 2003 amendments to select the rules to be followed but did not quote them here. If a more recent edition is in force when you use this workbook, you may find it useful to have a copy of the 2003 issue available for reference. Most rules do not change much over time, although the significance of some rule changes may be great. Second, we did not attempt to give any direction as to the creation of physical cards, or to include any practice with filing order. In a computer-based environment, operating systems and software govern filing order; when changes are needed they are made in these areas, and it is difficult (if not impossible) to override such basic elements of computer programs at the user end. If you need information in these areas—and there is certainly good material available—you may search in your library or on the Internet, or ask a librarian for assistance.

We have provided a very general form to be used in drafting cataloging records for all types of materials. You will need to add to it or change it when a field or subfield is missing or is to be repeated, but at least one tag is provided for most fields that are likely to be needed. The print version is included in this book see pp. xxi–xxii; it may be photocopied and reproduced as needed. An electronic version, which can also be used as a template, is available on the Web site <http://www.lu.com/workbook>. That form has advantages for adding and deleting, as well as for printing out copies of easily edited drafts.

The example pages are laid out with the chief source of information usually in the top left or center of the page. Additional images from various locations of the book or packaging are also included. We have provided information as to extent, measurements, and so on where these facts cannot be ascertained from the images shown. We have also listed *AACR2r* rules that we feel are needed for completing the catalog record. In listing rules, we have emphasized those in Chapter One, which applies to all formats. Rules from format-specific chapters are also included. Listed with the rules are references to some specific MARC fields that will be needed, such as MARC 010 for Library of Congress Control Number. Although two of the indexes are to *AACR2r* rule numbers, we have not attempted to include every possible use of a given rule in the index.

The examples are real items, but any workbook of this type is, of necessity, an artificial source for cataloging information. In the real world, you would have access to the item itself and could examine the contents carefully to determine subject headings, classification, and so forth. Within the constraints of the printed page we have attempted to provide as much information as possible for you to complete a catalog record for the item. MARC "answer" records are provided in the back of the book for some, but by no means all, of the exercises.

To know how much information to include, you should follow the guidelines for the various descriptive levels found in *AACR2* in rule 1.0D2; level two is the standard level. You may also follow the slightly modified "core" levels; links to these standards are included in the resource list. To the information required by these rules, add one or more subject terms and, when appropriate, terms for literary genre or form. Tools exist in print and online; for the most widely used, see the resource list. A list of genre terms is found in Appendix A. Finally, add the local call number, which can be based on the Dewey Decimal or Library of Congress classifications, or any other scheme used in a given library.

The amount and type of information provided in each record should satisfy the three objectives of the catalog: to find a known item, to find out what else is available, and to select from what is available (see p. xiv). To meet each objective we provide the actual or probable name or title of the item, the name of each responsible person or entity that is likely to be used for seeking the item, and any terms that may be considered to be the subject or form of the work and that might be sought by the catalog user. Many tools—compilations and lists in many languages—are available to aid in describing and assigning search terms and standardized forms of names so that the user's time in locating information is kept to a minimum (see p. xv) while their likelihood of success is maximized. This does not always save the time of the cataloger, but by following standards in each area one may conserve much time and provide maximum benefits to the future searcher. When the standard tools do not accommodate the nature of a particular work or item, there are groups to which one may refer to get excellent help in a short time. The largest of these is the AUTOCAT discussion list; members of the rulemaking bodies as well as compilers of the tools and instructors are available for assistance at all times when local resources have been exhausted. Please see the resource list for information on that list and others.

Unlock our Web site! http://www.lu.com/workbook.

Notes

[1] See Objectives of Cataloging (Cutter's ...), page xiv.
[2] See Ranganathan's Five Laws of Library Science (Ranganathan's ...), page xv.

Information for the Instructor

This book of examples and exercises is intended as a supplement to general cataloging textbooks. We hope it will be a source for assignments and testing.

The supplemental Web site includes reproductions of the graphic files, where they can be enlarged and studied more closely. Additional files, including enhanced MARC records for each exercise in the book, are also available on the Web site in a separate section for instructors. This section can be accessed by obtaining a password from Libraries Unlimited by e-mailing <workbook@lu.com>.

The order of the exercises on books is intended to reflect increasing difficulty; nonbook materials are grouped by format, rather than by difficulty. We have included several related groupings of materials in various formats that can be used for compare-and-contrast assignments. These include:

- Lord of the Rings and Tolkien—#40, 45, 50, 102, 103, 147, 148
- Mother Goose—#71, 72, 73
- Buffy the Vampire Slayer—#38, 44, 89, 149
- Graphic novels—#47, 89, 90, 91
- Non-English-language or bilingual materials—#21, 52, 66, 67, 69, 70, 80, 81, 98, 120, 135, 139, 140

Most exercises are laid out with the chief source of information in the upper left-hand corner or top center of the page. The CIP was excised from title page verso reproductions in most cases, except where exercise instructions require finding mistakes in the CIP. However, the full page is shown in the instructors' section of the related Web site.

We have included MARC records for approximately one-third of the examples in the workbook itself. The MARC records for all the examples can be found in the instructors' section of the Web site.

If you find mistakes or have suggestions for changes or improvements, please contact one of the authors via Libraries Unlimited. Comments are welcome.

Acknowledgments

We would like to acknowledge the assistance of the following graduate assistants in the School of Library and Information Science, University of Southern Mississippi: Linda Ginn, Suzanne Hays Mangrum, Sharon Davis, Patti Condon, Heather Weeden. These students checked rules, located materials, helped with scanning, and spent many hours proofreading. Stacey Chambers, in Texas, did a lot of the initial scanning, and we appreciate her help in getting started with this lengthy process.

The materials included were borrowed from the Georgetown Public Library (Texas); the Library of Hattiesburg, Petal and Forrest County (Mississippi); and the Cook Library of the University of Southern Mississippi if they were not owned by one of the authors. We appreciate the work of those who selected and cataloged them for those libraries. We borrowed two personally owned items from other individuals: the puppets from Rosemary Chance and the geode from Josh Chance, who also provided the detailed description. We benefited from their generosity.

Objectives of Cataloging

Objects, Means, and Reasons for Choice in a Dictionary Catalog

Charles A. Cutter*

Objects

1. To enable a person *to find a book* of which either
   (A) the author
   (B) the title
   (C) the subject is known.

2. To *show what the library has*
   (D) by a given by author
   (E) on a given subject
   (F) in a given kind of literature.

3. To *assist in the choice of a book*
   (G) as to its edition (bibliographically)
   (H) as to its character (literary or topical).

Means

1. Author-entry with the necessary references (for A and D).
2. Title-entry or title-reference (for B).
3. Subject-entry, cross-references, and classed subject-table (for C and E).
4. Form-entry and language-entry (for F).
5. Giving edition and imprint, with notes when necessary (for G).
6. Notes (for H).

Reasons for Choice

Among the several possible methods of attaining the OBJECTS, other things being equal, choose that entry

1. That will probably be first looked under by the class of people who use the library;

2. That is consistent with other entries, so that one principle can cover all;

3. That will mass entries least in places where it is difficult to so arrange them that they can be readily found, as under names of nations and cities.

This applies very slightly to entries under first words, because it is easy and sufficient to arrange them by the alphabet.

*Cutter, Charles A. *Rules for a Dictionary Catalog,* 4th ed., rewritten. Washington, D.C.: Government Printing Office, 1904. "General Remarks," pp. 11–12.

Ranganathan's Five Laws of Library Science

Books are for use.
Every book its reader.
Every reader his book.
Save the time of the reader.
A library is a growing organism.

"S. R. Ranganathan invented the term *library science*. He believed that all human activities were susceptible to analysis by using the scientific method and that such a careful examination of the phenomena of library work could lead to the formulation of empirical 'laws.' His are clearly not laws in the sense that, say, the Second Law of Thermodynamics is a law. However, they are more than mere generalities because they are founded on observation and analysis by a trained mind. (Dr. Ranganathan was originally a mathematician.) He, like that other genius of librarianship, Melvil Dewey, used high intelligence, the scientific approach, and considerable experience in his rethinking of our profession."*

*Gorman, Michael. *Our Singular Strengths: Meditations for Librarians.* Chicago: American Library Association, 1998. "Ranganathan's Five Laws," p. 55.

Keys You Need to Get Started Bibliography of Cataloging Tools and Aids

General

Cataloging Correctly for Kids: An Introduction to the Tools. Zuiderveld, Sharon, ed. 3rd ed. Chicago: American Library Assn., 1998. ISBN: 0-8389-3476-5. [Chapter 1 contains the Guidelines to be followed for "juvenile" catalogs] [*1 = ordering address] (out of print; 4th ed. forthcoming [2005])

AUTOCAT [electronic list for discussion of cataloging and authority topics]: http://ublib.buffalo.edu/libraries/units/cts/autocat/autocats.html

For Description of Materials

Basic

Anglo-American Cataloguing Rules (AACR2r). 2nd ed., 2002 revision. Ottawa: Canadian Library Assn.; Chicago: American Library Assn., 2002–. 1 v. ISBN: 0838935303 (loose-leaf without binder); 083893529X (loose-leaf with binder) [*1]

LC/NACO Authority Files. Online at LC: http://authorities.loc.gov/

Chart of PCC BIBCO Core Record Standards: http://www.loc.gov/catdir/pcc/bibco/core2002.html

Aids

Gorman, Michael. ***The Concise AACR2. 4th ed.*** Chicago: American Library Assn., 2004. [168 p.] ISBN: 0-8389-34943 (pbk.) [*1]

Maxwell, Robert L., with Margaret F. Maxwell. ***Maxwell's Handbook for AACR2R: Explaining and Illustrating the Anglo-American Cataloguing Rules and the 1993 Amendments.*** Chicago: American Library Assn., 1997. [522 p.] ISBN: 0-8389- [*1]

Olson, Nancy B. ***Cataloging of Audiovisual Materials and Other Special Materials: A Manual Based on AACR2.*** 4th ed., with addendum. DeKalb, Ill.: Minnesota Scholarly Press, 1998. [326 p.] ISBN: 0-933474-53-9 [*2]

For MARC Bibliographic Records

Basic

MARC 21: Format for Bibliographic Data, Including Guidelines for Content Designation. Washington, D.C.: Library of Congress. Cataloging Distribution Service, 1999. [2 v.] ISBN: 0-8444-0989-8 [*3]

Aids

Furrie, Betty. ***Understanding MARC Bibliographic: Machine-Readable Cataloging.*** 7th ed. Available online at http://www.loc.gov/marc/umb/ Paper copy [24 pp.] [ISBN 0-8444-1081-0] from Follett Software Co. (free) [*6], and Library of Congress [*3]

Piepenburg, Scott. ***Easy MARC: A Simplified Guide to Creating Catalog Records for Library Automation Systems Incorporating Format Integration.*** 4th ed. San Jose, Calif.: F&W Associates, 2002. [222 p.] ISBN: 0-9652126-2-9 (Distributed by LMC Source [*4])

Software

MARC Magician [cataloging template software]. Educational Version 2.0.5 (Windows only). Madison, Wis.: Information Transform, 2003. [CD-ROM + 1 manual] [*5] Trial version can be downloaded at http://www.mitinet.com/Support/s_mm_demo.htm

Classification

Basic

Abridged Dewey Decimal Classification and Relative Index. 14th ed. Dublin, Ohio: OCLC Online Computer Library Center, 2004. [1050 p.] ISBN: 0-910-60873-3 [*7]

Dewey Decimal Classification and Relative Index. Devised by Melvil Dewey. 22nd ed., edited by Joan S. Mitchell, *et al*. Dublin, Ohio : OCLC, 2003. [4 v.] ISBN: 0-910608-70-9 (set) [*7]

Aids

Davis, Sydney W., and Gregory R. New. ***Abridged 13 Workbook for Small Libraries Using Dewey Decimal Classification Abridged Edition 13.*** Albany, N.Y: Forest Press, 1997. [71 p.] ISBN: 0-910608-61-X (spiral pbk.) [*7] (Out of print; available via interlibrary loan)

Dewey 22: Summaries. http://www.oclc.org/dewey/resources/summaries/deweysummaries.pdf

Scott, Mona L. ***Dewey Decimal Classification, 22nd Edition: A Study Manual and Number Building Guide.*** Westport, CT: Libraries Unlimited, 1998. [198 p.] ISBN: 1-59158-210-5 (forthcoming May 2005) [*8]

Subject Headings

Basic

***Library of Congress Subject Headings* (LCSH).** 28th ed. Washington, D.C.: Library of Congress. Catalog Distribution Service, 2005. [5 v.] ISSN: 1086-8711 (updating information available at www.loc.gov. Orders: Fax 202-707-1334 or online at http://www.loc.gov/cds/ [*3]

Aids

Fountain, Joanna F. ***Subject Headings for School and Public Libraries: An LCSH/Sears Companion.*** 3rd ed. Englewood, Colo.: Libraries Unlimited, 2001. [208 p.] ISBN: 1-56308-853-3 [*9]

Guidelines on Subject Access to Fiction, Drama, Etc. 3rd ed. Chicago: American Library Assn., 2000. [67 p.] ISBN: 0-8389-3503-6. [*1]

People, Places & Things: A List of Popular Library of Congress Subject Headings with Dewey Numbers. Dublin, Ohio: OCLC Forest Press, 2001. [421 p.] ISBN: 0-910-60869-5 [*7]

Scott, Mona L. ***Conversion Tables, Volume 3: Subject Headings—LC and Dewey.*** 2nd ed. Englewood, Colo.: Libraries Unlimited, 1999. [250 p.] ISBN: 1-56308-849-5 [*8]

Šauperl, Alenka. ***Subject Determination during the Cataloging Process.*** Lanham, Md.: Scarecrow Press, 2002. [173 p.] ISBN: 0-8108-4289-0 [*9]

Subject Headings for Children. 2nd ed. Dublin, Ohio: OCLC Forest Press, 1998. [2 v.] ISBN: 0-910-608-58-X [*8] (Out of print; available via interlibrary loan)

Publisher and Distributor Addresses

1. ALA Editions: 50 E. Huron St., Chicago, IL 60611

2. Soldier Creek Press: P.O. Box 10, Belle Plaine, MN 56011. Send P.O. or check for $75. Voice: 507-726-2985; Fax: 952-873-2379.

3. Library of Congress, Cataloging Distribution Service, Washington, D.C. 20541-4912; Voice: 800-255-3666, 202-707-6100; Fax: 202-707-1334l; e-mail: cdsinfo@loc.gov)

4. LMC Source, P.O. Box 131266, Spring, TX 77393; Tel.: 800-873-3043

5. Information Transform, Inc., 6409 Odana Road, Madison, WI 53719-1125 (*MARC Magician* is also available from various other companies.)

6. OCLC/Forest Press, 6565 Frantz Road, Dublin, OH 43017-3395

7. Libraries Unlimited, P.O. Box 6926, Portsmouth, NH 03802-6926, or 88 Post Road West, Westport, CT 06881; 800-225-5800

8. Rowman & Littlefield Publishing Group, 15200 NBN Way, Blue Ridge Summit, PA 17214-0191; 800-462-6420

About MARC

This book is not the place to learn all about MARC. There are numerous sources available for that purpose. A brief introduction to MARC is useful, however.

MARC stands for MAchine Readable Cataloging. It was developed by the Library of Congress as a means of encoding bibliographic records so that they could be read and displayed, and shared by computers. The MARC 21 format is the standard used today for encoding catalog records in automated library catalog systems. MARC records are portable and can be imported and exported easily. The Library of Congress maintains and revises the MARC standards, and additional information can be found at http://www.loc.gov/marc/marcginf.html. There are variations in standard USMARC that are used by various countries and organizations, such as OCLC (Online Computer Library Catalog). These variations are usually minor and mostly concern such things as holdings fields and other local fields.

MARC records consist of fields (or tags), subfields, and indicators. There is a directory and leader field, as well as several fixed-length fields with coded information. The bibliographic content of the record is displayed in variable-length fields. A fuller explanation can be found in *Understanding MARC Bibliographic* (available on the Web at http://www.loc.gov/marc/umb/).

A MARC record as it is downloaded into your system is a collection of numbers and letters, an example of which follows. As you can see, some content is recognizable, but it is not easy to decipher. The directory (the long string of numbers at the beginning) contains the code that enables the computer to decipher the MARC record. Again, a fuller explanation can be found in *Understanding MARC Bibliographic.*

01185cam 2200301 a
450000100080000000500170000800800410002503500210006690600450008701000170
013202000250014904000180017404100110019204200090020305000230021208200120
023510000280024724000460027524500710032125000190039226000390041130000400
045050000530049052002290054365000280077270000210080099100620082l-2404562
-19920323074137.7-860306s1986 nyua j 000 1 eng – 9(DLC) 86005011- a7
bcbc corignew d1 eocip f19 gy-gencatlg- a 86005011 - a0399213112 :c$13.95-
aDLCcDLCdDLC-1 aengjpn- alcac-00aPZ7.A5875bAl 1986-00a[E]219-1 aAnno,
Mitsumasa,d1926—10aMarui chiky¯u no maru ichinichi.lEnglish-10aAll in a day /cby
Mitsumasa Anno and Raymond Briggs ... [et al.].- a1st U.S.A. ed.- aNew York
:bPhilomel Books,c1986.- a[22] p. :bcol. ill. ;c25 x 27 cm.- aTranslation of: Marui
chiky¯u no maru ichinichi.- aBrief text and illustrations by ten internationally well-
known artists reveal a day in the lives of children in eight different countries showing the
similarities and differences and emphasizing the commonality of humankind.-
1aBrotherlinessxFiction.-1 aBriggs, Raymond.- bc-GenCollhPZ7.A5875iAl
1986p00010212005tCopy 1wBOOKS-

In addition to its "raw" state (see above), there are two basic ways in which MARC records are displayed. One way can be described as horizontal, in that all of the subfields will be displayed in a horizontal line. The other way is vertical, with the subfields "stacked" in a vertical display. Following are examples of horizontal and vertical displays.

"Horizontal" Display

```
245 04    The adventures of Safety Frog. $p Fire safety $h [video-
          recording] / $c Century 21 Video, Inc.
246 30    Fire safety $h [videorecording]
260 ##    Van Nuys, Calif. : $b AIMS Media, $c 1988.
300 ##    1 videocassette (10 min.) : $b sd., col. ; $c 1/2   in.
```

"Vertical" Display

```
Title              245  10  $a Make the team.
                            $p Soccer :
                            $b a heads up guide to super soccer! /
                            $c Richard J. Brenner
Variant Title      246  30  $a Heads up guide to super soccer
Edition            250  ##  $a 1st ed.
Publication        260  ##  $a Boston :
                            $b Little, Brown,
                            $c c1990.
Phys Desc          300  ##  $a 127 p. :
                            $b ill. ;
                            $c 19 cm.
```

OCLC records normally appear with a workform format for the fixed fields, so that the fixed field tags and subfield codes do not actually appear. An example follows.

OCLC Workform

```
                                         ¶ CAT                    SID: 00033        OL
Beginning of record displayed.

OLUC

   OCLC:  NEW                      Rec stat:     n
   Entered:      19951207          Replaced:     19951207        Used:      19951207
 ▸ Type:   a     ELvl:   ■        Srce:   ■     Audn:          Ctrl:          Lang:  ■■■
   BLvl:   m     Form:            Conf:   0     Biog:          MRec:          Ctry:  ■■■
                 Cont:            GPub:         Fict:   0      Indx:   0
   Desc:   ■     Ills:            Fest:   0     DtSt:   ■      Dates:  ■■■■,        ¶
 ▸   1  010      ¶
 ▸   2  040      ‡c TRN ¶
 ▸   3  020      ¶
 ▸   4  041 ■    ‡h ‡b  ¶
 ▸   5  050 ■    ‡b  ¶
 ▸   6  090      ‡b  ¶
 ▸   7  049      TRNG ¶
 ▸   8  1■■ ■    ¶
 ▸   9  245 ■■   ‡b ‡c  ¶
 ▸  10  246 ■■   ¶
 ▸  11  250      ¶
 ▸  12  260      ‡b ‡c  ¶
 ▸  13  300      ‡b ‡c  ¶
```

In most on-screen displays of MARC records, the tag (or field number) is given to the left, followed by the indicators (if any) and the subfields. Some displays may have a brief field description at the far left. Consult the examples given here to locate these various parts, which as a group are called "content designation."

Delimiters are used to signal the computer that the next letter or number is a subfield code. Several different characters are used as delimiters: $, #, ‡, or |. In the examples provided above, $ is used as a delimiter.

An understanding of the basic MARC format is necessary before you can construct good catalog records in an automated environment. See the "Keys You Need to Get Started" section for resources that will help you learn about MARC.

This is an all-format workform. Add, omit, or repeat fields and subfields as needed. Give the preceding punctuation required at the end of the preceding subfield, even if it is a different field (see "vertical" Display, p. xx). Delimit each new subfield with a pipe mark (|) or dollar sign ($). For links to cataloging codes, see note 1.[1]

This workform will not yield an electronic record capable of being uploaded (imported) into a machine-readable catalog. To create a true MARC record you will need to use a MARC program. See the link that follows[2] to download a free trial copy of a stand-alone MARC template program.

You may use this file as a template for word processing by making a copy of it and renaming each copy, such as "Exercise1." You may also want to print one or more copies so that you can create draft records away from the computer.

<table>
<tr><td>006</td><td></td><td>_ _</td></tr>
<tr><td>007</td><td></td><td>_ _</td></tr>
<tr><td>008</td><td></td><td>_ _</td></tr>
<tr><td>010</td><td></td><td>|a</td></tr>
<tr><td>020</td><td></td><td>|a</td></tr>
<tr><td>02 _</td><td></td><td>|a</td></tr>
<tr><td></td><td></td><td>|?</td></tr>
<tr><td>03 _</td><td></td><td>|a</td></tr>
<tr><td></td><td></td><td>|?</td></tr>
<tr><td>040</td><td></td><td>|a</td></tr>
<tr><td></td><td></td><td>|c</td></tr>
<tr><td>04 _</td><td>_ _</td><td>|a</td></tr>
<tr><td></td><td></td><td>|?</td></tr>
<tr><td>050</td><td>_ _</td><td>|a</td></tr>
<tr><td></td><td></td><td>|b</td></tr>
<tr><td>082</td><td>_ _</td><td>|a</td></tr>
<tr><td></td><td></td><td>|2</td></tr>
<tr><td>100</td><td>_ _</td><td>|a</td></tr>
<tr><td></td><td></td><td>|d</td></tr>
<tr><td>110</td><td>_ _</td><td>|a</td></tr>
<tr><td></td><td></td><td>|b</td></tr>
<tr><td>130</td><td>_ _</td><td>|a</td></tr>
<tr><td>24_</td><td>_ _</td><td>|a</td></tr>
<tr><td></td><td></td><td>|l</td></tr>
<tr><td></td><td></td><td>|k</td></tr>
<tr><td>245</td><td>_ _</td><td>|a</td></tr>
<tr><td></td><td></td><td>|h</td></tr>
<tr><td></td><td></td><td>|b</td></tr>
<tr><td></td><td></td><td>|c</td></tr>
<tr><td>246</td><td>_ _</td><td>|a</td></tr>
<tr><td></td><td></td><td>|h</td></tr>
<tr><td>250</td><td></td><td>|a</td></tr>
<tr><td>25x</td><td></td><td>|a</td></tr>
<tr><td>260</td><td></td><td>|a</td></tr>
<tr><td></td><td></td><td>|b</td></tr>
<tr><td></td><td></td><td>|c</td></tr>
</table>

<table>
<tr><td>300</td><td></td><td>|a</td><td></td></tr>
<tr><td></td><td></td><td>|b</td><td></td></tr>
<tr><td></td><td></td><td>|c</td><td></td></tr>
<tr><td>440</td><td>_ _</td><td>|a</td><td></td></tr>
<tr><td>490</td><td>_ _</td><td>|a</td><td></td></tr>
<tr><td>5_ _</td><td></td><td>|a</td><td></td></tr>
<tr><td>5_ _</td><td></td><td>|a</td><td></td></tr>
<tr><td>6_ _</td><td></td><td>|a</td><td></td></tr>
<tr><td>6_ _</td><td></td><td>|a</td><td></td></tr>
<tr><td>7_ _</td><td></td><td>|a</td><td></td></tr>
<tr><td>7_ _</td><td></td><td>|a</td><td></td></tr>
<tr><td>852</td><td>_ _</td><td></td><td>|h</td></tr>
<tr><td></td><td></td><td>|i</td><td></td></tr>
<tr><td>856</td><td>_ _</td><td></td><td>|u</td></tr>
<tr><td></td><td></td><td>|?</td><td></td></tr>
</table>

Notes

1. *MARC content designation:* http://www.loc.gov/marc/marcdocz.html
   LC/NACO authority files: http://authorities.loc.gov/
   "Understanding MARC Bibliographic" tutorial: http://www.loc.gov/marc/umb/
   "MARC 21 Concise Format for Authority Data": http://www.loc.gov/marc/authority/ecadhome.html
2. http://www.mitinet.com/Support/s_mm_demo.htm

Exercises

Exercise 1

Title Page

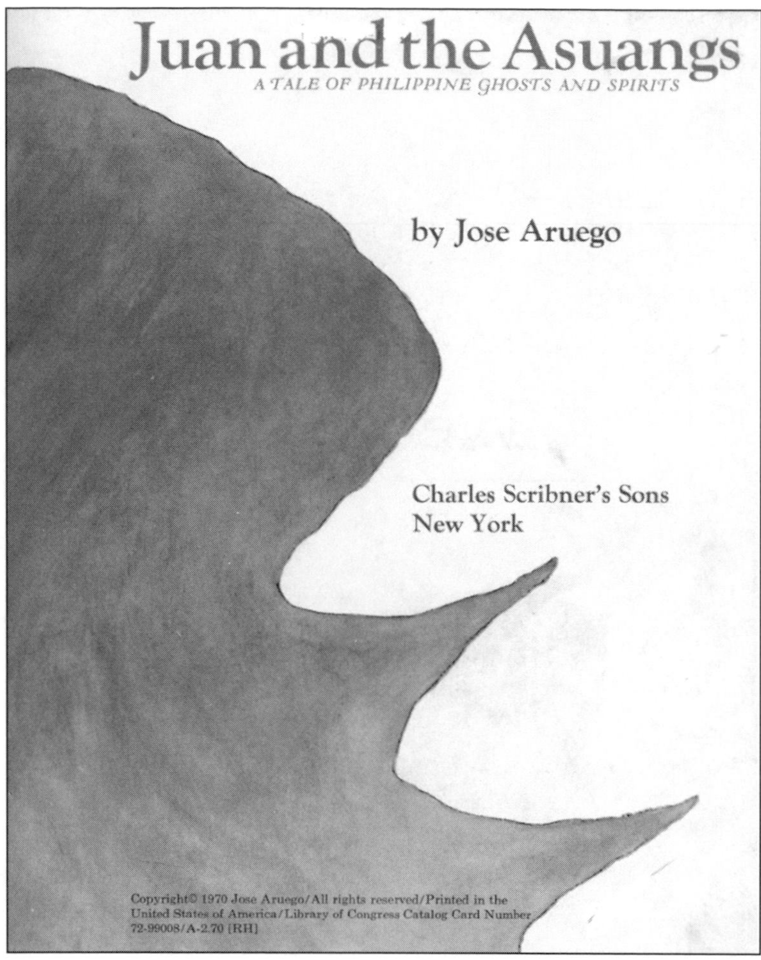

Juan and the Asuangs
A TALE OF PHILIPPINE GHOSTS AND SPIRITS
by Jose Aruego
Charles Scribner's Sons
New York
Copyright© 1970 Jose Aruego/All rights reserved/Printed in the United States of America/Library of Congress Catalog Card Number 72-99008/A-2.70 [RH]

Additional information:
32 unnumbered pages; colored illustrations; 27 cm.
Summary: A young Filipino boy makes the best of a bad situation in order to rescue his village's dogs and chickens from the terrible Asuangs, or jungle spirits.

Instructions: Prepare a catalog record for this work.

When cataloging this book, consider the following:
Why doesn't this book have an ISBN?
How is the date of publication treated?

***AACR2r* rules needed:** 1.1B1; 1.1F1; 1.4C1; 1.4D1; 1.5B2; 1.7B10; 1.8B1; 2.5B2; 2.5C3; 2.5D1; 2.7B17; 21.1A2; 22.5A1; MARC 010

Cover

Exercise 2

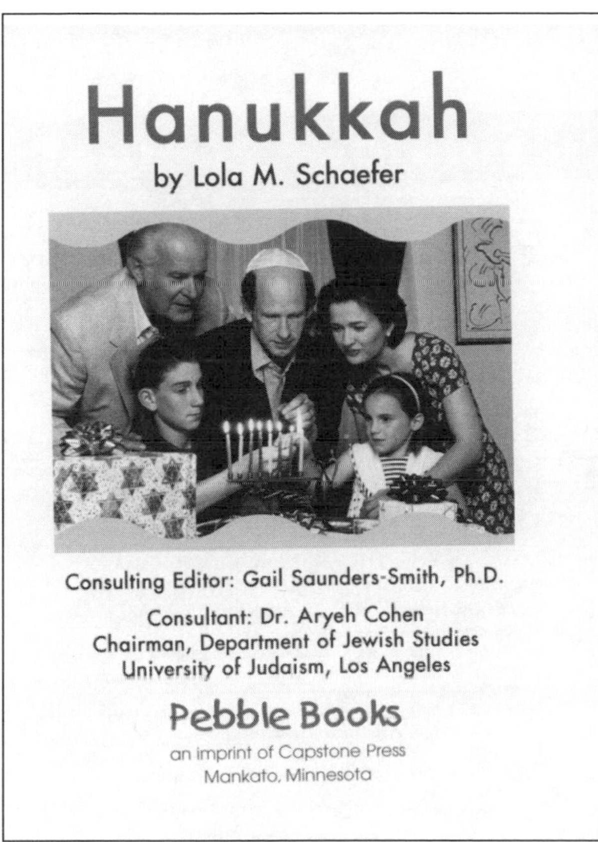

Hanukkah

by Lola M. Schaefer

Consulting Editor: Gail Saunders-Smith, Ph.D.

Consultant: Dr. Aryeh Cohen
Chairman, Department of Jewish Studies
University of Judaism, Los Angeles

Pebble Books
an imprint of Capstone Press
Mankato, Minnesota

Title Page

Pebble Books are published by Capstone Press
151 Good Counsel Drive, P.O. Box 669, Mankato, Minnesota 56002
http://www.capstone-press.com

Copyright © 2001 Capstone Press. All rights reserved.
No part of this book may be reproduced without written permission from the publisher. The publisher takes no responsibility for the use of any of the materials or methods described in this book, nor for the products thereof.
Printed in the United States of America.

1 2 3 4 5 6 06 05 04 03 02 01

Library of Congress Cataloging-in-Publication Data
Schaefer, Lola M., 1950–
Hanukkah/by Lola M. Schaefer.
p. cm.—(Holidays and celebrations)
Includes bibliographical references and index.
Summary: Presents, in simple text and photographs, the history of Hanukkah and how it is celebrated in the United States.
ISBN 0-7368-0662-8
1. Hanukkah—Juvenile literature. [1. Hanukkah. 2. Holidays.] I. Title. II. Series.
BM695.H3 S27 2001
394.267—dc21 00-023056

Note to Parents and Teachers

The Holidays and Celebrations series supports national social studies standards related to culture. This book describes Hanukkah and illustrates how it is celebrated in the United States. The photographs support early readers in understanding the text. The repetition of words and phrases helps early readers learn new words. This book also introduces early readers to subject-specific vocabulary words, which are defined in the Words to Know section. Early readers may need assistance to read some words and to use the Table of Contents, Words to Know, Read More, Internet Sites, and Index/Word List sections of the book.

Title Page Verso—Portion

Additional information:
24 pages; colored illustrations; 18 cm.; includes index
Summary: Presents, in simple text and photographs, the history of Hanukkah and how it is celebrated.

Instructions: Create a catalog record for this book.

When cataloging this book, consider the following:
Series

***AACR2r* rules needed:** 1.1B1; 1.1F1; 1.4C1; 1.4C3; 1.4D1; 1.4F6; 1.5B2; 1.5C1; 1.5D1; 1.6B1; 1.7B14; 1.7B17; 1.7B18; 2.5B2; 2.5C3; 2.5D1; 2.7B17; 2.7B18; 21.4A1; 22.5A1; MARC 010; MARC 020

Exercise 3

BABE DIDRIKSON ZAHARIAS

The Making of a Champion

BY RUSSELL FREEDMAN

Clarion Books ☆ New York

Title Page

CLARION BOOKS
a Houghton Mifflin Company imprint
215 Park Avenue South, New York, NY 10003

Copyright © 1999 by Russell Freedman

The text was set in 11-point Palatino.
Book design by Sylvia Frezzolini Severance.

All rights reserved.

For information about permission
to reproduce selections from this book,
write to Permissions, Houghton Mifflin Company,
215 Park Avenue South, New York, NY 10003.

Printed in the U.S.A.

Title Page Verso—Portion

Additional information:
192 pages; black and white illustrations; 27 cm.; bibliographical references (pp. 179-183); index; LCCN: 98-50208; ISBN: 0-395-63367-2
Summary: A biography of Babe Didrikson, who broke records in golf, track and field, and other sports, at a time when there were few opportunities for female athletes.

Instructions: Prepare a catalog record for this item.

When cataloging this item, consider the following:

- How is a bibliography treated in the MARC record?
- How does the presence of an index affect the treatment of the bibliography?

***AACR2r* rules needed**: 1.1B1; 1.1E2; 1.1F1; 1.4C1; 1.4D1; 1.4F6; 1.5B2; 1.5C1; 1.5D1; 2.5B2; 2.5C1; 2.5D1; 2.7B17; 2.

Exercise 4

WALTER DEAN MYERS

BAD BOY

a memoir

HarperCollins*Publishers*

Amistad

Title Page

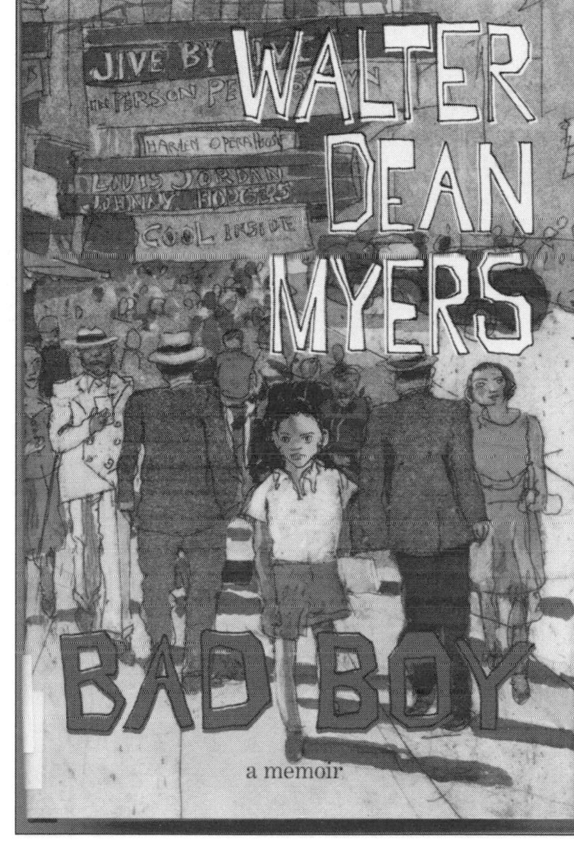

Cover

Bad Boy: A Memoir

Copyright © 2001 by Walter Dean Myers

All rights reserved. No part of this book may be used or reproduced in any manner whatsoever without written permission except in the case of brief quotations embodied in critical articles and reviews. Printed in the United States of America. For information address HarperCollins Children's Books, a division of HarperCollins Publishers, 1350 Avenue of the Americas, New York, NY 10019.

www.harperchildrens.com

Typography by Alison Donalty

1 3 5 7 9 10 8 6 4 2

◆ First Edition

Title Page Verso—Portion

Additional information:
214 pages; 22 cm.; LCCN: 00-52978; ISBN: 0-06-029523-6; 0-06-029524-4 (lib. bdg.)

Instructions: Prepare a catalog record for this item.

***AACR2r* rules needed:** 1.1B1; 1.1E1; 1.1F1; 1.2B1; 1.4C1; 1.4D2; 1.4F6; 1.5B2; 1.5D1; 2.5B2; 2.5D1; 21.1A2; 22.5A1; MARC 010; MARC 020

Exercise 5

GREAT
ACROSTICS

Martin Greif

Sterling Publishing Co., Inc. New York
A Sterling/Main Street Book

Title Page

Cover

Designed and Typeset by Sheila Kern, Cork, Ireland.

10 9 8 7 6 5 4 3 2 1

A Sterling/Main Street Book

Published in 1997 by Sterling Publishing Company, Inc.
387 Park Avenue South, New York, N.Y. 10016

Distributed in Canada by Sterling Publishing
c/o Canadian Manda Group, One Atlantic Avenue, Suite 105
Toronto, Ontario, Canada M6K 3E7
Distributed in Great Britain and Europe by Cassell PLC
Wellington House, 125 Strand, London WC2R 0BB, England
Distributed in Australia by Capricorn Link (Australia) Pty Ltd.
P.O. Box 6651, Baulkham Hills, Business Centre, NSW 2153, Australia

Manufactured in the United States of America

Sterling ISBN 0-8069-9471-1

Title Page Verso—Portion

Additional information:
128 pages; 22 cm; includes index; LCCN: 96-48043

Instructions: Prepare a catalog record for this item.

When cataloging this work, consider the following:

- The difference between a publisher and an imprint
- How information about an imprint is given

***AACR2r* rules needed:** 1.1B1; 1.1F1; 1.4C1; 1.4D1; 1.4D2; 1.4F1; 1.5B2; 1.5D1; 1.7B7; 1.7B18; 1.8B1; 2.5B2; 2.5D1; 2.7B18; 21.1A2; 22.5A1; MARC 010; MARC 020

Exercise 6

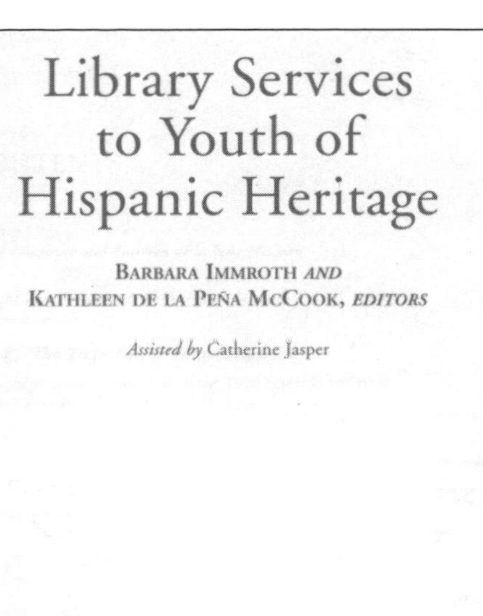

Library Services to Youth of Hispanic Heritage

BARBARA IMMROTH *AND* KATHLEEN DE LA PEÑA MCCOOK, *EDITORS*

Assisted by Catherine Jasper

McFarland & Company, Inc., Publishers
Jefferson, North Carolina, and London

Title Page

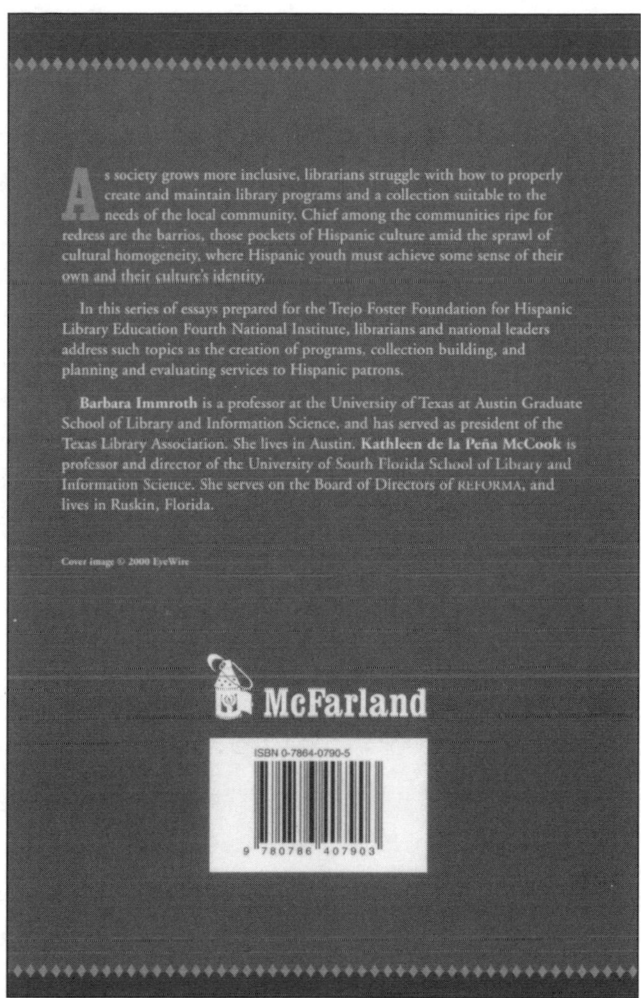

As society grows more inclusive, librarians struggle with how to properly create and maintain library programs and a collection suitable to the needs of the local community. Chief among the communities ripe for redress are the barrios, those pockets of Hispanic culture amid the sprawl of cultural homogeneity, where Hispanic youth must achieve some sense of their own and their culture's identity.

In this series of essays prepared for the Trejo Foster Foundation for Hispanic Library Education Fourth National Institute, librarians and national leaders address such topics as the creation of programs, collection building, and planning and evaluating services to Hispanic patrons.

Barbara Immroth is a professor at the University of Texas at Austin Graduate School of Library and Information Science, and has served as president of the Texas Library Association. She lives in Austin. **Kathleen de la Peña McCook** is professor and director of the University of South Florida School of Library and Information Science. She serves on the Board of Directors of REFORMA, and lives in Ruskin, Florida.

Cover image © 2000 EyeWire

McFarland

ISBN 0-7864-0790-5

9 780786 407903

Back Cover

Additional information:
ix, 197 pages; 26 cm.; bibliographic references, index; ISBN: 0-7864-0790-5 (softcover: #50 alkaline paper); LCCN: 00-37247

Instructions: Prepare a catalog record for this item.

***AACR2r* rules needed:** 1.1B1; 1.1F1; 1.1F4; 1.1F6; 1.4C1; 1.4C3; 1.4D1; 1.4D2; 1.5B2; 1.5D1; 1.7B14;1.7B17; 1.7B18; 2.5B2; 2.5D1; 2.7B14; 2.7B17; 2.7B18; 21.0D1; 21.6B1; 21.6B2; 22.5A1; App. B14; MARC 010; MARC 020

Cover image © 2000 EyeWire

©2000 Barbara Immroth and Kathleen de la Peña McCook.
All rights reserved

No part of this book may be reproduced or transmitted in any form or by any means, electronic or mechanical, including photocopying or recording, or by any information storage and retrieval system, without permission in writing from the publisher.

Manufactured in the United States of America

McFarland & Company, Inc., Publishers
Box 611, Jefferson, North Carolina 28640
www.mcfarlandpub.com

Title Page Verso—Portion

Exercise 7

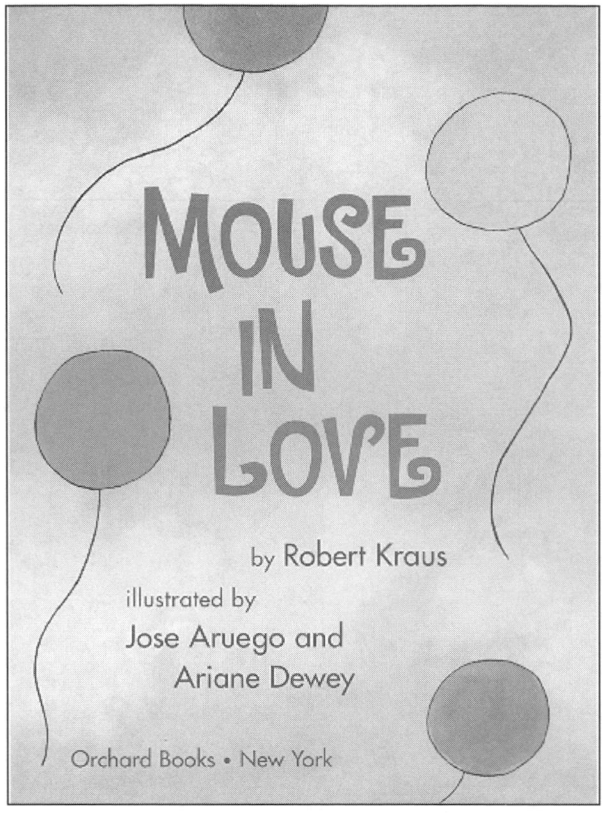

MOUSE
IN
LOVE
by Robert Kraus
illustrated by
Jose Aruego and
Ariane Dewey
Orchard Books • New York

Title Page

Text copyright © 2000 by Robert Kraus. Illustrations copyright © 2000 by Jose Aruego and Ariane Dewey.
All rights reserved. No part of this book may be reproduced or transmitted in any form or by any means, electronic or mechanical, including photocopying, recording, or by any information storage or retrieval system, without permission in writing from the Publisher.

Orchard Books, A Grolier Company, 95 Madison Avenue, New York, NY 10016

Manufactured in the United States of America. Printed and bound by Phoenix Color Corp.
Book design by Mina Greenstein. The text of this book is set in 24 point Futura Medium.
The illustrations are ink, watercolor, and pastels.
10 9 8 7 6 5 4 3 2 1

Title Page Verso—Portion

Additional information:
32 unnumbered pages; color illustrations; 27 cm.; LCCN: 99-58611; ISBN: 0-531-30297-0 (trade ; alk. paper); 0-531-33297-7 (lib bdg. : alk. paper)
Summary: Mouse searches high and low for his true love, only to find her right next door.

Instructions: Prepare a catalog record for this item.

***AACR2r* rules needed:** 1.1B1; 1.4C1; 1.1F6; 1.4D2; 1.4F6; 1.5B2; 1.5C1; 1.5D1; 1.7B17; 1.8B1; 1.8B2; 1.8E1; 2.5B7; 2.5C3; 2.5D1; 2.7B17; 21.1A2; 22.5A1; MARC 010; MARC 020

Exercise 8

Subject Headings for School and Public Libraries

An LCSH/Sears Companion

Third Edition

Joanna F. Fountain

2001
LIBRARIES UNLIMITED, INC.
Englewood, Colorado

Title Page

Copyright © 2001 Joanna F. Fountain
All Rights Reserved
Printed in the United States of America

No part of this publication may be reproduced, stored in a retrieval system, or transmitted, in any form or by any means, electronic, mechanical, photocopying, recording, or otherwise, without the prior written permission of the publisher.

Libraries Unlimited, Inc.
P.O. Box 6633
Englewood, CO 80155-6633
1-800-237-6124
www.lu.com

Title Page Verso—Portion

CONTENTS

Additional information:
xxxvi, 208 pages; 29 cm.; ISBN: 1-56308-853-3; LCCN: 00-066307

Instructions: Prepare a catalog record for this item.

When cataloging this item, consider the following:

- Contents

***AACR2r* rules needed:** 1.1B1; 1.1E2; 1.1F1; 1.2B1; 1.4C1; 1.4C3; 1.4D2; 1.4F1; 1.5B2; 1.5D1; 1.7B14; 1.7B17; 1.8B1; 2.5B2; 2.5D1; 21.1A2; 21.4A1; 22.5A1; App. B; App. C; MARC 010; MARC 020

Exercise 9

THE PERILOUS JOURNEY OF

The Donner Party

BY MARIAN CALABRO

CLARION BOOKS NEW YORK

Title Page

Cover

Title Page Verso—Portion

Clarion Books
a Houghton Mifflin Company imprint
215 Park Avenue South, New York, NY 10003
Copyright © 1999 by Marian Calabro

Book design by Sylvia Frezzolini Severance
The text is set in 13-point Bembo.
All rights reserved.

For information about permission
to reproduce selections from this book,
write to Permissions, Houghton Mifflin Company,
215 Park Avenue South, New York, NY 10003.

Printed in the U.S.A.

Additional information:
192 pages; black and white illustrations; 26 cm.; bibliographical references (pp. 184-187); index; map; ISBN: 0-395-86610-3; LCCN: 98-29610
Summary: Uses materials from letters and diaries written by survivors of the Donner Party to relate the experiences of that ill-fated group as they endured horrific circumstances on their way to California in 1846-47.

Instructions: Prepare a catalog record for this item.

When cataloging this book, consider the following:

- Capitalization within the title
- Physical description

AACR2r **rules needed:** 1.1B1; 1.1F1; 1.4C1; 1.4D1; 1.5B2; 1.5C1; 1.5D1; 1.7B17; 1.7B18; 1.8B1; 2.5B2; 2.5C2; 2.5D1; 2.7B17; 2.7B18; 22.5A1; 21.1A2; 21.29B; MARC 010; MARC 020

Exercise 10

BARBARA JORDAN

American Hero

MARY BETH ROGERS

BANTAM BOOKS

New York Toronto London
Sydney Auckland

Title Page

BARBARA JORDAN *American Hero*

A Bantam Book / December 1998

All rights reserved.
Copyright © 1998 by Mary Beth Rogers.

BOOK DESIGN BY GLEN M. EDELSTEIN

No part of this book may be reproduced or transmitted in any form or by any means, electronic or mechanical, including photocopying, recording, or by any information storage and retrieval system, without permission in writing from the publisher.
For information address: Bantam Books.

Photo on page ii courtesy of Frank Wolfe, Lyndon Baines Johnson Library Collection.
Photo on page 357 courtesy of Texas Senate Media Service.

Excerpts from FOR THE INWARD JOURNEY: THE WRITINGS OF HOWARD THURMAN by Anne Spencer Thurman, copyright © 1984 selected by Sue Bailey Thurman, reprinted by permission of Harcourt Brace & Company.

Published simultaneously in the United States and Canada

Bantam Books are published by Bantam Books, a division of Bantam Doubleday Dell Publishing Group, Inc. Its trademark, consisting of the words "Bantam Books" and the portrayal of a rooster, is Registered in U.S. Patent and Trademark Office and in other countries. Marca Registrada. Bantam Books, 1540 Broadway, New York, New York 10036.

PRINTED IN THE UNITED STATES OF AMERICA
BVG 10 9 8 7 6 5 4 3 2 1

Title Page Verso—Portion

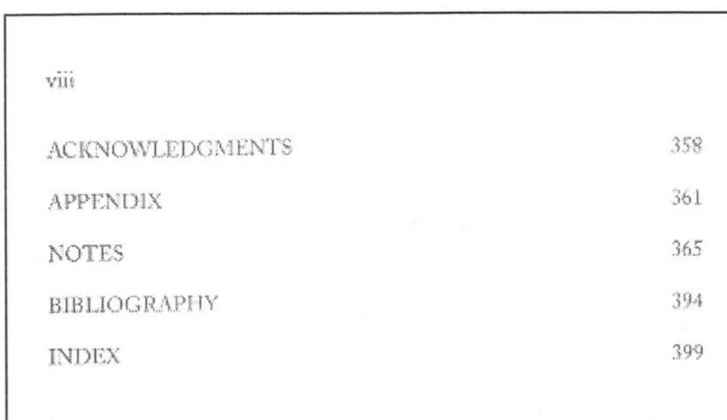
viii

Table of Contents (Portion)

Additional information:
xviii, 414 pages; black and white illustrations; 24 cm.; bibliographical references; index; ISBN: 0-553-10603-1; 0-553-38066-4 (pbk.); LCCN: 98-19996

Instructions: Prepare a catalog record for this item.

When cataloging this item, consider the following:

- How are the additional cities of publication treated?

***AACR2r* rules needed:** 1.1B1; 1.1E1; 1.1F1; 1.4C1; 1.4C5; 1.4D1; 1.4F1; 1.5B2; 1.5C1; 1.5D1; 1.7B18; 1.8B1; 2.5B2; 2.5C1; 2.5D1; 2.7B18; 21.1A2; 22.5A1; MARC 010; MARC 020

Exercise 11

THE
GRAND
COMPLICATION

ALLEN KURZWEIL

An Imprint of Hyperion
NEW YORK

Title Page

This book is a work of fiction. Names, characters, places, and incidents are products of the author's imagination or used fictitiously. Any resemblance to actual events, locales, or persons, living or dead, is entirely coincidental.

Copyright © 2001 Allen Kurzweil

Excerpt from "Unpacking My Library" in *Illuminations* by Walter Benjamin, copyright © 1955 by Suhrkamp Verlag, Frankfurt a.M., English translation by Harry Zohn copyright © 1968 and renewed 1966 by Harcourt, Inc., reprinted by permission of Harcourt, Inc.

Excerpt from *The Letters of Henry James, Volume IV, 1895–1916*, Cambridge, Mass.: The Belknap Press of Harvard University Press, Copyright © 1984 Leon Edel, Editorial, copyright © 1984, Alexander R. James, James copyright material, reprinted by permission of Harvard University Press.

A portion of this work appeared under the title "Slips of Love" in *Granta 54: Best of Young American Novelists, 1996.*

"Roll-Player" patent pending

All rights reserved. No part of this book may be used or reproduced in any manner whatsoever without the written permission of the Publisher. Printed in the United States of America. For information address: Hyperion, 77 W. 66th Street, New York, New York 10023-6298.

Title Page Verso—Portion

Additional information:
359 pages; 25 cm.; ISBN: 0-7868-6603-9; LCCN: 2001016811; first edition
Summary: Henry James Jesson III, a bibliophile, hires librarian Alexander Short for some after-hours research. The task: to render whole an incomplete cabinet of wonders chronicling the life of a mysterious eighteenth-century inventor.

Instructions: Prepare a catalog record for this item.

When cataloging this item, consider the following:

- How are the LC numbers from 2001 and later treated differently in the MARC record than earlier numbers?

***AACR2r* rules needed:** 1.1B1; 1.1F1; 1.2B1; 1.4C1; 1.4D1; 1.4F6; 1.5B2; 1.5D1; 1.7B17; 1.8B1; 2.5B2; 2.5D1; 2.7B17; 21.1A1; 22.5A1; App B.9; App C; MARC 010; MARC 020

Exercise 12

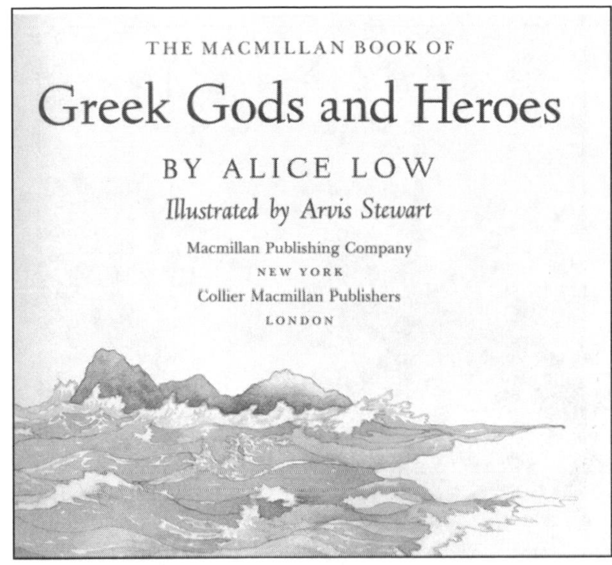

THE MACMILLAN BOOK OF

Greek Gods and Heroes

BY ALICE LOW

Illustrated by Arvis Stewart

Macmillan Publishing Company

NEW YORK

Collier Macmillan Publishers

LONDON

Title Page

Copyright © 1985 by Macmillan Publishing Company,
a division of Macmillan, Inc.
All rights reserved. No part of this book may be reproduced or transmitted in any form or by any means, electronic or mechanical, including photocopying, recording or by any information storage and retrieval system, without permission in writing from the Publisher.

Macmillan Publishing Company
866 Third Avenue, New York, N.Y. 10022
Collier Macmillan Canada, Inc.

Printed in the United States of America

10 9 8 7 6 5 4 3 2

Title Page Verso—Portion

Additional Information:
viii, 184 pages; colored and black and white illustrations; 29 cm.; index; LCCN: 85-7170; ISBN: 0-02-761390-9
Summary: Recreates the popular myths of ancient Greece, including the legend of Odysseus.

Instructions: Prepare a catalog record for this item.

When cataloging this work, consider the following:

- What impact, if any, the different font sizes on the title page have on how the title is entered
- What treatment an international publisher receives when listed on the title page
- Physical description
- The meaning of the number string at the bottom of the title page verso
- Alternate titles that might be given in the MARC record

***AACR2r* rules needed:** 1.1B1; 1.1B2; 1.1F1; 1.1F6; 1.4C1; 1.4C3; 1.4D2; 1.4F6; 1.5B2; 1.5C1; 1.5D1; 1.7B17; 1.8B1; 2.5B2; 2.5C3; 2.5D1; 2.7B17; 21.1A2; 22.5A1; MARC 010; MARC 020

Exercise 13

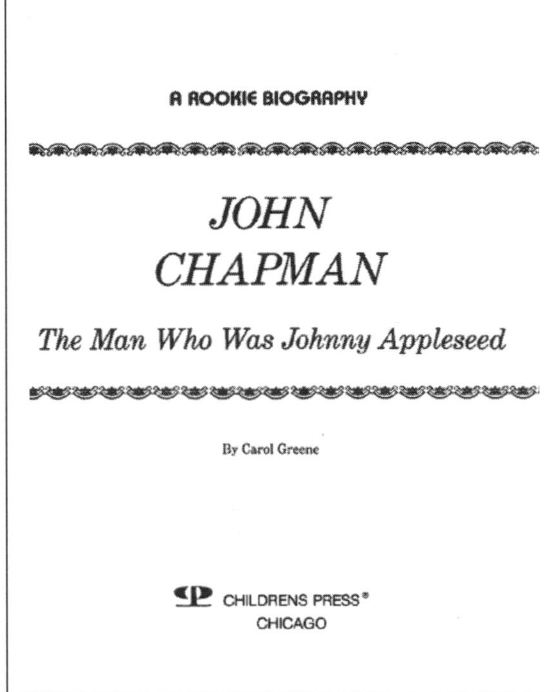
A ROOKIE BIOGRAPHY

JOHN
CHAPMAN

The Man Who Was Johnny Appleseed

By Carol Greene

CHILDRENS PRESS®
CHICAGO

Title Page

Cover

Printed in the United States of America.
4 5 6 7 8 9 10 R 00 99 98 97 96 95 94

Title Page Verso—Portion

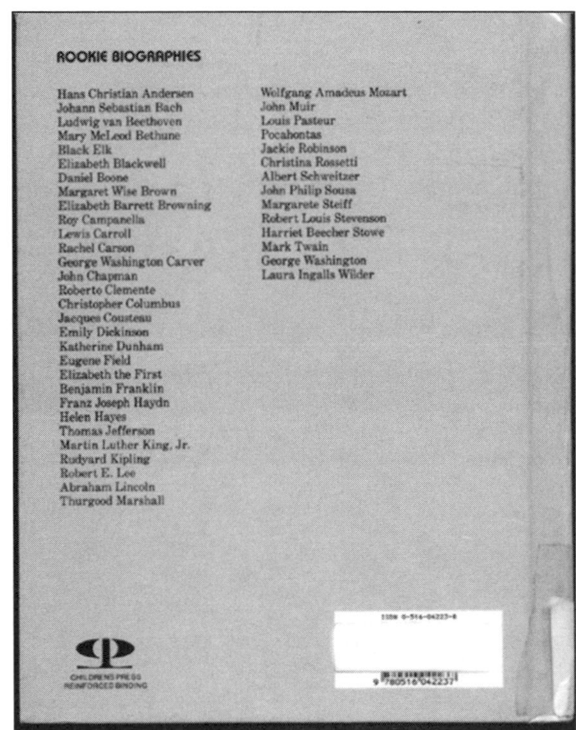
ROOKIE BIOGRAPHIES

Hans Christian Andersen
Johann Sebastian Bach
Ludwig van Beethoven
Mary McLeod Bethune
Black Elk
Elizabeth Blackwell
Daniel Boone
Margaret Wise Brown
Elizabeth Barrett Browning
Roy Campanella
Lewis Carroll
Rachel Carson
George Washington Carver
John Chapman
Roberto Clemente
Christopher Columbus
Jacques Cousteau
Emily Dickinson
Katherine Dunham
Eugene Field
Elizabeth the First
Benjamin Franklin
Franz Joseph Haydn
Helen Hayes
Thomas Jefferson
Martin Luther King, Jr.
Rudyard Kipling
Robert E. Lee
Abraham Lincoln
Thurgood Marshall
Wolfgang Amadeus Mozart
John Muir
Louis Pasteur
Pocahontas
Jackie Robinson
Christina Rossetti
Albert Schweitzer
John Philip Sousa
Margarete Steiff
Robert Louis Stevenson
Harriet Beecher Stowe
Mark Twain
George Washington
Laura Ingalls Wilder

Back Cover

Additional information:
47 pages; black and white and color illustrations; portrait; 24 cm.; index; LCCN: 91-2649; ISBN: 0-516-04223-8 (reinforced binding)

Instructions: Prepare a catalog record for this item.

When cataloging this item, consider the following:

- Physical description
- Series information
- Personal name subject heading

***AACR2r* rules needed:** 1.1B1; 1.1E1; 1.1F1; 1.4C1; 1.4D1; 1.4D2; 1.4F6; 1.5B2; 1.5C1; 1.5D1; 1.6B1; 1.7B17; 1.7B18; 1.8B1; 2.5B2; 2.5B3; 2.5C3; 2.5D1; 2.7B18; 21.1A2; 22.5A1; MARC 010; MARC 020

Exercise 14

33 things every girl should know

STORIES, SONGS, POEMS, AND SMART TALK
BY 33 EXTRAORDINARY WOMEN
edited by TONYA BOLDEN

CROWN PUBLISHERS, INC.
NEW YORK

Title Page

Copyright © 1998 by Tonya Bolden
Front cover photograph copyright ©1997 by Jim Cummins / FPG International

All rights reserved. No part of this book may be reproduced or transmitted in any form or by any means, electronic or mechanical, including photocopying, recording, or by any information storage and retrieval system, without permission in writing from the publisher.

Photographic acknowledgments: The Body Shop, UK: pages 16, 17, 18. Tanya Burnett, copyright © 1997, courtesy of Lauren Hutton: page 54. Elizabeth Jenkins-Sahlin: page 102. The Office of the Architect of the Capitol: page 105. Dana Lixenberg, copyright © 1995: page 143. Gretchen Rosenkranz: pages 22, 24, 25, 27. Vera Wang Ltd.: pages 39, 40, 41, 42.

Acknowledgments for permission to reprint previously published material can be found on pages 158–159.

Published by Crown Publishers, Inc., a Random House company, 201 East 50th Street, New York, New York 10022.

CROWN is a trademark of Crown Publishers, Inc.

Book design by Elizabeth Van Itallie

http://www.randomhouse.com/

Printed in the United States of America

Title Page Verso—Portion

Additional information:
159 pages; black and white illustrations; 23 cm; LCCN: 97-29431; ISBN: 0-517-70936-8 (tr. pb.); ISBN: 0-517-70999-6 (lib. bdg.)
Summary: A mix of short stories, essays, a comic strip, a speech, an interview, poems, and more that offer insights and advice for girls.

Instructions: Prepare a catalog record for this item.

***AACR2r* rules needed:** 1.1B1; 1.1E1; 1.1F1; 1.1F6; 1.2B1; 1.4C3; 1.4D2; 1.4F6; 1.5B2; 1.5C1; 1.5D1; 1.7B17; 1.8B1; 1.8B2; 1.8E1; 2.1B1; 2.5B2; 2.5C1; 2.5D1; 2.7B17; App. B; App. C; MARC 010; MARC 020

Exercise 15

Children's and Young Adult Literature by Latino Writers: A Guide for Librarians, Teachers, Parents, and Students

Sherry York

Linworth PUBLISHING, INC.

Title Page

Table of Contents

Table of Contents v

Table of Contents

Published by Linworth Publishing, Inc.
480 East Wilson Bridge Road, Suite L
Worthington, Ohio 43085

ISBN 1-58683-062-7
5 4 3 2 1

Title Page Verso—Portion

Across the Great River

- **Author:** Irene Beltrán Hernández
- **Publication:** Houston, TX: Arte Público Press, 1989
- **LC#:** 89000289
- **Editions:**
0934770964 pb.
- **Description:** 136 pages, 22 cm. Cover illustration by Mark Piñón.
- **Chapters:** 10
- **Summary:** Katarina Campos and her family are separated while illegally crossing the border from Mexico to Texas.
- **Subjects:**
Emigration and immigration—Fiction
Immigrants—Texas—Fiction
Mexican Americans—Fiction
- **Interest Level:** young adult
- **Reading Level:** 4.3
- **Tests:** Accelerated Reader
- **Reviewed:** *The Book Report*, *Booklist*, *ALAN Review*, *San Francisco Chronicle*
- **Lists:** *Brave Girls and Strong Women*
- **Web site:**
<www.unigiessen.de/~ga52/seminarP/mcyal98/grRiver.htm>
<http://ladb.unm.edu/retanet/plans/search/retrieve.php3?ID[0]=442>
- **Note:** Features a female protagonist.

Alicia's Treasure

- **Author:** Diane Gonzales Bertrand
- **Publication:** Houston, TX: Piñata Books, 1996
- **LC#:** 95037669
- **Editions:**
1558850856 hc. Arte Público
1558850864 pb. Arte Público
0613179587 hc. Econo-Clad
- **Description:** 123 pages, 23 cm. Illustrated by Daniel Lechón.
- **Chapters:** 13
- **Summary:** When ten-year-old Alicia accompanies her brother and his girlfriend to the beach, she experiences many things for the first time and gains new insights into herself.
- **Subjects:**
Beaches—Fiction
Brothers and Sisters—Fiction
Mexican Americans—Fiction
- **Interest Level:** ages 8–12, 9–12, grades 3–4, 4–6
- **Reading Level**: 3.9
- **Tests:** Accelerated Reader
- **Reviewed:** *Booklist*, *Horn Book*
- **Awards:** Tomás Rivera nominee 1996

Breaking Through

- **Author:** Francisco Jiménez
- **Publication:** Boston: Houghton Mifflin, 2001
- **LC#:** 2001016941
- **Editions:**
0618011730 hc.
- **Description:** 208 pages, 19 cm.
- **Chapters:** 25
- **Summary:** Having come from Mexico to California ten years ago, fourteen-year-old Francisco is still working in the fields but is

Latino Novels and Chapter Books 11

Sample Page

Additional information:
v, 184 pages; 28 cm.; bibliographic references and index; LCCN: 2002067112; ISBN: 1586830627 (pbk.)

Instructions: Prepare a catalog record for this item.

***AACR2r* rules needed:** 1.1B1; 1.1E1; 1.1F1; 1.4C1; 1.4C3; 1.4D1; 1.4D2; 1.4F6; 1.5B2; 1.5C1; 1.5D1; 1.7B17; 1.7B18; 1.8B1; 2.5B2; 2.5D1; 2.7B17; 2.7B18; MARC 010; MARC 020

Exercise 16

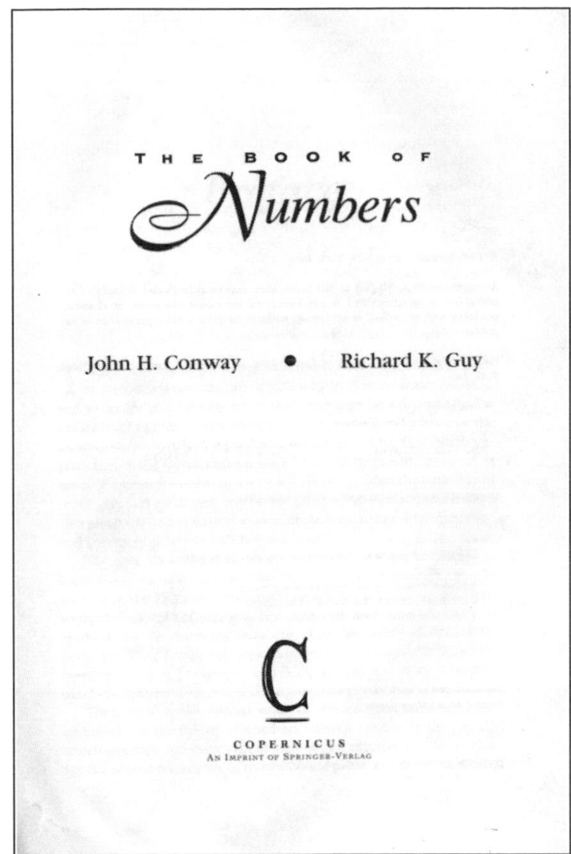

Title Page

Additional information:
ix, 310 pages; black and white and color illustrations; 24 cm.; bibliographical references; index; LCCN: 95-32588; ISBN: 0-387-97993-X (harcover: alk. paper)
Summary: Guides readers at different levels of mathematical sophistication in understanding the origins, patterns, and interrelationships of numbers.

Instructions: Prepare a catalog record for this item.

When cataloging this work, consider the following:

- Publisher information
- Physical description

***AACR2r* rules needed:** 1.1B1; 1.1F1; 1.1F6; 1.4D1; 1.4F6; 1.5B1; 1.5B2; 1.5C1; 1.5D1; 1.7B7; 1.7B17; 1.8B1; 2.5B2; 2.5C1; 2.5C3; 2.5D1; 2.7B18; 21.1A2; 22.5A1; MARC 010; MARC 020

© 1996 Springer-Verlag New York, Inc.

All rights reserved. No part of this publication may be reproduced, stored in a retrieval system, or transmitted, in any form or by any means, electronic, mechanical, photocopying, recording, or otherwise, without the prior written permission of the publisher.

Published in the United States by Copernicus, an imprint of Springer-Verlag New York, Inc.

Copernicus
Springer-Verlag New York, Inc.
175 Fifth Avenue
New York, NY 10010

Title Page Verso—Portion

Exercise 17

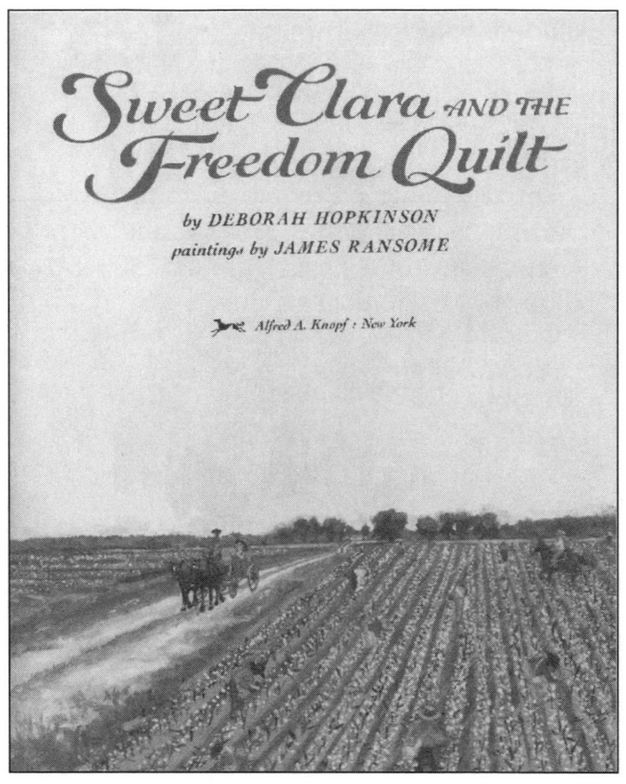
Sweet Clara and the Freedom Quilt

by DEBORAH HOPKINSON

paintings by JAMES RANSOME

Alfred A. Knopf : New York

Title Page

THIS IS A BORZOI BOOK
PUBLISHED BY ALFRED A. KNOPF, INC.

Text copyright © 1993 by Deborah Hopkinson
Illustrations copyright © 1993 by James Ransome
All rights reserved under International and Pan-American Copyright Conventions.
Published in the United States by Alfred A. Knopf, Inc., New York, and simultaneously in Canada by Random House of Canada Limited, Toronto.
Distributed by Random House, Inc., New York.

Manufactured in the United States of America
Book design by Mina Greenstein 6 7 8 9 10

Title Page Verso—Portion

Additional information:
Unpaged (approximately 32 pages); color illustrations; 28 cm.; LCCN: 91-11601; ISBN: 0-679-82311-5 (trade); ISBN: 0-679-92311-X (lib. bdg.)
Summary: A young slave stitches a quilt with a map pattern that guides her to freedom in the North.

Instructions: Prepare a catalog record for this item.

When cataloging this item, consider the following:

- Physical description
- Publisher information

***AACR2r* rules needed:** 1.1B1; 1.1F1; 1.1F6; 1.4C3; 1.4D1; 1.4D2; 1.4D3; 1.4F6; 1.5B2; 1.5C1; 1.5D1; 1.7B7; 1.7B17; 1.8B1; 1.8B2; 1.8E1; 2.4D1; 2.5B7; 2.5C3; 2.5D1; 2.7B7; 2.7B17; 21.4A1; 21.30K2; 22.5A1; MARC 010; MARC 020

Exercise 18

SLAP, SQUEAK & SCATTER

HOW ANIMALS COMMUNICATE

STEVE JENKINS

HOUGHTON MIFFLIN COMPANY
BOSTON 2001

Title Page

Additional information:
32 unnumbered pages; color illustrations; 25 x 26 cm.; bibliography (verso of title page); LCCN: 00-061402; ISBN: 0-618-03376-9
Summary: Explains some of the many ways that animals communicate with one another.

Instructions: Prepare a catalog record for this item.

When cataloging this item, consider the following:

- Title
- Bibliography
- Physical description

***AACR2r* rules needed:** 1.1B1; 1.1E1; 1.1F1; 1.4C1; 1.4D1; 1.4D2; 1.4F1; 1.5B2; 1.5C1; 1.5D1; 1.7B17; 1.7B18; 1.8B1; 2.5B2; 2.5C3; 2.5D2; 2.7B17; 2.7B18; 21.1A2; 21.29B; 21.30J2; 22.5A1; MARC 010; MARC 020

For Jamie, Alec, and Page

Bibliography

Bailey, Jill. *Animal Life.*
New York: Oxford University Press, 1994.

Caras, Roger. *The Private Lives of Animals.*
New York: Grosset & Dunlap Publishers, 1974.

Casale, Paolo. *Animal Behavior.*
Florence, Italy: Barron's Educational Series, 1999.

Facklam, Margery. *Bees Dance and Whales Sing.*
San Francisco: Sierra Books for Children, 1992.

Gould, Dr. Edwin, and Dr. George McKay, eds. *Encyclopedia of Mammals.*
2nd edition. San Diego: Academic Press, 1998.

Wyckoff, Betsy. *Talking Apes & Dancing Bees.*
Barrytown, New York: Station Hill/Barrytown, 1999.

Copyright © 2001 by Steve Jenkins

All rights reserved. For information about permission to reproduce selections from this book, write to Permissions, Houghton Mifflin Company, 215 Park Avenue South, New York, New York 10003.

www.houghtonmifflinbooks.com

The text of this book is set in Palatino.
The section introductions are set in Franklin Gothic Condensed.
The illustrations are collages of cut and torn paper.

Title Page Verso—Portion

Exercise 19

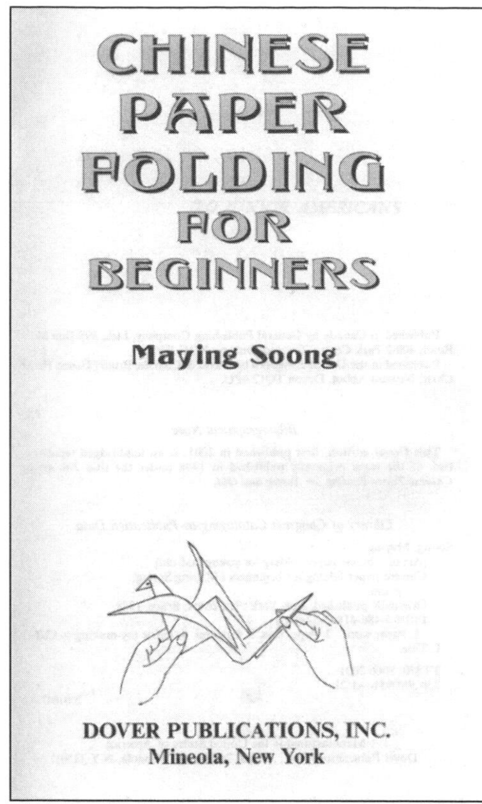

CHINESE PAPER FOLDING FOR BEGINNERS

Maying Soong

DOVER PUBLICATIONS, INC.
Mineola, New York

Title Page

CHINESE PAPER FOLDING FOR BEGINNERS

Maying Soong

Though nowadays people usually refer to paper folding by its Japanese name, origami, the art most likely originated in China. Even today, youngsters in that country are taught this craft at a very early age by mothers or grandmothers.

In this charming, instructive book, the author shares her knowledge of this rewarding craft by providing clear instructions and simple diagrams for folding gaily colored party hats, a pagoda-shaped bookmark, toy boats made of waterproof paper, decorative candy boxes, a bird with wings that flap when its tail is pushed in and out, a Chinese fishing boat, a monkey, steamboats—even a three-piece living room set and other items of tiny furniture for a doll's house. All can be made without using scissors or paste, and projects are arranged from easiest to those requiring more skill.

Children and adults alike will find this book fascinating and will be delighted by the imaginative works they're able to create from a single sheet of paper. ". . . fine entertainment for a child alone, for a group, for a family kept indoors by rain."—*Chicago Sun*.

Unabridged Dover (2001) republication of the work originally published as *The Art of Chinese Paper Folding for Young and Old* by Harcourt, Brace & World, Inc., New York, 1948. 230 black-and-white illustrations by the author. xii+132pp. 5⅜ x 8½. Paperbound.

ALSO AVAILABLE

ORIGAMI FOR BEGINNERS, Vicente Palacios. 80pp. 6⅛ x 9¼. 40284-3
PAPER TOY MAKING, Margaret W. Campbell. 79pp. 6⅛ x 9¼. 21662-4

Free Dover Crafts, Needlework and Cooking Catalog (59111-5) available upon request.

For current price information write to Dover Publications, or log on to **www.doverpublications.com**—and see every Dover book in print.

ISBN 0-486-41806-5

UPC

$4.95 IN USA

EAN

90000

Back Cover

Published in Canada by General Publishing Company, Ltd., 895 Don Mills Road, 400-2 Park Centre, Toronto, Ontario M3C 1W3.
Published in the United Kingdom by David & Charles, Brunel House, Forde Close, Newton Abbot, Devon TQ12 4PU.

Bibliographical Note

This Dover edition, first published in 2001, is an unabridged republication of the work originally published in 1948 under the title *The Art of Chinese Paper Folding for Young and Old*.

Originally published: New York : Harcourt, Brace, 1948.
ISBN 0-486-41806-5 (pbk.)

2001047367

Manufactured in the United States of America
Dover Publications, Inc., 31 East 2nd Street, Mineola, N.Y. 11501

Title Page Verso—Portion

Additional information:
xii, 132 pages; black and white illustrations; 8½ in.

Instructions: Prepare a catalog record for this item.

When cataloging this work, consider the following:

- How is the publication history of this item described?
- Translate the height dimension from inches to centimeters.

***AACR2r* rules needed:** 1.1B1; 1.1F1; 1.2B1; 1.4C1; 1.4C3; 1.4D1; 1.4D2; 1.5B2; 1.5C1; 1.5D1; 1.7A4; 1.7B4; 1.7B7; 1.7B17; 1.8B1; 1.8D1; 2.5B2; 2.5C1; 2.5D1; 21.2A1; 21.4A1; MARC 010; MARC 020

Exercise 20

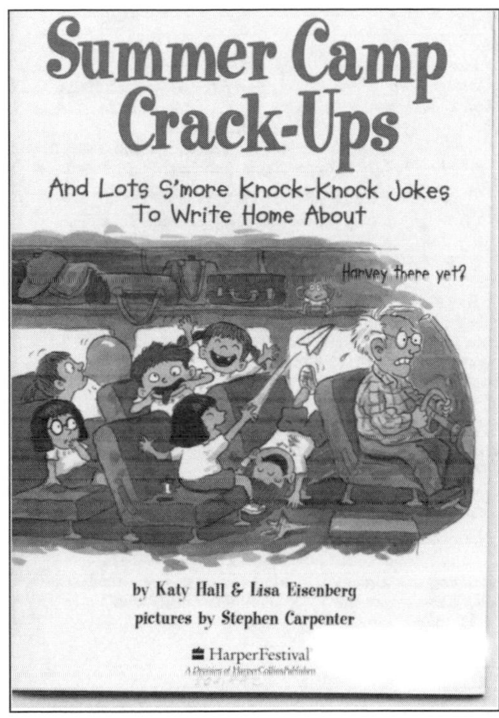

Title Page

Cover

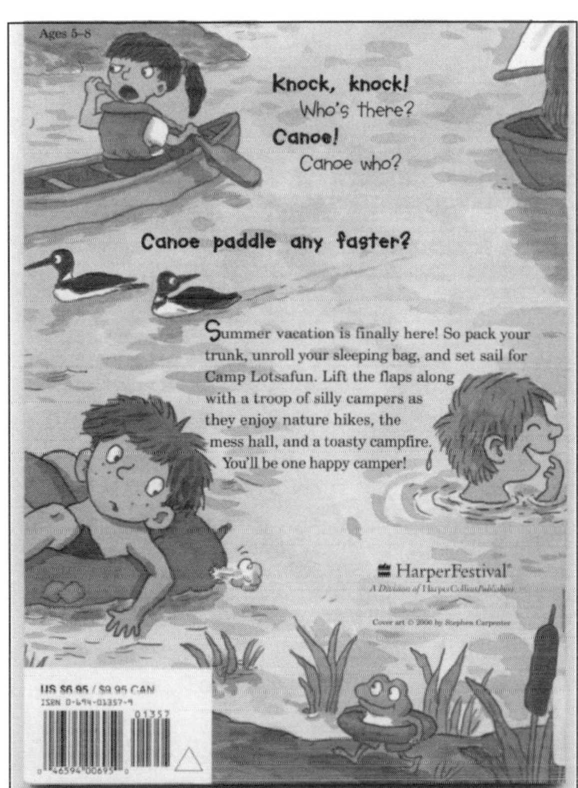

Back Cover

Summer Camp Crack-Ups
And Lots S'more Knock-Knock Jokes To Write Home About
Text copyright © 2001 by Katy Hall and Lisa Eisenberg
Illustrations copyright © 2001 by Stephen Carpenter
Library of Congress catalog card number: 00-106532
Printed in China. All rights reserved.
HarperCollins®, ®, and HarperFestival® are registered trademarks of HarperCollins Publishers Inc.
www.harperchildrens.com

Title Page Verso

Additional information:
16 unnumbered pages; color illustrations; 22 cm.; LCCN: 00-106532

Instructions: Prepare a catalog record for this item.

When cataloging this work, consider the following:

- Difference between a publisher and a publisher's imprint

***AACR2r* rules needed:** 1.1B1; 1.1E1; 1.1F1; 1.1F6; 1.4D1; 1.4F6; 1.5B2; 1.5C1; 1.5D1; 1.6B1; 1.7B10; 1.7B14; 1.8B1; 1.8D1; 2.5B7; 2.5C3; 2.5D1; 21.0D1; 21.29B; 21.30B1; 21.30K2; 22.5A1; MARC 010; MARC 020

Exercise 21

LET'S SPEAK SPANISH!

A FIRST BOOK OF WORDS

EDITED BY **KATHERINE FARRIS**

ILLUSTRATED BY **LINDA HENDRY**

VIKING

Title Page

VIKING
Published by the Penguin Group
Penguin Books USA Inc., 375 Hudson Street, New York, New York 10014, U.S.A.
Penguin Books Ltd, 27 Wrights Lane, London W8 5TZ, England
Penguin Books Australia Ltd, Ringwood, Victoria, Australia
Penguin Books Canada Ltd, 10 Alcorn Avenue, Toronto, Ontario, Canada M4V 3B2
Penguin Books (N.Z.) Ltd, 182–190 Wairau Road, Auckland 10, New Zealand

Penguin Books Ltd, Registered Offices: Harmondsworth, Middlesex, England

First published in 1993 by Viking, a division of Penguin Books USA Inc.

10 9 8 7 6 5 4 3 2 1

Text copyright © Kids Can Press Ltd., 1991
Illustrations copyright © Linda Hendry, 1991
Spanish translation and pronunciation guide copyright © Viking, a division of Penguin Books USA Inc., 1993
All rights reserved

Adapted from *The Kids Can Press French & English Word Book*, first published in Canada by The Kids Can Press, 1991
Translated by Arshes Anasal

Printed in Hong Kong Set in Century Schoolbook
Without limiting the rights under copyright reserved above, no part of this publication may be reproduced, stored in or introduced into a retrieval system, or transmitted, in any form or by any means (electronic, mechanical, photocopying, recording or otherwise), without the prior written permission of both the copyright owner and the above publisher of this book.

Title Page Verso—Portion

Additional information:
48 pages; color illustrations; 32 cm.; LCCN: 92-41736; ISBN: 0-670-84994-4
Summary: Labeled pictures in Spanish and English introduce vocabulary for familiar objects and events, as well as concepts such as colors, numbers, and opposites.

Instructions: Prepare a catalog record for this item.

When cataloging this work, consider the following:

- What information from the title page verso needs to be included in the cataloging record?

***AACR2r* rules needed:** 1.0C1; 1.1B1; 1.1E1; 1.1F6; 1.4C3; 1.4D1; 1.4F1; 1.4F6; 1.5B2; 1.5C1; 1.5D1; 1.7B2; 1.7B6; 1.7B7; 1.7B17; 1.7B22; 2.5B2; 2.5C3; 2.5D1; 2.7B17; 21.0D1; 21.30D1; 21.30G1; 21.30K2a; 22.5A1; MARC 010; MARC 020

Exercise 22

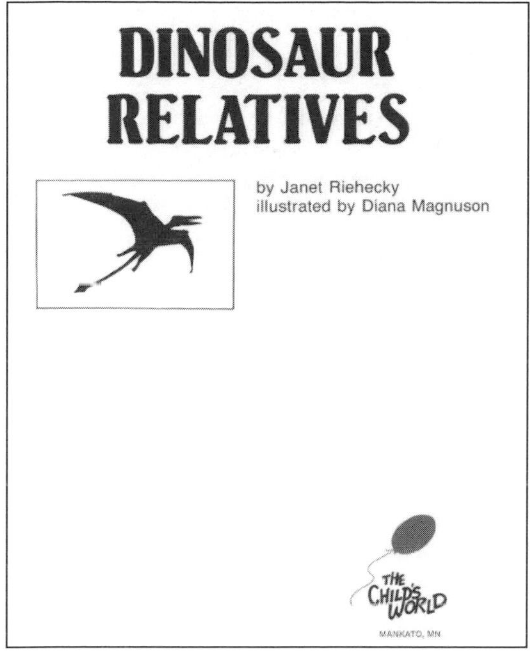

DINOSAUR RELATIVES

by Janet Riehecky
illustrated by Diana Magnuson

THE CHILD'S WORLD
MANKATO, MN

Title Page

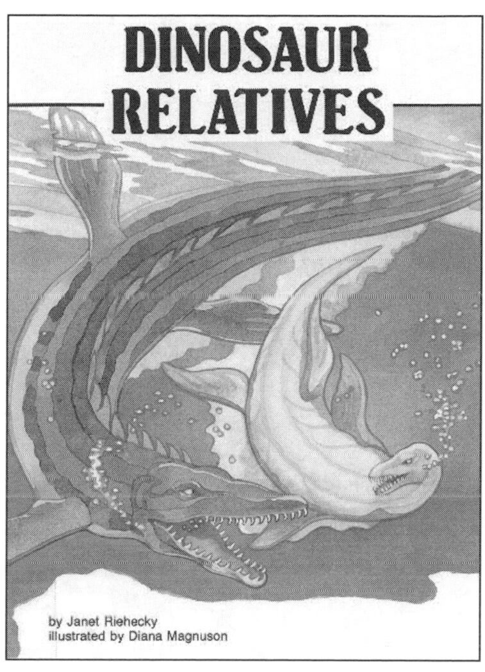

DINOSAUR RELATIVES

by Janet Riehecky
illustrated by Diana Magnuson

Cover

© 1991 The Child's World, Inc.
Mankato, MN
All rights reserved. Printed in U.S.A.

Summary: Describes other reptiles that were alive during the age of dinosaurs, including creatures that lived in the sea and those that flew through the skies.
ISBN 0-89565-626-4

Title Page Verso—Portion

DINOSAUR BOOKS

ALLOSAURUS
ANATOSAURUS
ANKYLOSAURUS
APATOSAURUS
BARYONYX
BRACHIOSAURUS
COELOPHYSIS
COMPSOGNATHUS
DEINONYCHUS
DINOSAUR RELATIVES
DISCOVERING DINOSAURS
DIPLODOCUS
HYPSILOPHODON
IGUANODON
MAIASAURA
MEGALOSAURUS
ORNITHOMIMUS
OVIRAPTOR
PACHYCEPHALOSAURUS
PARASAUROLOPHUS
PROTOCERATOPS
SALTASAURUS
STEGOSAURUS
TRICERATOPS
TROODON
TYRANNOSAURUS

0-89565-626-4

Back Cover

Additional information:
32 pages; black and white and color illustrations; 26 cm.; LCCN: 90-43744
Summary: Describes other reptiles that were alive during the age of dinosaurs, including creatures that lived in the sea and those that flew through the skies.

Instructions: Prepare a catalog record for this item.

When cataloging this work, consider the following:

- What information can we obtain by looking at the back cover of the book?
- Series authority record

***AACR2r* rules needed:** 1.1B1; 1.1F1; 1.1F6; 1.4C1; 1.4C3; 1.4D1; 1.4D2; 1.4D3; 1.4F6; 1.5B2; 1.5C1; 1.5D1; 1.7B17; 1.7B18; 1.8B1; 2.5B2; 2.5C3; 2.5D1; 2.7B17; 2.7B18; 21.1A2; 22.5A1; MARC 010; MARC 020

Exercise 23

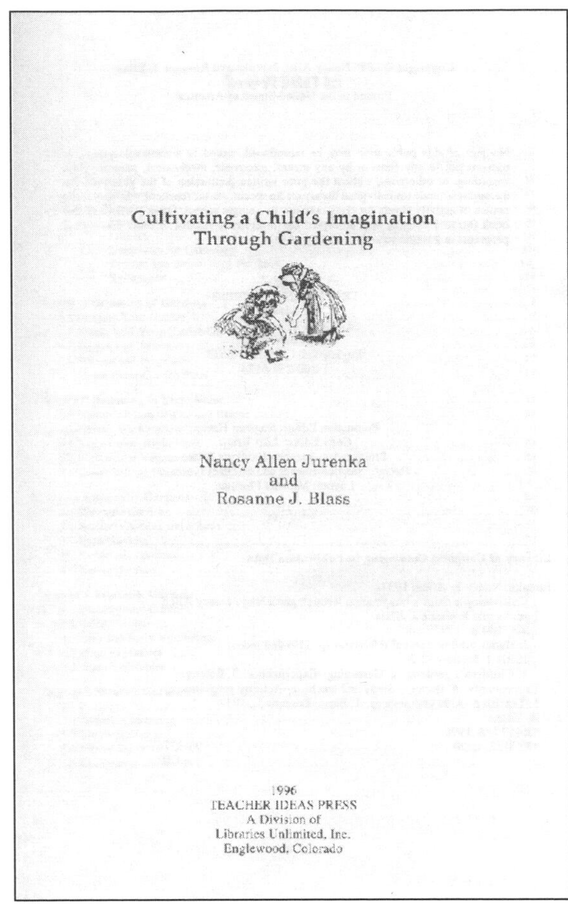
Cultivating a Child's Imagination
Through Gardening

Nancy Allen Jurenka
and
Rosanne J. Blass

1996
TEACHER IDEAS PRESS
A Division of
Libraries Unlimited, Inc.
Englewood, Colorado

Title Page

Copyright © 1996 Nancy Allen Jurenka and Rosanne J. Blass
All Rights Reserved
Printed in the United States of America

No part of this publication may be reproduced, stored in a retrieval system, or transmitted, in any form or by any means, electronic, mechanical, photocopying, recording, or otherwise, without the prior written permission of the publisher. An exception is made for individual library media specialists and teachers, who may make copies of activity sheets for classroom use in a single school. Other portions of this book (up to 15 pages) may be copied for in-service programs or other educational programs in a single school.

TEACHER IDEAS PRESS
A Division of
Libraries Unlimited, Inc.
P.O. Box 6633
Englewood, CO 80155-6633
1-800-237-6124

Production Editor: Stephen Haenel
Copy Editor: Lori Kranz
Proofreader: Suzanne Hawkins Burke
Design: Stephen Haenel and Michael Florman
Layout: Michael Florman

Title Page Verso—Portion

Along the Garden Path to Literacy and Learning

Cultivate learning in students with imaginative projects on the theme of gardens—and watch their interest grow! Each of these 45 lessons focuses on a specific book about plants, gardens, or growing and offers a variety of engaging activities that enhance creativity and build literacy skills. Whether it's building a bird house, listening to a garden poem, performing in a play, making a garden calendar, or planting a friendship garden, these activities will motivate and inform young learners. Recipes for treats also accompany the lessons. This is a unique and fun resource with many classroom possibilities.

Grades K–6

Back Cover—Portion

Additional information:
xiv, 142 pages; illustrations; 28 cm.; includes bibliographical references (pp. 119-132) and indexes to authors, subjects, and activities; LCCN: 96-32747; ISBN: 1-56308-452-X (pbk.)

Instructions: Prepare a catalog record for this item.

When cataloging this work, consider the following:

- Summary
- Use the LC Authorities file to find the proper entries for the authors

***AACR2r* rules needed:** 1.1B1; 1.1F1; 1.1F4; 1.4C1; 1.4C3; 1.4D1; 1.4F1; 1.5B2; 1.5C1;1.5D1; 1.7B14; 1.7B17; 1.7B18; 2.5B2; 2.5C1; 2.5D1; 2.7B14; 2.7B17; 2.7B18; 21.6A1a; 21.30B1; 22.5A1; MARC 010; MARC 020

Exercise 24

RADCLIFFE BIOGRAPHY SERIES

HELEN and TEACHER

The Story of Helen Keller and Anne Sullivan Macy

JOSEPH P. LASH

A Merloyd Lawrence Book

Addison-Wesley Publishing Company, Inc.
Reading, Massachusetts Menlo Park, California New York
Don Mills, Ontario Harlow, England Amsterdam Bonn
Sydney Singapore Tokyo Madrid San Juan
Paris Seoul Milan Mexico City Taipei

Title Page

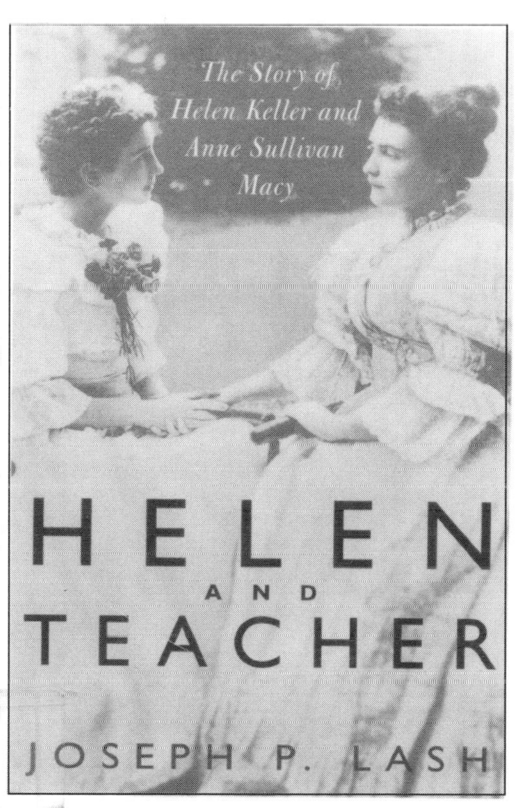

Cover

Additional information:
xvii, 811 pages; [40] pages of plates; illustrations; portraits; 24 cm.; bibliographical references (pages 787-789); index; Radcliffe biography series
Summary: Biography of Helen Keller focusing on her relationship with her teacher Annie Sullivan covering the years from Sullivan's childhood in an almshouse in the 1860s to Keller's death in 1968.

Instructions: Prepare a catalog record for this item.

When cataloging this work, consider the following:

- Publishing history
- Physical description

***AACR2r* rules needed:** 1.1B1; 1.1C1; 1.1F1; 1.4C1; 1.4C3; 1.4C5; 1.4D1; 1.4D2; 1.4F6; 1.5B2; 1.5C1; 1.5D1; 1.6B1; 1.7B7; 1.7B17; 1.7B18; 1.8B1; 1.8E1; 2.5B2; 2.5C2; 2.5D1; 2.7B7; 2.7B17; 2.7B18; 21.1A2; 22.5A1; MARC 020

Pebble Books are published by Capstone Press
151 Good Counsel Drive, P.O. Box 669, Mankato, Minnesota 56002
http://www.capstone-press.com

Copyright © 2001 Capstone Press. All rights reserved
No part of this book may be reproduced without written permission from the publisher. The publisher takes no responsibility for the use of any of the materials or methods described in this book, nor for the products thereof.
Printed in the United States of America.

1 2 3 4 5 6 06 05 04 03 02 01

Library of Congress Cataloging-in-Publication Data
Schaefer, Lola M., 1950–
Hanukkah/by Lola M. Schaefer.
p. cm.—(Holidays and celebrations)
Includes bibliographical references and index.
Summary: Presents, in simple text and photographs, the history of Hanukkah and how it is celebrated in the United States.
ISBN 0-7368-0662-8
1. Hanukkah—Juvenile literature. [1. Hanukkah. 2. Holidays.] I. Title. II. Series.
BM695.H3 S27 2001
394.267—dc21 00-023056

Note to Parents and Teachers

The Holidays and Celebrations series supports national social studies standards related to culture. This book describes Hanukkah and illustrates how it is celebrated in the United States. The photographs support early readers in understanding the text. The repetition of words and phrases helps early readers learn new words. This book also introduces early readers to subject-specific vocabulary words, which are defined in the Words to Know section. Early readers may need assistance to read some words and to use the Table of Contents, Words to Know, Read More, Internet Sites, and Index/Word List sections of the book.

Title Page Verso—Portion

Exercise 25

Necessary Journeys

Letting Ourselves Learn From Life

Nancy L. Snyderman, M.D., and Peg Streep

HYPERION
New York

Title Page

Excerpt from Anne Morrow Lindbergh's *Gift from the Sea*, reprinted by permission of Pantheon Books. Copyright © 1955, 1976.

Photograph on page 230 by Alfred Sandstedt. Copyright © Gayle Workman.

The Zen parable was reprinted in *Zen Flesh, Zen Bones*, translated by Paul Reps.

Printed in the United States of America.
For information address:
Hyperion, 77 West 66th Street,
New York, New York 10023.

ISBN: 0-7868-6513-X

Book design by Richard Oriolo

FIRST EDITION

10 9 8 7 6 5 4 3 2 1

Title Page Verso

Contents

Table of Contents

U.S. $19.95
Canada $27.95

Compassionate wisdom and inspiration on the challenges of living a woman's life from one of America's leading medical authorities

For years, Nancy Snyderman has been a familiar and trusted presence in the lives of women all over the country, both as a well-known correspondent on *Good Morning America* and *20/20* and as the author of the highly successful *Dr. Nancy Snyderman's Guide to Good Health*. Now, in a new book filled with warmth and honesty, she turns her attention to those continuing journeys of self-discovery and fulfillment that are part of every woman's life.

Filled with her own heartfelt and revealing stories, *Necessary Journeys* illuminates the joys and challenges of women's everyday lives and shows us how every experience can be an opportunity for emotional and spiritual growth. At the heart of this book are the real

(continued on back flap)

(continued from front flap)

issues women ages 35–60 confront, no matter which path they have chosen: issues of confidence and self-esteem, love and relationships, health and aging, parenting and self-fulfillment. Nancy Snyderman has written that rare book of insight, encouragement, and support, one that reminds all women that we already possess what we need to give voice to our inner selves in each stage of our lives.

Dr. Nancy L. Snyderman is a mother of three, a wife, and a surgeon who specializes in otolaryngology. She is a medical correspondent for ABC News, *20/20*, and *Good Morning America*.

Peg Streep is the mother of a daughter and the author of *Spiritual Gardening*, among other books.

Jacket design by Cathy Saska
Jacket photograph by Deborah Feingold

HYPERION

5/00
www.hyperionbooks.com

Jacket Flaps

Additional information:
248 pages; 20 cm.; bibliographic references (pp. 241–243); LCCN: 00-029584

Instructions: Prepare a catalog record for this item.

***AACR2r* rules needed:** 1.1B1; 1.1E1; 1.1F1; 1.1F6; 1.2B1; 1.4C1; 1.4D1; 1.4F6; 1.5B2; 1.5D1; 1.7B18; 2.5B2; 2.5B3; 2.5D1; 2.7B18; 21.1A2; 21.30B1; 22.5A1; App. B; App. C; MARC 020

Exercise 26

Straight Talk on
INVESTING
What You Need to Know

Jack Brennan
with
Marta McCave

John Wiley & Sons, Inc.

Title Page

Published by John Wiley & Sons, Inc., Hoboken, New Jersey.

Published simultaneously in Canada.

For general information on our other products and services, or technical support, please contact our Customer Care Department within the United States at 800-762-2974, outside the United States at 317-572-3993 or fax 317-572-4002.

Wiley also publishes its books in a variety of electronic formats. Some content that appears in print may not be available in electronic books.

ISBN 0-471-26579-9

Printed in the United States of America

10 9 8 7 6 5 4 3 2 1

Title Page Verso

Cover

Additional information:
xiv, 239 pages; black and white illustrations; 24 cm.; index; bibliographic references (pages 233-234); LCCN: 2002014899

Instructions: Prepare a catalog record for this item.

***AACR2r* rules needed:** 1.1B1; 1.1E1; 1.1F1; 1.1F5; 1.4C1; 1.4C3; 1.4D1; 1.4D2; 1.4F6; 1.5B2; 1.5C1; 1.5D1; 1.7B18; 2.5B2; 2.5C1; 2.5D1; 2.7B18; 21.1A2; 21.30B1; 21.30J2; 22.5A1; MARC 020

Exercise 27

Title Page

Cover

Text copyright © 1981 by Arnold Lobel. Illustrations copyright © 1981 by Anita Lobel. All rights reserved. No part of this book may be reproduced or utilized in any form or by any means, electronic or mechanical, including photocopying, recording or by any information storage and retrieval system, without permission in writing from the Publisher, Greenwillow Books, a division of William Morrow & Company, Inc., 105 Madison Avenue, New York, N.Y. 10016.

Printed in the United States of America   First Edition   10 9 8 7 6 5 4 3 2 1

Library of Congress Cataloging in Publication Data   Lobel, Arnold.   On Market Street.
Summary: A child buys presents from A to Z in the shops along Market Street.
[1. Shopping–Fiction. 2. Alphabet. 3. Stories in rhyme] I. Lobel, Anita. II. Title.
PZ8.3.L820m   [E]   80-21418   ISBN 0-688-80309-1   ISBN 0-688-84309-3 (lib. bdg.)

Title Page Verso—Portion

Additional information:
40 unnumbered pages; mostly colored illustrations; 26 cm.
Summary: A child buys presents from A to Z in the shops along Market Street.

Instructions: Prepare a catalog record for this item.

When cataloging this work, consider the following:

- The main entry
- Physical description
- Does the CIP agree with *AACR2r* rules? Why or why not?

***AACR2r* rules needed:** 1.1B1; 1.1F1; 1.1F6; 1.2B1; 1.4C1; 1.4D1; 1.4F6; 1.5B2; 1.5C1; 1.5D1; 1.7B17; 1.8B1; 1.8E1; 2.5B2; 2.5C3; 2.5D1; 2.7B17; 21.6A1a; 21.6B1; 22.5A1; MARC 010; MARC 020

Exercise 28

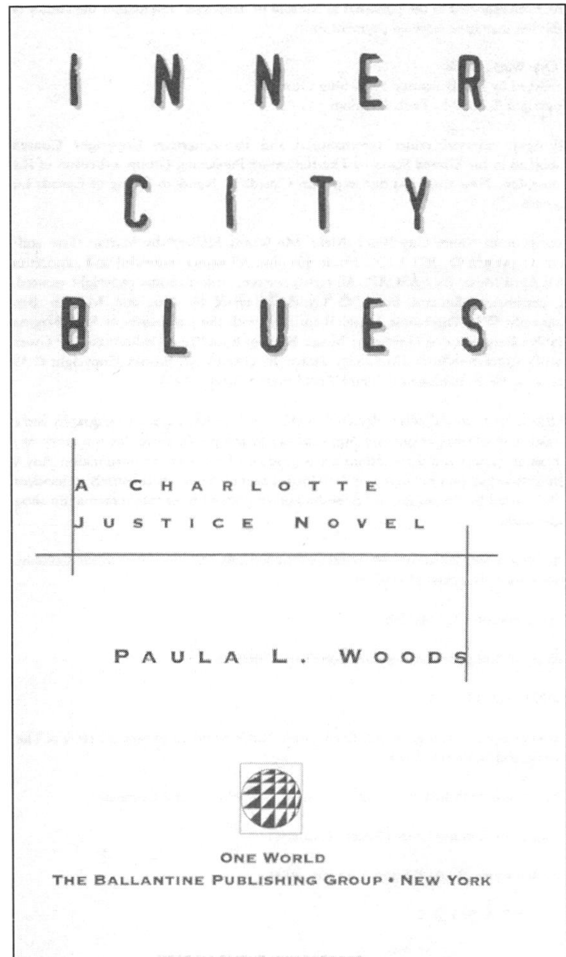

INNER
CITY
BLUES

A CHARLOTTE
JUSTICE NOVEL

PAULA L. WOODS

ONE WORLD
THE BALLANTINE PUBLISHING GROUP • NEW YORK

Title Page

Sale of this book without a front cover may be unauthorized. If this book is coverless, it may have been reported to the publisher as "unsold or destroyed" and neither the author nor the publisher may have received payment for it.

A One World Book
Published by The Ballantine Publishing Group
Copyright © 1999 by Paula L. Woods

All rights reserved under International and Pan-American Copyright Conventions. Published in the United States by The Ballantine Publishing Group, a division of Random House, Inc., New York, and distributed in Canada by Random House of Canada Limited, Toronto.

Excerpt from "Inner City Blues (Make Me Wanna Holler)" by Marvin Gaye and James Nyx. Copyright © 1971 Jobete Music Co., Inc. All rights controlled and administered by EMI April Music Inc. (ASCAP). All rights reserved. International copyright secured. Used by permission. Excerpt from "O Cantador," lyrics by Alan and Marilyn Bergman. Copyright © by Threesome Music. Reprinted with the permission of Alan Bergman and Marilyn Bergman, c/o Threesome Music. Excerpt from "Two Dedications," by Gwendolyn Brooks. Quotation from *The Chicago Picasso*, by Gwendolyn Brooks. Copyright © 1991, in her book *Blacks*, published by Third World Press, Chicago, 1991.

While some historical events depicted in this novel are factual, as are geography and certain locales, and certain persons and organizations in the public view, this is a work of fiction whose characters and their actions are a product of the author's imagination. Any resemblance to actual persons, living or dead, organizations, or events is entirely coincidental and not intended by the author, nor does the author pretend to private information about such individuals.

One World and Ballantine are registered trademarks and the One World Colophon is a trademark of Random House, Inc.

www.randomhouse.com/BB/

Library of Congress Catalog Card Number: 99-69500

ISBN 0-345-43793-4

Cover design and collage by Kristine V. Mills-Noble based on photos courtesy of The Stock Market and Definitive Stock

This edition published by arrangement with W.W. Norton and Company.

Manufactured in the United States of America

First Ballantine Books Edition: February 2000

10 9 8 7 6 5 4 3 2

Title Page Verso

Additional information:
316 pages; 21 cm.
Summary: This is a mystery/suspense novel.

Instructions: Prepare a catalog record for this item.

When cataloging this work, consider the following:

- Publisher
- Genre subject heading(s)

***AACR2r* rules needed:** 1.1B1; 1.1F1; 1.1F6; 1.2B1; 1.4C1; 1.4D2; 1.5B2; 1.5D1; 1.7B7; 1.7B9; 1.8B1; 2.5B2; 2.5D1; 2.7B7; 2.7B9; 21.0B1; 22.5A1; MARC 010; MARC 020

Exercise 29

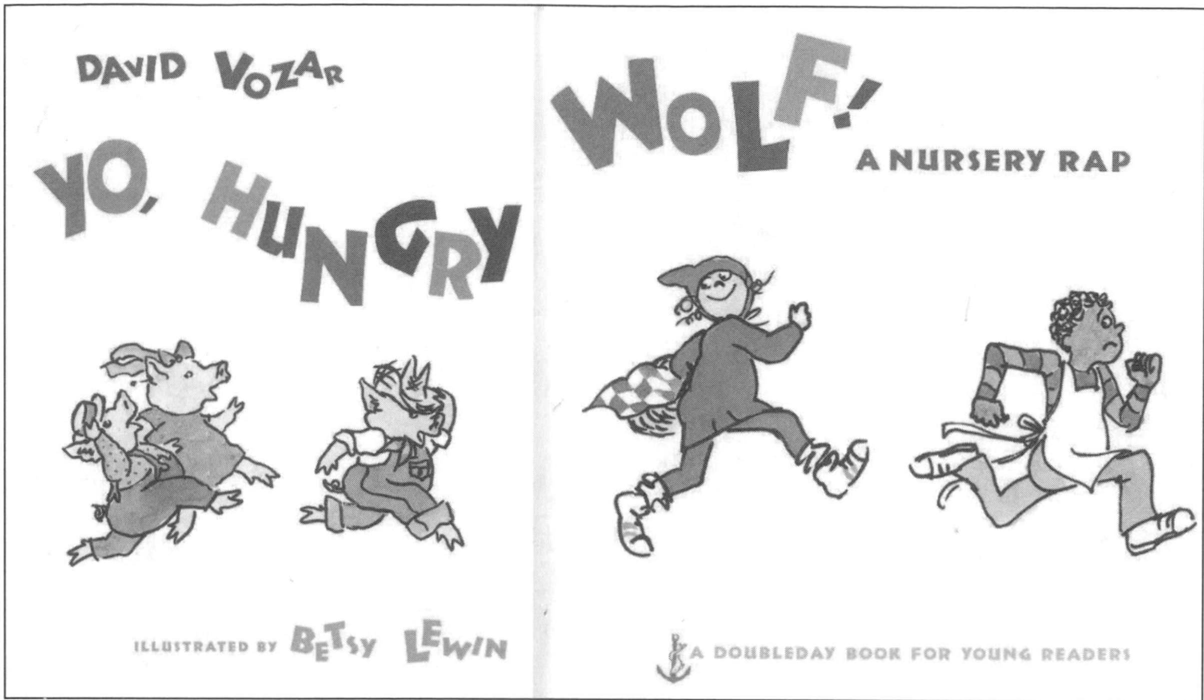

DAVID VOZAR

YO, HUNGRY WOLF!

A NURSERY RAP

ILLUSTRATED BY BETSY LEWIN

A DOUBLEDAY BOOK FOR YOUNG READERS

Facing Title Page

A Doubleday Book for Young Readers
Published by
Delacorte Press
Bantam Doubleday Dell Publishing Group, Inc.
666 Fifth Avenue
New York, New York 10103
Doubleday and the portrayal of an anchor with a dolphin are trademarks of
Bantam Doubleday Dell Publishing Group, Inc.
Text copyright © 1993 by David Vozar
Illustrations copyright © 1993 by Betsy Lewin
All rights reserved. No part of this book may be reproduced or transmitted in any form or by any means, electronic or mechanical, including photocopying, recording, or by any information storage and retrieval system, without the written permission of the Publisher, except where permitted by law.

Title Page Verso—Portion

Additional information:
48 unnumbered pages; color illustrations; 28 cm.; LCCN: 91-46264; ISBN: 0-385-30452-8
Summary: A retelling in rap verse of "The Three Little Pigs," "Little Red Riding Hood," and "The Boy Who Cried Wolf."

Instructions: Prepare a catalog record for this item.

When cataloging this work, consider the following:

- Chief source of information
- Publisher

***AACR2r* rules needed:** 1.1B1; 1.1E1; 1.1F1; 1.1F6; 1.4C1; 1.4C3; 1.4D1; 1.4F6; 1.5B2; 1.5C1; 1.5D1; 1.7B9; 1.7B17; 1.8B1; 2.0B1; 2.5B7; 2.5C3; 2.5D1; 2.7B9; 2.7B17; 2.7B18; 21.1A2; 21.29B; 21.30K2; 22.5A1; MARC 010; MARC 020

Exercise 30

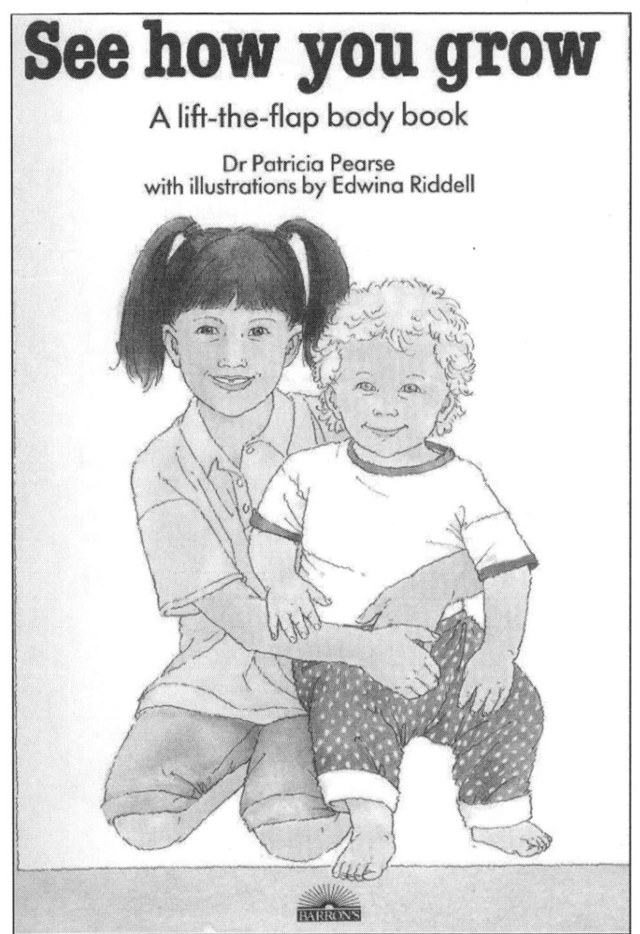

See how you grow

A lift-the-flap body book

Dr Patricia Pearse
with illustrations by Edwina Riddell

BARRON'S

Title Page

First edition for the United States, the Philippines, and Canada published 1988 by Barron's Educational Series, Inc.

Text and illustrations © Frances Lincoln 1988

See How You Grow was conceived, edited and produced by Frances Lincoln Limited, 4 Torriano Mews, Torriano Avenue, London, England.

All rights reserved.
No part of this book may be reproduced in any form by photostat, microfilm, xerography, or any other means, or incorporated into any information retrieval system, electronic or mechanical, without the written permission of the copyright owner.

All inquiries should be addressed to:
Barron's Educational Series, Inc.
250 Wireless Boulevard
Hauppauge, New York 11788

International Standard Book No. 0-8120-5936-0
Library of Congress Catalog Card No. 87-33268
Printed and bound in Singapore

Design and Art Direction Debbie MacKinnon
Editors Pippa Rubinstein
Sarah Mitchell
5 9870 9876

Title Page Verso—Portion

Additional information:
32 unnumbered pages; color illustrations; 29 cm.

Instructions: Prepare a catalog record for this item.

When cataloging this work, consider the following:

- Publishing history

***AACR2r* rules needed:** 1.1B2; 1.1E1; 1.1F1; 1.1F6; 1.1F7; 1.2B1; 1.4C1; 1.4C3; 1.4D1; 1.4D2; 1.4F1; 1.5B2; 1.5C1; 1.5D1; 1.7B6; 1.8B1; 2.5B7; 2.5C3; 2.5D1; 21.1A2; 21.29B; 21.30H1; 21.30K2; 22.5A1; App C; MARC 010; MARC 020

Exercise 31

The Texas Cherokees

A People Between Two Fires 1819–1840

by Dianna Everett

University of Oklahoma Press : Norman and London

Title Page

The Texas Cherokees: A People Between Two Fires, 1819–1840, is Volume 203 in The Civilization of the American Indian Series.

The paper in this book meets the guidelines for permanence and durability of the Committee on Production Guidelines for Book Longevity of the Council on Library Resources, Inc. ♾

2 3 4 5 6 7 8 9 10 11

Title Page Verso

Additional information:
xiv, 173 pages; black and white illustrations; maps; 23 cm.; bibliographical references (pages 155-166); index; LCCN: 90-50233; ISBN: 0-8061-2296-X

Instructions: Prepare a catalog record for this item.

When cataloging this work, consider the following:

- Title statement
- Series statement

***AACR2r* rules needed:** 1.1B1; 1.1E1; 1.1E2; 1.1F1; 1.4C1; 1.4C3; 1.4F6; 1.5B2; 1.5C1; 1.5D1; 1.6B1; 1.6G1; 1.8B1; 2.5B2; 2.5C2; 2.5D1; 21.4A1; 22.5A1; App C; MARC 010; MARC 020

Exercise 32

Achievements of the
Left Hand: Essays on the
Prose of John Milton

Edited by Michael Lieb
and John T. Shawcross

The University of Massachusetts Press
Amherst

Title Page

Library of Congress Catalog Card Number 73-79506
ISBN Number 0-87023-125-1
Printed in the United States of America
University of Massachusetts Press
Amherst, Massachusetts 01002
Publication of this book has been financially assisted
by the American Council of Learned Societies under
a grant from the Andrew W. Mellon Foundation.

Title Page Verso

Table of Contents (two pages combined)

(Continued on Next Page)

Exercise 32

LC Control Number: 73079506
000 00954cam 2200265 450
001 3142808
005 20010417100910.0
008 740506s1974 mau b 000 0 eng
035 __ |**9** (DLC) 73079506
906 __ |**a** 7 |**b** cbc |**c** orignew |**d** 2 |**e** opcn |**f** 19 |**g** y-gencatlg
010 __ |**a** 73079506
020 __ |**a** 0870231251
040 __ |**a** DLC |**c** DLC |**d** DLC
050 00 |**a** PR3581 |**b** .L47
082 00 |**a** 824/.4
100 1_ |**a** Lieb, Michael, |**d** 1940-
245 10 |**a** Achievements of the left hand: essays on the prose of John Milton. |**c** Edited by Michael Lieb and John T. Shawcross.
260 __ |**a** Amherst, |**b** University of Massachusetts Press |**c** [1974]
300 __ |**a** viii, 396 p. |**c** 25 cm.
350 __ |**a** $12.50
504 __ |**a** Bibliography: p. [393]-394.
600 10 |**a** Milton, John, |**d** 1608-1674 |**x** Prose.
650 _0 |**a** English prose literature |**y** Early modern, 1500-1700 |**x** History and criticism.
700 1_ |**a** Shawcross, John T., |**e** joint author.

Additional information:
viii, 396 pages; 24 cm.; bibliography (pages 393-394); other bibliographic references.

Instructions: The MARC record shown has several errors in it according to today's rules. Edit the record so that it is correct.

When cataloging this work, consider the following:

- Main entry
- Notes needed

***AACR2r* rules needed:** 1.1B1; 1.1E1; 1.1F4; 1.4D2; 1.4D3; 1.4F6; 1.5B1; 1.5D1; 1.7B18; 1.8B1; 2.5B2; 2.5D1; 2.7B18; 21.0D1; 21.30D; 21.30D1; 22.5A1; MARC 010; MARC 020; MARC 600

Exercise 33

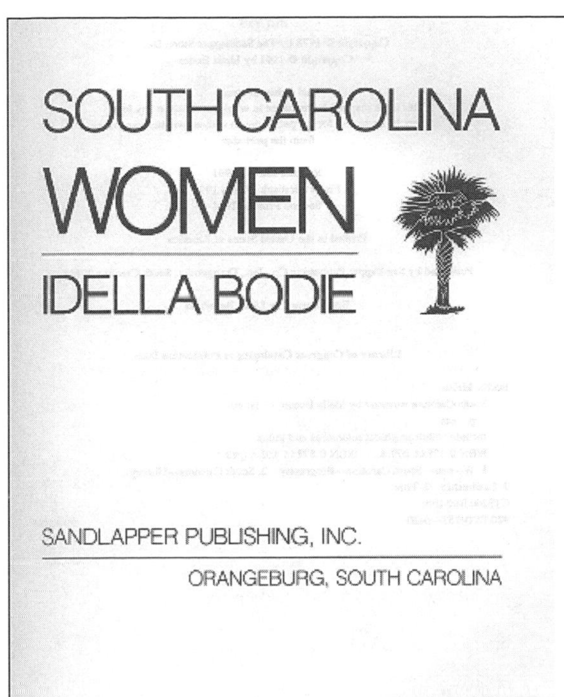

SOUTH CAROLINA
WOMEN
IDELLA BODIE

SANDLAPPER PUBLISHING, INC.
ORANGEBURG, SOUTH CAROLINA

Title Page

Revised Edition 1991
First Paperback Edition 1991
Second Printing 1994

Printed in the United States of America

Published by Sandlapper Publishing Co., Inc., Orangeburg, South Carolina 29115

Book design by Linda Benefield

Title Page Verso—Portion

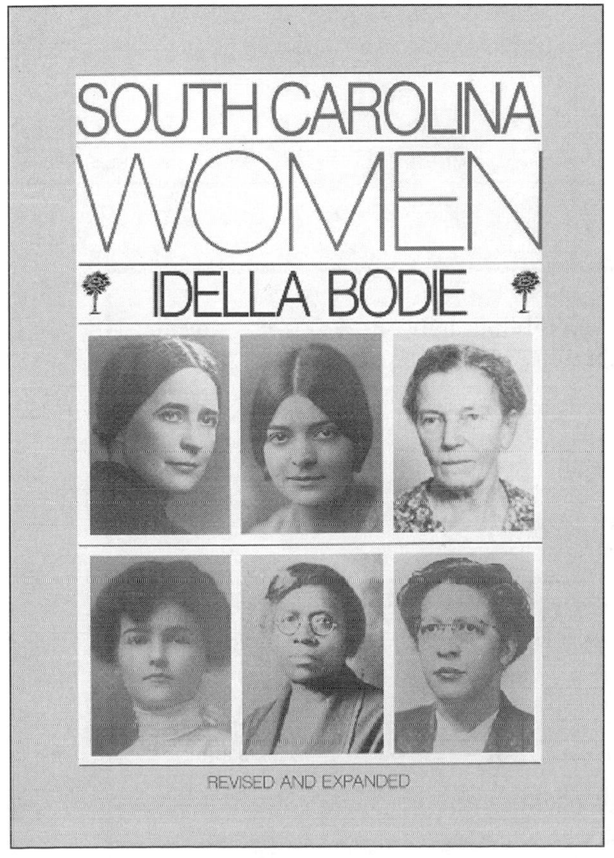

Cover

South Carolina Women profiles fifty-one notable women of the Palmetto state. Written to appeal to readers of all ages, the book is especially intended to help young people appreciate the contributions women have made to this state and the nation.

The stories of South Carolina's leading women are told in lively, narrative form. Readers first meet **Judith Giton Manigault**, a French Huguenot who wielded an ax clearing land for her new home in South Carolina in the 1600s. Though she was to be the founder of a great family, she wrote in a letter, "I have been six months without tasting bread."

Then, in chronological order, come stories of women black and white, young and old, wartime heroines and leaders in medicine, education, the arts, the civil rights movement, sports, and government:

Eliza Lucas Pinckney, who at sixteen took over running her family's three plantations when her father was called away, and later was the first planter in the state to successfully grow indigo. . . . **Emily Geiger**, the eighteen-year-old who carried a message through the British lines to the Patriot army during the Revolutionary War, a mission that was considered too dangerous for a Patriot soldier to attempt. . . . **Sarah and Angelina Grimké**, the daughters of a wealthy Charleston judge, who became leading abolitionists. . . . **Matilda Arabella Evans**, who started life in poverty, picking cotton in the fields, but whose determination to get an education carried her through high school, college, and medical school to become the first native black woman doctor in the state.

A final chapter provides basic biographical data on many other distinguished South Carolina women, and a bibliography is included to encourage further reading.

SANDLAPPER PUBLISHING CO., INC.
ORANGEBURG, SOUTH CAROLINA 29115

ISBN 0-87844-102-6

9 780878 441020

10102
1495

Back Cover

(*Continued on Next Page*)

Exercise 33

Contents

x Contents

Additional information:
x, 178 pages; illustrations; portraits; 27 cm.; bibliographical references (pages 163-172); index; LCCN: 90-48424; ISBN: 0-87844-079-8; 0-87844-102-6 (pbk.)

Instructions: Prepare a catalog record for this item.

When cataloging this work, consider the following:

- Edition
- Physical description
- Notes needed

***AACR2r* rules needed:** 1.1B1; 1.1F1; 1.2B1; 1.4C1; 1.4C3; 1.4D1; 1.4D2; 1.5B2; 1.5C1; 1.5D1; 1.7B17; 1.7B18; 1.8B1; 1.8B2; 1.8E1; 2.5B2; 2.5C2; 2.5D1; 2.7B18; 21.1A2; 22.5A1; App. B9; App. B14; MARC 010; MARC 020

Exercise 34

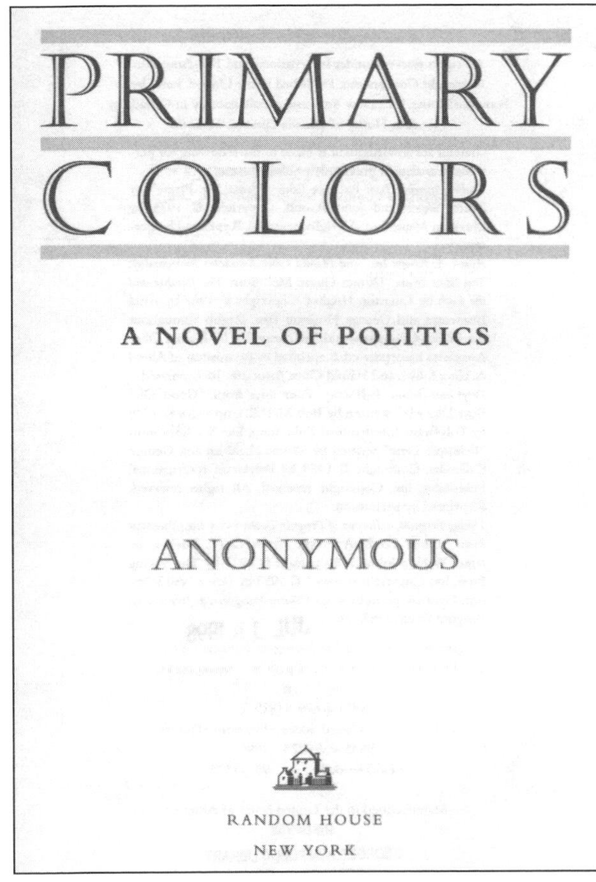

Title Page

Copyright © 1996 by Machiavelliana, Inc.

All rights reserved under International and Pan-American Copyright Conventions. Published in the United States by Random House, Inc., New York and simultaneously in Canada by Random House of Canada Limited, Toronto.

Grateful acknowledgment is made to the following for permission to reprint previously published material:
Carlin America, Inc.: Excerpt from "Please Mr. Please" by Bruce Welch and John Rostill. Copyright © 1975 by Bluegum Music Ltd. All rights reserved. Reprinted by permission.
Alfred A. Knopf, Inc., and Harold Ober Associates Incorporated: Ten lines from "Dinner Guest: Me" from *The Panther and the Lash* by Langston Hughes. Copyright © 1967 by Arna Bontemps and George Houston Bass. Rights throughout the British Commonwealth are controlled by Harold Ober Associates Incorporated. Reprinted by permission of Alfred A. Knopf, Inc., and Harold Ober Associates Incorporated.
PolyGram Music Publishing: Four lines from "Good Ole' Boys Like Me" written by Bob McDill. Copyright © 1979 by PolyGram International Publishing, Inc. Six lines from "Primrose Lane" written by Wayne Shanklin and George Callender. Copyright © 1958 by PolyGram International Publishing, Inc. Copyright renewed. All rights reserved. Reprinted by permission.
Viking Penguin, a division of Penguin Books USA Inc.: Excerpt from "Listen Lord—A Prayer" from *God's Trombone* by James Weldon Johnson. Copyright © 1927 by The Viking Press, Inc. Copyright renewed © 1955 by Grace Nail Johnson. Used by permission of Viking Penguin, a division of Penguin Books USA Inc.

Title Page Verso

Additional information:
366 pages; 25 cm.; ISBN: 0-679-44859-4; LCCN: 95-39823
Summary: When a former congressional aide becomes part of the staff of the governor of a small southern state, he watches in horror, admiration, and amazement, as the governor mixes calculation and sincerity in his not-so-above-board campaign for the presidency.

Instructions: Prepare a catalog record for this item.

***AACR2r* rules needed:** 1.1B1; 1.1E1; 1.1F1; 1.4C1; 1.4D1; 1.5B2; 1.5D1; 1.7B17; 1.8B1; 2.5B2; 2.5D1; 2.7B17; 21.1A2; 21.4A1; 22.2B1; MARC 010; MARC 020

Exercise 35

ITALIAN NEIGHBORS

OR,

A LAPSED
ANGLO-SAXON
IN VERONA

Tim Parks

Fawcett Columbine • New York

Title Page

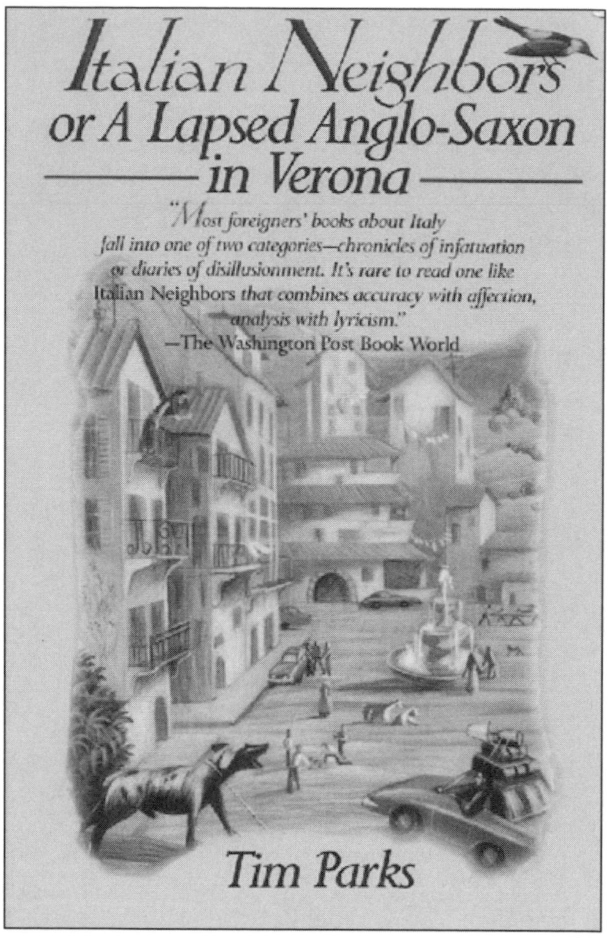

Cover

To protect the privacy of individuals, some names have been altered.

A Fawcett Columbine Book
Published by Ballantine Books

This edition published by arrangement with Grove Press, Inc.

Library of Congress Catalog Card Number: 92-97332

ISBN: 0-449-90818-6

Cover design by Georgia Morrissey
Illustration by Mark Strathy

Manufactured in the United States of America

First Ballantine Books Edition: July 1993

10 9 8 7 6 5

Title Page Verso

Additional information:
vi, 272 pages, 21 cm.

Instructions: Prepare a catalog record for this item.

When cataloging this work, consider the following:

- Title
- Additional added entries (other than subject headings) that might be needed for this record

***AACR2r* rules needed:** 1.1B1; 1.1F1; 1.2B1; 1.4C1; 1.4C3; 1.4D1; 1.4F1; 1.5B1; 1.5B2; 1.5D1; 1.6D1; 1.8B1; 2.5B2; 2.5D1; 21.1A2; 22.5A1; MARC 010; MARC 020

Exercise 36

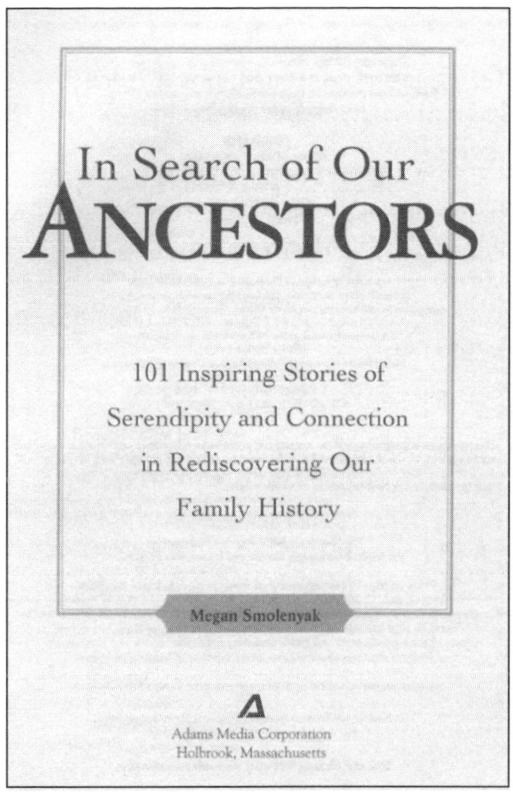

In Search of Our
ANCESTORS

101 Inspiring Stories of
Serendipity and Connection
in Rediscovering Our
Family History

Megan Smolenyak

Adams Media Corporation
Holbrook, Massachusetts

Title Page

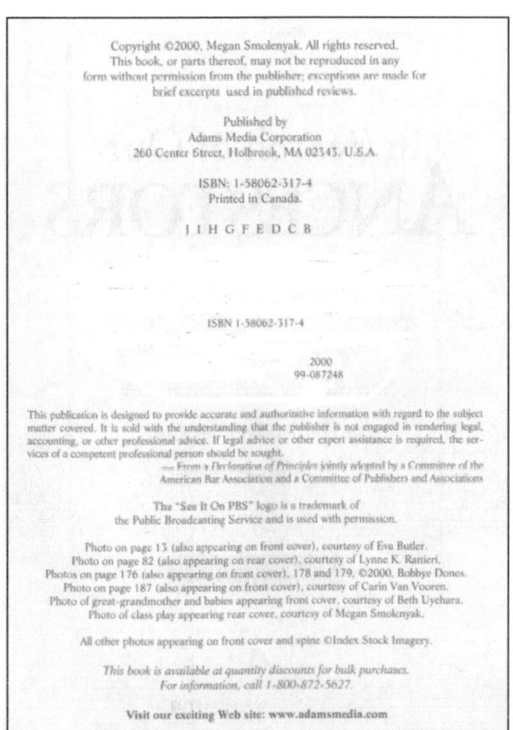

Published by
Adams Media Corporation
260 Center Street, Holbrook, MA 02343. U.S.A.

ISBN: 1-58062-317-4
Printed in Canada.

J I H G F E D C B

ISBN 1-58062-317-4

2000
99-087248

This publication is designed to provide accurate and authoritative information with regard to the subject matter covered. It is sold with the understanding that the publisher is not engaged in rendering legal, accounting, or other professional advice. If legal advice or other expert assistance is required, the services of a competent professional person should be sought.

— *From a Declaration of Principles* jointly adopted by a Committee of the American Bar Association and a Committee of Publishers and Associations

The "See It On PBS" logo is a trademark of
the Public Broadcasting Service and is used with permission.

Photo on page 13 (also appearing on front cover), courtesy of Eva Butler.
Photo on page 82 (also appearing on rear cover), courtesy of Lynne K. Ranieri.
Photos on page 176 (also appearing on front cover), 178 and 179, ©2000, Bobbye Dones.
Photo on page 187 (also appearing on front cover), courtesy of Carin Van Vooren.
Photo of great-grandmother and babies appearing front cover, courtesy of Beth Uyehara.
Photo of class play appearing rear cover, courtesy of Megan Smolenyak.

All other photos appearing on front cover and spine ©Index Stock Imagery.

*This book is available at quantity discounts for bulk purchases.
For information, call 1-800-872-5627.*

Visit our exciting Web site: www.adamsmedia.com

Title Page Verso—Portion

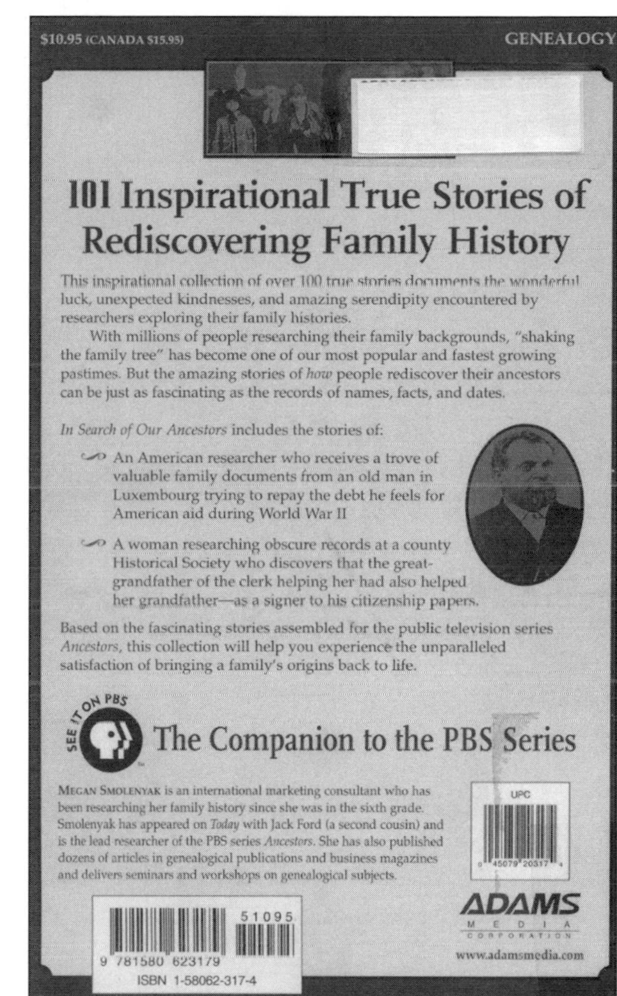

$10.95 (CANADA $15.95) GENEALOGY

101 Inspirational True Stories of Rediscovering Family History

This inspirational collection of over 100 true stories documents the wonderful luck, unexpected kindnesses, and amazing serendipity encountered by researchers exploring their family histories.

With millions of people researching their family backgrounds, "shaking the family tree" has become one of our most popular and fastest growing pastimes. But the amazing stories of *how* people rediscover their ancestors can be just as fascinating as the records of names, facts, and dates.

In Search of Our Ancestors includes the stories of:

- An American researcher who receives a trove of valuable family documents from an old man in Luxembourg trying to repay the debt he feels for American aid during World War II
- A woman researching obscure records at a county Historical Society who discovers that the great-grandfather of the clerk helping her had also helped her grandfather—as a signer to his citizenship papers.

Based on the fascinating stories assembled for the public television series *Ancestors*, this collection will help you experience the unparalleled satisfaction of bringing a family's origins back to life.

SEE IT ON PBS

The Companion to the PBS Series

MEGAN SMOLENYAK is an international marketing consultant who has been researching her family history since she was in the sixth grade. Smolenyak has appeared on *Today* with Jack Ford (a second cousin) and is the lead researcher of the PBS series *Ancestors*. She has also published dozens of articles in genealogical publications and business magazines and delivers seminars and workshops on genealogical subjects.

UPC

0 45079 20317 4

51095

9 781580 623179

ISBN 1-58062-317-4

ADAMS MEDIA CORPORATION

www.adamsmedia.com

Back Cover

Additional information:
x, 241 pages; black and white illustrations; 22 cm.

Instructions: Prepare a MARC record for this item.

When cataloging this work, consider the following:

- Notes needed for this record

***AACR2r* rules needed:** 1.1B1; 1.1E1; 1.1E3; 1.1F1; 1.1F6; 1.4C1; 1.4C3; 1.4D1; 1.5B2; 1.5C1; 1.5D1; 1.7B7; 1.7B17; 1.8B1; 2.5B2; 2.5C1; 2.5D1; 2.7B1; 21.1A2; 22.5A1; App B.9; App B.14; MARC 010; MARC 020

Exercise 37

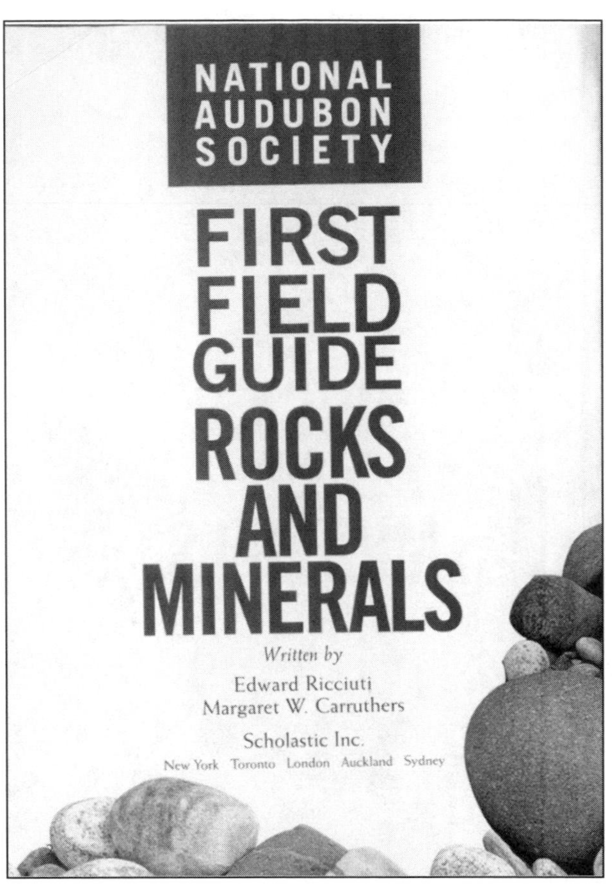

NATIONAL AUDUBON SOCIETY

FIRST FIELD GUIDE

ROCKS AND MINERALS

Written by

Edward Ricciuti

Margaret W. Carruthers

Scholastic Inc.

New York Toronto London Auckland Sydney

Title Page

Additional information:
159 pages; color illustrations; 19 cm.; index; ISBN: 0590054635; 0590054848 (pbk.) LCCN: 97-17991

Instructions: Prepare a catalog record for this item.

When cataloging this work, consider the following:

- Title

***AACR2r* rules needed:** 1.1B1; 1.1E1; 1.1F1; 1.1F6; 1.4D1; 1.4D2; 1.4F6; 1.5B2; 1.5C1; 1.5D1; 2.5B2; 2.5C3; 2.5D1; 21.4A1; 21.29C; 22.5A1; 24.1A; 24.5C1; MARC 010; MARC 020

The National Audubon Society, established in 1905, has 550,000 members and more than 500 chapters nationwide. Its mission is to conserve and restore natural ecosystems, focusing on birds and other wildlife, and these guides are part of that mission. Celebrating the beauty and wonders of nature, Audubon looks toward its second century of educating people of all ages.

For information about Audubon membership, contact:
National Audubon Society
700 Broadway
New York, NY 10003-9562
212-979-3000 800-274-4201
http://www.audubon.org

Title Page Verso—Portion

Exercise 38

IMMORTAL

A Buffy the Vampire Slayer™ Novel

by

Christopher Golden

&

Nancy Holder

POCKET BOOKS

New York London Toronto Sydney Tokyo Singapore

Title Page

This book is a work of fiction. Names, characters, places and incidents are products of the author's imagination or are used fictitiously. Any resemblance to actual events or locales or persons, living or dead, is entirely coincidental.

POCKET BOOKS, a division of Simon & Schuster Inc.
1230 Avenue of the Americas, New York, NY 10020

™ and copyright © 1999 by Twentieth Century Fox Film Corporation. All rights reserved.

All rights reserved, including the right to reproduce this book or portions thereof in any form whatsoever. For information address Pocket Books, 1230 Avenue of the Americas, New York, NY 10020

ISBN: 0-671-04117-7

First Pocket Books hardcover printing October 1999

10 9 8 7 6 5 4 3 2 1

POCKET and colophon are registered trademarks of Simon & Schuster Inc.

Printed in the U.S.A.

Title Page Verso

Buffy the Vampire Slayer™

Child of the Hunt
Return to Chaos
The Gatekeeper Trilogy
  Book 1: Out of the Madhouse
  Book 2: Ghost Roads
  Book 3: Sons of Entropy
Obsidian Fate
Immortal

The Watcher's Guide: The Official Companion to the Hit Show
The Postcards
The Essential Angel
The Sunnydale High Yearbook

Available from POCKET BOOKS

Buffy the Vampire Slayer young adult books

Buffy the Vampire Slayer (movie tie-in)
The Harvest
Halloween Rain
Coyote Moon
Night of the Living Rerun
The Angel Chronicles, Vol. 1
Blooded
The Angel Chronicles, Vol. 2
The Xander Years, Vol. 1
Visitors
Unnatural Selection
The Angel Chronicles, Vol. 3
Power of Persuasion

Available from ARCHWAY Paperbacks

Series Information

Additional information:
309 pages; 22 cm.; LCCN: 00504559; Cover statement: An original novel based on the hit TV series created by Joss Whedon.

Instructions: Prepare a catalog record for this item.

***AACR2r* rules needed:** 1.1B1; 1.1F1; 1.1F4; 1.4C1; 1.4C5; 1.4D1; 1.4F1; 1.5B1; 1.5B2; 1.5D1; 1.6B1; 1.7B12; 1.7B16; 1.7B17; 1.8B1; 1.8D1; 2.5B2; 2.5D1; 21.1A2; 22.5B1; MARC 010; MARC 020

Exercise 39

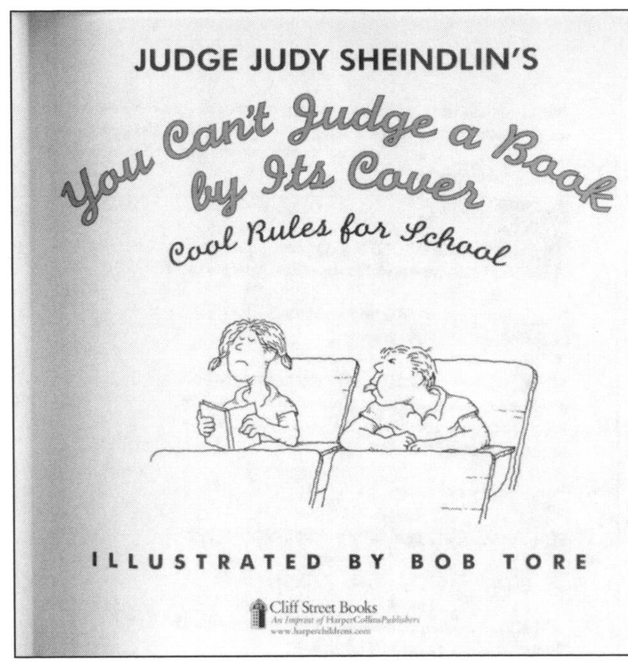

Title Page

Judge Judy Sheindlin's You Can't Judge a Book by Its Cover
Text copyright © 2001 by Judge Judy Sheindlin
Illustrations copyright © 2001 by Bob Tore
Printed in the U.S.A. All rights reserved.
www.harperchildrens.com

Library of Congress Cataloging-in-Publication Data is available.

ISBN 0-06-029483-3 — ISBN 0-06-029484-1 (lib. bdg.)

Typography by Matt Adamec

1 2 3 4 5 6 7 8 9 10

❖

First Edition

Title Page Verso

Additional information:
95 unnumbered pages; black and white illustrations; 24 cm.; LCCN: 00-053512
Summary: Examines the deeper meaning behind popular sayings such as "Never put off to tomorrow what you can do today" and "You can't judge a book by its cover," and applies these rules of thumb to familiar school situations.

Instructions: Prepare a catalog record for this item.

When cataloging this work, consider the following:

- Title

***AACR2r* rules needed:** 1.1B1; 1.1B2; 1.1E1; 1.1F1; 1.2B1; 1.4D1; 1.4F6; 1.5B2; 1.5C1; 1.5D1; 1.7B17; 1.8B1; 1.8B2; 1.8E1; 2.5B7; 2.5C1; 2.5D1; 2.7B17; 21.1A2; 21.29B; 21.30K2; 22.5A1; MARC 010; MARC 020

Exercise 40

The Fellowship of the Ring

BEING THE FIRST PART OF

THE LORD OF THE RINGS

BY

J. R. R. TOLKIEN

Second Edition

HOUGHTON MIFFLIN COMPANY BOSTON

The Riverside Press Cambridge

1967

Title Page

THE LORD OF THE RINGS

BY J. R. R. TOLKIEN

PART I

THE FELLOWSHIP OF THE RING

PART II

THE TWO TOWERS

PART III

THE RETURN OF THE KING

Page Facing Title Page

FIRST PRINTING W

COPYRIGHT © 1966 BY GEORGE ALLEN & UNWIN LTD.
ALL RIGHTS RESERVED INCLUDING THE RIGHT TO
REPRODUCE THIS BOOK OR PARTS THEREOF IN ANY FORM
LIBRARY OF CONGRESS CATALOG CARD NUMBER: 67-12274
PRINTED IN THE UNITED STATES OF AMERICA

Title Page Verso

Additional information:
423 pages; 23 cm; black and white illustrations; map; additional folded two-color map tipped in before last page (41 x 45 cm.)

Instructions: Prepare a catalog record for this item.

When cataloging this item, consider the following:

- Title statement
- Physical description

***AACR2r* rules needed:** 1.1B1; 1.1B9; 1.1F1; 1.2B1; 1.4C1; 1.4D1; 1.4D2; 1.4F1; 1.5B1; 1.5B2; 1.5C1; 1.5D1; 1.7B10; 2.5B2; 2.5C2; 2.5C6; 2.5D1; 21.1A2; 22.5A1; App. B; App. C; MARC 010

Exercise 41

Title Page

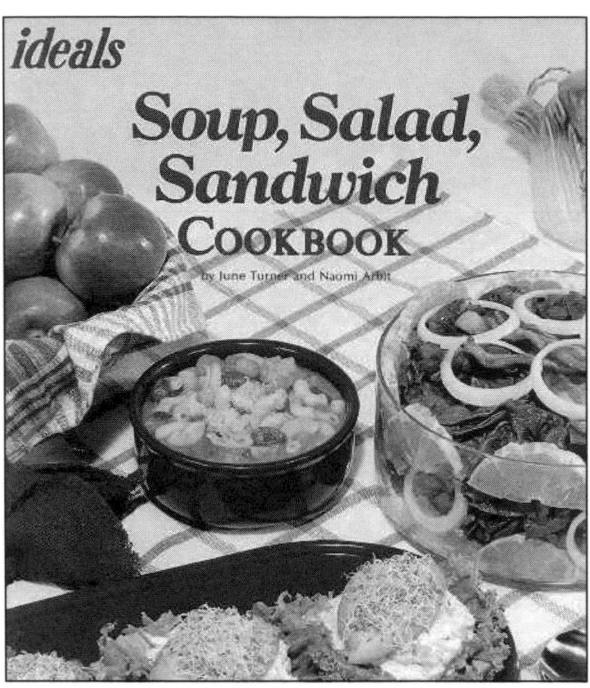

Cover

ISBN 0-8249-3001-0

Copyright © MCMLXXXI by Naomi Arbit and June Turner
All rights reserved.
Printed and bound in the United States of America

Published by Ideals Publishing Corporation
11315 Watertown Plank Road
Milwaukee, WI 53226
Published simultaneously in Canada

Title Page Verso

Additional information:
63 pages; color illustrations; 29 cm.; index

Instructions: Prepare a catalog record for this item.

When cataloging this work, consider the following:

- Title

***AACR2r* rules needed:** 1.1B1; 1.1F1; 1.1F4; 1.4D1; 1.4D2; 1.4F1; 1.4F6; 1.5B2; 1.5C1; 1.5D1; 1.8B1; 2.5B2; 2.5C3; 2.5D1; 21.29B; 21.29C; 21.30B1; 21.30J2; 22.5A1; MARC 020

Contents

Exercise 42

Title Page

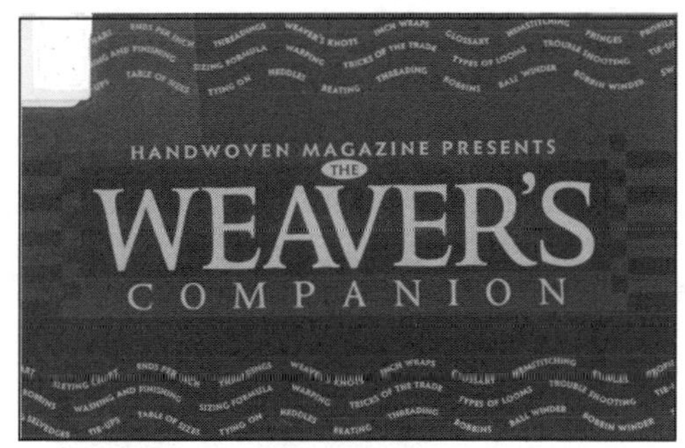

Cover

The Weaver's Companion
Presented by *Handwoven* Magazine

Editors: Linda Ligon, Marilyn Murphy
Managing Editor: Marilyn Murphy
Research Editor: Bobbie Irwin

Interweave Press
201 East Fourth Street
Loveland, Colorado 80537
USA
www.interweave.com

Printed in Singapore.

Proofreaders: Stephen Beal, Nancy Arndt
Editorial and Production Assistant: Nancy Arndt
Book Design and Production: Dean Howes
Illustrations: Gayle Ford
Print Manager: Kathé Hayden

Copyright © 2001, Interweave Press, Inc.

Title Page Verso—Portion

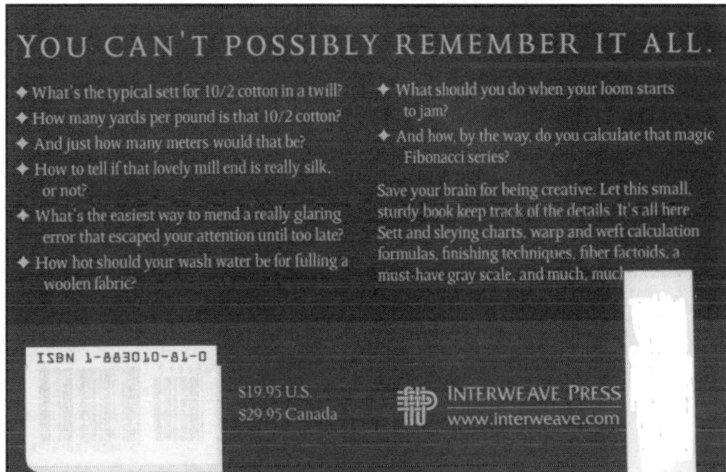

Back Cover

Additional information:
112 pages; black and white illustrations; 14 x 18 cm.; ISBN: 1-883010-81-0; LCCN: 00-05035; Spiral bound; Glossary; Bibliography (pages 107-108); Index; Lists of associations, Web sites and Web lists

Instructions: Prepare a MARC record for this item.

When cataloging this work, consider the following:

- Titles
- Notes

***AACR2r* rules needed:** 1.1B1; 1.1F1; 1.4C1; 1.4C3; 1.4D1; 1.4F6; 1.5B1; 1.5C1; 1.5D1; 1.7B4; 1.7B18; 1.8B1; 2.5B2; 2.5C1; 2.5D2; 2.7B18; 21.29B; 21.30E1; 24.1A; MARC 010; MARC 020

Exercise 43

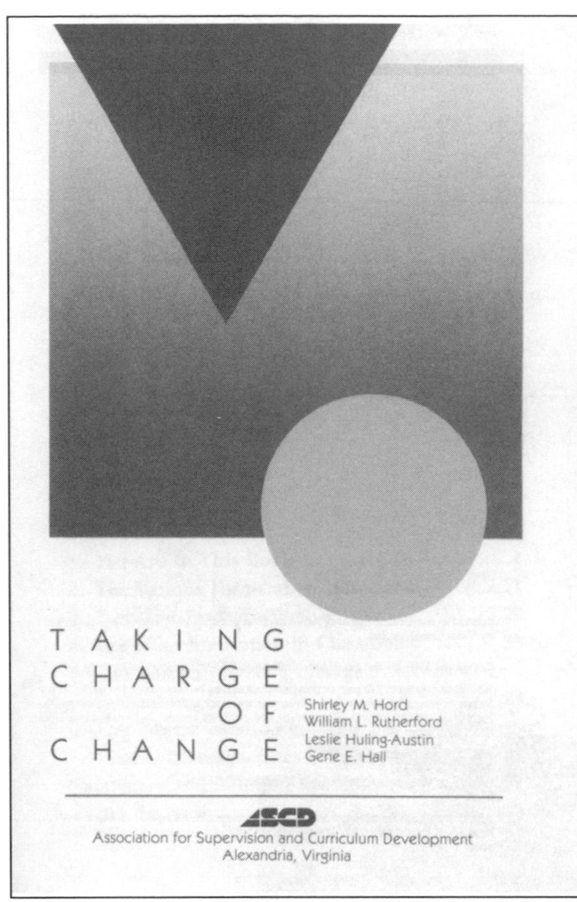

TAKING CHARGE OF CHANGE

Shirley M. Hord
William L. Rutherford
Leslie Huling-Austin
Gene E. Hall

ASCD
Association for Supervision and Curriculum Development
Alexandria, Virginia

Title Page

Printed in the United States of America. First printing 1987; second printing 1989 by VictorGraphics, Inc.

Copyright 1987 by the Southwest Educational Development Laboratory.

All rights reserved. No part of this publication may be reproduced or transmitted in any form or by any means, electronic or mechanical, including photocopy, recording, or any information storage and retrieval system, without permission in writing from SEDL (211 East 7th Street, Austin, TX 78710).

ASCD Stock Number: 611-87022
ISBN: 0-87120-144-5
Library of Congress Catalog Card Number: 87-070644
$8.00

ASCD publications present a variety of viewpoints. The views expressed or implied in this publication are not necessarily official positions of the Association.

Title Page Verso

Additional information:
98 pages; black and white illustrations; 23 cm.; bibliography (pages 91-97).

Instructions: Prepare a catalog record for this item.

When cataloging this work, consider the following:

- Main entry

***AACR2r* rules needed:** 1.1B1; 1.1F5; 1.4C3; 1.4D2; 1.4F6; 1.5B2; 1.5C1; 1.5D1; 1.7B18; 1.8B1; 1.8B3; 1.8D1; 2.5B2; 2.5C1; 2.5D1; 21.6C2; 22.5A1; App B.9; MARC 010; MARC 020

Exercise 44

Buffy the Vampire Slayer and Philosophy

Fear and Trembling in Sunnydale

Edited by
JAMES B. SOUTH

OPEN COURT
Chicago and La Salle, Illinois

Title Page

vii

Partial Contents

Popular Culture and Philosophy
General Editor: William Irwin

Series Information

Volume 4 in the series, Popular Culture and Philosophy

To order books from Open Court, call toll free 1-800-815-2280, or visit our website at www.opencourtbooks.com.

Open Court Publishing Company is a division of Carus Publishing Company.

Copyright ©2003 by Carus Publishing Company

First printing 2003

All rights reserved. No part of this publication may be reproduced, stored in a retrieval system, or transmitted, in any form or by any means, electronic, mechanical, photocopying, recording, or otherwise, without the prior written permission of the publisher, Open Court Publishing Company, a division of Carus Publishing Company, 315 Fifth Street, P.O. Box 300, Peru, Illinois, 61354-0300.

Printed and bound in the United States of America

Cover design: Joan Sommers Design

Title Page Verso—Portion

Additional information:
xi, 335 pages; 23 cm.; bibliographical references; index; lists of episodes for the television series *Buffy the Vampire Slayer* and *Angel;* LCCN 2003001134; ISBN 0-8126-9530-5 (hardcover); 0-8126-0531-3 (pbk.)

Instructions: Prepare a catalog record for this item.

***AACR2r* rules needed:** 1.1B1; 1.1E1; 1.1F1; 1.4C1; 1.4C5; 1.4D1; 1.4D5; 1.4F1; 1.5B2; 1.5D1; 1.5B2; 1.6B1; 1.6G1; 1.8B1; 1.8D1; 2.5B2; 2.5D1; 2.7B18; 21.0D1; 21.1C1b; 21.6C2; 21.7A1; 22.5A1; App. A; App. C; MARC 010; MARC 020

Exercise 45

The Hobbit

or

There and Back Again

by

J. R. R. Tolkien

Illustrated by the Author

Houghton Mifflin Company, Boston

The Riverside Press

Cambridge

Title Page

Cover

Twenty-third Printing c

Title Page Verso—Complete

Additional information:
315 pages; black and white illustrations; 21cm.; maps on end pages. No date of publication is given anywhere in this item. Book acquired during 1960s.
Summary: Bilbo Baggins, a respectable, well-to-do hobbit, lives comfortably in his hobbit-hole until the day the wandering wizard Gandalf chooses him to take part in an adventure from which he may never return.

Instructions: Prepare a catalog record for this item.

When cataloging this work, consider the following:

- Date of publication

***AACR2r* rules needed:** 1.1B1; 1.1F1; 1.1F6; 1.4C1; 1.4C5; 1.4D1; 1.4D4; 1.5B2; 1.5C1; 1.5D1; 1.7B17; 2.5B2; 2.5C2; 2.5D1; 2.7B17; 21.1A2; 22.5A1

Exercise 46

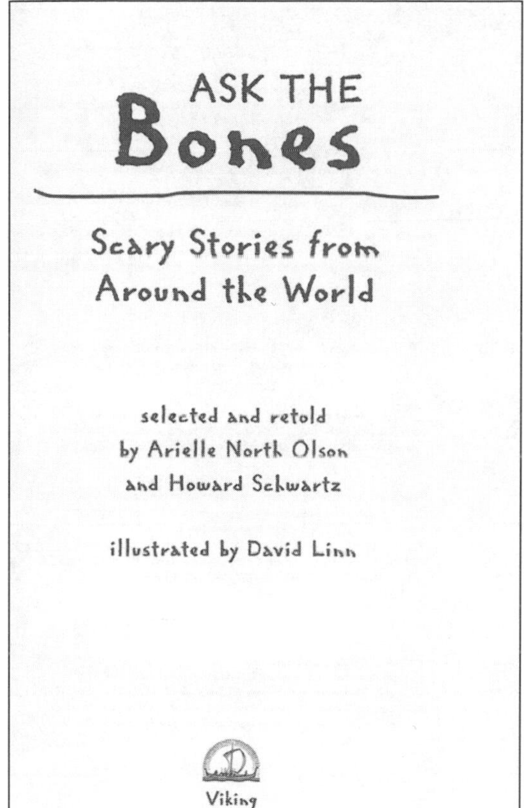

ASK THE
Bones

Scary Stories from
Around the World

selected and retold
by Arielle North Olson
and Howard Schwartz

illustrated by David Linn

Viking

Title Page

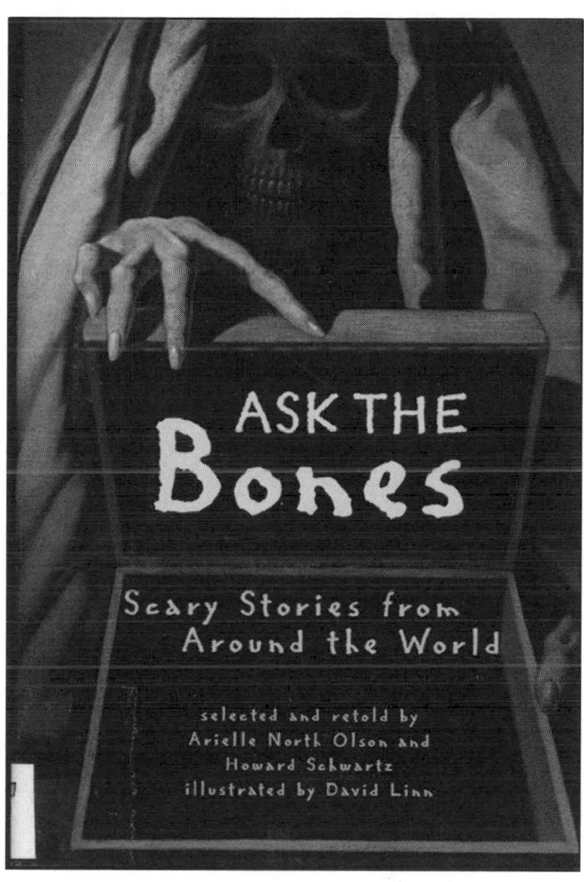

Cover

VIKING
Published by the Penguin Group
Penguin Putnam Books for Young Readers, 345 Hudson Street, New York, New York 10014, U.S.A.
Penguin Books Ltd, 27 Wrights Lane, London W8 5TZ, England
Penguin Books Australia Ltd, Ringwood, Victoria, Australia
Penguin Books Canada Ltd, 10 Alcorn Avenue, Toronto, Ontario, Canada M4V 3B2
Penguin Books (N.Z.) Ltd, 182–190 Wairau Road, Auckland 10, New Zealand

Penguin Books Ltd, Registered Offices: Harmondsworth, Middlesex, England

First published in 1999 by Viking, a member of Penguin Putnam Books for Young Readers.

1 3 5 7 9 10 8 6 4 2

Text copyright © Arielle North Olson and Howard Schwartz, 1999
Illustrations copyright © David Linn, 1999
All rights reserved

Title Page Verso—Portion

Additional information:
ix, 145 pages; black and white illustrations; 23 cm.; LCCN: 98-19108; ISBN: 0-670-87581-3; bibliographic references (pages 141-145).
Summary: A collection of scary folktales from countries around the world including China, Russia, Spain, and the United States.

Instructions: Prepare a catalog record for this item.

When cataloging this work, consider the following:

- What is the main entry and why?

***AACR2r* rules needed:** 1.1B1; 1.1E1; 1.1F4; 1.1F6; 1.5B1; 1.5C1; 1.5D1; 1.7B17; 1.7B18; 1.8B1; 2.5B2; 2.5C1; 2.5D1; 2.7B17; 2.7B18; 21.10A; 21.30B1; 21.30K2; MARC 010; MARC 020

Exercise 47

GETTING GRAPHIC!

Using Graphic Novels
to Promote Literacy
with Preteens
and Teens

Michele Gorman

With a foreword by Jeff Smith, creator of *Bone*

Title Page

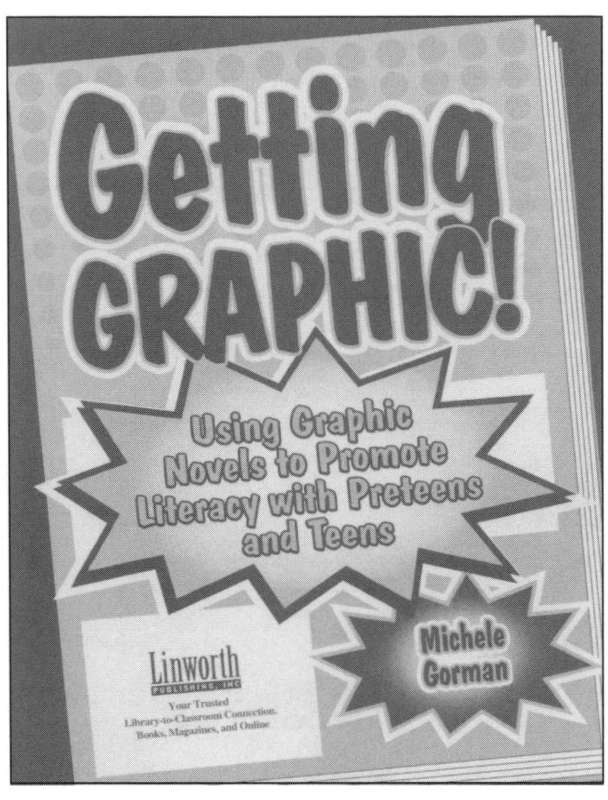

Cover

TABLE OF CONTENTS

Table of Contents iii

iv *Getting Graphic! Using Graphic Novels to Promote Literacy with Preteens and Teens*

(*Continued on Next Page*)

Exercise 47

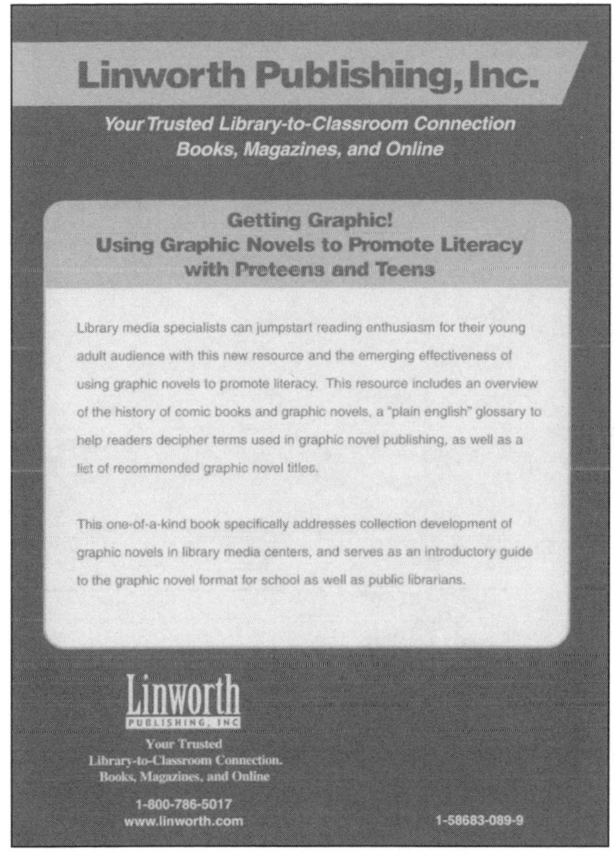

Back Cover

Published by Linworth Publishing, Inc.
480 East Wilson Bridge Road, Suite L
Worthington, Ohio 43085

Copyright © 2003 by Linworth Publishing, Inc.

All rights reserved. Purchasing this book entitles a librarian to reproduce activity sheets for use in the library within a school or entitles a teacher to reproduce activity sheets for single classroom use within a school. Other portions of the book (up to 15 pages) may be copied for staff development purposes within a single school. Standard citation information should appear on each page. The reproduction of any part of this book for an entire school or school system or for commercial use is strictly prohibited. No part of this book may be electronically reproduced, transmitted or recorded without written permission from the publisher.

ISBN: 1-58683-089-9

5 4 3 2 1

Title Page Verson—Portion

Additional information:
xii, 100 pages; black and white illustrations; 28 cm.; index; bibliographic references (pages 91-92); LCCN: 2003013199; ISBN 1-58683-089-0 (pbk.)

Instructions: Prepare a catalog record for this item.

***AACR2r* rules needed:** 1.0C1; 1.1B1; 1.1E2; 1.1F1; 1.1F6; 1.4C1; 1.4C3; 1.4D1; 1.4D2; 1.4F6; 1.5B2; 1.5C1; 1.5D1; 1.7B17; 1.7B18; 1.8B1; 2.5B2; 2.5C1; 2.5D1; 2.7B17; 2.7B18; 2.8B1; 2.8D1; 21.1A2; 22.5A1; App. B.14; MARC 010; MARC 020

Exercise 48

Chemistry for Every Kid

101 Easy Experiments That Really Work

Janice Pratt VanCleave

John Wiley & Sons, Inc.
New York · Chichester · Brisbane · Toronto · Singapore

Title Page

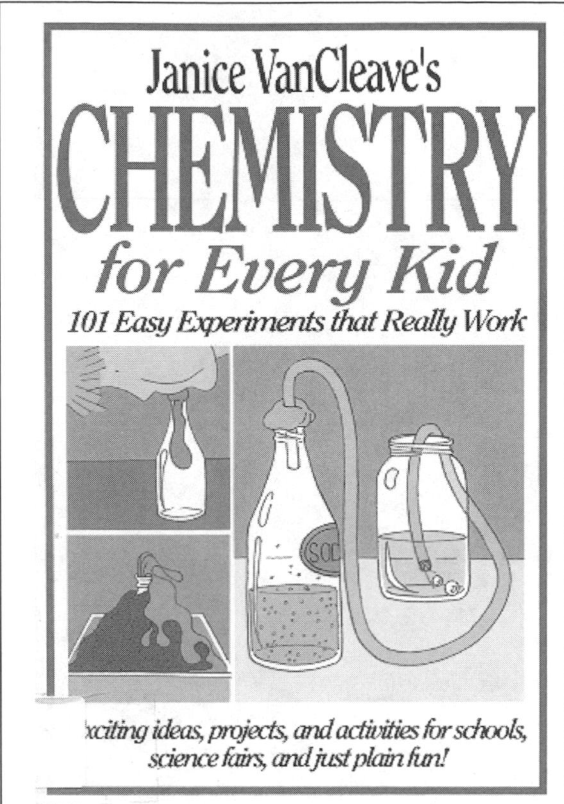

Front Cover

Publisher: Stephen Kippur
Editor: David Sobel
Managing Editor: Corinne McCormick
Composition: Vail-Ballou Press, Inc.
Illustrator: April Blair Stewart

The publisher and the author have made every reasonable effort to assure that the experiments and activities in this book are safe when conducted as instructed but assume no responsibility for any damage caused or sustained while performing the experiments or activities in CHEMISTRY FOR EVERY KID. Parents, guardians and/or teachers should supervise young readers who undertake the experiments and activities in this book.

Copyright © 1989 by John Wiley & Sons, Inc.

All rights reserved. Published simultaneously in Canada.

Reproduction or translation of any part of this work beyond that permitted by section 107 or 108 of the 1976 United States Copyright Act without the permission of the copyright owner is unlawful. Requests for permission or further information should be addressed to the Permission Department, John Wiley & Sons, Inc.

ISBN 0471-50974-4
ISBN 0-471-62085-8 (pbk.)

88-27540

Printed and bound by Courier Companies, Inc.

10 9 8

Title Page Verso—Portion

Additional information:
xx, 232 pages; black and white illustrations; 21 cm.; bibliography (p. 223); index
Summary: Instructions for experiments, each introducing a different chemistry concept and demonstrating that chemistry is a part of our everyday life.

Instructions: Prepare a MARC record for this item.

When cataloging this work, consider the following:

- Variant title(s)

***AACR2r* rules needed:** 1.1B1; 1.1B2; 1.1E1; 1.1F1; 1.4C1; 1.4D1; 1.4F6; 1.5B2; 1.5C1; 1.5D1; 1.6B1; 1.7B17; 1.8B1; 1.8B2; 1.8E1; 2.5B2; 2.5C1; 2.5D1; 2.7B17; 21.1A2; 21.30J2; 21.30L1; 22.5D1; MARC 010; MARC 020

Exercise 49

All IN A DAY

by Mitsumasa Anno

and

Raymond Briggs

Ron Brooks

Eric Carle

Gian Calvi

Zhu Chengliang

Leo and Diane Dillon

Akiko Hayashi

Nicolai Ye. Popov

Philomel Books • New York

Title Page

The publishers gratefully acknowledge the assistance of Kazuko Shiraishi and Susan Tsumura in the translation of the text for this book.

First U.S.A. edition 1986. Published by Philomel Books, a member of The Putnam Publishing Group, 51 Madison Avenue, New York, N.Y. 10010.
Text translation copyright © 1986 by Philomel Books. Original Japanese edition published in 1986 by Dowaya, Tokyo, copyright © 1986 by Kuso-Kubo, Raymond Briggs, Ron Brooks, Gian Calvi, Eric Carle, Leo & Diane Dillon, Akiko Hayashi, Nicolai Ye. Popov, & Zhu Chengliang. All rights reserved.
Translation rights were arranged with Dowaya through the Japan Foreign Rights Centre (JFC). Printed in Japan.

Translation of: Marui chikyū no maru ichinichi. Summary: Brief text and illustrations by ten internationally well-known artists reveal a day in the lives of children in eight different countries showing the similarities and differences and emphasizing the commonality of humankind.

Title Page Verso—Portion

Back Cover

Additional information:
22 unnumbered pages; color illustrations; 25 x 27 cm.; ISBN: 0-399-21311-2; LCCN: 86-5011

Instructions: Prepare a catalog record for this item.

When cataloging this work, consider the following:

- Main entry

***AACR2r* rules needed:** 1.1B1; 1.1F1; 1.1F5; 1.2B1; 1.4D1; 1.5B2; 1.5C1; 1.5D1; 1.7B7; 1.7B17; 1.8B1; 2.5B7; 2.5C3; 2.5D2; 2.7B17; 21.1A2; 22.5A1; MARC 010; MARC 020

Exercise 50

TOLKIEN

The Lord
of the Rings

by

J.R.R. TOLKIEN

HOUGHTON MIFFLIN COMPANY
Boston • New York

Title Page

J.R.R. TOLKIEN

THE LORD OF THE RINGS

THE COMPLETE BEST-SELLING CLASSIC
NOW AN EPIC MOTION PICTURE TRILOGY

Cover

Additional information:
xviii, 1137 pages; 7 unnumbered pages of black and white maps; black and white illustrations; 22 cm.; includes indexes; maps on verso of book jacket; includes "Note on the text" revised 1994 from the 1987 edition.

Instructions: Prepare a catalog record for this item. Construct a summary from the information on the book jacket flap.

When cataloging this item, consider the following:

- Contents
- Physical description
- Publishing history

***AACR2r* rules needed:** 1.1B1; 1.1F1; 1.4C1; 1.4C5; 1.4D1; 1.4D2; 1.5B1; 1.5B2; 1.5C1; 1.5D1; 1.7B7; 1.7B9; 1.7B10; 1.7B17; 1.7B18; 2.5B2; 2.5B3; 2.5B8b; 2.5C2; 2.5C4; 2.5D1; 2.7B17; 2.7B18; 25.1A; 25.3A; 21.1A2; 22.5A1; MARC 020

(*Continued on Next Page*)

Exercise 50

Featuring maps of Middle-earth →

IN ANCIENT TIMES the Rings of Power were crafted by the Elven-smiths, and Sauron, the Dark Lord, forged the One Ring, filling it with his own power so that he could rule all others. But the One Ring was taken from him, and though he sought it throughout Middle-earth, it remained lost to him. After many ages, it fell by chance into the hands of the hobbit Bilbo Baggins.

From his fastness in the Dark Tower of Mordor, Sauron's power spread far and wide. He gathered all the Great Rings to him, but always he searched for the One Ring that would complete his dominion.

On Bilbo's eleventy-first birthday, he disappeared, bequeathing to his young cousin, Frodo, the Ruling Ring and a perilous quest: to journey across Middle-earth, deep into the shadow of the Dark Lord, and destroy the Ring by casting it into the Cracks of Doom.

The Lord of the Rings tells of the great quest undertaken by Frodo and the Fellowship of the Ring: Gandalf the Wizard; the hobbits Merry, Pippin, and Sam; Gimli the Dwarf; Legolas the Elf; Boromir of Gondor; and a tall, mysterious stranger called Strider.

1103

Inside Jacket Flap (negative image)

This edition of *The Lord of the Rings*
was first published in Great Britain by HarperCollinsPublishers 1994.

The Fellowship of the Ring
Copyright © 1954, 1965, 1966 by J.R.R. Tolkien
1954 edition copyright © renewed 1982 by Christopher R. Tolkien,
Michael H. R. Tolkien, John F. R. Tolkien and Priscilla M.A.R. Tolkien
1965/1966 editions copyright © renewed 1993, 1994 by Christopher R. Tolkien,
John F. R. Tolkien and Priscilla M.A.R. Tolkien

The Two Towers
Copyright © 1954, 1965, 1966 by J.R.R. Tolkien
1954 edition copyright © renewed 1982 by Christopher R. Tolkien,
Michael H. R. Tolkien, John F. R. Tolkien and Priscilla M.A.R. Tolkien
1965/1966 editions copyright © renewed 1993, 1994 by Christopher R. Tolkien,
John F. R. Tolkien and Priscilla M.A.R. Tolkien

The Return of the King
Copyright © 1955, 1965, 1966 by J.R.R. Tolkien
1955 edition copyright © renewed 1983 by Christopher R. Tolkien,
Michael H. R. Tolkien, John F. R. Tolkien and Priscilla M.A.R. Tolkien
1965/1966 editions copyright © renewed 1993, 1994 by Christopher R. Tolkien,
John F. R. Tolkien and Priscilla M.A.R. Tolkien

Note on the Text copyright © 1987 by Houghton Mifflin Company
Revised Note on the Text copyright © 1994 by Douglas A. Anderson

® is a registered trademark of the
J.R.R. Tolkien Estate Limited.

ISBN 0-618-26024-2
ISBN 0-618-26025-0 (pbk.)
Library of Congress Cataloging-in-Publication Data is available.

For information about permission to reproduce selections from this book, write to Permissions, Houghton Mifflin Company, 215 Park Avenue South, New York, New York 10003.
Visit our Web Site: www.houghtonmifflinbooks.com.

Printed in the United States of America
KPT 10 9 8 7 6 5 4 3 2 1

Title Page Verso

NOTE ON THE TEXT

The Lord of the Rings **is often erroneously called a trilogy, when it is in fact a single novel, consisting of six books plus appendices, sometimes published in three volumes.**

Excerpt from "Note on the Text"

Exercise 51

Sanditon

Jane Austen

and Another Lady

Boston

HOUGHTON MIFFLIN COMPANY

1975

Title Page

A PORTION OF THIS BOOK HAS APPEARED IN *REDBOOK*.

FIRST PRINTING V

COPYRIGHT © 1975 BY HOUGHTON MIFFLIN COMPANY. ALL RIGHTS RESERVED. NO PART OF THIS WORK MAY BE REPRODUCED OR TRANSMITTED IN ANY FORM BY ANY MEANS, ELECTRONIC OR MECHANICAL, INCLUDING PHOTOCOPYING AND RECORDING, OR BY ANY INFORMATION STORAGE OR RETRIEVAL SYSTEM, WITHOUT PERMISSION IN WRITING FROM THE PUBLISHER.

Title Page Verso—Portion

Additional information:
329 pages; 24 cm.; ISBN: 0-395-20284-1; LCCN: 74-20584
Marie Dobbs has written short stories and novels under various pseudonyms, her most successful being Anne Telscombe.

Instructions: Prepare a catalog record for this item.

When cataloging this work, consider the following:

- What is the main entry for this work?
- Authority Files

***AACR2r* rules needed:** 1.1B1; 1.1F4; 1.4C3; 1.4D2; 1.4F1; 1.5B1; 1.5D1; 2.5B2; 2.5D1; 21.30B1; 22.5A1; 22.11A; MARC 010; MARC 020

Exercise 52

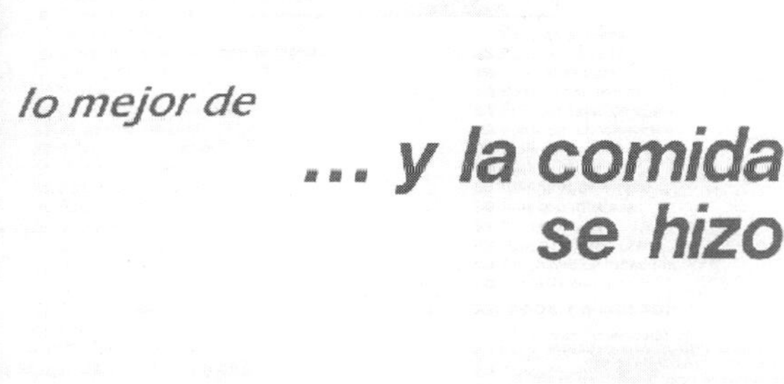

lo mejor de

... y la comida
se hizo

Title Page

Cover

Title Page Verso—Portion

La presentación y disposición en conjunto de
LO MEJOR DE ...Y LA COMIDA SE HIZO
son propiedad del editor. Ninguna parte de esta obra
puede ser reproducida o trasmitida, mediante ningún sistema
o método, electrónico o mecánico (incluyendo el fotocopiado,
la grabación o cualquier sistema de recuperación y almacenamiento
de información), sin consentimiento por escrito del editor

Derechos reservados
© 1994, Editorial Trillas, S. A. de C. V.,
Av. Río Churubusco 385, Col. Pedro María Anaya,
C. P. 03340, México, D. F.

División Comercial, Calz. de la Viga 1132, C.P. 09439
México, D. F. Tel. 6330995, FAX 6330870

Miembro de la Cámara Nacional de la
Industria Editorial. Reg. núm. 158

Primera edición (edición especial SEP), mayo 1994
ISBN 968-24-5066-7

Impreso en México
Printed in Mexico

Esta obra se terminó de imprimir y encuadernar
el 4 de mayo de 1994,
en los talleres de Litografía Magno Graf, S. A. de C. V.,
Calle E núm. 6, Parque Industrial Puebla 2000,
C. P. 72200, Puebla, Puebla.
Se tiraron
130 000 ejemplares, más sobrantes de reposición.
KF 90

Additional information:
79 pages; color photographs; 27 cm.; index
CIP gives the following as authors: Beatriz L. Fernández, Maria Yani and Margarita Zafiro.
Summary: This is a general, basic cookbook in Spanish.

Instructions: Prepare a catalog record for this item.

When cataloging this work, consider the following:

- Main entry
- Variant title(s)

***AACR2r* rules needed:** 1.1B1; 1.2B1; 1.4C1; 1.4C3; 1.4D1; 1.4F1; 1.5B2; 1.5C1; 1.5D1; 1.7B2; 1.8B1; 2.5B2; 2.5C1; 2.5C3; 2.5D1;21.1C1c; App B.9; App C; MARC 020

Exercise 53

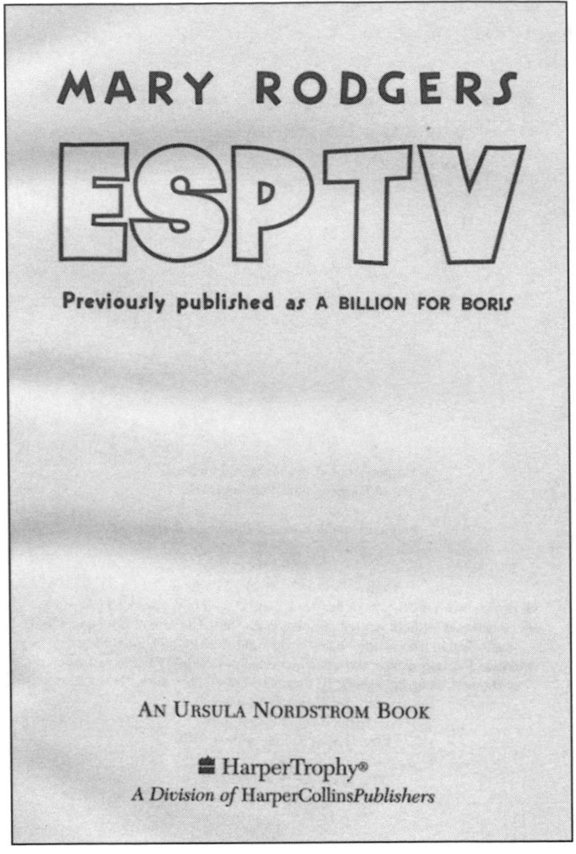
MARY RODGERS

ESP TV

Previously published as A BILLION FOR BORIS

An Ursula Nordstrom Book

HarperTrophy®

A Division of HarperCollins*Publishers*

Title Page

Harper Trophy® is a registered trademark
of HarperCollins Publishers Inc.

Previously published as *A Billion for Boris*

ESP TV
Copyright © 1974 by Mary Rodgers
All rights reserved. No part of this book may be used or reproduced in any manner whatsoever without written permission except in the case of brief quotations embodied in critical articles and reviews. Printed in the United States of America. For information address HarperCollins Children's Books, a division of HarperCollins Publishers, 10 East 53rd Street, New York, NY 10022.
LC Number: 74-3586
ISBN 0-06-440838-8 (pbk.)
First Harper Trophy edition, 1976

Visit us on the World Wide Web!
http://www.harperchildrens.com

Title Page Verso

Additional information:
216 pages; 20 cm; LCCN: 99-71634; "A Freaky Friday book" on cover.

Instructions: Prepare a catalog record for this item.

When cataloging this work, consider the following:

- How is the original title treated?

***AACR2r* rules needed:** 1.1F3; 1.1F6; 1.4D1; 1.4F6; 1.5B1; 1.5D1; 1.7B7; 1.7B9; 1.8B1; 2.5B2; 2.5D1; 2.7B9; 21.1A2; 21.2B1; 22.5A1; MARC 010; MARC 020

Exercise 54

BEATRIX POTTER'S
LETTERS

Selected and introduced
by Judy Taylor

FREDERICK WARNE

Title Page

FREDERICK WARNE

Published by the Penguin Group
27 Wrights Lane, London W8 5TZ, England
Viking Penguin Inc., 40 West 23rd Street, New York, New York 10010, USA
Penguin Books Australia Ltd, Ringwood, Victoria, Australia
Penguin Books Canada Ltd, 2801 John Street, Markham, Ontario, Canada L3R 1B4
Penguin Books (NZ) Ltd, 182–190 Wairau Road, Auckland 10, New Zealand

Penguin Books Ltd, Registered Offices: Harmondsworth, Middlesex, England

First published 1989
1 3 5 7 9 10 8 6 4 2

Notes and introduction © Judy Taylor, 1989
Beatrix Potter's original illustrations copyright © Frederick Warne & Co.,
1901, 1902, 1903, 1904, 1905, 1908, 1909, 1910, 1912, 1913, 1917, 1918, 1922, 1925,
1928, 1929, 1930, 1946, 1955, 1971, 1978, 1985, 1986, 1987, 1989

Copyright in all countries signatory to the Berne Convention

Designed by Ron Callow

All rights reserved. Without limiting the rights under copyright reserved above, no part of this publication may be reproduced, stored in or introduced into a retrieval system, or transmitted, in any form or by any means (electronic, mechanical, photocopying, recording or otherwise), without the prior written permission of both the copyright owner and the above publisher of this book.

British Library Cataloguing in Publication Data available

ISBN 0 7232 3437 X

Typeset, printed and bound in Great Britain by William Clowes Limited, Beccles and London

Title Page Verso

Additional information:
480 pages; [8] pages of color plates; 24 cm.; includes index, bibliography (pages 469-470), black and white illustrations, facsimiles of letters.

Instructions: Prepare a catalog record for this item.

When cataloging this work, consider the following:

- Main entry
- Physical description

***AACR2r* rules needed:** 1.1B1; 1.1B2; 1.1F6; 1.4D1; 1.4D2, 1.4D4d; 1.4E1a; 1.4F1; 1.5B2; 1.5C1; 1.5D1; 1.7B9; 1.7B18; 1.8B1; 2.5B2; 2.5C3; 2.5D1; 2.7B18; 21.1A2; 21.30D1; 22.5A1; MARC 020

Exercise 55

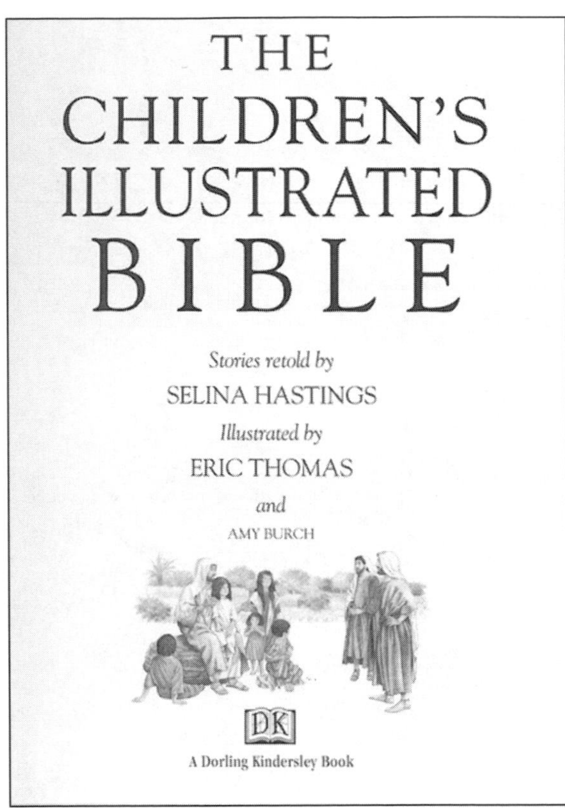

THE
CHILDREN'S
ILLUSTRATED
BIBLE

Stories retold by
SELINA HASTINGS
Illustrated by
ERIC THOMAS
and
AMY BURCH

DK
A Dorling Kindersley Book

Title Page

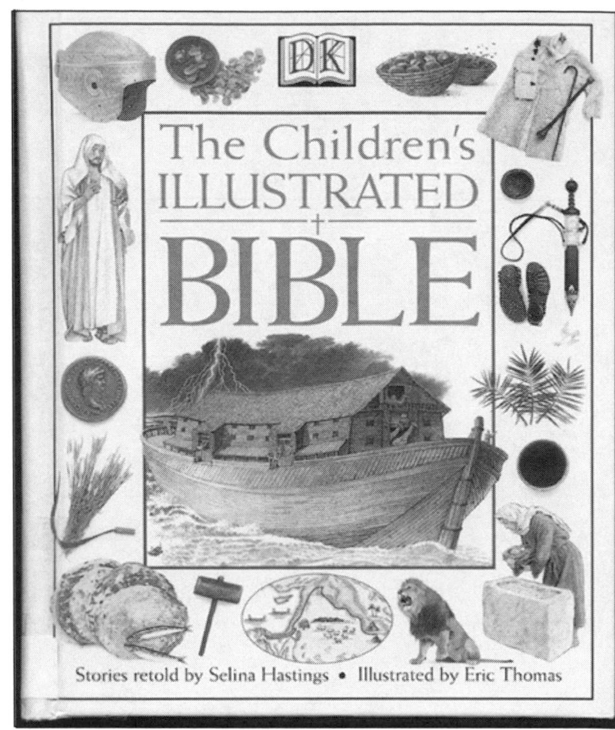

Cover

Dorling Kindersley
LONDON, NEW YORK, DELHI, SYDNEY

Art Editor Shirley Gwillym
Project Editor Marie Greenwood
Senior Editor Emma Johnson
Designer Sarah Cowley
Additional design by
Heather Blackham, Muffy Dodson
Production Ruth Cobb, Marguerite Fenn
Managing Editor Susan Peach
Managing Art Editor Jacquie Gulliver
US Editor B. Alison Weir

Published in the United States by
Dorling Kindersley Publishing, Inc., 95 Madison Avenue
New York, New York 10016

This edition first published in 2000

10 9 8 7 6 5 4 3 2 1

Copyright © 1994 Dorling Kindersley Limited, London
Text copyright © 1994 Selina Hastings
The right of Selina Hastings to be identified as the Author of this Work has been asserted by her in accordance with the Copyright Designs and Patents Act 1988.

All rights reserved under International and Pan-American Copyright Conventions. No part of this publication may be reproduced, stored in a retrieval system, or transmitted in any form or by any means, electronic, mechanical, photocopying, recording, or otherwise, without the prior written permission of the copyright owner. Published in Great Britain by Dorling Kindersley Limited.

ISBN 0-7894-5331-2

93-30814

For our complete catalog visit WWW.dk.com
Reproduced by Colourscan, Singapore
Printed and bound in China by L. Rex Printing Company

CONSULTANTS

Religious Consultants
Reverend John Glover
Rabbi Joseph Potasnik
Sister K.C. Young
Mary Evans
Jenny Nemko
Reverend Stephen Motyer
Bernadette Chapman
Father Philip Walshe

Educational Consultant
Geoffrey Marshall-Taylor

Historical Consultant, Old Testament
Jonathan Tubb,
Western Asiatic Department,
British Museum, London

Historical Consultant, New Testament
Carole Mendleson,
Western Asiatic Department,
British Museum, London

Editor's Note
The dates listed in this book are chronicled BC, meaning "before Christ," and AD, meaning "anno Domini," or "in the year of the Lord." However, much of the non-Christian world uses CE ("Common Era") and BCE ("Before the Common Era") to designate eras.

Introduction and section openers written by Geoffrey Marshall-Taylor

Title Page Verso—Portion

Additional information:
320 pages; color illustrations; color maps; 17 cm.; index; section titled "Who's Who in the Bible Stories" (pages 310-313).

Instructions: Prepare a catalog record for this item.

When cataloging this work, consider the following:

- Main entry

***AACR2r* rules needed:** 1.1B1; 1.1F1; 1.1F6; 1.4C1; 1.4F1; 1.4F5; 1.5B1; 1.5C1; 1.5D1; 1.7B9; 1.7B18; 1.8B1; 2.5B2; 2.5C2; 2.5C3; 2.5D1; 2.7B9; 2.7B18; 21.10A; 21.30K2; 22.5A1; MARC 010; MARC 020

Exercise 56

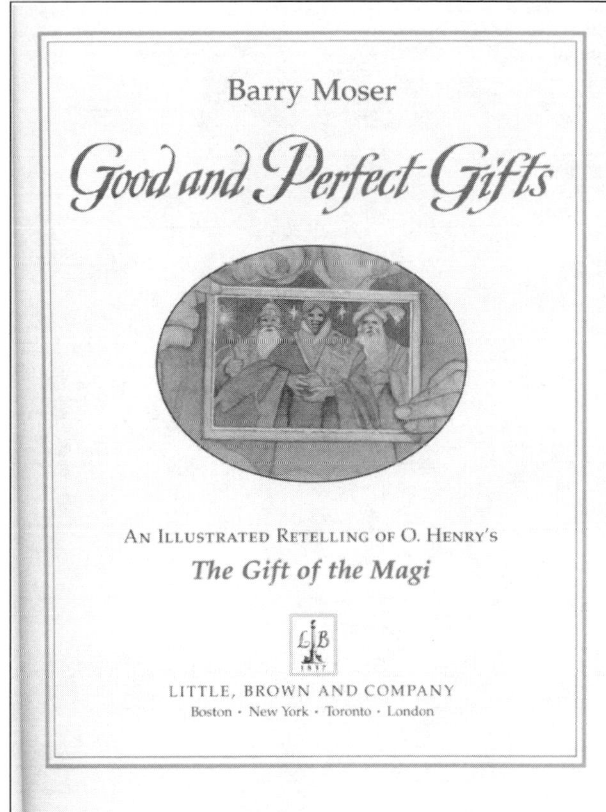

Barry Moser

Good and Perfect Gifts

AN ILLUSTRATED RETELLING OF O. HENRY'S

The Gift of the Magi

LITTLE, BROWN AND COMPANY

Boston · New York · Toronto · London

Title Page

Additional information:
22 pages; color illustrations; 24 cm.
Summary: Based on the classic story in which a husband and wife sacrifice treasured possessions to buy each other Christmas presents.

Instructions: Prepare a catalog record for this item.

When cataloging this work, consider the following:

- Main entry
- How is the original title handled in the MARC record?

***AACR2r* rules needed:** 1.1B1; 1.1E1; 1.1E4; 1.1F1; 1.2B1; 1.4C1; 1.4C5; 1.4D1; 1.4D2; 1.4F6; 1.5B2; 1.5C1; 1.5D1; 1.7B17;1.8B1; 2.5B2; 2.5C3; 2.5D1; 2.7B17; 21.10A; 21.30G1; 21.30J1; 22.5A1; MARC 010; MARC 020

Copyright © 1997 by Barry Moser

All rights reserved. No part of this book may be reproduced in any form or by any electronic or mechanical means, including information storage and retrieval systems, without permission in writing from the publisher, except by a reviewer who may quote brief passages in a review.

First Edition

ISBN 0-316-58543-2

94-39168

10 9 8 7 6 5 4 3 2

IM

Published simultaneously in Canada by Little, Brown & Company (Canada) Limited

Printed in Singapore

Title Page Verso—Portion

Exercise 57

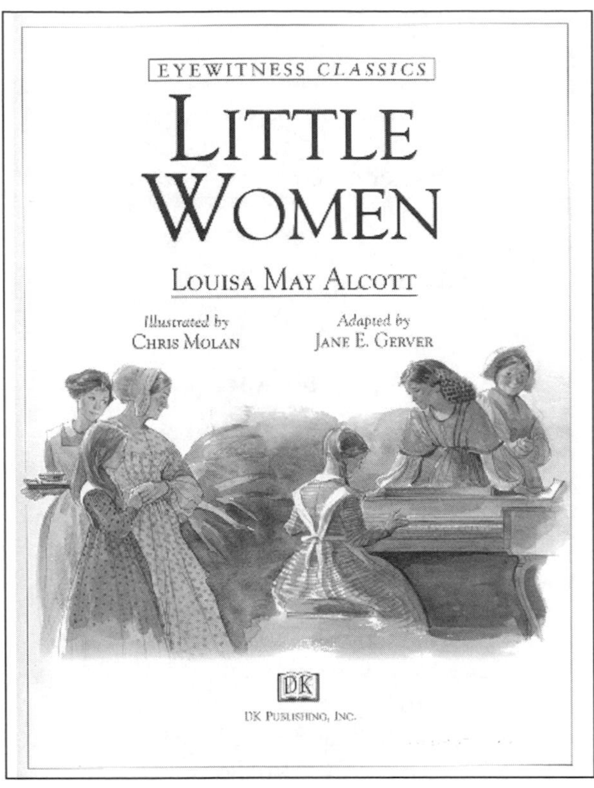
EYEWITNESS CLASSICS

LITTLE WOMEN

LOUISA MAY ALCOTT

Illustrated by CHRIS MOLAN

Adapted by JANE E. GERVER

DK

DK PUBLISHING, INC.

Title Page

ALREADY PUBLISHED

EYEWITNESS CLASSICS

LITTLE WOMEN

The inspiring, heartwarming story of four sisters growing up in New England during the Civil War, *Little Women* is one of the best loved of all novels.

This Eyewitness Classic edition, with its innovative use of photography and narrative illustration, reveals the fascinating historical background to this timeless tale.

DK

DK PUBLISHING, INC.
www.dk.com

ISBN 0-7894-4767-3

90000>

9 780789 447678

Back Cover

DK

A DK PUBLISHING BOOK
www.dk.com

A RETELLING FOR YOUNG READERS

Produced by Leapfrog Press Ltd

Project Editor Caryn Jenner
Art Editor Penny Lamprell

For DK Publishing
Senior Editor Alastair Dougall
Managing Art Editor Jacquie Gulliver
Picture Research Liz Moore
Production Steve Lang
US Editors Lilan Patri, Connie Robinson

First American Edition, 1999
2 4 6 8 10 9 7 5 3

Published in the United States by DK Publishing, Inc.
95 Madison Avenue New York, New York 10016

Copyright © 1999 Dorling Kindersley Limited

All rights reserved under International and Pan-American Copyright Conventions. No part of this publication may be reproduced, stored in a retrieval system, or transmitted in any form or by any means, electronic, mechanical, photocopying, recording, or otherwise, without the prior written permission of the copyright owner. Published in Great Britain by Dorling Kindersley Limited.

Title Page Verso—Portion

Additional information:
64 pages; color illustrations; 26 cm.; LCCN: 99-14752; ISBN: 0-7894-4767-3
Summary: Chronicles the joys and sorrows of the four March sisters as they grow into young women in nineteenth-century New England. Illustrated notes throughout the text explain the historical background of the story.

Instructions: Prepare a catalog record for this item.

When cataloging this item, consider the following:

- Main entry

***AACR2r* rules needed:** 1.1B1; 1.1F1; 1.1F6; 1.2B1; 1.4C1; 1.4F6; 1.5B2; 1.5C1; 1.5D1; 1.6B1; 1.7B4; 1.7B17; 1.8B1; 2.5B2; 2.5C3; 2.5D1; 2.7B17; 21.10A; 21.30K2; 22.5A1; App C; MARC 010; MARC 020

Exercise 58

Booknotes

LIFE STORIES

Notable Biographers on the People Who Shaped America

Brian Lamb

NEW YORK

Title Page

The author is directing all of his royalties from the sales of this book to the not-for-profit C-SPAN Education Foundation.

Copyright © 1999 by National Cable Satellite Corporation

All rights reserved under International and Pan-American Copyright Conventions.
Published in the United States by Times Books, a division of Random House, Inc., New York, and simultaneously in Canada by Random House of Canada Limited, Toronto.

98-41374

Random House website address: www.atrandom.com

Printed in the United States of America on acid-free paper

98765432

First Edition

Book design by Robert C. Olsson

ISBN 0-8129-3081-9 (HC : alk. paper)

Title Page Verso—Portion

Contents

Additional information:
xxiii, 471 pages; black and white and color illustrations; 25 cm.; index
Summary: Collection of essays by various biographers based on interviews originally held on the television program *Booknotes*.

Instructions: Prepare a catalog record for this item.

When cataloging this work, consider the following:

- Title
- Added entries

***AACR2r* rules needed:** 1.1B1; 1.1E1; 1.1E3; 1.1F1; 1.2B1; 1.4C1; 1.4D1; 1.4F6; 1.7B17; 1.7B18; 1.8B1; 2.5B2; 2.5C3; 2.5D1; 2.7B17; 2.7B18; 21.1A2; 22.5A1; App B.9; App C; MARC 010; MARC 020

Exercise 59

Lydia Cassatt
Reading
the Morning Paper

a novel by

Harriet Scott Chessman

a copublication of The Permanent Press
and Seven Stories Press
NEW YORK • LONDON • TORONTO • SYDNEY

Title Page

Lydia Cassatt Reading the Morning Paper

HARRIET SCOTT CHESSMAN

Cover

Copyright © 2001 by Harriet Scott Chessman

A Permanent Press/Seven Stories Press FIRST EDITION

All rights reserved.
No part of this book may be reproduced, stored in a retrieval system, or transmitted in any form, by any means, including mechanical, electric, photocopying, recording or otherwise, without the prior written permission of the publisher.

For inquiries related to English-language distribution and North American rights contact:

Seven Stories Press
140 WATTS STREET, NEW YORK, NY 10013
info@sevenstories.com

For editorial inquiries, or matters related to foreign-language rights or film rights, contact:

The Permanent Press
4170 NOYAC ROAD, SAG HARBOR, NY 11963
shepard@thepermanentpress.com

In Canada:
HUSHION HOUSE, 36 NORTHLINE ROAD, TORONTO, ONTARIO M4B 3E2

In the U.K.:
TURNAROUND PUBLISHER SERVICES LTD., UNIT 3, OLYMPIA TRADING ESTATE
COBURG ROAD, WOOD GREEN, LONDON N22 6TZ

In Australia:
TOWER BOOKS, 9/19 RODBOROUGH ROAD, FRENCHS FOREST NSW 2086

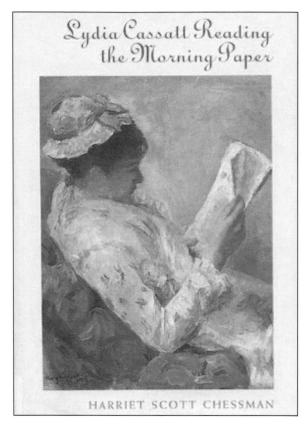

Title Page Verso—Portion

Additional information:
164 pages plus 4 unnumbered leaves of col. plates; 19 cm.; ISBN: 1-58322-272-3; LCCN: 2001032111
Summary: A fictional first-person account by Lydia Cassatt of her life and activities as a model for Mary Cassatt's paintings.

Instructions: Prepare a catalog record for this item.

When cataloging this work, consider the following:

- Physical description
- Publisher information

***AACR2r* rules needed:** 1.1B2; 1.1E1; 1.1E6; 1.1F1; 1.2B1; 1.4C5; 1.4D1; 1.4D4; 1.4F6; 1.5B1; 1.5C1; 1.5D1; 1.7B17; 1.8B1; 2.5B9; 2.5C3; 2.5D1; 2.7B17; 21.30; 22.5A1; MARC 010; MARC 020

Exercise 60

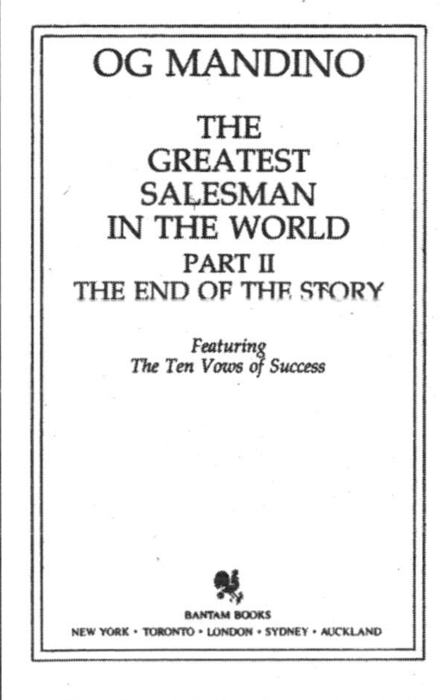
OG MANDINO

THE GREATEST SALESMAN IN THE WORLD

PART II

THE END OF THE STORY

Featuring

The Ten Vows of Success

BANTAM BOOKS

NEW YORK • TORONTO • LONDON • SYDNEY • AUCKLAND

Title Page

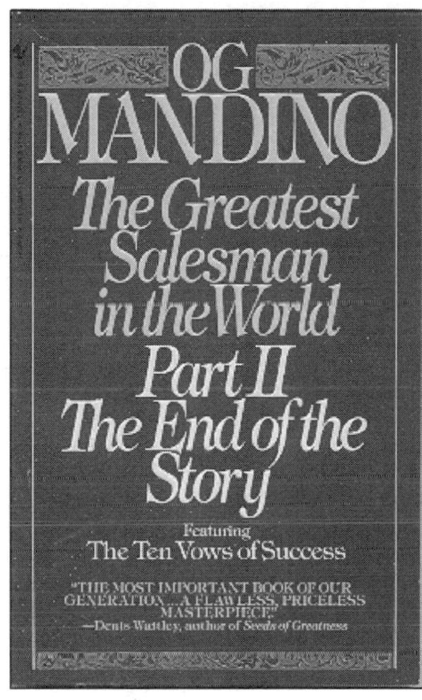

Front Cover

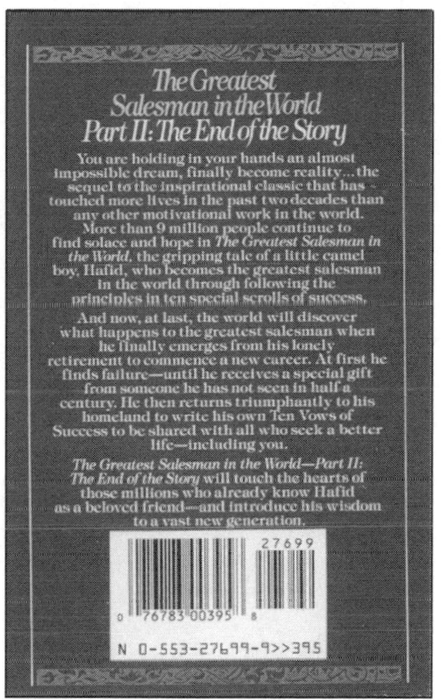

Back Cover

THE GREATEST SALESMAN IN THE WORLD, PART II

A Bantam Book

Bantam hardcover edition/March 1988

Five printings through March 1988

Bantam paperback edition/April 1989

All rights reserved.

Copyright © 1988 by Og Mandino.

Cover design © 1989 by Bantam Books.

No part of this book may be reproduced or transmitted in any form or by any means, electronic or mechanical, including photocopying, recording, or by any information storage and retrieval system, without permission in writing from the publisher.

For information address: Bantam Books.

Title Page Verso—Portion

Additional information:

7 unnumbered preliminary pages, 134 numbered pages; [p. 135] biographical sketch of author; [p. 136] ads. Inside the back cover is a black and white photo of the author; 17.4 cm.; LCCN: 87-47795

Instructions: Prepare a catalog record for this item.

When cataloging this work, consider the following:

- How would you handle the various titles of this book?
- Notes

***AACR2r* rules needed:** 1.1B1; 1.1E1; 1.1F1; 1.2B1; 1.4C1; 1.4C5; 1.4D1; 1.4F1; 1.4F6; 1.5B1; 1.5B2; 1.5D1; 1.7B5; 1.7B17; 1.8B1; 2.5B2; 2.5B3; 2.5D1; 21.1A2; 21.29B; 21.29C; 21.31M1; 22.5A1; MARC 010; MARC 020

Exercise 61

James Thomson (B.V.)

A CRITICAL STUDY

Imogene B. Walker

CORNELL UNIVERSITY PRESS

ITHACA, NEW YORK, 1950

Title Page

Copyright 1950 by Cornell University

Cornell University Press

London: Geoffrey Cumberlege

Oxford University Press

PRINTED IN THE UNITED STATES OF AMERICA BY

THE VAIL-BALLOU PRESS, INC., BINGHAMTON, N. Y.

Title Page Verso

Additional information:
ix, 212 pages; 22 cm.; bibliography (pages 175-200). LCCN: 50-7773
Summary: A critical assessment of the works of "B.V.," a pseudonym of James Thomson.

Instructions: Prepare a catalog record for this item.

When cataloging this work, consider the following:

- What do the initials "B.V." stand for?

***AACR2r* rules needed:** 1.1B3; 1.1E1; 1.1F1; 1.4C3; 1.4D1; 1.4F1; 1.5B1; 1.5D1; 1.7B18; 2.5B2; 2.5D1; 2.7B18; 21.10A; 21.30A1; 21.30D1; 26.2B2; MARC 010; References

Exercise 62

LOUIS L'AMOUR

THE RIDERS
OF
HIGH ROCK

A HOPALONG CASSIDY NOVEL

BANTAM BOOKS
NEW YORK • TORONTO • LONDON • SYDNEY • AUCKLAND

A Bantam Large Print Edition

Title Page

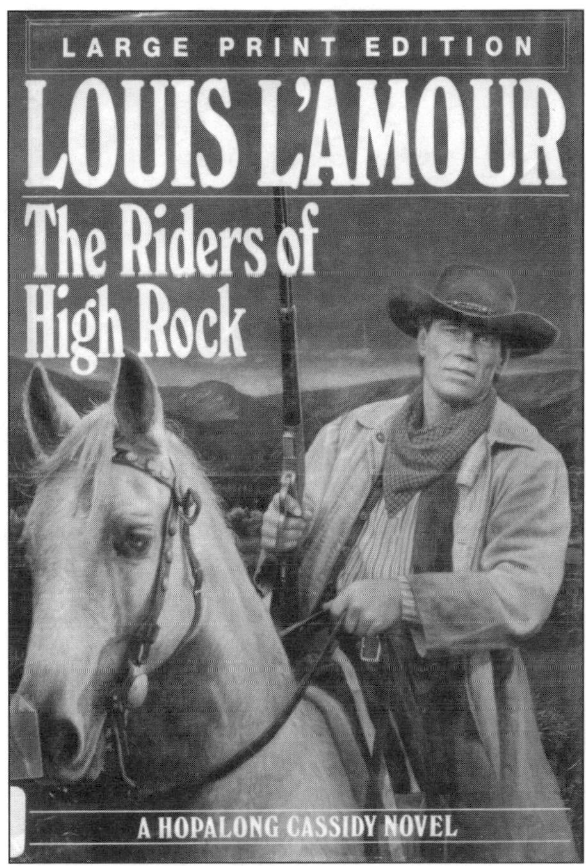

Cover

THE RIDERS OF HIGH ROCK
A Bantam Book / July 1993

Previously published as *Hopalong Cassidy and the Riders of High Rock* by Louis L'Amour (writing as Tex Burns).

All rights reserved.
Copyright © 1951, renewed © 1979 by Bantam Books.
Note copyright © 1993 by Beau L'Amour.
No part of this book may be reproduced or transmitted in any form or by any means, electronic or mechanical, including photocopying, recording, or by any information storage and retrieval system, without permission in writing from the publisher.
For information address: Bantam Books.

Published simultaneously in the United States and Canada

Bantam Books are published by Bantam Books, a division of Bantam Doubleday Dell Publishing Group, Inc. Its trademark, consisting of the words "Bantam Books" and the portrayal of a rooster, is Registered in U.S. Patent and Trademark Office and in other countries. Marca Registrada. Bantam Books, 1540 Broadway, New York, New York 10036.

PRINTED IN THE UNITED STATES OF AMERICA

ISBN 0-385-47040-1 92-37034

Title Page Verso—Portion

Additional information:
338 numbered, and [6] pages (six unnumbered pages in back of volume—a note of explanation and thanks—2 pp; biographical sketch—4 pp); 23.5 cm.

Instructions: Prepare a catalog record for this item.

When cataloging this work, consider the following:

- Physical description
- Edition statement

AACR2r **rules needed:** 1.1B1; 1.1F1; 1.2B1; 1.4C1; 1.4D1; 1.4F1; 1.4F5; 1.5B1; 1.5B2; 1.5D1; 1.7B7; 1.7B10; 1.7B12; 1.8B1; 2.5B2; 2.5B3; 2.5D1; 2.5B23; 21.1A2; 21.29C; 21.30G1; 22.5A1; App B.9; MARC 010; MARC 020

Exercise 63

Aesop & Company

WITH SCENES FROM HIS LEGENDARY LIFE

Prepared by Barbara Bader Pictured by Arthur Geisert

HOUGHTON MIFFLIN COMPANY

BOSTON

Title Page

Walter Lorraine Books

Text copyright © 1991 by Barbara Bader
Illustrations copyright © 1991 by Arthur Geisert

All rights reserved. For information about permission to reproduce selections from this book, write to Permissions, Houghton Mifflin Company, 215 Park Avenue South, New York, New York 10003.

RNF ISBN 0-395-50597-6 PAP ISBN 0-395-97496-8

90-4838

Printed in the United States of America
HOR 10 9 8 7 6 5 4 3 2

Title Page Verso—Portion

Additional information:
64 pages; colored illustrations; 26 cm.
Summary: A collection of concise stories told by the Greek slave, Aesop. Includes facts and legends about his life and commentary on the timeless appeal of his fables.

Instructions: Prepare a catalog record for this item.

***AACR2r* rules needed:** 1.1B1; 1.1F1; 1.1F6; 1.4C1; 1.4D1; 1.4D2; 1.4F6; 1.5B2; 1.5C1; 1.5D1; 1.7B7; 1.7B8; 1.8B1; 1.8B2; 1.8E1; 2.5B2; 2.5C3; 2.5D1; 21.1A2; 21.30J2; 22.5A1; MARC 010; MARC 020

Exercise 64

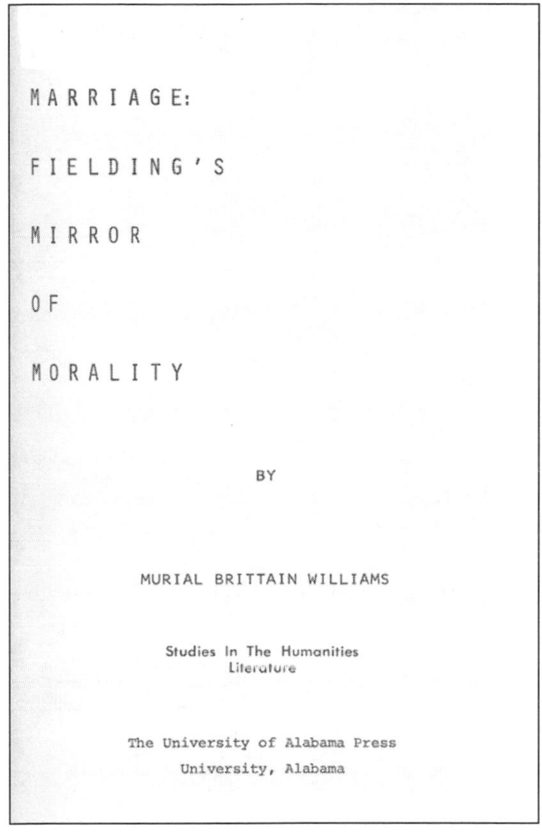

MARRIAGE:

FIELDING'S

MIRROR

OF

MORALITY

BY

MURIAL BRITTAIN WILLIAMS

Studies In The Humanities
Literature

The University of Alabama Press
University, Alabama

Title Page

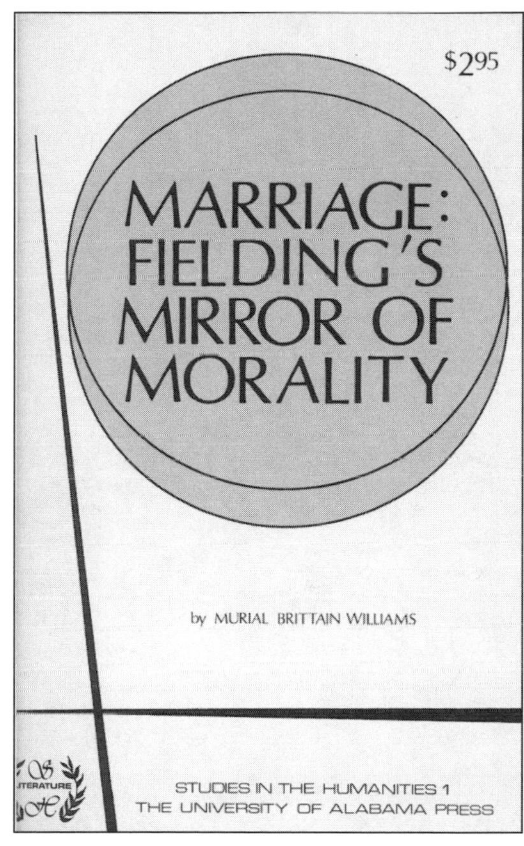

$2.95

MARRIAGE: FIELDING'S MIRROR OF MORALITY

by MURIAL BRITTAIN WILLIAMS

STUDIES IN THE HUMANITIES 1
THE UNIVERSITY OF ALABAMA PRESS

Cover

For

D.L., David, and Mark

Copyright (c) 1973
By University of Alabama Press
ISBN Number 0-8173-7311-X
Library of Congress Catalog Card Number 73-56
Manufactured in the United States of America

Title Page Verso

Additional information:
vi, 168 pages; 21 cm; bibliography (pp. 153–163); index

Instructions: Prepare a catalog record for this item.

When cataloging this work, consider the following:

- Series

***AACR2r* rules needed:** 1.1B1; 1.1E1; 1.1F1; 1.4C3; 1.4D1; 1.4F6; 1.5B1; 1.5D1; 1.6B1; 1.6D1; 1.7B12; 1.8E2; 2.4D1; 2.5B2; 2.5D1; 2.7B18; 20.4; 21.4A1; 21.28B1; 21.30G1; 21.30J1; 21.30L1; 22.5A1; MARC 010 MARC 020

Exercise 65

How to Do Things Right

THE REVELATIONS OF A FUSSY MAN

Three incomparable books of wit, charm, and wisdom finally available in one volume, as revised, edited, and enhanced by the author

L. Rust Hills

D·R·G

DAVID R. GODINE, PUBLISHER
Boston

Title Page

First published in this form in 1993 by
David R. Godine, Publisher, Inc.
Horticultural Hall
300 Massachusetts Avenue
Boston, Massachusetts 02115

Copyright © 1972, 1973, 1970, 1993 by L. Rust Hills
Originally published, in slightly different form, as three volumes
How to Do Things Right,
How to Retire at Forty-One,
and *How to Be Good,*
by Doubleday & Company, Inc.

All rights reserved. No part of this book may be used or reproduced in any manner whatsoever without written permission, except in the case of brief quotations embodied in critical articles and reviews.

BJ1581.2.H548 1993 93-15086
170′.44—dc20 CIP

ISBN 0-87923-968-9 (HC)
ISBN 0-87923-969-7 (SC)

First printing
Printed in the United States of America

Title Page Verso—Portion

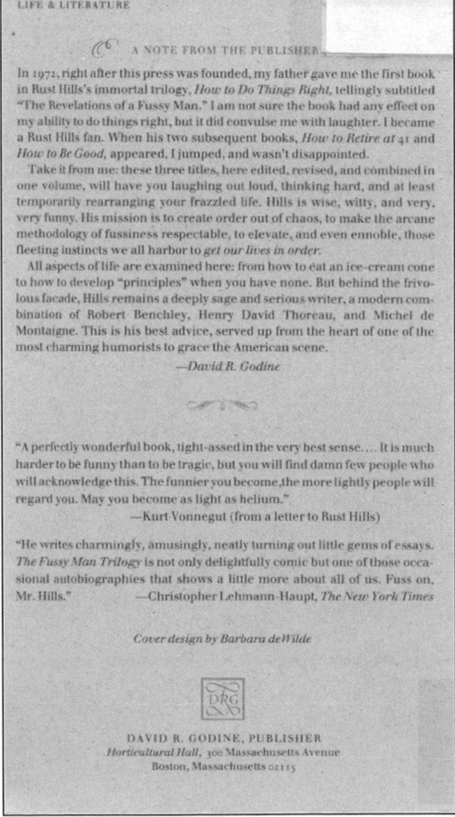

LIFE & LITERATURE

A NOTE FROM THE PUBLISHER

In 1972, right after this press was founded, my father gave me the first book in Rust Hills's immortal trilogy, *How to Do Things Right,* tellingly subtitled "The Revelations of a Fussy Man." I am not sure the book had any effect on my ability to do things right, but it did convulse me with laughter. I became a Rust Hills fan. When his two subsequent books, *How to Retire at* 41 and *How to Be Good,* appeared, I jumped, and wasn't disappointed.

Take it from me: these three titles, here edited, revised, and combined in one volume, will have you laughing out loud, thinking hard, and at least temporarily rearranging your frazzled life. Hills is wise, witty, and very, very funny. His mission is to create order out of chaos, to make the arcane methodology of fussiness respectable, to elevate, and even ennoble, those fleeting instincts we all harbor to *get our lives in order.*

All aspects of life are examined here: from how to eat an ice-cream cone to how to develop "principles" when you have none. But behind the frivolous facade, Hills remains a deeply sage and serious writer, a modern combination of Robert Benchley, Henry David Thoreau, and Michel de Montaigne. This is his best advice, served up from the heart of one of the most charming humorists to grace the American scene.

—*David R. Godine*

"A perfectly wonderful book, tight-assed in the very best sense.... It is much harder to be funny than to be tragic, but you will find damn few people who will acknowledge this. The funnier you become,the more lightly people will regard you. May you become as light as helium."

—Kurt Vonnegut (from a letter to Rust Hills)

"He writes charmingly, amusingly, neatly turning out little gems of essays. *The Fussy Man Trilogy* is not only delightfully comic but one of those occasional autobiographies that shows a little more about all of us. Fuss on, Mr. Hills." —Christopher Lehmann-Haupt, *The New York Times*

Cover design by Barbara deWilde

DRG

DAVID R. GODINE, PUBLISHER
Horticultural Hall, 300 Massachusetts Avenue
Boston, Massachusetts 02115

Back Cover

Additional information:
259 pages; illustrations; 23 cm.

Instructions: Prepare a catalog record for this item.

When cataloging this work, consider the following:

- How are the titles of the individual works in this volume handled?

***AACR2r* rules needed:** 1.1E1; 1.1F1; 1.1G1; 1.1G4; 1.2B1; 1.2B3; 1.4C1; 1.4D1; 1.4F6; 1.5B2; 1.5C1; 1.5D1; 1.7B7; 1.7B17; 1.7B18; 1.8B1; 1.8B2; 1.8E1; 2.5B2; 2.5C1; 2.5D1; 21.0B1; 22.5A1; MARC 010; MARC 020

Exercise 66

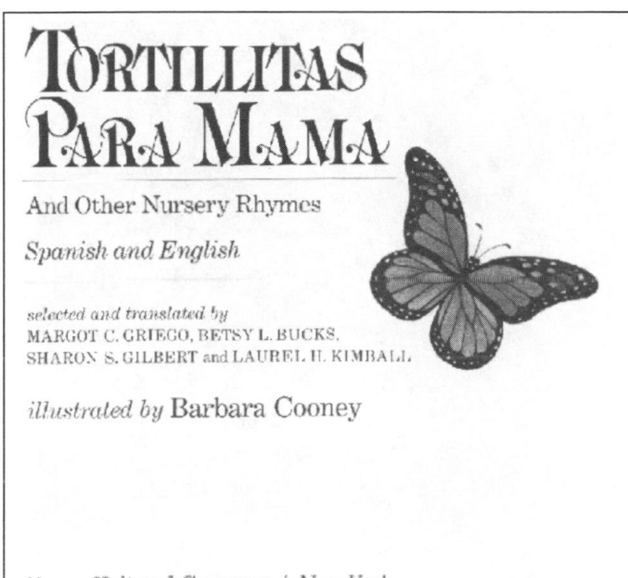

TORTILLITAS PARA MAMA

And Other Nursery Rhymes

Spanish and English

selected and translated by
MARGOT C. GRIEGO, BETSY L. BUCKS,
SHARON S. GILBERT and LAUREL H. KIMBALL

illustrated by Barbara Cooney

Henry Holt and Company / *New York*

Title Page

Text copyright © 1981 by Margot Griego, Betsy Bucks,
Sharon Gilbert, Laurel Kimball
Illustrations copyright © 1981 by Barbara Cooney
All rights reserved, including the right to reproduce
this book or portions thereof in any form.
Published by Henry Holt and Company, Inc.,
115 West 18th Street, New York, New York 10011.
Published in Canada by Fitzhenry & Whiteside Limited,
91 Granton Drive, Richmond Hill, Ontario L4B 2N5.

Title Page Verso—Portion

Additional information:
32 unnumbered pages; color illustrations; 22 cm.; LCCN: 81-4823; ISBN: 0-8050-0285-5 (hardcover); 0-8050-0317-7 (pbk)
Summary: A collection of nursery rhymes, each in both English and Spanish, collected from the Spanish community in the Americas, many with instructions for accompanying finger plays or other activities.

Instructions: Prepare a catalog record for this item.

***AACR2r* rules needed:** 1.0G1; 1.1B1; 1.1E1; 1.1E2; 1.1F5; 1.1F6; 1.4B4; 1.4C3; 1.4D2; 1.4F6; 1.5B2; 1.5C1; 1.5D1; 1.7B2; 1.7B17; 1.8B1; 1.8B2; 1.8E1; 2.5B7; 2.5C3; 2.5D1; 2.7B2; 2.7B17; 21.6C2; 21.30K2; 22.5A1; App A.51; MARC 010; MARC 020; MARC 041

Exercise 67

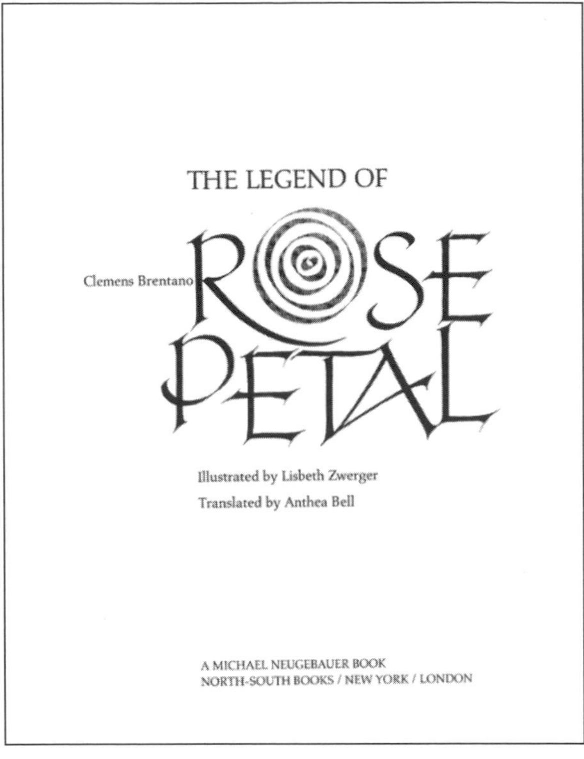

THE LEGEND OF

Clemens Brentano ROSE PETAL

Illustrated by Lisbeth Zwerger

Translated by Anthea Bell

A MICHAEL NEUGEBAUER BOOK
NORTH-SOUTH BOOKS / NEW YORK / LONDON

Title Page

Cover

Colophon—Portion

Illustrations copyright © 1978 by Michael Neugebauer Verlag AG, Gossau Zürich, Switzerland.
First published in Switzerland under the title *Das Märchen von Rosenblättchen*
English translation copyright © 1985 by Michael Neugebauer Verlag AG

All rights reserved. No part of this book may be reproduced or utilized in any form or by any means, electronic or mechanical, including photocopying, recording, or any information storage and retrieval system, without permission in writing from the publisher.

Originally published in the United States, Canada, Great Britain, Australia, and New Zealand in 1985 by Picture Book Studio. Reissued in 1995 by North-South Books, an imprint of Nord-Süd Verlag AG, Gossau Zürich, Switzerland.

Distributed in the United States by North-South Books Inc., New York.

Additional information:
28 unnumbered pages; color illustrations; 34 cm.; LCCN: 84-27386;
ISBN: 1-55858-484-6
Summary: A lover of roses with most of her kingdom made into a rose garden, Princess Rosalina makes a pact with an old enchantress to obtain the most beautiful rosebush of all.

Instructions: Prepare a catalog record for this item.

When cataloging this item, consider the following:

- Publishing history

***AACR2r* rules needed:** 1.1B1; 1.1F1; 1.1F6; 1.4C1; 1.4C5; 1.4D1; 1.4F1; 1.4F5; 1.5B1; 1.5B2; 1.5C1; 1.5D1; 1.7B2; 1.7B12; 1.7B17; 2.5B1; 2.5B7; 2.5C3; 2.5D1; 2.7B17; 21.30J2; 21.30K1; 21.30K2; 22.5A1; 25.1A; 25.2C1; 25.5C1; MARC 010; MARC 020

Exercise 68

THE PHYSICISTS

by

FRIEDRICH DÜRRENMATT

Translated from the German by

James Kirkup

GROVE PRESS, INC. / NEW YORK

Title Page

Original German version by Friedrich Dürrenmatt
copyright © 1962 by Peter Schifferli,
Verlags AG "Die Arche,"
Zurich, Switzerland

English translation copyright © 1964 by James Kirkup
All Rights Reserved

Originally published in Switzerland under the title
Die Physiker

Library of Congress Catalog Card Number: 63-17001

Second Printing 1964

CAUTION: This play is fully protected, in whole, in part or in any form under the copyright laws of the United States of America, the British Empire including the Dominion of Canada, and all other countries of the Copyright Union, and is subject to royalty. All rights, including professional, amateur, motion picture, radio, television, recitation, public reading, are strictly reserved. All inquiries should be addressed to the author's representative: Dr. Jan van Loewen Ltd., 81-83 Shaftesbury Avenue, London, W.1.

MANUFACTURED IN THE UNITED STATES OF AMERICA
BY THE BOOK PRESS, BRATTLEBORO, VERMONT

Title Page Verso

Additional information:
94 pages, 21 cm.
Summary: In this two-act comedy, Dürrenmatt addresses the broad themes of a person's responsibility in a world in which the individual appears to have less and less influence, and what a scientist's responsibility is for the uses to which his or her research is put.

Instructions: Prepare a catalog record for this item.

When cataloging this item, consider the following:

- Original title

***AACR2r* rules needed:** 1.1B1; 1.1F1; 1.1F6; 1.4C1; 1.4D1; 1.4D2; 1.4F6; 1.5B2; 1.5D1; 1.7B1; 1.7B2; 1.7B4; 1.7B7; 2.5B2; 2.5D1; 2.7B2; 2.7B7; 21.0D1; 21.1A2; 21.30G1; 21.30J2; 22.5A1; 25.2A; 25.2C1; 25.2E1; MARC 010

Exercise 69

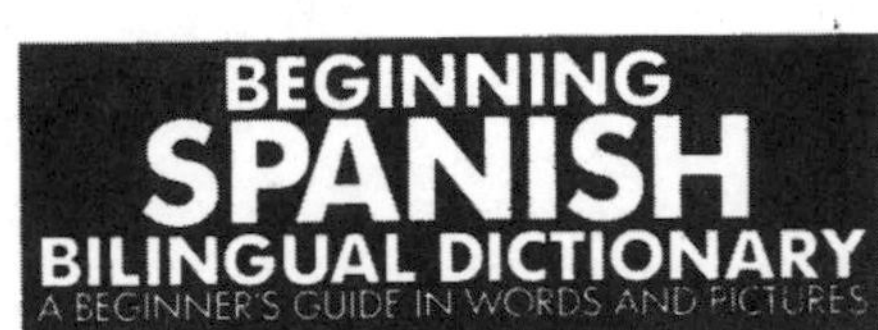
BEGINNING
SPANISH
BILINGUAL DICTIONARY
A BEGINNER'S GUIDE IN WORDS AND PICTURES

Gladys C. Lipton
Coordinator of Foreign Language Workshops
Department of Modern Languages and Linguistics
University of Maryland, Baltimore County
Baltimore, Maryland

Olivia Muñoz
Director of Foreign Languages
Board of Education, Houston Public Schools,
Houston, Texas

Second Edition

Barron's Educational Series, Inc.
New York • London • Toronto • Sydney

Title Page

Dedicated, with affection, to
Robert Lipton and Raúl Muñoz

© Copyright 1989 by Barron's Educational Series, Inc.
Prior editions © Copyright 1979, 1975 by Barron's Educational Series, Inc.

All rights reserved.
No part of this book may be reproduced in any form, by photostat, microfilm, xerography or any other means, or incorporated into any information retrieval system, electronic or mechanical, without the written permission of the copyright owner.

All inquiries should be addressed to:
Barron's Educational Series, Inc.
250 Wireless Boulevard
Hauppauge, New York 11788

Library of Congress Catalog Card No. 89-6850

International Standard Book No. 0-8120-4274-3

Title Page Version—Portion

Sample Pages

el abogado

A

a A preposition at, in, to
Ellos van a México.
They are going to Mexico.

a causa de a-KAU-sa-de adverb because of
A causa de esta fiebre, tengo que ver al doctor.
Because of this fever, I have to see the doctor.

a la derecha a-la-de-RE-cha preposition to the right
El auto dobla a la derecha.
The car turns to the right.

a la izquierda a-la-is-KYER-da to the left
Enrique se sienta a la izquierda de Carlos.
Henry sits to the left of Charles.

el abanico a-ba-NEE-co noun, masc. fan
Usa el abanico porque hace calor.
She uses the fan because it's hot.

la abeja a-BE-ja noun, fem. bee
A la abeja le gustan las flores.
The bee likes flowers.

abierto a-BYER-to adjective, masc. open
abierta (fem.)
La caja está abierta.
The box is open.

el abogado a-bo-GA-do noun, masc. lawyer, attorney
Mi papá es abogado.
My father is a lawyer.

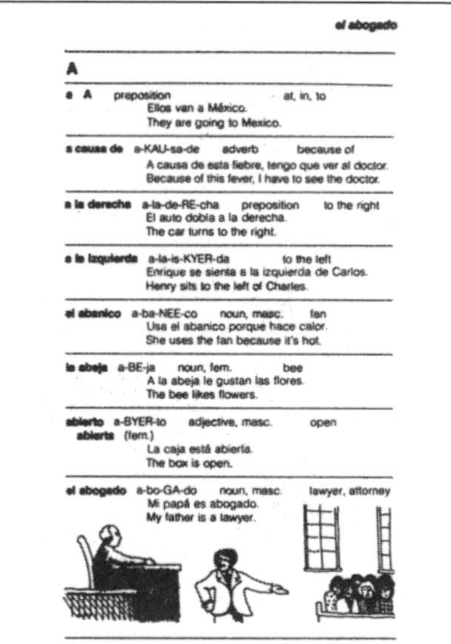

1

Table of Contents
Tabla de materias

Additional information:
x, 405 pages; black and white illustrations; 17.7 cm.

Instructions: Prepare a catalog record for this item.

When cataloging this item, consider the following:

- Size of item

***AACR2r* rules needed:** 1.1B1; 1.1E1; 1.1F1; 1.1F6; 1.2B1; 1.4F6; 1.5B2; 1.5C1; 1.5D1; 1.6B1; 1.7B14; 1.7B17; 1.8B1; 2.5B4; 2.5C1; 2.5D1; 21.1A2; 21.6A1; 21.30B1; 22.5A1; App B.9; App C; MARC 010; MARC 020

(*Continued on Next Page*)

Exercise 69

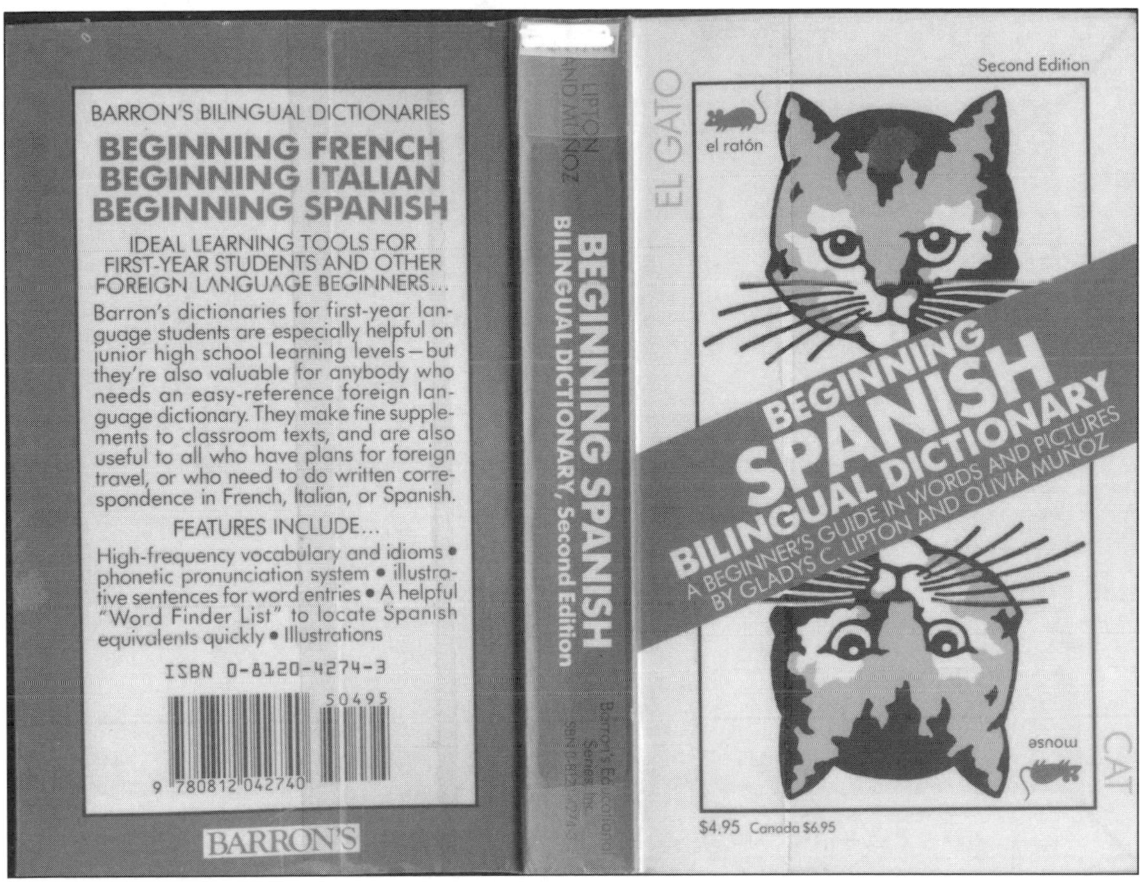

Cover

Special Features

The dictionary has a number of unique features.

1. The controlled vocabulary and idiomatic listings make it highly usable for beginners because they are not overwhelmed by too many words, explanations, and definitions. Other dictionaries of this type have tended to discourage beginners from consulting them because the definitions have all been in Spanish or English.
2. The pronunciation key,* pictures, definitions, and sentences in Spanish and English will aid the student in using this dictionary independently. The use of both languages will facilitate understanding and will promote activities of exploration and self-instruction.
3. The selection of words and idiomatic expressions has been based on frequency lists, content of courses, and reading materials at the beginning language student's level and on the natural interests of young people. It should be noted that

*The *phonemic* alphabet is based on a comparative analysis of English and Spanish sounds; it uses only Roman letters, with minimal modifications.

current words have been included to appeal to expanding interests and experiences.

4. Several special sections have been included to extend the interests of students of Spanish and English. Among these are:
   a. personal names in Spanish and English
   b. parts of speech in Spanish and English
   c. numbers 1-100 in Spanish and English
   d. days of the week, months of the year in Spanish and English
   e. Spanish verb supplement

HOW TO USE THIS DICTIONARY

The dictionary contains approximately 1300 entries in the Spanish-English vocabulary listing and an equal number of English words and expressions in the English-Spanish vocabulary listing. Each Spanish entry consists of the following:

1. Spanish word
2. phonemic transcription
3. part of speech
4. English definition(s)
5. use of word in Spanish sentence
6. English translation of Spanish sentence

Each English entry consists of the following:

1. English word
2. phonemic transcription
3. part of speech
4. Spanish definition(s)
5. use of word in English sentence
6. Spanish translation of English sentence

In addition, many word entries in both the English and Spanish sections include an illustration.

Introduction—Portion

Exercise 70

ERICH KÄSTNER

WHEN I WAS A LITTLE BOY

TRANSLATED FROM THE GERMAN
BY ISABEL AND FLORENCE MCHUGH
ILLUSTRATED BY HORST LEMKE

JONATHAN CAPE · LONDON

Title Page

Page Facing Title Page

FIRST PUBLISHED IN GREAT BRITAIN 1959
TRANSLATED FROM THE GERMAN
Als Ich Ein Kleiner Junge War
© 1957 BY ATRIUM VERLAG A. G. ZÜRICH
ENGLISH VERSION © 1959 BY JONATHAN CAPE LTD
30 BEDFORD SQUARE, LONDON W.C.I

PRINTED IN GREAT BRITAIN IN THE CITY OF OXFORD
AT THE ALDEN PRESS
ON PAPER MADE BY JOHN DICKINSON & CO. LTD
BOUND BY A. W. BAIN & CO. LTD, LONDON

Title Page Verso

Additional information:
187 pages; black and white illustrations; 21 cm.;
LCCN: 59-2626

Instructions: Prepare a catalog record for this item.

When cataloging this item, consider the following:

- Original title

***AACR2r* rules needed:** 1.1B1; 1.1F1; 1.1F6; 1.4C1; 1.4D1; 1.4F6; 1.5B2; 1.5C1; 1.5D1; 1.7B2; 2.5B2; 2.5C1; 2.5D1; 2.7B2; 21.0D1; 21.1A2; 21.30G1; 21.30K; 21.30K2; 22.5A1; 25.2A; 25.2C1; 25.2E2; MARC 010

Exercise 71

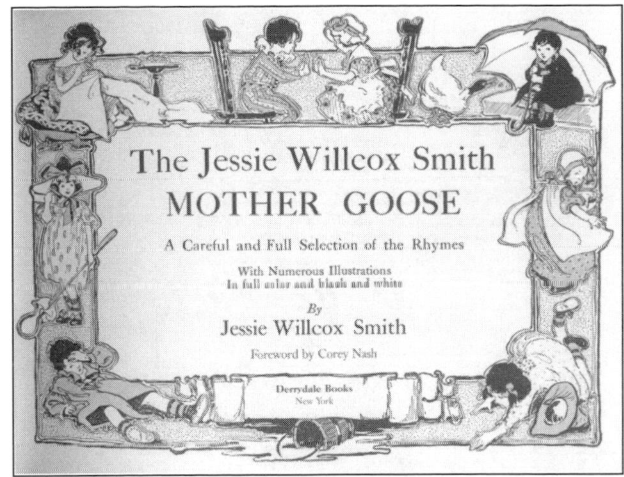

The Jessie Willcox Smith
MOTHER GOOSE

A Careful and Full Selection of the Rhymes

With Numerous Illustrations
In full color and black and white

By
Jessie Willcox Smith

Foreword by Corey Nash

Derrydale Books
New York

Title Page

This 1991 edition is published by Derrydale Books, distributed by Outlet Book Company, Inc., a Random House Company, 225 Park Avenue South, New York, New York 10003.

Printed and Bound in the United States of America

Summary: An illustrated collection of over 600 Mother Goose nursery rhymes, including both the well-known and the less familiar rhymes.

86-16673

ISBN 0-517-60357-8

10 9 8 7 6 5

Title Page Verso—Portion

Cover

Additional information:
173 pages; 22 pages of plates (unnumbered); illustrations in both black and white and color; 23 x 27 cm.
Summary: An illustrated collection of more than six hundred Mother Goose nursery rhymes including both the well-known and the less familiar rhymes.

Instructions: Prepare a catalog record for this item.

When cataloging this work, consider the following:

- Main entry
- Physical description

***AACR2r* rules needed:** 1.1B1; 1.1B2; 1.1E1; 1.1F6; 1.1F13; 1.2B1; 1.4C1; 1.4D2; 1.4D5; 1.4F6; 1.5B2; 1.5C1; 1.5D1; 1.7B4; 1.7B17; 1.8B1; 2.5B2; 2.5C3; 2.5D2; 2.7B17; 21.1A2; 25.12A; MARC 010; MARC 020

Exercise 72

MOTHER GOOSE
NURSERY RHYMES

ILLUSTRATED BY
ARTHUR RACKHAM

A STUDIO BOOK
THE VIKING PRESS · NEW YORK

Title Page

Copyright © 1913 by A. Rackham
Renewed 1941 by Edyth Rackham
Published in 1975 by The Viking Press, Inc.
625 Madison Avenue, New York, N.Y. 10022
Printed in U.S.A.

Includes index.
Summary: A collection of 162 nursery rhymes illustrated by Arthur Rackham.

75-16242
ISBN 0-670-49003-2

Title Page Verso—Portion

Additional information:
153 pages; six leaves of plates (unnumbered); black and white and colored illustrations; 25 cm.; index
Summary: A collection of 162 nursery rhymes illustrated by the well-known illustrator Arthur Rackham.

Instructions: Prepare a catalog record for this item.

When cataloging this work, consider the following:

- Main entry
- Treatment of illustrator
- Physical description

***AACR2r* rules needed:** 1.1B1; 1.1F1; 1.4C1; 1.4D2; 1.4F1; 1.4F5; 1.5B2; 1.5C1; 1.5D1; 1.7B7; 1.7B17; 1.7B18; 1.8B1; 2.5B2; 2.5B9; 2.5C3; 2.5D1; 2.7B17; 2.7B18; MARC 010; MARC 020

Exercise 73

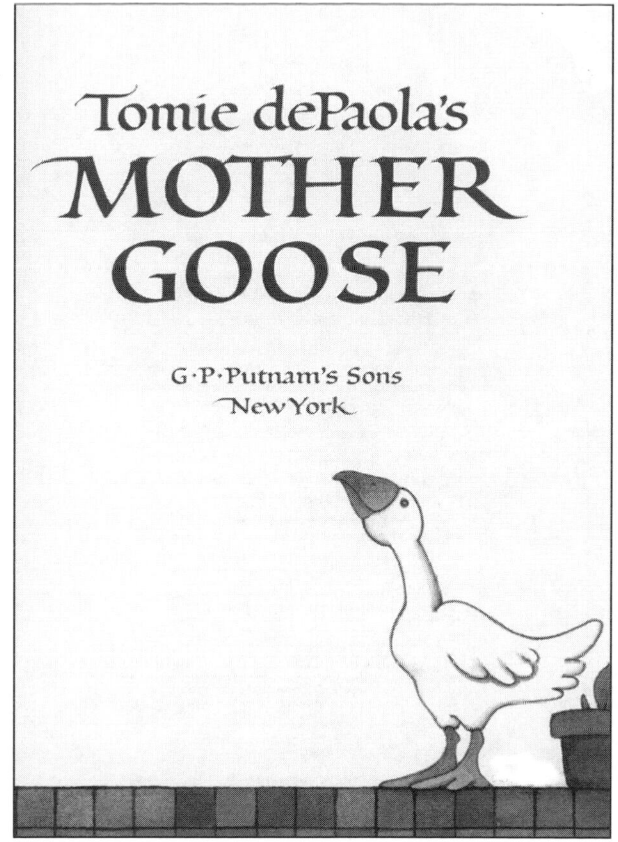

Tomie dePaola's
MOTHER
GOOSE

G·P·Putnam's Sons
New York

Title Page

Wherever possible, the Mother Goose rhymes
in this book are the classic versions
collected by Peter and Iona Opie.

Illustrations copyright © 1985 by Tomie dePaola
All rights reserved. Published simultaneously in Canada.
Printed in Hong Kong by South
China Printing Co. (1988) Ltd.
Typography by Nanette Stevenson
Calligraphy by Jeanyee Wong

Includes index.
Summary: An illustrated collection of over 200 Mother Goose nursery
rhymes, including well-known ones such as "Little Boy Blue"
and less familiar ones such as "Charlie Warlie and his cow."

84-26314
ISBN 0-399-21258-2

Title Page Verso—Portion

Additional information:
127 pages; color illustrations; 29 cm.; index of first lines
Summary: An illustrated collection of 204 Mother Goose nursery rhymes, including such less familiar ones as "Charlie Warlie and His Cow" and popular rhymes such as "Little Boy Blue."

Instructions: Prepare a catalog record for this item.

When cataloging this item, consider the following:

- Main entry

***AACR2r* rules needed:** 1.1B2; 1.4C1; 1.4D1; 1.4F3; 1.4F6; 1.5B2; 1.5C1; 1.5D1; 1.7B17; 1.7B18; 1.8B1; 2.5B2; 2.5C3; 2.5D1; 2.7B17; 2.7B18; 21.1A2; 21.29C; 21.30J2; 25.1A; MARC 010; MARC 020

Exercise 74

THE POEMS AND PROSE
OF
Mary, Lady Chudleigh

EDITED BY
Margaret J. M. Ezell

New York Oxford
OXFORD UNIVERSITY PRESS
1993

Title Page

Oxford University Press

Oxford New York Toronto
Delhi Bombay Calcutta Madras Karachi
Kuala Lumpur Singapore Hong Kong Tokyo
Nairobi Dar es Salaam Cape Town
Melbourne Auckland Madrid
and associated companies in
Berlin Ibadan

Published by Oxford University Press, Inc.,
200 Madison Avenue, New York, New York 10016

Oxford is a registered trademark of Oxford University Press

Library of Congress Cataloging-in-Publication Data

Chudleigh, Mary, Lady. 1656–1710.
The Poems and Prose of Mary, Lady Chudleigh:
edited by Margaret J. M. Ezell
p. cm. -- (Women writers in English 1350–1850)
1. Women—England—Literary collections. 2. Women and literature—England—History—17th century.
I. Ezell, Margaret J. M. II. Title. III. Series.
PR3346.C6A6 1993 828'.409–dc20 92-16922
ISBN 0-19-507874-8 (cloth)
ISBN 0-19-508360-1 (paper)

This volume was supported in part by the National Endowment for the Humanities, an independent federal agency.

Printing (last digit):
9 8 7 6 5 4 3 2 1

Printed in the United States of America
on acid-free paper

Title Page Verso

WOMEN WRITERS IN ENGLISH
1350–1850

GENERAL EDITOR
Susanne Woods

MANAGING EDITOR
Elaine Brennan

EDITORS
Patricia Caldwell
Stuart Curran
Margaret J. M. Ezell
Elizabeth H. Hageman
Elizabeth D. Kirk

WOMEN WRITERS PROJECT
Brown University

Page Facing Title Page

Additional information:
xxxvi, 392 pages; 21 cm.; index; LCCN: 92-16922; ISBN:0-19-507874-8 (cloth); 0-19-508360-1 (paper)

Instructions: Prepare a catalog record for this item.

When cataloging this work, consider the following:

- Proper form of main entry
- What errors are present in the CIP?
- Collective uniform title

***AACR2r* rules needed:** 1.1B2; 1.1F1; 1.1F6; 1.4C5; 1.4D1; 1.4F1; 1.5B1; 1.5D1; 1.7B18; 1.8B1; 1.8B2; 1.8E1; 2.5B2; 2.5D1; 2.7B18; 21.0D1; 21.4A1; 21.15B; 22.5A1; 22.6A1; MARC 010; MARC 020

Exercise 75

Title Page Vol. 1

Title Page Last Vol.

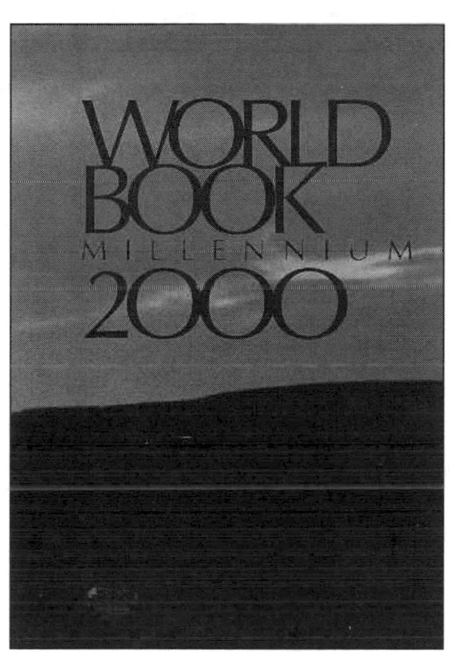

Cover Vol. 1

The World Book Encyclopedia

© World Book, Inc. All rights reserved. This volume may not be reproduced in whole or in part in any form without prior written permission from the publisher.

World Book, Inc.
233 North Michigan
Chicago, IL 60601

www.worldbook.com

"World Book" Reg. U.S. Pat. & T.M. Off. Marca Registrada

Copyright © 2000, 1999, 1998, 1997, 1996, 1995, 1994, 1993, 1992, 1991, 1990, 1989, 1988, 1987, 1986, 1985, 1984, 1983 by World Book, Inc.
Copyright © 1982, 1981, 1980, 1979, 1978 by World Book-Childcraft International, Inc.
Copyright © 1977, 1976, 1975, 1974, 1973, 1972, 1971, 1970, 1969, 1968, 1967, 1966, 1965, 1964, 1963, 1962, 1961, 1960, 1959, 1958, 1957 by Field Enterprises Educational Corporation.
Copyright © 1957, 1956, 1955, 1954, 1953, 1952, 1951, 1950, 1949, 1948 by Field Enterprises, Inc.
Copyright 1948, 1947, 1946, 1945, 1944, 1943, 1942, 1941, 1940, 1939, 1938 by The Quarrie Corporation.
Copyright 1937, 1936, 1935, 1934, 1933, 1931, 1930, 1929 by W. F. Quarrie & Company.
The World Book, Copyright 1928, 1927, 1926, 1925, 1923, 1922, 1921, 1919, 1918, 1917 by W. F. Quarrie & Company.
Copyrights renewed 1990, 1989, 1988, 1987, 1986, 1985, 1984, 1983 by World Book, Inc.
Copyrights renewed 1982, 1981, 1980, 1979, 1978 by World Book-Childcraft International, Inc.
Copyrights renewed 1977, 1976, 1975, 1974, 1973, 1972, 1971, 1970, 1969, 1968, 1967, 1966, 1965, 1964, 1963, 1962, 1961, 1960, 1958 by Field Enterprises Educational Corporation.
Copyrights renewed 1957, 1956, 1955, 1954, 1953, 1952, 1950 by Field Enterprises, Inc.

International Copyright © 1999, 1998, 1997, 1996, 1995, 1994, 1993, 1992, 1991, 1990, 1989, 1988, 1987, 1986, 1985, 1984, 1983 by World Book, Inc.
International Copyright © 1982, 1981, 1980, 1979, 1978 by World Book-Childcraft International, Inc.
International Copyright © 1977, 1976, 1975, 1974, 1973, 1972, 1971, 1970, 1969, 1968, 1967, 1966, 1965, 1964, 1963, 1962, 1961, 1960, 1959, 1958, 1957 by Field Enterprises Educational Corporation.
International Copyright © 1957, 1956, 1955, 1954, 1953, 1952, 1951, 1950, 1949, 1948 by Field Enterprises, Inc.
International Copyright 1948, 1947 The Quarrie Corporation

ISBN 0-7166-0100-1

00 5 4 3 2 1

Library of Congress Catalog Card Number 99-62063

Printed in the United States of America

Title Page Verso, Vol. 22

Additional information:
22-volume set of encyclopedias; 26 cm.; bibliographical references; ISBN is for the set; black and white and color illustrations; maps

Instructions: Prepare a MARC record for this item.

When cataloging this work, consider the following:

- Physical description for a multivolume set of books.

***AACR2r* rules needed:** 1.1B1; 1.1F6; 1.4C1; 1.4C3; 1.4D1; 1.4D2; 1.5B1; 1.5B3; 1.5C1; 1.5D1; 1.7B7; 1.7B18; 1.8B1; 1.8B2; 2.5B16; 2.5C3; 2.5D1; 2.7B18; 21.1C1; 21.29B; 21.30E1; 24.1A; 24.5C1; MARC 010; MARC 020

Exercise 76

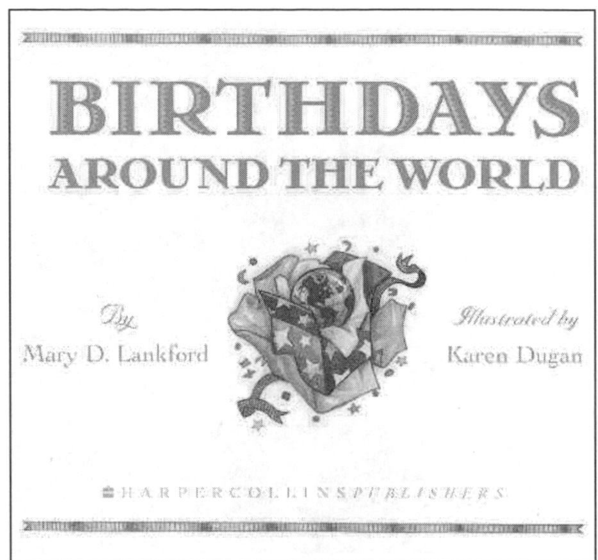

Title Page

Birthdays Around the World
Text copyright © 2002 by Mary D. Lankford
Illustrations copyright © 2002 by Karen Dugan
Printed in Hong Kong. All rights reserved.
www.harperchildrens.com

Colophon

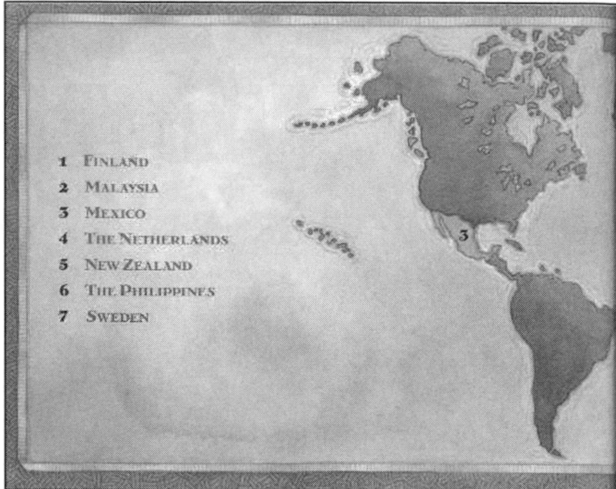

Verso of Title Page (1 page of 2-page spread)

Additional information:
32 pages; color illustrations; color map; 21 x 26 cm.; LCCN: 99-49779; ISBN: 0-688-15431-X (tr. bdg.); ISBN 0-688-15432-8 (lib. bdg.); first edition; bibliographic references and index
Summary: Describes the way birthdays have been celebrated in the past and the customs used to mark these special occasions in such countries as Finland, Malaysia, Mexico, New Zealand, and others.

Instructions: Prepare a catalog record for this item.

When cataloging this work, consider the following:

- Subject headings for this work—should you use AC or LCSH headings and why?
- The publication and CIP information is not found on the title-page verso. Does this make a difference in how it is treated in the catalog record?

***AACR2r* rules needed:** 1.1B1; 1.1F1; 1.1F6; 1.4C3; 1.4D2; 1.4F6; 1.5B2; 1.5C1; 1.5D1; 1.7B17; 1.7B18; 1.8B1; 2.5B2; 2.5C3; 2.5D1; 2.5D2; 2.7B17; 2.7B18; 2.8B1; 2.8D1; 21.1A2; 21.11A1; 22.5A1; App. B.14; MARC 010; MARC 020

Exercise 77

The Texas Library Connection Network: Usage by School Library Media Specialists Related to the Stages of Concern
by

Dorothy Elizabeth Haynes, B.A., B.S., M.L.S.
Dissertation
Presented to the Faculty of the Graduate School of
The University of Texas at Austin
in Partial Fulfillment
of the Requirements
for the Degree of
Doctor of Philosophy
The University of Texas at Austin
August, 1999

Title Page

Abstract: The Texas Library Connection (TLC) is a statewide network serving school library media centers with a bibliographic database of member library holdings and access to selected commercial indexing and full-text databases. To ascertain the impact of selected factors on the use of TLC and on the concerns of library media specialists about using TLC, a survey was constructed which contains the Stages of Concern Questionnaire (SoCQ), a part of the Concerns-Based Adoption Model (CBAM). Research questions include: 1) relationship between size of district, frequency of usage and type of usage of TLC; 2) relationship between TLC training and SoC scores; 3) relationship between the type of usage of TLC and SoC scores; 4) relationship between the presence of district library leadership and SoC scores; 5) relationship between the type of Internet connection and frequency of TLC usage; and 6) relationship between district presence of centralized processing and type of TLC usage. The population is composed of library media specialists whose campuses became members of TLC during years one and two of the project. Campuses were stratified into four groups based on size of school district student population, and surveys were sent to 25% of each subgroup. Important findings include: a strong relationship between size of district and most-used TLC function, and size of district and least-used TLC function; a positive relationship between TLC training and means of SoC scores; and lower SoC means for those respondents who didn't have a librarian as administrator than for those respondents who did. TLC is used for a variety of purposes and appears to meet the needs of librarians in different situations and sizes of districts. Research recommendations included replication of the study at a point when interlibrary loan is more strongly established, investigation of why some librarians don't use TLC, and a study validating use of SoCQ with school librarians. Policy recommendations included differentiation of TLC training to meet user concerns, strengthening campus access to funds for technology infrastructure, and continuing investigation of ways to add useful components to TLC.

Additional information:
This is an unpublished manuscript. xii, 133 leaves; 28 cm.; bibliographical references (pages 127-131); biographical information

Instructions: Prepare a catalog record for this item.

When cataloging this item, consider the following:

- Special rules relating to dissertations and unpublished manuscripts

***AACR2r* rules needed:** 1.1B1; 1.1C1; 1.1E1; 1.1F1; 1.1F7; 1.4C8; 1.4D8; 1.4F1; 1.4F9; 1.5B1; 1.5D1; 1.7B1; 1.7B13; 1.7B17; 1.7B18; 4.1B1; 4.1C1; 4.1E1; 4.1F1; 4.4B1; 4.5B1; 4.5D1; 4.7B1; 4.7B13; 4.7B17; 4.7B18; 21.1A2; 21.4A1; 22.1A; 22.5A1

Exercise 78

WHAT WE SAW | *CBS News, with an Introduction by Dan Rather*

SIMON & SCHUSTER
NEW YORK LONDON TORONTO SYDNEY SINGAPORE

Title Page

SIMON & SCHUSTER
Rockefeller Center
1230 Avenue of the Americas
New York, NY 10020

Permissions acknowledgments appear on page 142.

For information about special discounts for bulk purchases, please contact Simon & Schuster Special Sales:
1-800-456-6798 or business@simonandschuster.com

Edited by Susan Ellingwood
Design by VERTIGO DESIGN, NYC

Manufactured in the United States of America

10 9 8 7 6 5 4 3 2 1

Title Page Verso—Portion

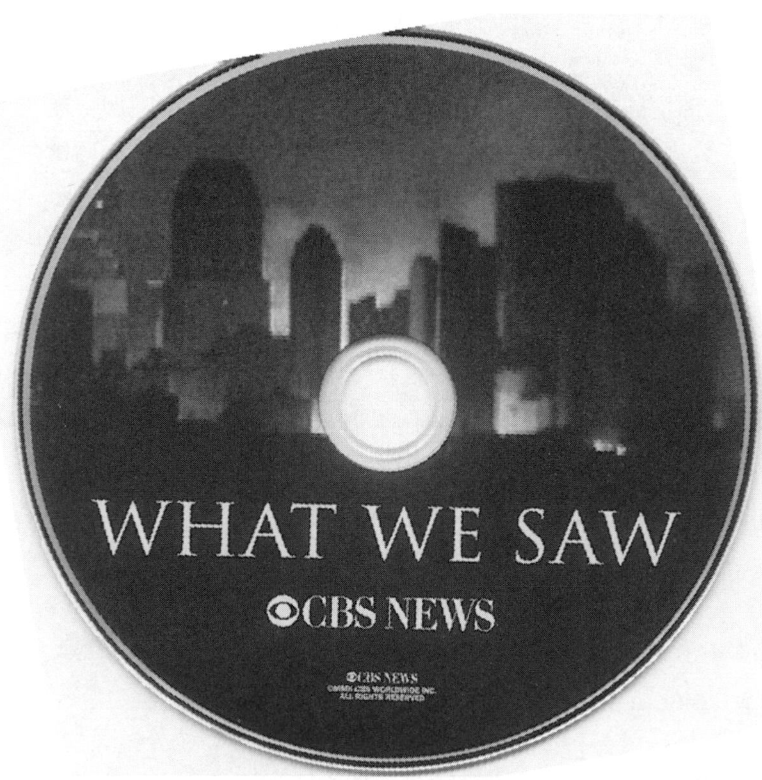

Accompnying DVD

(*Continued on Next Page*)

Exercise 78

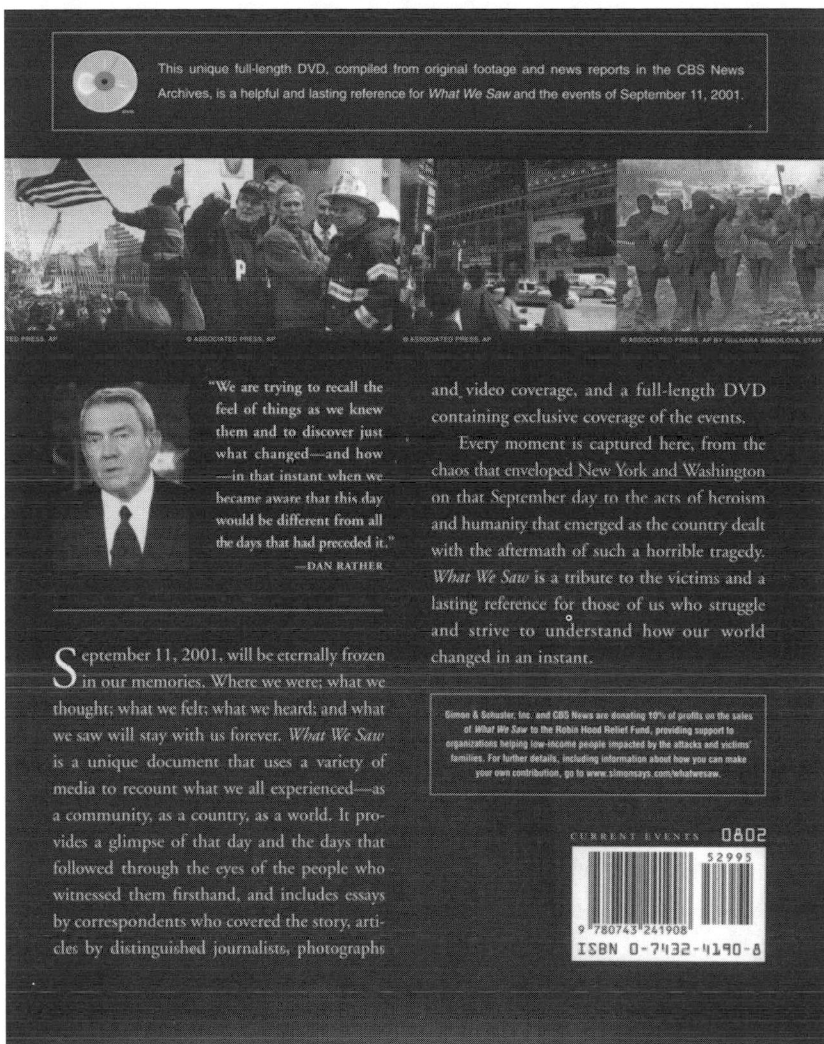

Back Cover

Additional information:
143 pages; black and white photographs; 24 cm.; accompanying DVD in pocket in back of book; LCCN: 2002075811; ISBN: 0-7432-4190-8

Instructions: Prepare a catalog record for this item.

When cataloging this work, consider the following:

- Physical description
- Construct a summary

***AACR2r* rules needed:** 1.1B1; 1.1F1; 1.1F6; 1.4C1; 1.4C5; 1.4D1; 1.4F1; 1.4F6; 1.5B2; 1.5C1; 1.5D1; 1.5E1d; 1.7B17; 2.5B2; 2.5C1; 2.5D1; 2.5E1; 2.7B17; 21.1C1; 21.29B; 21.29C; 21.30D1; 21.30F1; 22.5A1; MARC 010; MARC 020

Exercise 79

SELECTIONS FROM

The Female Spectator

by Eliza Haywood

Edited by

Patricia Meyer Spacks

New York Oxford

Oxford University Press

1999

Title Page

Oxford University Press

Oxford New York

Athens Auckland Bangkok Bogotá Buenos Aires Calcutta
Cape Town Chennai Dar es Salaam Delhi Florence Hong Kong Istanbul
Karachi Kuala Lumpur Madrid Melbourne Mexico City Mumbai
Nairobi Paris São Paulo Singapore Taipei Tokyo Toronto Warsaw

and associated companies in
Berlin Ibadan

Copyright © 1999 by Oxford University Press, Inc.

Published by Oxford University Press, Inc.
198 Madison Avenue, New York, New York 10016

Oxford is a registered trademark of Oxford University Press.

All rights reserved. No part of this publication may be reproduced, stored in a retrieval system or transmitted, in any form or by any means, electronic, mechanical, photocopying recording, or otherwise, without the prior permission of Oxford University Press.

1 3 5 7 8 6 4 2

Printed in the United States of America
on acid-free paper.

Title Page Verso—Portion

Additional information:
xxii, 313 pages; 21 cm.; bibliography, pages xxi–xxii; LCCN: 98-18306; ISBN: 0-19-510921-X (cloth : alk. paper); ISBN: 0-19 510922-8 (pbk.); Series: Women writers in English 1350-1850 (from cover)

Instructions: Prepare a catalog record for this item.

When cataloging this work, consider the following:

- Main entry
- Title statement
- What was *The Female Spectator*? How would this information affect your added entries and subject headings?
- The typestyles and appearance of the title page give us clues about interpreting the information given. What are those clues?

***AACR2r* rules needed:** 1.1B2; 1.1F6; 1.4C5; 1.4D1; 1.4F1; 1.5B1; 1.5D1; 1.6B1; 1.7B18; 2.5B2; 2.5D1; 2.7B18; 21.4A1; 22.5A1; MARC 010; MARC 020

Exercise 80

GEORGE WASHINGTON

Una biografía ilustrada con fotografías

Texto: T. M. Usel
Traducción: Dr. Martín Luis Guzmán Ferrer
Revisión de la traducción: María Rebeca Cartes

Consultora de la traducción:
Dra. Isabel Schon, Directora
Centro para el Estudio de Libros
Infantiles y Juveniles en Español
California State University-San Marcos

Bridgestone Books
an imprint of Capstone Press
Mankato, Minnesota

Title Page

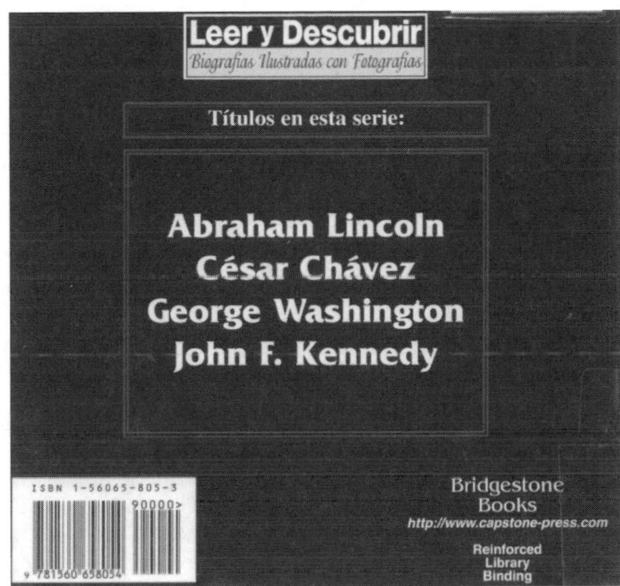

Leer y Descubrir
Biografías Ilustradas con Fotografías
Títulos en esta serie:
Abraham Lincoln
César Chávez
George Washington
John F. Kennedy
ISBN 1-56065-805-3
90000>
9 781560 658054
Bridgestone Books
http://www.capstone-press.com
Reinforced Library Binding

Back Cover

Datos sobre George Washington

- George Washington fue el primer presidente de los Estados Unidos.
- Él diseñó la ciudad de Washington, D.C., el edificio del Capitolio y la Casa Blanca.
- Su rostro está en la moneda de 25 centavos y el billete de un dólar.
- Él liberó a sus esclavos en su testamento.

Bridgestone Books are published by Capstone Press
818 North Willow Street, Mankato, Minnesota 56001 • http://www.capstone-press.com
Copyright © 1999 by Capstone Press. All rights reserved.
No part of this book may be reproduced without written permission from the publisher.
The publisher takes no responsibility for the use of any of the materials
or methods described in this book, nor for the products thereof.
Printed in the United States of America.

Editorial Credits
Martha E. Hillman, translation project manager; Timothy Halldin, cover designer
Historical Consultant
Steve Potts, Professor of History
Photo Credits
Archive Photos, 4, 6, 8, 10, 12, 14, 16, 18, 20
Ed Carlin, cover

Title Page Verso—Portion

Additional information:
24 pages, black and white and color illustrations; 23 x 22 cm.; bibliographic references (page 24) and index; LCCN: 98-19958

Instructions: Prepare a MARC record for this item by altering the MARC record for the English version which is supplied.

***AACR2r* rules needed:** 1.0D2; 1.0G1; 1.1B1; 1.1E1; 1.1F1; 1.1F6; 1.4C1; 1.4C3; 1.4D1; 1.4F6; 1.5B1; 1.5C1; 1.6B1; 1.6D1; 1.7B2; 1.7B19; 1.8B1; 1.8E1; 2.5B1; 2.5C1; 2.5C3; 2.5D1; 21.1A2; 21.29C; 21.30J2; App A.33A; MARC 010; MARC 020

(*Continued on Next Page*)

Exercise 80

AS DOWNLOADED FROM LC

```
Leader01419cam  2200337 a  4500
005       20040507213505.1
008       951026s1996    mnua   j b    001 0beng
010       a    95046666
020       a 156065340X
040       a DLC ‡c DLC ‡d DLC
042       a lcac
043       a n-us--
050 00 a E312.66 ‡b. U84 1996
082 00 a 973.4/1/092 ‡a B ‡2 20
100 1  a Usel, T. M.
245 10 a George Washington : ‡b a photo-illustrated biographies / ‡c T.M.
Usel ; historical consultant Steve Potts.
260       a Mankato, Minn. : ‡b Bridgestone Books, ‡c c1996.
300       a 24 p. : ‡b ill. (some col.) ; ‡c 23 cm.
440  0 a Read and discover photo-illustrated biographies
504       a Includes bibliographical references (p. 24) and index.
520       a Presents the life story of the first president of the United
States.
600 10 a Washington, George, ‡d 1732-1799 ‡x Juvenile literature.
650  0 a Presidents ‡z United States ‡x Biography ‡x Juvenile literature.
650  0 a Presidents ‡z United States ‡x Pictorial works ‡x Juvenile litera-
ture.
600 11 a Washington, George, ‡d 1732-1799.
650  1 a Presidents.
```

Exercise 81

Title Page

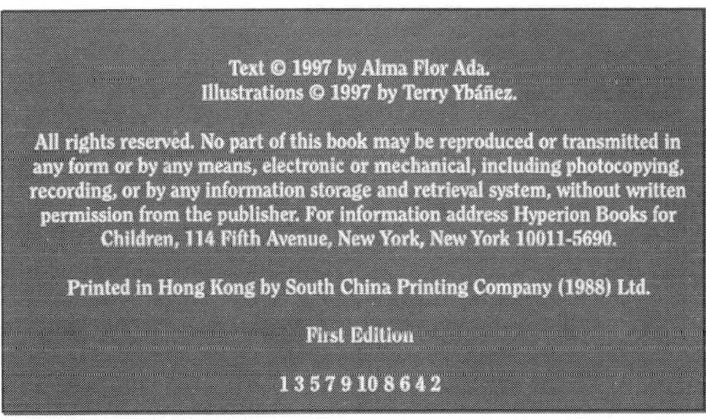

Text © 1997 by Alma Flor Ada.
Illustrations © 1997 by Terry Ybáñez.

All rights reserved. No part of this book may be reproduced or transmitted in any form or by any means, electronic or mechanical, including photocopying, recording, or by any information storage and retrieval system, without written permission from the publisher. For information address Hyperion Books for Children, 114 Fifth Avenue, New York, New York 10011-5690.

Printed in Hong Kong by South China Printing Company (1988) Ltd.

First Edition

1 3 5 7 9 10 8 6 4 2

Title Page Verso—Portion

Additional information:
32 unnumbered pages; colored illustrations; 27 cm.; ISBN: 0-7868-2123-X (lib. bdg.); 0-7868-0151-4 (trade); LCCN: 96-38218
Summary: A cumulative rhyme describes the decorating of the family Christmas tree.

Instructions: Prepare a MARC record for this item. In addition, access the Library of Congress catalog record for this book and state whether you agree or disagree with the way that LC has cataloged the book and why.

When cataloging this work, consider the following:

- Title statement

***AACR2r* rules needed:** 1.1B1; 1.1B8; 1.1D2; 1.1E1; 1.1F1; 1.2B1; 1.4C1; 1.4D1; 1.4D3b; 1.4F6; 1.5B2; 1.5C1; 1.5D1; 1.7B18; 1.8B1; 2.5B3; 2.5C3; 2.5D1; 2.7B17; 21.1A2; 22.1D1; 22.5A1;MARC 010; MARC 020

Exercise 82

The
BEST AMERICAN ESSAYS
of the Century

Joyce Carol Oates EDITOR
Robert Atwan COEDITOR

WITH AN INTRODUCTION
BY JOYCE CAROL OATES

HOUGHTON MIFFLIN COMPANY
BOSTON · NEW YORK 2000

Title Page

Contents ix

Table of Contents (Part)

Henry Adams
Jane Addams
James Agee
Maya Angelou
James Baldwin
Saul Bellow
Randolph Bourne
Rachel Carson
John Jay Chapman
Joan Didion
Annie Dillard
W.E.B. Du Bois
Gerald Early
Gretel Ehrlich
Loren Eiseley
T. S. Eliot
F. Scott Fitzgerald
Robert Frost
William H. Gass
Stephen Jay Gould
Donald Hall
Elizabeth Hardwick
Ernest Hemingway
Michael Herr
Edward Hoagland
Langston Hughes
Zora Neale Hurston
William James
Martin Luther King, Jr.
Maxine Hong Kingston
William Manchester
Mary McCarthy
John McPhee
H. L. Mencken
N. Scott Momaday
John Muir
Vladimir Nabokov
Joyce Carol Oates
Cynthia Ozick
S. J. Perelman
Katherine Anne Porter
Adrienne Rich
Richard Rodriguez
Susan Sontag
Gertrude Stein
Lewis Thomas
James Thurber
Mark Twain
John Updike
Alice Walker
Eudora Welty
E. B. White
Edmund Wilson
Tom Wolfe
Richard Wright

ISBN 0-618-04370-5 90000

Back of Dust Jacket

Contents

Table of Contents—
Last Page

(*Continued on Next Page*)

Exercise 82

Copyright © 2000 by Houghton Mifflin Company
Introduction copyright © 2000 by The Ontario Review Inc.

ALL RIGHTS RESERVED

No part of this work may be reproduced or transmitted in any form or by any means, electronic or mechanical, including photocopying and recording, or by any information storage or retrieval system without the prior written permission of the copyright owner unless such copying is expressly permitted by federal copyright law. With the exception of nonprofit transcription in Braille, Houghton Mifflin is not authorized to grant permission for further uses of copyrighted selections reprinted in this book without the permission of their owners. Permission must be obtained from the individual copyright owners as identified herein. Address requests for permission to make copies of Houghton Mifflin material to Permissions, Houghton Mifflin Company, 215 Park Avenue South, New York, New York 10003. For permission to reprint the essays included in this volume, see below.

Visit our Web site: www.houghtonmifflinbooks.com.

ISSN 0888-3742   ISBN 0-618-04370-5

Book design by Robert Overholtzer

Printed in the United States of America

QUM 10 9 8 7 6 5 4 3 2 1

Ernest Hemingway, "Pamplona in July." First published as "World's Series of Bull Fighting a Mad, Whirling Carnival" in the *Toronto Star Weekly*, 1923; collected in *By-Line: Ernest Hemingway*, edited by William White, 1967. Reprinted with permission of Scribner, a Division of Simon & Schuster, from *By-Line: Ernest Hemingway*, edited by William White. Copyright © 1967 by Mary Hemingway. • H. L. Mencken, "The Hills of Zion." From *Prejudices, 5th Series* by H. L. Mencken. First published as a dispatch to the *Baltimore Evening Sun* in July 1925. Collected in *Prejudices, 5th Series*, 1926. Copyright 1926 by Alfred A. Knopf, Inc., and renewed 1954 by H. L. Mencken. Reprinted by permission of Alfred A. Knopf, a division of Random House, Inc. • Zora Neale Hurston, "How It Feels to Be Colored Me." From *World Tomorrow* (May 1928). Used with the permission of the Estate of Zora Neale Hurston. • Edmund Wilson, "The Old Stone House." First published in *Scribner's*, 1933; collected in *Travels in Two Democracies*, 1936, and in *The American Earthquake*, 1958, by Edmund Wilson. Copyright © 1958 by Edmund Wilson. Copyright renewed © 1986 by Helen Miranda Wilson. Reprinted by permission of Farrar, Straus & Giroux, LLC. • Gertrude Stein, "What Are Master-pieces and Why Are There So Few of Them." Used by permission. • F. Scott Fitzgerald, "The Crack-Up." From *The Crack-Up*, edited by Edmund Wilson. Copyright 1945 by New Directions Publishing Corp. First published in *Esquire*, February–April 1936; collected in Fitzgerald, *The Crack-Up*, edited by Edmund Wilson, 1945. Reprinted by permission of New Directions Publishing Corp. • James Thurber, "Sex Ex Machina." From *Let Your Mind Alone! And Other More or Less Inspirational Pieces* by James Thurber (New York: Harper & Bros., 1937). First published in *The New Yorker*, 1937. Used by permission. • Richard Wright, "The Ethics of Living Jim Crow: An Autobiographical Sketch." From *Uncle Tom's Children* by Richard Wright. Copyright 1937 by Richard Wright. Copyright renewed © 1965 by Ellen Wright. First published in *American Stuff: WPA Writers' Anthology*, 1937; reprinted as the introduction to the second printing of *Uncle Tom's Children*, 1940. Reprinted by permission of HarperCollins Publishers, Inc. • James Agee, "Knoxville: Summer of 1915." First published in *Partisan Review*, 1938; reprinted as the prologue to Agee's posthumously published novel *A Death in the Family*. Copyright © 1957 by The James Agee Trust, renewed 1985 by Mia Agee. Used by permission of Grosset & Dunlap, Inc., a division of Penguin Putnam Inc. • Robert Frost, "The Figure a Poem Makes." From *The Selected Prose of Robert Frost*, edited by Hyde Cox and Edward Connery Lathem. Copyright 1946, © 1956, 1959 by Robert Frost. Copyright 1949, 1954, © 1966 by Henry Holt & Co., LLC. Reprinted by permission of Henry Holt & Co., LLC. • E. B. White, "Once More to the Lake." From *One Man's Meat* by E. B. White. Text copyright 1941 by E. B. White. Reprinted by permission of Tilbury House, Publishers, Gardiner, Maine. • S. J. Perelman, "Insert Flap 'A' and Throw Away." From *The Most of S. J. Perelman* by S. J. Perelman (New York: Simon & Schuster, 1958). First published in *The New Yorker*, 1944. Copyright 1944 by S. J. Perelman. Reprinted by permission of Harold Ober Associates Inc. • Langston Hughes, "Bop." First published in *The Chicago Defender*, 1949; revised and collected in *Simple Takes a Wife*, 1953, and in *The Best of Simple*, 1961. Copyright © 1961 by Langston Hughes. Copyright renewed © 1989 by George Houston Bass. Reprinted by permission of Hill and Wang, a division of Farrar, Straus & Giroux, LLC, and by permission of Harold Ober Associates Inc. • Katherine Anne Porter, "The Future Is Now." From *The Collected Essays and Occasional Writings of Katherine Anne Porter* (New York: Delacorte Press/Seymour Lawrence, 1970). Originally published in *Mademoiselle* (November 1950). Reprinted with the permission of Barbara Thompson Davis, Literary Trustee for the Estate of Katherine Anne Porter, c/o The Permissions Company, High Bridge, New Jersey, USA. • Mary McCarthy, "Artists in Uniform." First published in *Harper's Magazine*, 1953; collected in *On the Contrary* by Mary McCarthy, 1961. Copyright © by The Mary McCarthy Literary Trust. Reprinted by permission of The Mary McCarthy Literary Trust. • Rachel Carson, "The Marginal World." From *The Edge of the Sea* by Rachel Carson (Boston: Houghton Mifflin, 1955). Used by permission. • James Baldwin, "Notes of a Native Son." From *Notes of a Native Son* by James Baldwin. Copyright © 1955, renewed 1983, by James Baldwin. First published in *Harper's Magazine*, 1955; collected in *Notes of a Native Son*, 1955. Reprinted by permission of Beacon Press, Boston. • Loren Eiseley, "The Brown Wasps." First published in *Gentry*, 1956–57; collected in *The Night Country*, 1971. Reprinted with permission of Scribner, a Division of Simon & Schuster, from *The Night Country* by Loren Eiseley. Copy-

Title Page Verso

Additional information:
6 unnumbered preliminary pages, vii–xxviii, 596 pages; biographical notes (pages [569]-590); Appendix [Notable Twentieth-Century American Literary Nonfiction] pp. [591]-596; 23½ cm. 55 essays included. LCCN: 87-650062

Instructions: Prepare a catalog record for this item. Find the LCCN for this record.

When cataloging this work, consider the following:

- How is an ISSN handled?

***AACR2r* rules needed:** 1.1B1; 1.1F1; 1.1F6; 1.4C1; 1.4D1; 1.4D2; 1.4F6; 1.5B2; 1.5D1; 1.6B1; 1.6F1; 1.7B17; 1.7B18; 1.8B1; 1.8B2; 1.8E1; 2.5B2; 2.5D1; 2.7B18; 21.0D1; 21.1C1; 21.30B1; 21.30D1; 22.5A1; MARC 010; MARC 020; MARC 022

Exercise 83

Short Masterpieces by
TOLSTOY

TRANSLATED BY MARGARET WETTLIN

Introduction by F. D. Reeve

A LAUREL EDITION

Title Page

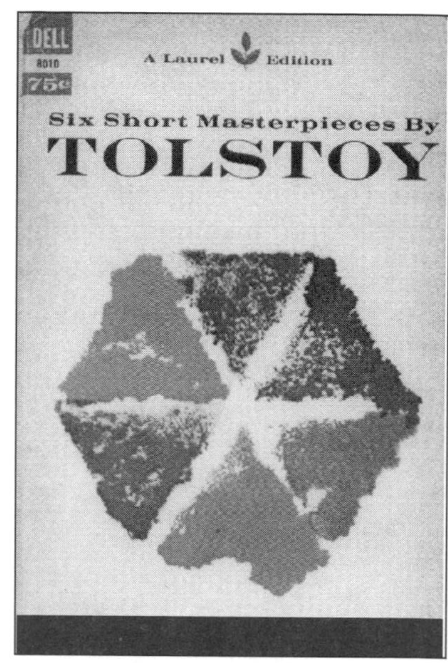

Front Cover

CONTENTS

NOTES

TWO HUSSARS:
Written in 1856. First published in the same year.

A HAPPY MARRIED LIFE:
Work on this story was begun in 1858. It was first published in 1859.

YARDSTICK:
The story was conceived in 1856, but written only in 1863. After writing it, Tolstoy laid it aside until 1885, when he introduced changes into the text. It was first published in 1886.

THE DEATH OF IVAN ILYICH:
Written from 1884 to 1886. First published in 1886.

THE KREUTZER SONATA:
Written from 1887 to 1889. The censor prevented its publication until 1891.

AFTER THE BALL:
The first sketch was written in 1903. It appeared posthumously in 1911.

Published by DELL PUBLISHING CO., INC.
750 Third Avenue, New York 17, N.Y.

Introduction © Copyright, 1963 by F. D. Reeve

Laurel ® TM 674623, Dell Publishing Co., Inc.

All rights reserved

First printing—October, 1963

Printed in U.S.A.

Title Page Verso

Additional information:
380 pages; 16.2 cm.; page 1 has a biographical sketch of Tolstoy.

Instructions: Prepare a catalog record for this item.

When cataloging this work, consider the following:

- Title variations
- Contents

***AACR2r* rules needed:** 1.1B1; 1.1B2; 1.1F1; 1.1F6; 1.4C1; 1.4C3; 1.4D1; 1.4D2; 1.4F1; 1.5B2; 1.5D1; 1.7B12; 1.7B17; 1.7B18; 1.8B3; 2.5B2; 2.5D1; 21.15B; 21.29C; 21.29D; 21.30D1; 21.30H1; 21.30K1c; 22.5A1

Exercise 84

NORTHANGER ABBEY

AND

PERSUASION

BY

JANE AUSTEN

WITH AN INTRODUCTION

BY

AUSTIN DOBSON

ILLUSTRATED

BY

HUGH THOMSON

MACMILLAN AND CO., LIMITED
ST MARTIN'S STREET LONDON
1926

Title Page

COPYRIGHT

First Edition with Hugh Thomson's Illustrations 1897
First printed in Illustrated Pocket Classics 1904
Reprinted 1906, 1909, 1912, 1916, 1923, 1926

PRINTED IN GREAT BRITAIN

Title Page Verso

Additional information:
xvi, 443 pages (last page not numbered 444); black and white illustrations; 18 cm.

Instructions: Prepare a catalog record for this item.

When cataloging this work, consider the following:

- Title statement
- Varying titles

***AACR2r* rules needed:** 1.1F1; 1.1F6; 1.1G3; 1.2B1; 1.4C1; 1.4D1; 1.4F1; 1.4F4; 1.5B1; 1.5C1; 1.5D1; 1.6B1; 1.7B7; 2.5B2; 2.5C1; 2.5D1; 21.0D1; 21.15B; 21.30G1; 21.30K2; 21.30M1; 22.5A1; App. B; App. C

Exercise 85

Persuasion

NEW YORK
E. P. DUTTON & CO. INC.

Title Page

Made in Great Britain
at The Temple Press Letchworth
for
J. M. Dent & Sons Ltd.
Aldine House Bedford St. London
First Published 1818
First Published in this Edition 1934

Title Page Verso

THE WORKS OF JANE AUSTEN
Illustrated by Maximilien Vox

Series Title Page

Additional information:
v, 219 pages; 8 unnumbered colored plates including frontispiece facing title page; 19 cm.; LCCN: 36-10905

Instructions: Prepare a catalog record for this item. Research this title to prepare a summary and add subject headings.

When cataloging this work, consider the following: What do you do when the author is known but is not given on the title page?

***AACR2r* rules needed:** 1.1B1; 1.1F6; 1.4C3; 1.4D2; 1.4F1; 1.5B1; 1.5C1; 1.5D1; 1.6B1; 1.6E1; 2.5B2; 2.5B9; 2.5C3; 2.5D1; 21.4A1; 21.30K2; 22.5A1; MARC 010

Exercise 86

George Darley

The Errors of Ecstasie

Sylvia

Nepenthe

with an introduction
for the Garland edition by
Donald H. Reiman

Garland Publishing, Inc., New York & London

1978

Title Page

Bibliographical note:

these facsimiles were made from copies in the British Library *The Errors of Ecstasie* T1059.(10) and the Yale University Library *Sylvia* (In.D249.827) *Nepenthe* (In.D249.835)

The copy of *Nepenthe* reprinted here contains autograph notes by the author.

Title Page Verso—Portion

A Garland Series

ROMANTIC CONTEXT: POETRY

Significant Minor Poetry 1789-1830

Printed in photo-facsimile
in 128 volumes

selected and arranged by
Donald H. Reiman
The Carl H. Pforzheimer Library

Series Title Page

Additional information:
Reprint of the 1822 edition of *The Errors of Ecstasie,* printed for G. and W. B. Whittaker, London; the 1827 edition of *Sylvia,* published for J. Taylor and sold by J. A. Hessey, London; and the 1835 edition of *Nepenthe,* published by the author, London. vii, various pagings (43 pages; vii, 217 pages; 69 pages); 21 cm.; LCCN: 75-31193; ISBN: 0-8240-2144-4

Instructions: Prepare a catalog record for this item.

When cataloging this work, consider the following:

- Title statement
- Varying titles
- Series
- Added entries

***AACR2r* rules needed:** 1.1E1; 1.1F3; 1.1F6; 1.1G3; 1.4B4; 1.4C5; 1.4D1; 1.4D2; 1.4F1; 1.5B1; 1.5D1; 1.6B1; 1.6B2; 1.6D1; 1.6E1; 1.6H1; 1.6J1; 1.7B7; 1.7B10; 2.5B8a; 2.5B8b; 2.5D1; 2.6B1; 2.7B7; 21.0D1; 21.1A2; 21.29C; 21.29D1; 21.30H1; 21.30M1; 22.5A1; MARC 010; MARC 020

Exercise 87

The Winged Skull

PAPERS FROM THE LAURENCE STERNE BICENTENARY CONFERENCE

AT THE UNIVERSITY OF YORK

and sponsored by

McMASTER UNIVERSITY

THE UNIVERSITY OF YORK

THE NEW PALTZ COLLEGE OF THE STATE UNIVERSITY OF NEW YORK

Edited by Arthur H. Cash
and John M. Stedmond

THE KENT STATE UNIVERSITY PRESS

Title Page

Contents

Contents—Two Pages Combined

ISBN 0-87338-102-5
Library of Congress Card Catalog Number 70:114668

Published simultaneously in Great Britain
by Methuen & Co. Ltd.
11 New Fetter Lane London EC4

Designed by Ruari McLean
Printed in England by Westerham Press
Westerham Kent

Title Page Verso

Additional information:
xix, 315 pages; includes frontispiece and 8 unnumbered pages of plates, including 1 plate of music; 26 cm.; bibliographies (pages 279-315)

Instructions: Prepare a catalog record for this item.

When cataloging this work, consider the following:
This is a publication resulting from a conference.

***AACR2r* rules needed:** 1.1B1; 1.1F4; 1.4A2; 1.4B1; 1.4C6; 1.4D2; 1.4F4; 1.4F6; 1.5B1; 1.5D1; 1.7B18; 1.8B1; 2.4D1; 2.5B2; 2.5B3; 2.5C2; 2.5D1; 21.0D1; 21.1B2d; 21.30A1; 21.30D; 21.30D1; 22.5A1; 24.1A; 24.7B4; 24.13A6; MARC 010; MARC 020

Exercise 88

HELBECK
OF BANNISDALE

Mary Augusta Ward

Garland Publishing, Inc., New York & London

1975

Title Page of this Edition

HELBECK OF BANNISDALE

BY

MRS HUMPHRY WARD

. . . metus ille . . . . Acheruntis. . . .
Funditus humanam qui vitam turbat ab imo

LONDON
SMITH, ELDER, & CO., 15 WATERLOO PLACE
1898

[All rights reserved]

Second Title Page (Facsimile)

A
Garland Series

VICTORIAN
FICTION

NOVELS OF FAITH
AND DOUBT

A collection of 121 novels
in 92 volumes, selected by
Professor Robert Lee Wolff,
Harvard University,
with a separate introductory volume
written by him
especially for this series.

Series Information

Bibliographical note:

this facsimile has been made from a copy in the
Yale University Library
(Ip.W215.898)

Library of Congress Cataloging in Publication Data

Ward, Mary Augusta Arnold, 1851-1920.
Helbeck of Bannisdale.

(Victorial fiction : Novels of faith and doubt ;
v. 19)
Reprint of the 1898 ed. published by Smith, Elder,
London.
I. Title. II. Series.
PZ3.W215He15 [PR5714] 823'.8 75-465
ISBN 0-8240-1543-6

Printed in the United States of America

Title Page Verso

Additional information:
464 pages; 19 cm.; ISBN 0-8240-1543-6; LCCN: 75-465
Summary: Laura Fountain, the daughter of a "liberated" Cambridge professor, comes to Bannisdale with her invalid widowed stepmother, Augustina, the older sister of Alan Helbeck. Alan, a devout Catholic, and Laura discover their love for each other, but Alan's desire to glorify that love by converting Laura to his faith threatens her individuality.

Instructions: Prepare a catalog record for this item.

When cataloging this work, consider the following:
What is the main entry for this work? How did you determine the main entry?

***AACR2r* rules needed:** 1.1B1; 1.1F1; 1.1F7; 1.2B4; 1.4C1; 1.4D2; 1.4F1; 1.5B2; 1.5D1; 1.6B1; 1.6B2; 1.6D1; 1.6E1; 1.7A4; 1.7B6; 1.7B7; 1.7B9; 1.7B22; 1.8B1; 1.11D; 1.11F; 2.5B2; 2.5D1; 21.1A2; 21.4A1; 21.30D1; 22.2C1; 22.5A1; MARC 010; MARC 020

Exercise 89

Buffy the Vampire Slayer

the blood of carthage

based on the television series created by JOSS WHEDON

writer CHRISTOPHER GOLDEN

penciller CLIFF RICHARDS

inker JOE PIMENTEL

Sunnydale flashbacks by CHYNNA CLUGSTON-MAJOR

Carthage flashbacks by PAUL LEE & BRIAN HORTON

colorist GUY MAJOR

letterers AMADOR CISNEROS & DRAGON MONKEY

This story takes place during Buffy the Vampire Slayer's third season.

dark horse comics

Title Page (negative image)

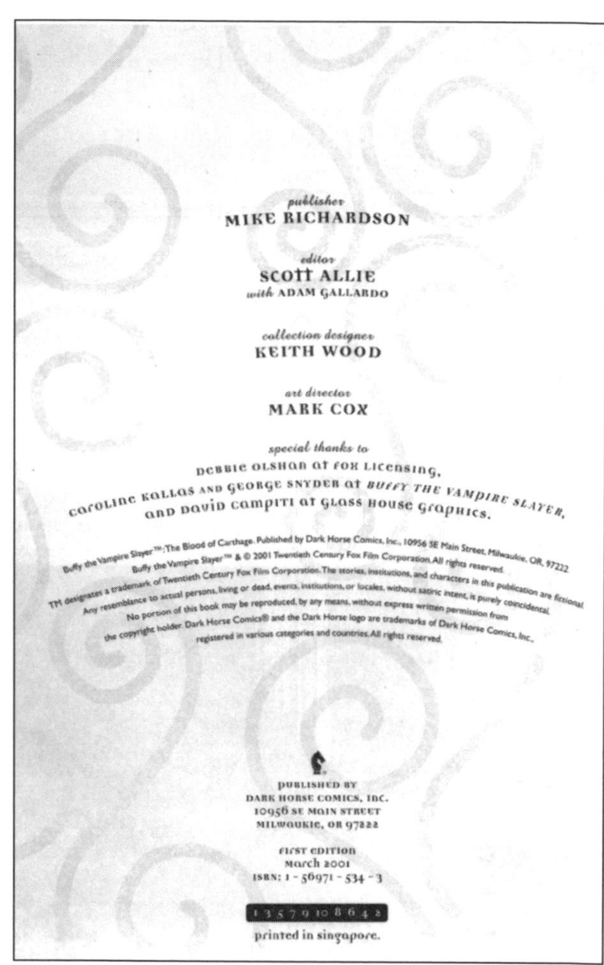

publisher
MIKE RICHARDSON

editor
SCOTT ALLIE
with ADAM GALLARDO

collection designer
KEITH WOOD

art director
MARK COX

special thanks to
DEBBIE OLSHAN AT FOX LICENSING,
CAROLINE KALLAS AND GEORGE SNYDER AT *BUFFY THE VAMPIRE SLAYER*,
AND DAVID CAMPITI AT GLASS HOUSE GRAPHICS.

Buffy the Vampire Slayer™: The Blood of Carthage. Published by Dark Horse Comics, Inc., 10956 SE Main Street, Milwaukie, OR, 97222
Buffy the Vampire Slayer™ & © 2001 Twentieth Century Fox Film Corporation. All rights reserved.
TM designates a trademark of Twentieth Century Fox Film Corporation. The stories, institutions, and characters in this publication are fictional.
Any resemblance to actual persons, living or dead, events, instiutions, or locales, without satiric intent, is purely coincidental.
No portion of this book may be reproduced, by any means, without express written permission from
the copyright holder. Dark Horse Comics® and the Dark Horse logo are trademarks of Dark Horse Comics, Inc.,
registered in various categories and countries. All rights reserved.

PUBLISHED BY
DARK HORSE COMICS, INC.
10956 SE MAIN STREET
MILWAUKIE, OR 97222

FIRST EDITION
MARCH 2001
ISBN: 1-56971-534-3

1 3 5 7 9 10 8 6 4 2

printed in singapore.

Title Page Verso (negative image)

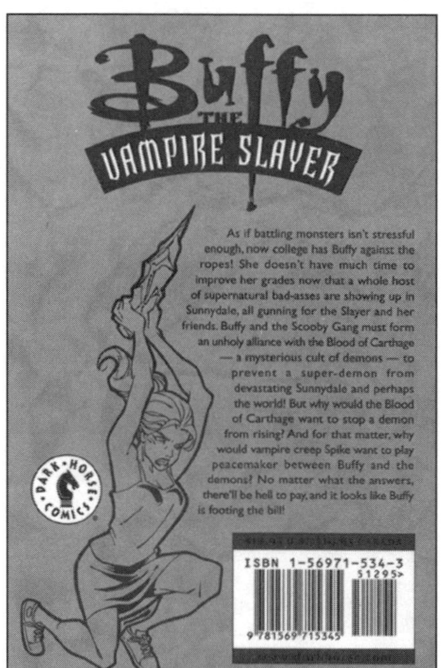

Buffy the Vampire Slayer

As if battling monsters isn't stressful enough, now college has Buffy against the ropes! She doesn't have much time to improve her grades now that a whole host of supernatural bad-asses are showing up in Sunnydale, all gunning for the Slayer and her friends. Buffy and the Scooby Gang must form an unholy alliance with the Blood of Carthage — a mysterious cult of demons — to prevent a super-demon from devastating Sunnydale and perhaps the world! But why would the Blood of Carthage want to stop a demon from rising? And for that matter, why would vampire creep Spike want to play peacemaker between Buffy and the demons? No matter what the answers, there'll be hell to pay, and it looks like Buffy is footing the bill!

ISBN 1-56971-534-3
51295>
9 781569 715345

Back Cover

Additional information:
128 unnumbered pages; mostly color illustrations; 26 cm.
Summary: An original graphic novel based on the television series *Buffy the Vampire Slayer.*

Instructions: Prepare a catalog record for this item.

When cataloging this item, consider the following:

- Physical description
- Genre headings

***AACR2r* rules needed:** 1.1B1; 1.1B9; 1.1C1; 1.1F1; 1.1F6; 1.2B1; 1.4C1; 1.4C3; 1.4F1; 1.5B1; 1.5C1; 1.5D1; 1.7B6; 1.7B17; 1.8B1; 2.5B7; 2.5C3; 2.5C5; 2.5D1; 2.7B17; 21.0D1; 21.1A2; 21.6B2; 21.30F1; 21.30G1; 21.30H1; 21.30K2; 22.5A1; App. B; MARC 020

Exercise 90

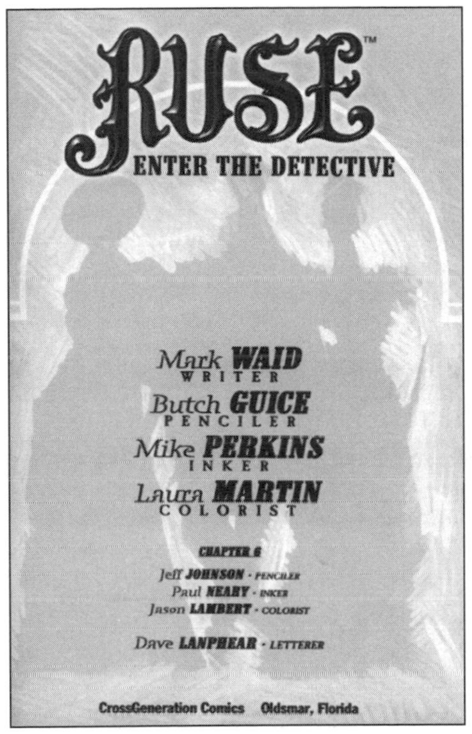

RUSE™
ENTER THE DETECTIVE
Mark WAID
WRITER
Butch GUICE
PENCILER
Mike PERKINS
INKER
Laura MARTIN
COLORIST
CHAPTER 6
Jeff JOHNSON · PENCILER
Paul NEARY · INKER
Jason LAMBERT · COLORIST
Dave LANPHEAR · LETTERER
CrossGeneration Comics Oldsmar, Florida

Title Page

ENTER THE DETECTIVE
features Chapters One through Six
from the ongoing series RUSE.

Page After Title Page

The
CrossGen
Universe
created by
Mark Alessi &
Gina M. Villa

RUSE™ Traveler Edition: Enter the Detective, Vol. 1, MARCH 2003. FIRST PRINTING. Originally published in single magazine form as Ruse™ Vol. 1, Issues #1-#6. Copyright © 2001 and 2002. All rights reserved. Published by CG Entertainment, Inc. Office of publication: 4023 Tampa Road, Suite 2400, Oldsmar, Florida 34677. CrossGen®, CrossGen Comics®, CrossGeneration®, CrossGeneration Comics®, and the CrossGen sigil® are registered trademarks of CrossGeneration Comics, Inc. CG Entertainment™, the CGE logo™, Ruse™ and all prominent characters are ™ and © 2002 CrossGeneration Comics, Inc. ALL RIGHTS RESERVED. The entire contents of this book are ™ and © 2003 CrossGeneration Comics, Inc. The stories, incidents and characters in this publication are fictional. Any similarities to persons living or dead are purely coincidental. With the exception of artwork used for review purposes, none of the contents of this book may be reproduced in any form without the express written consent of CrossGeneration Comics, Inc. PRINTED IN CANADA.

Inside Front Cover (negative image)

Additional information:
Various pagings by chapter—1.1–1.32, 2.1–2.22, 3.1–3.22, 4.1–4.22, 5.1–5.22, 6.1–6.22; mostly color illustrations; 21 cm.; an original graphic novel; LCCN: 2004297236; ISBN: 1-59314-012-6
Summary: Detective Simon Archard and his assistant Emma Bishop begin to suspect that Partington's newest resident may be responsible for a rash of serial killings.

Instructions: Prepare a catalog record for this item.

When cataloging this item, consider the following:

- Statement of responsibility
- Physical description

***AACR2r* rules needed:** 1.1B1; 1.1B9; 1.1F1; 1.1F6; 1.2B1; 1.4D4b; 1.4F1; 1.4F5; 1.5B1; 1.5B2; 1.5C1; 1.5D1; 1.6B1; 1.6G1; 1.7B6; 1.7B22; 1.8B1; 1.8D1; 2.5B8b; 2.5C3; 2.5C5; 2.5D1; 21.6A1a; 21.6B1; 21.29B; 21.30F1; 21.30J2; 21.30L1; 22.5A1; App. B; MARC 020

Exercise 91

Last Page

Executive Producer: Yasuyoshi Tokuma
Planning: Tatsumi Yamashita, Hideo Ogata
Animation Supervisor: Tsukasa Niwauchi
Art Direction: Toshiro Nozaki, Nizo Yamamoto
Music: Joe Hisaishi
Recording and Sound Mixing: Shuji Inoue
Camera: Hirokata Takahashi
Editor: Takeshi Seyama
Sound Director: Shigeharu Shiba
Sound Engineer: Shuji Inoue
Sound Effects: Kazutoshi Sato

Production: Toru Hara, Studio Ghibli
Producer: Isao Takahata

Original Story · Screenwriter · Director: Hayao Miyazaki

Colophon

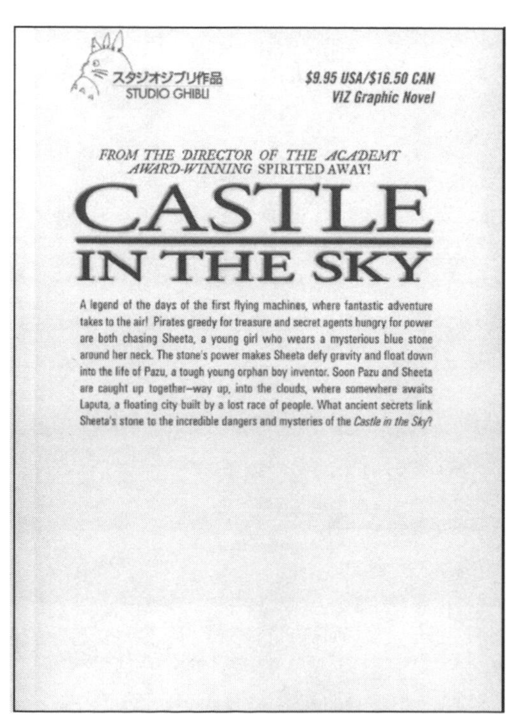

Front Cover

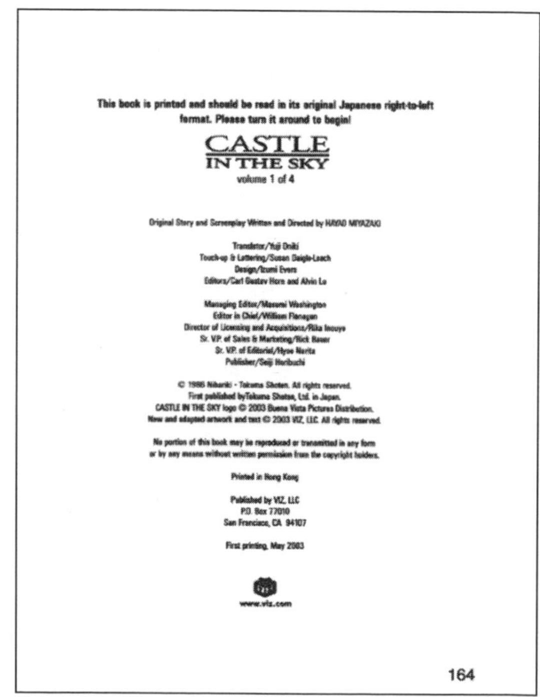

This book is printed and should be read in its original Japanese right-to-left format. Please turn it around to begin!

CASTLE
IN THE SKY
volume 1 of 4

Original Story and Screenplay Written and Directed by HAYAO MIYAZAKI

Translator/Yuji Oniki
Touch-up & Lettering/Susan Daigle-Leach
Design/Izumi Evers
Editors/Carl Gustav Horn and Alvin Lu

Managing Editor/Masumi Washington
Editor in Chief/William Flanagan
Director of Licensing and Acquisitions/Rika Inouye
Sr. V.P. of Sales & Marketing/Rick Bauer
Sr. V.P. of Editorial/Hyoe Narita
Publisher/Seiji Horibuchi

© 1986 Nibariki · Tokuma Shoten. All rights reserved.
First published byTokuma Shoten, Ltd. in Japan.
CASTLE IN THE SKY logo © 2003 Buena Vista Pictures Distribution.
New and adapted artwork and text © 2003 VIZ, LLC. All rights reserved.

No portion of this book may be reproduced or transmitted in any form or by any means without written permission from the copyright holders.

Printed in Hong Kong

Published by VIZ, LLC
P.O. Box 77010
San Francisco, CA 94107

First printing, May 2003

www.viz.com

164

First Page

(*Continued on Next Page*)

Exercise 91

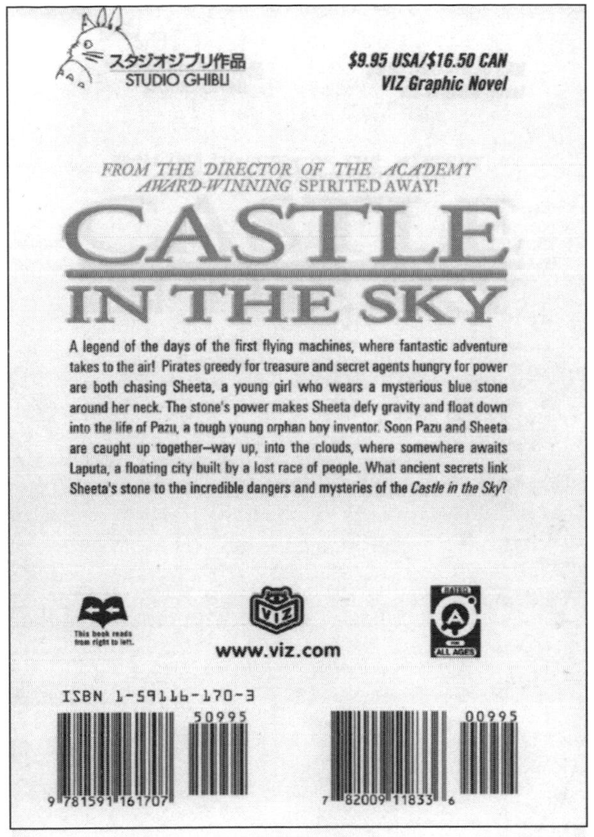

Front Jacket Cover

Back Jacket Cover

Additional information:
This is a "manga" graphic novel. 164 pages; color illustrations; 182 mm.

Instructions: Prepare a catalog record for this item.

When cataloging this item, consider the following:

- What is significant about this item being a manga?
- What is the chief source of information for this book?

***AACR2r* rules needed:** 1.1B1; 1.1B9; 1.1C1; 1.1F1; 1.1F6; 1.4C1; 1.4C3; 1.4D1; 1.4D2; 1.4F1; 1.5B1; 1.5B2; 1.5C1; 1.5D1; 1.7B1; 1.7B2; 1.7B14; 1.7B17; 1.7B20; 1.8B1; 1.8D1; 2.0B1; 2.5B2; 2.5C5; 2.5C3; 2.5D2; 2.7B3; 2.7B10; 21.1A1; 21.30K1; 21.30K2; 21.30L1; 22.4B2; 22.5A1; MARC 020; MARC 041

Exercise 92

Title Page

Accompanying CD

Amistad is an imprint of HarperCollins Publishers Inc.

God Bless the Child
Words and music copyright © 1941 by Edward B. Marks Music Company.
Copyright renewed. Used by permission. All rights reserved. Illustrations copyright © 2004 by Jerry Pinkney
Printed in the U.S.A.
All rights reserved. www.harperchildrens.com

Typography by Matt Adamec 1 2 3 4 5 6 7 8 9 10 ❖ First Edition

Title Page Verso—Portion

Additional information:
36 unnumbered pages, color illustrations, 29 cm.; ISBN: 0-06-028797-7, 0-06-029487-6 (lib. bdg.); LCCN: 00-063200; includes an accompanying CD in pocket inside the back cover; HarperCollins is in New York City. Note: The second ISBN number is transcribed correctly but was incorrect in the book.
Summary: A swing spiritual based on the proverb "God blessed the child that's got his own."

Instructions: Prepare a catalog record for this item.

***AACR2r* rules needed:** 1.1B1; 1.1F1; 1.1F4; 1.1F6; 1.2B1; 1.4C6; 1.4D2; 1.4D3; 1.4F1; 1.5B2; 1.5B4; 1.5C1; 1.5D1; 1.5E1(d); 1.7B9; 1.7B11; 1.7B14; 1.7B17; 1.8B1; 1.8B2; 1.8E1; 2.5B7; 2.5C3; 2.5D1; 2.5E1; 2.5E2; 2.7B11; 2.7B17; 6.1F2; 6.5B1; 6.5B2; 6.5C2; 6.5D2; 6.7B6; 6.7B7; 21.0D1; 21.1A2; 21.29B; 21.29C; 21.30K2; 22.5A1; MARC 010; MARC 020

Exercise 93

Cassette

HarperCollins®, ®, Harper Trophy®, and I Can Read Book®
are trademarks of HarperCollins Publishers Inc.

Bathtime for Biscuit
Text copyright © 1998 by Alyssa Satin Capucilli
Illustrations copyright © 1998 by Pat Schories
Printed in the U.S.A. All rights reserved.

Summary: Biscuit the puppy runs away from his bath with his puppy friend Puddles.
ISBN 0-06-027937-0. — ISBN 0-06-027938-9 (lib. bdg.)
ISBN 0-06-444264-0 (pbk.)

97-49663

First Harper Trophy edition, 1999

Title Page Verso—Portion

Title Page

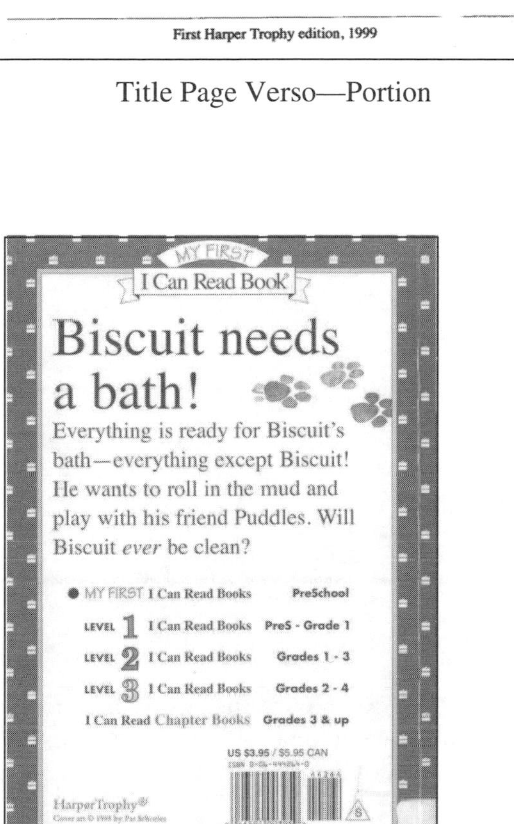

Back Cover

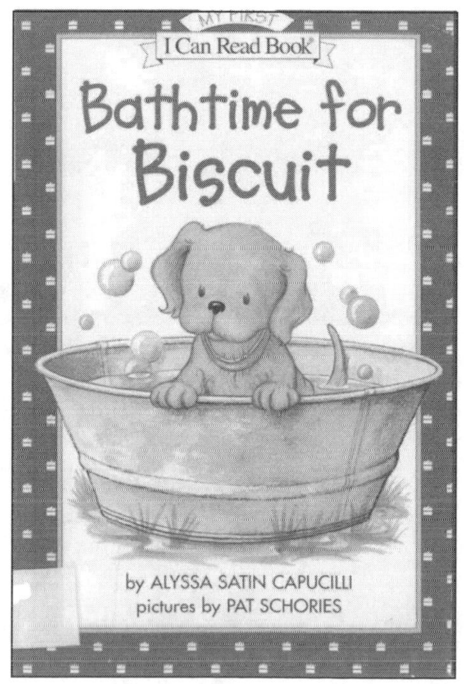

Front Cover

(*Continued on Next Page*)

Exercise 93

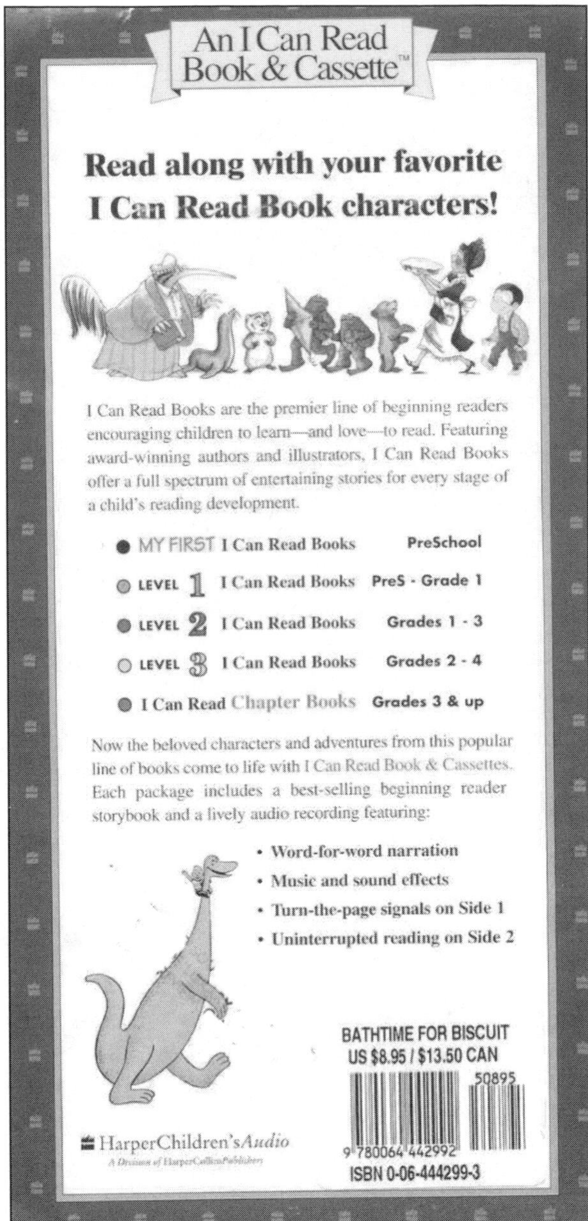

Container Liner

Additional information:
Book has 28 pages; colored illustrations, 23 cm.; in plastic bag.

Instructions: Prepare a catalog record for this item. Find the MARC record for this item on the Library of Congress Web site. Do you agree with the way this is cataloged? What changes would need to be made to catalog the item as a sound recording with accompanying book?

***AACR2r* rules needed:** 1.1B1; 1.1F1; 1.1F6; 1.4C1; 1.4C3; 1.4D1; 1.4D2; 1.4F6; 1.5B1; 1.5B4; 1.5C1; 1.5D1; 1.5D2; 1.5E1(d); 1.7A4; 1.7B10; 1.7B11; 1.7B14; 1.7B17; 1.7B19; 1.8B1; 1.8B2; 1.8B3; 6.7B10; 6.7B11; 6.7B14; 6.7B17; 6.7B19; 21.1A2; 22.5A1; MARC 010; MARC 020; MARC 028

Exercise 94

Cassette

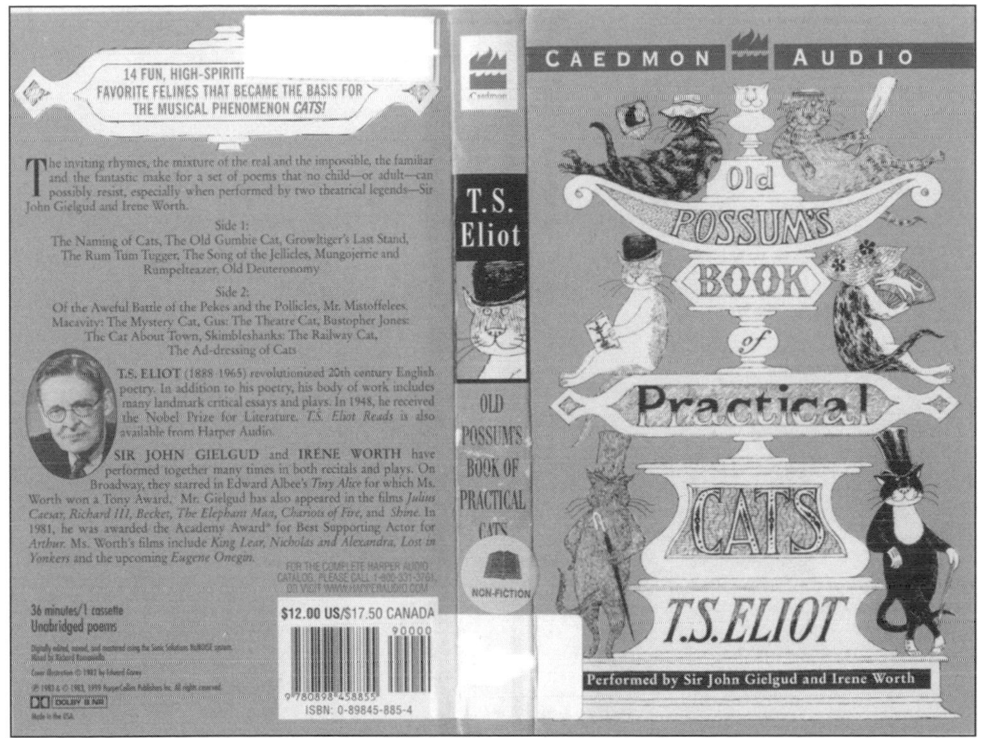

Container Cover

Additional information: Container size: 19 cm.

Instructions: Prepare a catalog record for this item.

***AACR2r* rules needed:** 1.1B1; 1.1C1; 1.1F1; 1.1F6; 1.1F7d; 1.4C1; 1.4C3; 1.4D1; 1.4F6; 1.5B1; 1.5B4; 1.6B2; 1.7B1; 1.7B10; 1.7B17; 1.7B18; 1.8B1; 1.8D1; 6.0B1; 6.5B1; 6.5B2; 6.5C2; 6.5C8; 21.1A2; 21.29B; 21.29C; 21.30E1; 22.1B; 22.5A1; MARC 020

Exercise 95

Front Cover

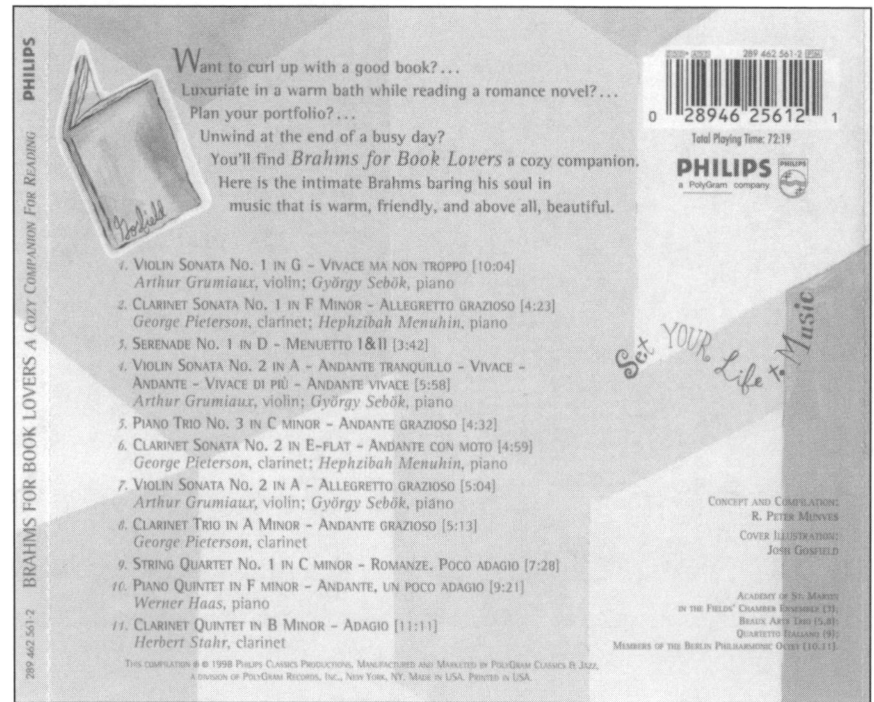

Back Cover

Instructions: Prepare a catalog record for this item.

***AACR2r* rules needed:** 1.1B1; 1.1B2; 1.1E1; 1.1F2; 1.4D1; 1.4F6; 1.5B1; 1.5B4a; 1.5D1; 1.7B18; 1.7B19; 6.5B1; 6.5B2; 6.5D2; 6.7B18; 6.7B19; 21.0B1; 21.23B1; 21.29C; 21.30D1; 22.5A1; MARC 028

Exercise 96

Dr. Laura Schlessinger
HOW COULD YOU DO THAT?!
Read by the Author
Harper Audio
CPN 2549
Tape
40:04
4
℗ 1996 HarperCollins Publishers, Inc.
10 East 53rd Street, New York, N.Y. 10022
All rights reserved. Made in the USA.

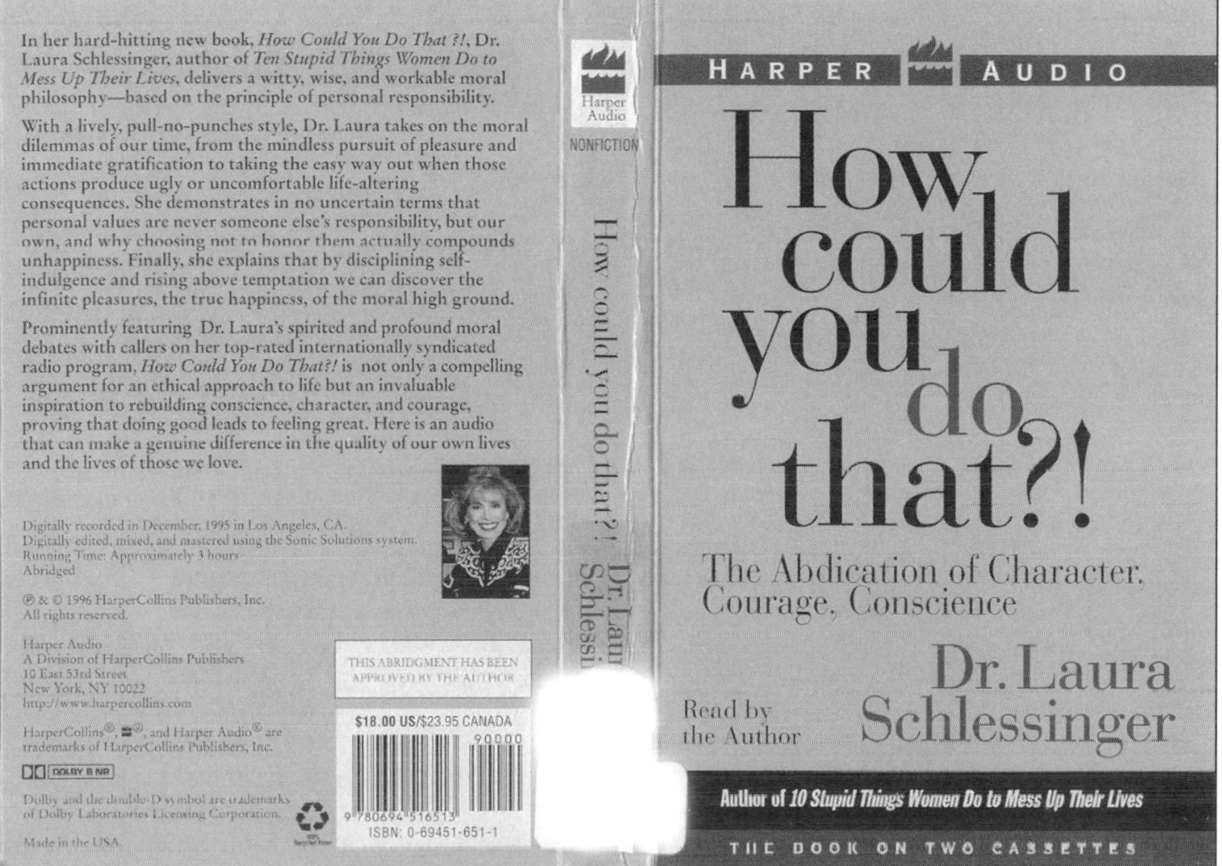

In her hard-hitting new book, *How Could You Do That ?!*, Dr. Laura Schlessinger, author of *Ten Stupid Things Women Do to Mess Up Their Lives*, delivers a witty, wise, and workable moral philosophy—based on the principle of personal responsibility.
With a lively, pull-no-punches style, Dr. Laura takes on the moral dilemmas of our time, from the mindless pursuit of pleasure and immediate gratification to taking the easy way out when those actions produce ugly or uncomfortable life-altering consequences. She demonstrates in no uncertain terms that personal values are never someone else's responsibility, but our own, and why choosing not to honor them actually compounds unhappiness. Finally, she explains that by disciplining self-indulgence and rising above temptation we can discover the infinite pleasures, the true happiness, of the moral high ground.
Prominently featuring Dr. Laura's spirited and profound moral debates with callers on her top-rated internationally syndicated radio program, *How Could You Do That?!* is not only a compelling argument for an ethical approach to life but an invaluable inspiration to rebuilding conscience, character, and courage, proving that doing good leads to feeling great. Here is an audio that can make a genuine difference in the quality of our own lives and the lives of those we love.
Digitally recorded in December, 1995 in Los Angeles, CA.
Digitally edited, mixed, and mastered using the Sonic Solutions system.
Running Time: Approximately 3 hours
Abridged
℗ & © 1996 HarperCollins Publishers, Inc.
All rights reserved.
Harper Audio
A Division of HarperCollins Publishers
10 East 53rd Street
New York, NY 10022
http://www.harpercollins.com
HarperCollins®, ®, and Harper Audio® are trademarks of HarperCollins Publishers, Inc.
DOLBY B NR
Dolby and the double-D symbol are trademarks of Dolby Laboratories Licensing Corporation.
Made in the USA.
THIS ABRIDGMENT HAS BEEN APPROVED BY THE AUTHOR
$18.00 US/$23.95 CANADA
90000
9 780694 516513
ISBN: 0-69451-651-1
Harper Audio
NONFICTION
How could you do that?!
Dr. Laura Schlessinger
HARPER AUDIO
How could you do that?!
The Abdication of Character, Courage, Conscience
Read by the Author
Dr. Laura Schlessinger
Author of 10 Stupid Things Women Do to Mess Up Their Lives
THE BOOK ON TWO CASSETTES

Cassette Case

(*Continued on Next Page*)

Exercise 96

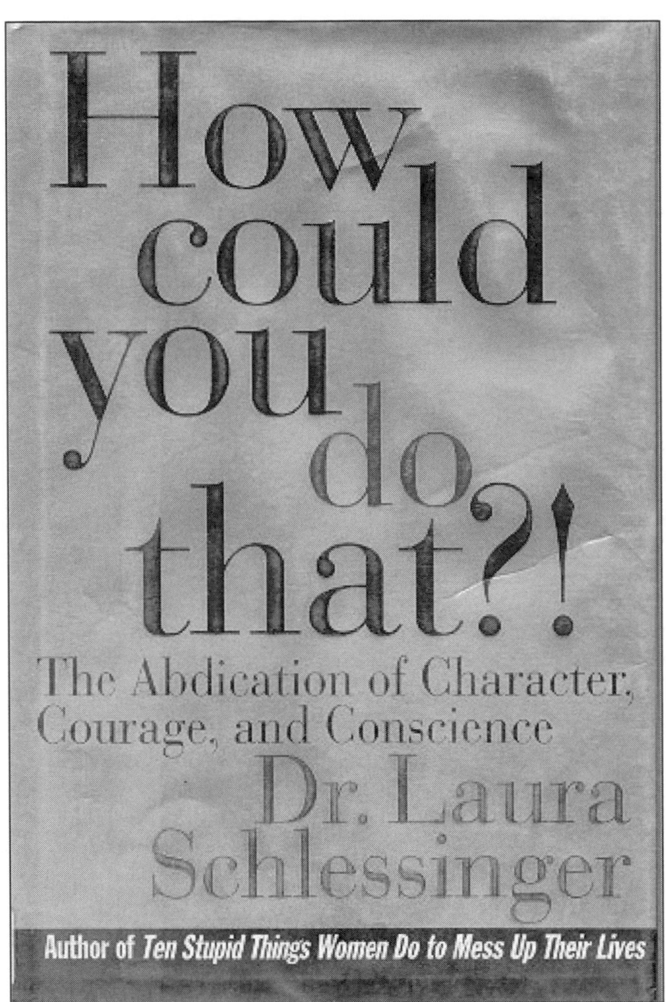

Book Front Cover

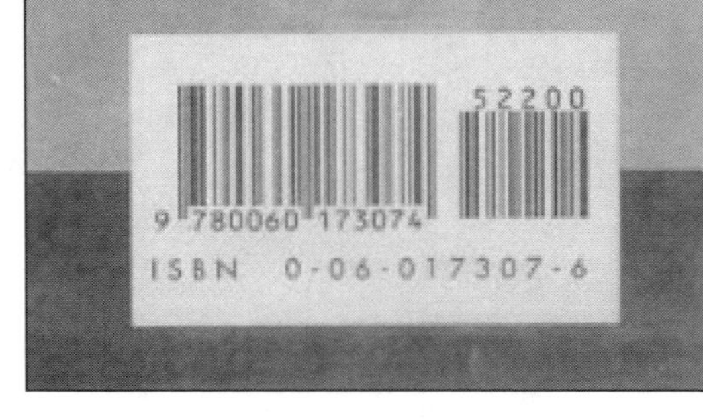

Back Cover Detail

Instructions: This item has been issued as both a book and on audiocassette. Find a MARC record for the book and indicate what changes should be made to the record to make a correct record for the audiocassettes. Compare and contrast the two records.

***AACR2r* rules needed:** 1.0C1; 1.1B1; 1.1C1; 1.1F1; 1.1F3; 1.1F6; 1.1F7; 1.2B4; 1.4C1; 1.4C3; 1.4D1; 1.4D2; 1.4D3b; 1.4F6; 1.5B1; 1.5B3; 1.5B4; 1.5C1; 1.7B4; 1.8B1; 1.8B3; 1.8D1; 6.5B1; 6.5C1; 6.5C2; 6.5C3; 6.5C8; 6.5D5; 6.7B19; 6.8B2; 21.1A2; 22.5A1; 22.15C; MARC 020

Exercise 97

Front Cover

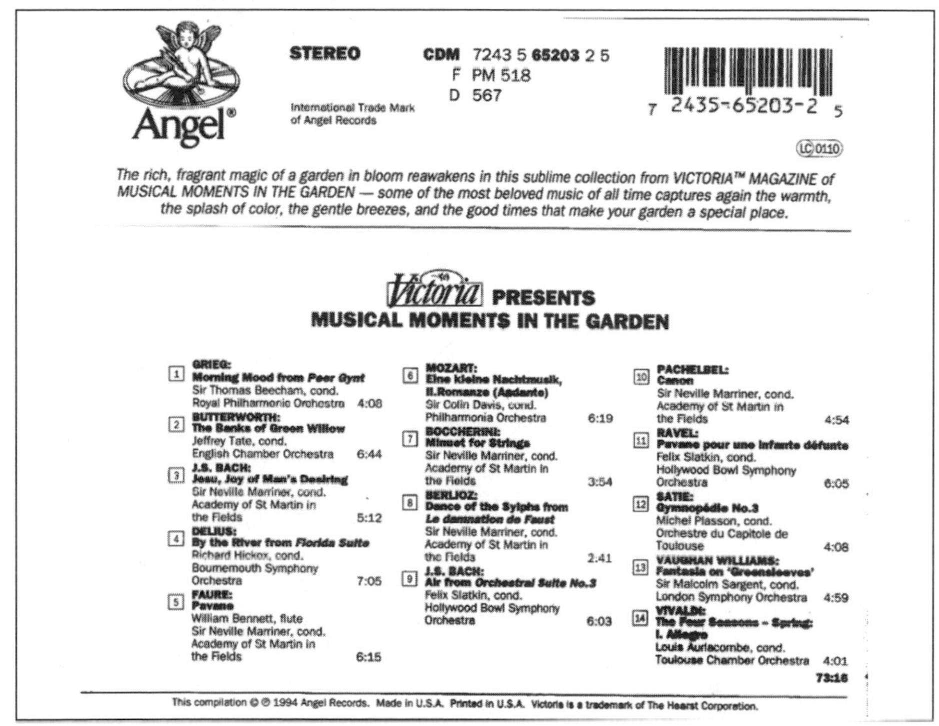

Back Cover

Additional information: LCCN: 99-588391; program notes by David Foil, laid in container

Instructions: Prepare a catalog record for this item.

***AACR2r* rules needed:** 1.1B1; 1.1B2; 1.4C1; 1.4C6; 1.4D1; 1.4F6; 1.5B1; 1.5B4; 1.5C1; 1.5D1; 1.7B4; 1.7B10; 1.7B17; 1.7B18; 1.7B19; 6.5B1; 6.5B2; 6.5C2; 6.5C7; 6.5C8; 6.5D2; 6.7B4; 21.7B1; 21.23C1; 21.30D1; 21.30E1; 21.30M1; MARC 010; MARC 024; MARC 028

Exercise 98

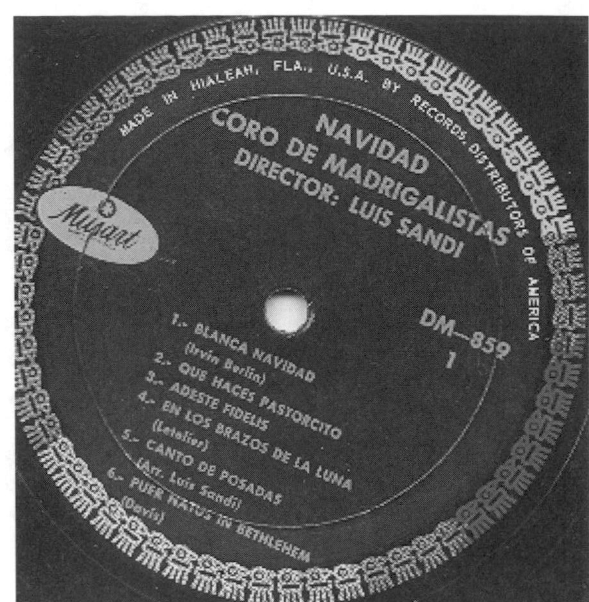

Record Labels

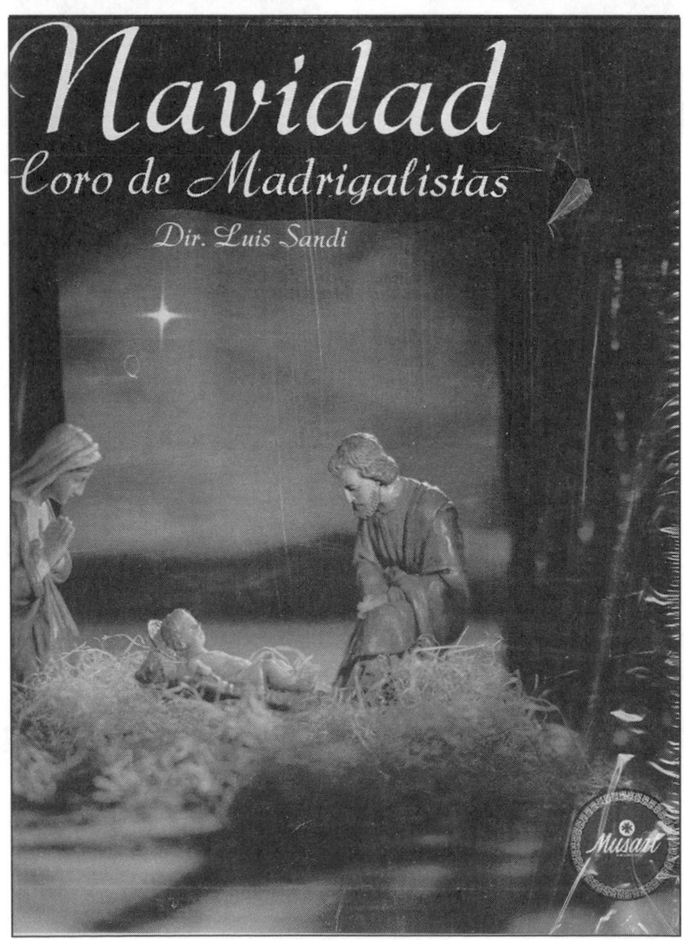

Album Cover

(*Continued on Next Page*)

Exercise 98

Back of Album Cover

Additional information: 12 inches; 33 1/3 rpm. The recording group was formed in 1938. The album was acquired sometime during the 1970s. The probable date of publication was during the 1960s. Musart is in Mexico.

Instructions: Prepare a catalog record for this item.

***AACR2r* rules needed:** 1.1B1; 1.1C1; 1.1F1; 1.1F6; 1.4C1; 1.4C3; 1.4D1; 1.4D2; 1.4D3; 1.4F7; 1.5B1; 1.5B4; 1.7B18; 1.7B19; 6.0B1; 6.5B1; 6.5B2; 6.5C1; 6.5C2; 6.5C3; 6.5D2; 21.1B1; 21.29B; 21.30F1; 22.5A1; 22.5C1; 24.1A; 24.5C1

Exercise 99

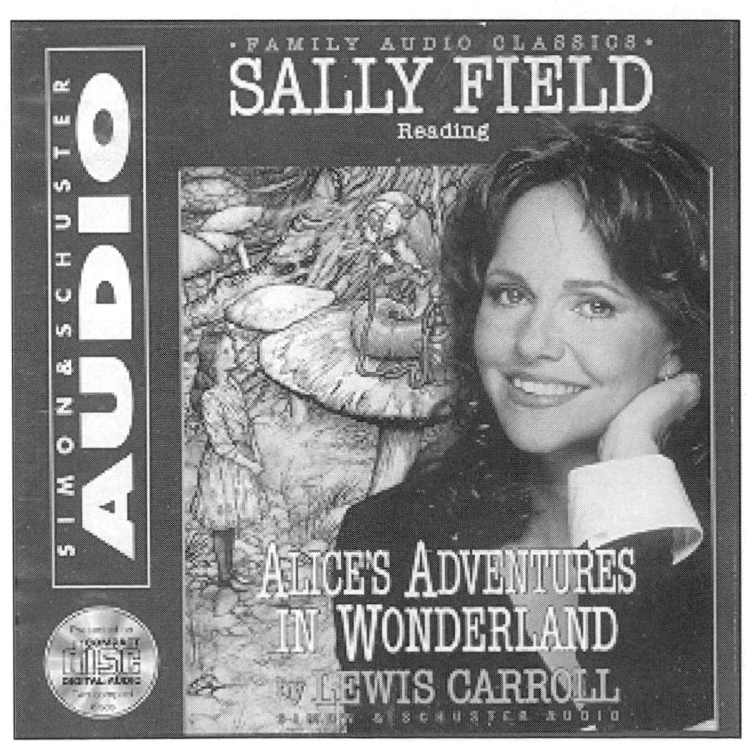

Container Front Cover

(*Continued on Next Page*)

Exercise 99

AUDIO CLASSIC

...LY FIELD

READING

ALICE'S ADVENTURES IN WONDERLAND

by Lewis Carroll

In an enchanting performance, two-time Academy Award® winner Sally Field takes us on a topsy-turvy adventure through Wonderland. Irresistibly delightful, fascinating and funny, Ms. Field's stunning interpretation brings Alice, the Mad Hatter, the White Rabbit, the Cheshire Cat and all of Lewis Carroll's remarkable characters to life.

Produced in a simple manner that allows imaginations to soar, Carroll's triumph will charm the entire family. Destined to become an instant classic, this audiobook will help introduce your family to the unique pleasure of classic literature.

A portion of the proceeds from this audiobook will be donated to the National Center for Family Literacy, a non-profit organization that improves the lives of tens of thousands of families annually by creating and assisting programs that teach the entire family basic literacy skills that expand their economic and social well-being.

RUNNING TIME: APPROX. 2.5 HOURS

DOLBY SYSTEM ®

An abridgement of *Alice's Adventures in Wonderland*.
℗ © 2000 Power Studios Inc. All rights reserved.
Visit Power Studios website at: www.powerstudios.com
AUDIOWORKS is an imprint of Simon & Schuster
Audio Division, Simon & Schuster, Inc.
1230 Avenue of the Americas
New York, NY 10020
AUDIOWORKS is a registered trademark of
Simon & Schuster, Inc.

Container Back Cover

Additional information: The number on the discs is an ISBN number. LCCN: 2002574035; copyright 2002

Instructions: Prepare a catalog record for this item.

When cataloging this work, consider the following:

- What is the main entry?

***AACR2r* rules needed:** 1.1B1; 1.1B2; 1.1C1; 1.4C1; 1.4C3; 1.4D1; 1.4F6; 1.5B1; 1.5B4; 1.5D1; 1.6B1; 1.7B4; 1.7B5; 1.7B10; 1.7B17; 1.8B1; 6.0B1; 6.5B1; 6.5B2; 6.5D2; 21.1A2; 21.29B; 21.30F1; 21.30J2; 22.5A1; MARC 010; MARC 020; MARC 024; MARC 028

Exercise 100

Disc One of Seven

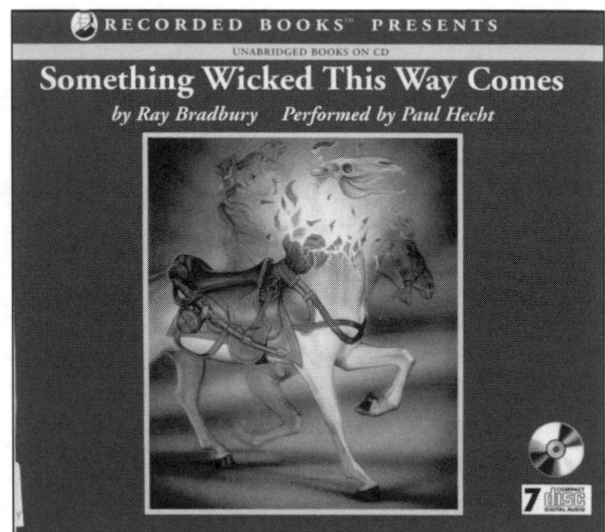

Container Front Cover

Container Back Cover

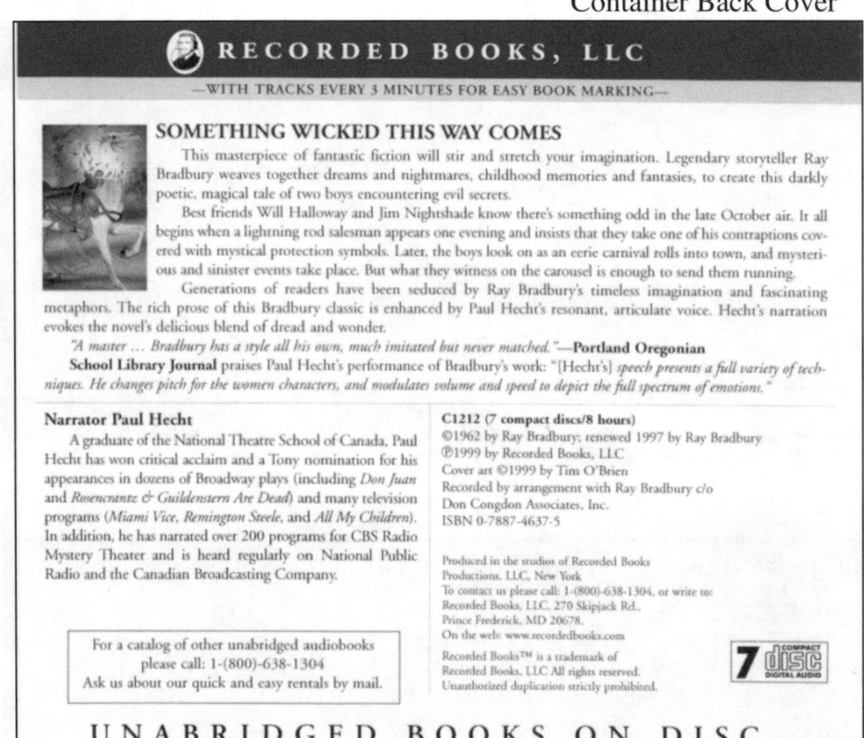

RECORDED BOOKS, LLC

—WITH TRACKS EVERY 3 MINUTES FOR EASY BOOK MARKING—

SOMETHING WICKED THIS WAY COMES

This masterpiece of fantastic fiction will stir and stretch your imagination. Legendary storyteller Ray Bradbury weaves together dreams and nightmares, childhood memories and fantasies, to create this darkly poetic, magical tale of two boys encountering evil secrets.

Best friends Will Halloway and Jim Nightshade know there's something odd in the late October air. It all begins when a lightning rod salesman appears one evening and insists that they take one of his contraptions covered with mystical protection symbols. Later, the boys look on as an eerie carnival rolls into town, and mysterious and sinister events take place. But what they witness on the carousel is enough to send them running.

Generations of readers have been seduced by Ray Bradbury's timeless imagination and fascinating metaphors. The rich prose of this Bradbury classic is enhanced by Paul Hecht's resonant, articulate voice. Hecht's narration evokes the novel's delicious blend of dread and wonder.

"A master … Bradbury has a style all his own, much imitated but never matched."—**Portland Oregonian**

School Library Journal praises Paul Hecht's performance of Bradbury's work: "[Hecht's] *speech presents a full variety of techniques. He changes pitch for the women characters, and modulates volume and speed to depict the full spectrum of emotions."*

Narrator Paul Hecht

A graduate of the National Theatre School of Canada, Paul Hecht has won critical acclaim and a Tony nomination for his appearances in dozens of Broadway plays (including *Don Juan* and *Rosencrantz & Guildenstern Are Dead*) and many television programs (*Miami Vice*, *Remington Steele*, and *All My Children*). In addition, he has narrated over 200 programs for CBS Radio Mystery Theater and is heard regularly on National Public Radio and the Canadian Broadcasting Company.

For a catalog of other unabridged audiobooks
please call: 1-(800)-638-1304
Ask us about our quick and easy rentals by mail.

C1212 (7 compact discs/8 hours)
©1962 by Ray Bradbury; renewed 1997 by Ray Bradbury
℗1999 by Recorded Books, LLC
Cover art ©1999 by Tim O'Brien
Recorded by arrangement with Ray Bradbury c/o
Don Congdon Associates, Inc.
ISBN 0-7887-4637-5

Produced in the studios of Recorded Books Productions, LLC, New York
To contact us please call: 1-(800)-638-1304, or write to:
Recorded Books, LLC, 270 Skipjack Rd.,
Prince Frederick, MD 20678.
On the web: www.recordedbooks.com

Recorded Books™ is a trademark of
Recorded Books, LLC All rights reserved.
Unauthorized duplication strictly prohibited.

7 COMPACT disc DIGITAL AUDIO

UNABRIDGED BOOKS ON DISC

Instructions: Prepare a catalog record for this item.

***AACR2r* rules needed:** 1.1B1; 1.1C1; 1.1F1; 1.1F6; 1.4C1; 1.4C3; 1.4D1; 1.4D2; 1.4F1; 1.4F5; 1.5B1; 1.5B4; 1.5C1; 1.7B4; 1.7B7; 1.7B8; 1.7B10; 1.7B17; 1.7B19; 1.8B1; 6.1C1; 6.5B1; 6.5B2; 6.5D2; 21.1A2; 22.5A1; MARC 020

Exercise 101

Cassette One of Two

npr PEABODY AWARD WINNING RADIO SERIES
"An astounding documentary series." — The Washington Post
LOST & FOUND SOUND
Radio Stories From NPR's
ALL THINGS CONSIDERED
LOST & FOUND sound
An American Record
VOLUME ONE
TWO AUDIOCASSETTES

Cover of Container

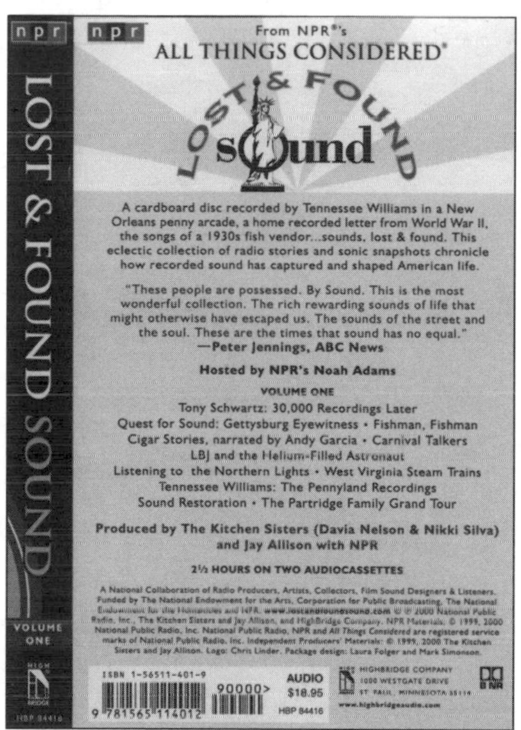

npr
LOST & FOUND SOUND
VOLUME ONE
From NPR®'s
ALL THINGS CONSIDERED®
LOST & FOUND sound
A cardboard disc recorded by Tennessee Williams in a New Orleans penny arcade, a home recorded letter from World War II, the songs of a 1930s fish vendor...sounds, lost & found. This eclectic collection of radio stories and sonic snapshots chronicle how recorded sound has captured and shaped American life.
"These people are possessed. By Sound. This is the most wonderful collection. The rich rewarding sounds of life that might otherwise have escaped us. The sounds of the street and the soul. These are the times that sound has no equal."
—Peter Jennings, ABC News
Hosted by NPR's Noah Adams
VOLUME ONE
Tony Schwartz: 30,000 Recordings Later
Quest for Sound: Gettysburg Eyewitness • Fishman, Fishman
Cigar Stories, narrated by Andy Garcia • Carnival Talkers
LBJ and the Helium-Filled Astronaut
Listening to the Northern Lights • West Virginia Steam Trains
Tennessee Williams: The Pennyland Recordings
Sound Restoration • The Partridge Family Grand Tour
Produced by The Kitchen Sisters (Davia Nelson & Nikki Silva) and Jay Allison with NPR
2½ HOURS ON TWO AUDIOCASSETTES
ISBN 1-56511-401-9
AUDIO
$18.95
HBP 84416
HIGHBRIDGE COMPANY

Back Cover and Spine of Container

Additional information: LCCN: 2004569359

Instructions: Prepare a catalog record for this item.

***AACR2r* rules needed:** 1.1B1; 1.1B9; 1.1C1; 1.1E1; 1.1E2; 1.1F2; 1.4C1; 1.4C2; 1.4C3; 1.5B1; 1.5B3; 1.5B4; 1.5C1; 1.5D1; 1.5D2; 1.7B3; 1.7B5; 1.7B6; 1.7B7; 1.7B18; 6.1B1; 6.5B1; 6.5B2; 6.5C2; 6.5C3; 6.5C6; 6.5C8; 6.5D5; 6.7B3; 6.7B5; 6.7B7; 21.30E1; 21.30G1; 21.30H1; 22.5A1; 24.1A; MARC 020; MARC 028

(*Continued on Next Page*)

Exercise 101

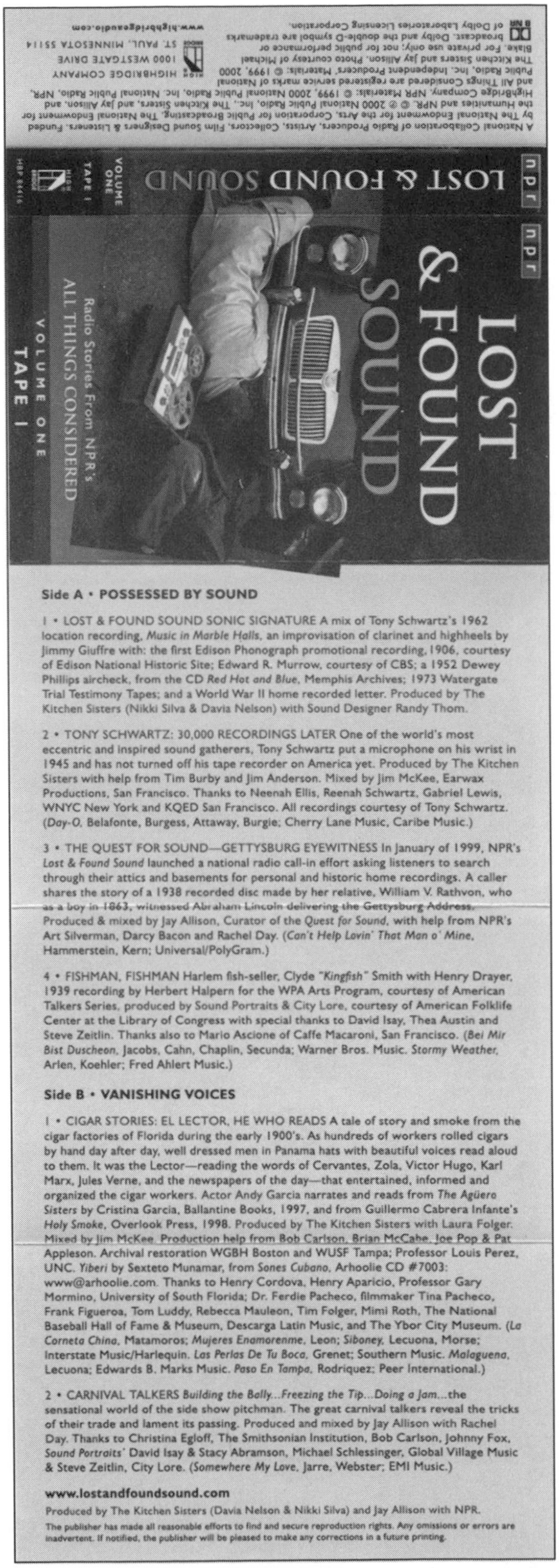

LOST & FOUND SOUND

Radio Stories From NPR's ALL THINGS CONSIDERED

VOLUME ONE

TAPE 1

Side A • POSSESSED BY SOUND

1 • LOST & FOUND SOUND SONIC SIGNATURE A mix of Tony Schwartz's 1962 location recording, *Music in Marble Halls*, an improvisation of clarinet and highheels by Jimmy Giuffre with: the first Edison Phonograph promotional recording, 1906, courtesy of Edison National Historic Site; Edward R. Murrow, courtesy of CBS; a 1952 Dewey Phillips aircheck, from the CD *Red Hot and Blue*, Memphis Archives; 1973 Watergate Trial Testimony Tapes; and a World War II home recorded letter. Produced by The Kitchen Sisters (Nikki Silva & Davia Nelson) with Sound Designer Randy Thom.

2 • TONY SCHWARTZ: 30,000 RECORDINGS LATER One of the world's most eccentric and inspired sound gatherers, Tony Schwartz put a microphone on his wrist in 1945 and has not turned off his tape recorder on America yet. Produced by The Kitchen Sisters with help from Tim Burby and Jim Anderson. Mixed by Jim McKee, Earwax Productions, San Francisco. Thanks to Neenah Ellis, Reenah Schwartz, Gabriel Lewis, WNYC New York and KQED San Francisco. All recordings courtesy of Tony Schwartz. (*Day-O*, Belafonte, Burgess, Attaway, Burgie; Cherry Lane Music, Caribe Music.)

3 • THE QUEST FOR SOUND—GETTYSBURG EYEWITNESS In January of 1999, NPR's *Lost & Found Sound* launched a national radio call-in effort asking listeners to search through their attics and basements for personal and historic home recordings. A caller shares the story of a 1938 recorded disc made by her relative, William V. Rathvon, who as a boy in 1863, witnessed Abraham Lincoln delivering the Gettysburg Address. Produced & mixed by Jay Allison, Curator of the *Quest for Sound*, with help from NPR's Art Silverman, Darcy Bacon and Rachel Day. (*Can't Help Lovin' That Man o' Mine*, Hammerstein, Kern; Universal/PolyGram.)

4 • FISHMAN, FISHMAN Harlem fish-seller, Clyde *"Kingfish"* Smith with Henry Drayer, 1939 recording by Herbert Halpern for the WPA Arts Program, courtesy of American Talkers Series, produced by Sound Portraits & City Lore, courtesy of American Folklife Center at the Library of Congress with special thanks to David Isay, Thea Austin and Steve Zeitlin. Thanks also to Mario Ascione of Caffe Macaroni, San Francisco. (*Bei Mir Bist Duscheon*, Jacobs, Cahn, Chaplin, Secunda; Warner Bros. Music. *Stormy Weather*, Arlen, Koehler; Fred Ahlert Music.)

Side B • VANISHING VOICES

1 • CIGAR STORIES: EL LECTOR, HE WHO READS A tale of story and smoke from the cigar factories of Florida during the early 1900's. As hundreds of workers rolled cigars by hand day after day, well dressed men in Panama hats with beautiful voices read aloud to them. It was the Lector—reading the words of Cervantes, Zola, Victor Hugo, Karl Marx, Jules Verne, and the newspapers of the day—that entertained, informed and organized the cigar workers. Actor Andy Garcia narrates and reads from *The Agüero Sisters* by Cristina Garcia, Ballantine Books, 1997, and from Guillermo Cabrera Infante's *Holy Smoke*, Overlook Press, 1998. Produced by The Kitchen Sisters with Laura Folger. Mixed by Jim McKee. Production help from Bob Carlson, Brian McCabe, Joe Pop & Pat Appleson. Archival restoration WGBH Boston and WUSF Tampa; Professor Louis Perez, UNC. *Yiberi* by Sexteto Munamar, from *Sones Cubano*, Arhoolie CD #7003: www@arhoolie.com. Thanks to Henry Cordova, Henry Aparicio, Professor Gary Mormino, University of South Florida; Dr. Ferdie Pacheco, filmmaker Tina Pacheco, Frank Figueroa, Tom Luddy, Rebecca Mauleon, Tim Folger, Mimi Roth, The National Baseball Hall of Fame & Museum, Descarga Latin Music, and The Ybor City Museum. (*La Corneta China*, Matamoros; *Mujeres Enamorenme*, Leon; *Siboney*, Lecuona, Morse; Interstate Music/Harlequin. *Las Perlas De Tu Boca*, Grenet; Southern Music. *Malaguena*, Lecuona; Edwards B. Marks Music. *Paso En Tampa*, Rodriquez; Peer International.)

2 • CARNIVAL TALKERS *Building the Bally...Freezing the Tip...Doing a Jam*...the sensational world of the side show pitchman. The great carnival talkers reveal the tricks of their trade and lament its passing. Produced and mixed by Jay Allison with Rachel Day. Thanks to Christina Egloff, The Smithsonian Institution, Bob Carlson, Johnny Fox, *Sound Portraits'* David Isay & Stacy Abramson, Michael Schlessinger, Global Village Music & Steve Zeitlin, City Lore. (*Somewhere My Love*, Jarre, Webster; EMI Music.)

www.lostandfoundsound.com

Produced by The Kitchen Sisters (Davia Nelson & Nikki Silva) and Jay Allison with NPR.

The publisher has made all reasonable efforts to find and secure reproduction rights. Any omissions or errors are inadvertent. If notified, the publisher will be pleased to make any corrections in a future printing.

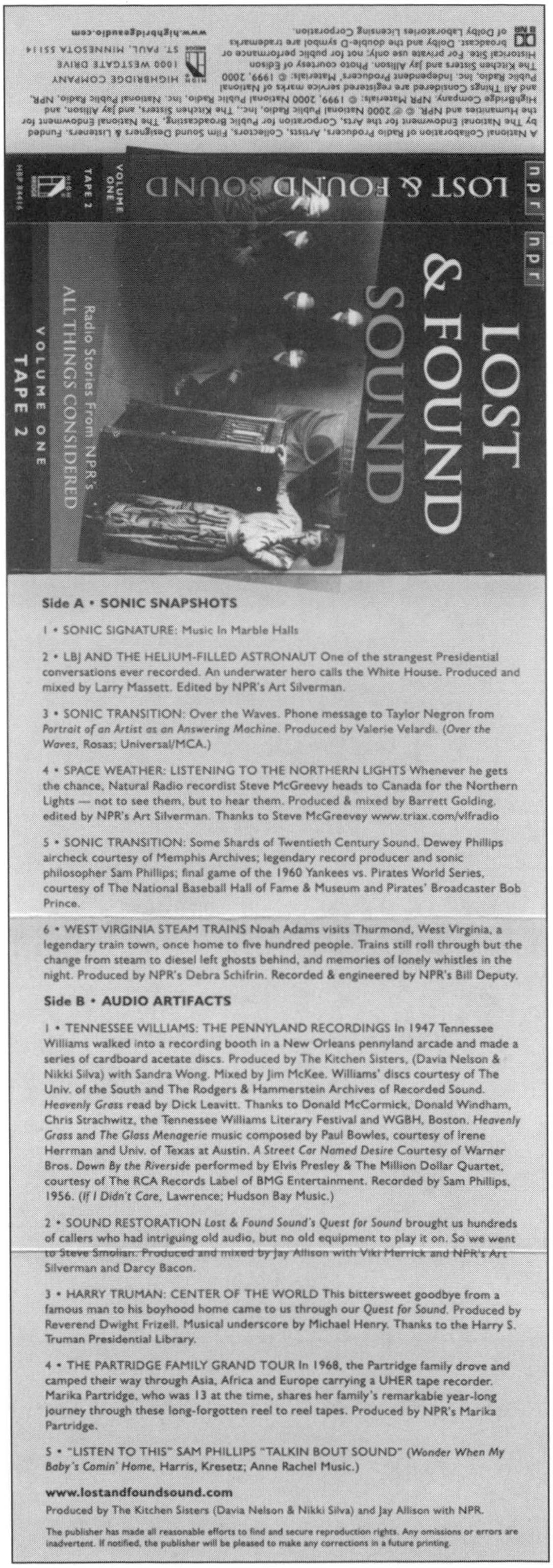

LOST & FOUND SOUND

Radio Stories From NPR's ALL THINGS CONSIDERED

VOLUME ONE

TAPE 2

Side A • SONIC SNAPSHOTS

1 • SONIC SIGNATURE: Music In Marble Halls

2 • LBJ AND THE HELIUM-FILLED ASTRONAUT One of the strangest Presidential conversations ever recorded. An underwater hero calls the White House. Produced and mixed by Larry Massett. Edited by NPR's Art Silverman.

3 • SONIC TRANSITION: Over the Waves. Phone message to Taylor Negron from *Portrait of an Artist as an Answering Machine*. Produced by Valerie Velardi. (*Over the Waves*, Rosas; Universal/MCA.)

4 • SPACE WEATHER: LISTENING TO THE NORTHERN LIGHTS Whenever he gets the chance, Natural Radio recordist Steve McGreevy heads to Canada for the Northern Lights — not to see them, but to hear them. Produced & mixed by Barrett Golding, edited by NPR's Art Silverman. Thanks to Steve McGreevey www.triax.com/vlfradio

5 • SONIC TRANSITION: Some Shards of Twentieth Century Sound. Dewey Phillips aircheck courtesy of Memphis Archives; legendary record producer and sonic philosopher Sam Phillips; final game of the 1960 Yankees vs. Pirates World Series, courtesy of The National Baseball Hall of Fame & Museum and Pirates' Broadcaster Bob Prince.

6 • WEST VIRGINIA STEAM TRAINS Noah Adams visits Thurmond, West Virginia, a legendary train town, once home to five hundred people. Trains still roll through but the change from steam to diesel left ghosts behind, and memories of lonely whistles in the night. Produced by NPR's Debra Schifrin. Recorded & engineered by NPR's Bill Deputy.

Side B • AUDIO ARTIFACTS

1 • TENNESSEE WILLIAMS: THE PENNYLAND RECORDINGS In 1947 Tennessee Williams walked into a recording booth in a New Orleans pennyland arcade and made a series of cardboard acetate discs. Produced by The Kitchen Sisters, (Davia Nelson & Nikki Silva) with Sandra Wong. Mixed by Jim McKee. Williams' discs courtesy of The Univ. of the South and The Rodgers & Hammerstein Archives of Recorded Sound. *Heavenly Grass* read by Dick Leavitt. Thanks to Donald McCormick, Donald Windham, Chris Strachwitz, the Tennessee Williams Literary Festival and WGBH, Boston. *Heavenly Grass* and *The Glass Menagerie* music composed by Paul Bowles, courtesy of Irene Herrman and Univ. of Texas at Austin. *A Street Car Named Desire* Courtesy of Warner Bros. *Down By the Riverside* performed by Elvis Presley & The Million Dollar Quartet, courtesy of The RCA Records Label of BMG Entertainment. Recorded by Sam Phillips, 1956. (*If I Didn't Care*, Lawrence; Hudson Bay Music.)

2 • SOUND RESTORATION *Lost & Found Sound's Quest for Sound* brought us hundreds of callers who had intriguing old audio, but no old equipment to play it on. So we went to Steve Smolian. Produced and mixed by Jay Allison with Viki Merrick and NPR's Art Silverman and Darcy Bacon.

3 • HARRY TRUMAN: CENTER OF THE WORLD This bittersweet goodbye from a famous man to his boyhood home came to us through our *Quest for Sound*. Produced by Reverend Dwight Frizell. Musical underscore by Michael Henry. Thanks to the Harry S. Truman Presidential Library.

4 • THE PARTRIDGE FAMILY GRAND TOUR In 1968, the Partridge family drove and camped their way through Asia, Africa and Europe carrying a UHER tape recorder. Marika Partridge, who was 13 at the time, shares her family's remarkable year-long journey through these long-forgotten reel to reel tapes. Produced by NPR's Marika Partridge.

5 • "LISTEN TO THIS" SAM PHILLIPS "TALKIN BOUT SOUND" (*Wonder When My Baby's Comin' Home*, Harris, Kresetz; Anne Rachel Music.)

www.lostandfoundsound.com

Produced by The Kitchen Sisters (Davia Nelson & Nikki Silva) and Jay Allison with NPR.

The publisher has made all reasonable efforts to find and secure reproduction rights. Any omissions or errors are inadvertent. If notified, the publisher will be pleased to make any corrections in a future printing.

Cassette Liners (1 and 2)

Exercise 102

The Fellowship of the Ring
by J.R.R. Tolkien
read by Rob Inglis
Disc 1
Recorded Books, LLC
The Lord of the Rings ©1955, 1965 J.R.R. Tolkien; renewed 1982, 1983 ℗1990 Recorded Books, LLC

Disc One of Sixteen

Container Cover

Instructions: Prepare a catalog record for this item.

***AACR2r* rules needed:** 1.1B1; 1.1C1; 1.1F1; 1.1F6; 1.4C1; 1.4C3; 1.4D1; 1.4D2; 1.4F6; 1.5B1; 1.5B3; 1.5B4; 1.5C1; 1.5D1; 1.5D2; 1.7B3; 1.7B17; 1.7B19; 1.8B1; 1.8D1; 7.5B1; 7.5B2; 7.5C3; 7.5C4; 7.5D4; 7.7B17; 7.7B19; MARC 020

Container Back Cover

WWW.RECORDEDBOOKS.COM

THE FELLOWSHIP OF THE RING
Being the First Part of *The Lord of the Rings*
J.R.R. Tolkien • narrated by Rob Inglis

From his fortress tower in Mordor, the evil sorcerer Sauron sends forth a darkness that creeps across the enchanted land of Middle-earth. Men and elves and dwarves have raised armies in futile efforts to combat this evil. Great wizards have failed to keep it in check. Sauron's shadow threatens to engulf all.

But in the peaceful, far-off Shire, a hobbit named Frodo Baggins holds a ring that may be the key to defeating Sauron. Joining together in a fellowship of his closest friends and a mix of unlikely allies, under the guidance of the wizard Gandalf, Frodo prepares for a perilous journey in a desperate quest that may be the only hope for restoring light to the land.

Let master narrator Rob Inglis guide you through all the awesome beauty and terrifying evil of J.R.R. Tolkien's timeless world.

Author J.R.R. Tolkien was born in South Africa and raised in England, eventually becoming a professor at Oxford University. His magical tales of the land of Middle-earth—including *The Lord of the Rings* trilogy—continue to enjoy immense, widespread popular appeal and fierce loyalty among their many fans.

Narrator Rob Inglis has appeared with the Royal Shakespeare and Royal Court Theatre companies playing such roles as the Ghost and Claudius in *Hamlet* and Mr. Bumble in *Oliver*. He regularly tours Europe and the U.S. with his repertoire of Chaucer, Shakespeare, Dickens, and Tolkien dramatizations.

U.S. $49.99 Canada $78.00
16 CDs/19.25 hours
For other Recorded Books titles,
call toll free at 1-800-638-1304
or visit www.recordedbooks.com

Container Body Flap

00212 (16 CDs/19.25 hours)
The Lord of Rings ©1955, 1965 by J.R.R. Tolkien; renewed 1982, 1983 by Christopher R. Tolkien, Michael H.R. Tolkien, John F.R. Tolkien, and Priscilla M.A.R. Tolkien. All rights reserved under the Berne and Buenos Aires Copyright Conventions.
℗1990 by Recorded Books, LLC. Produced and directed by Claudia Howard
Cover art ©1979 by The Brothers Hildebrandt; used by arrangement with Spiderweb Art, Inc. Cover design by Cynthia Rudzis
Published in book form in the United States by Houghton Mifflin Company and worldwide by Unwin Hyman Limited.
ISBN 0-7887-8981-3

Produced in the studios of Recorded Books Productions, LLC, New York
Recorded Books, LLC, 270 Skipjack Rd., Prince Frederick, MD 20678.

Recorded Books™ is a trademark of
Recorded Books, LLC. All rights reserved.
Unauthorized duplication strictly prohibited.

Exercise 103

CD Disc

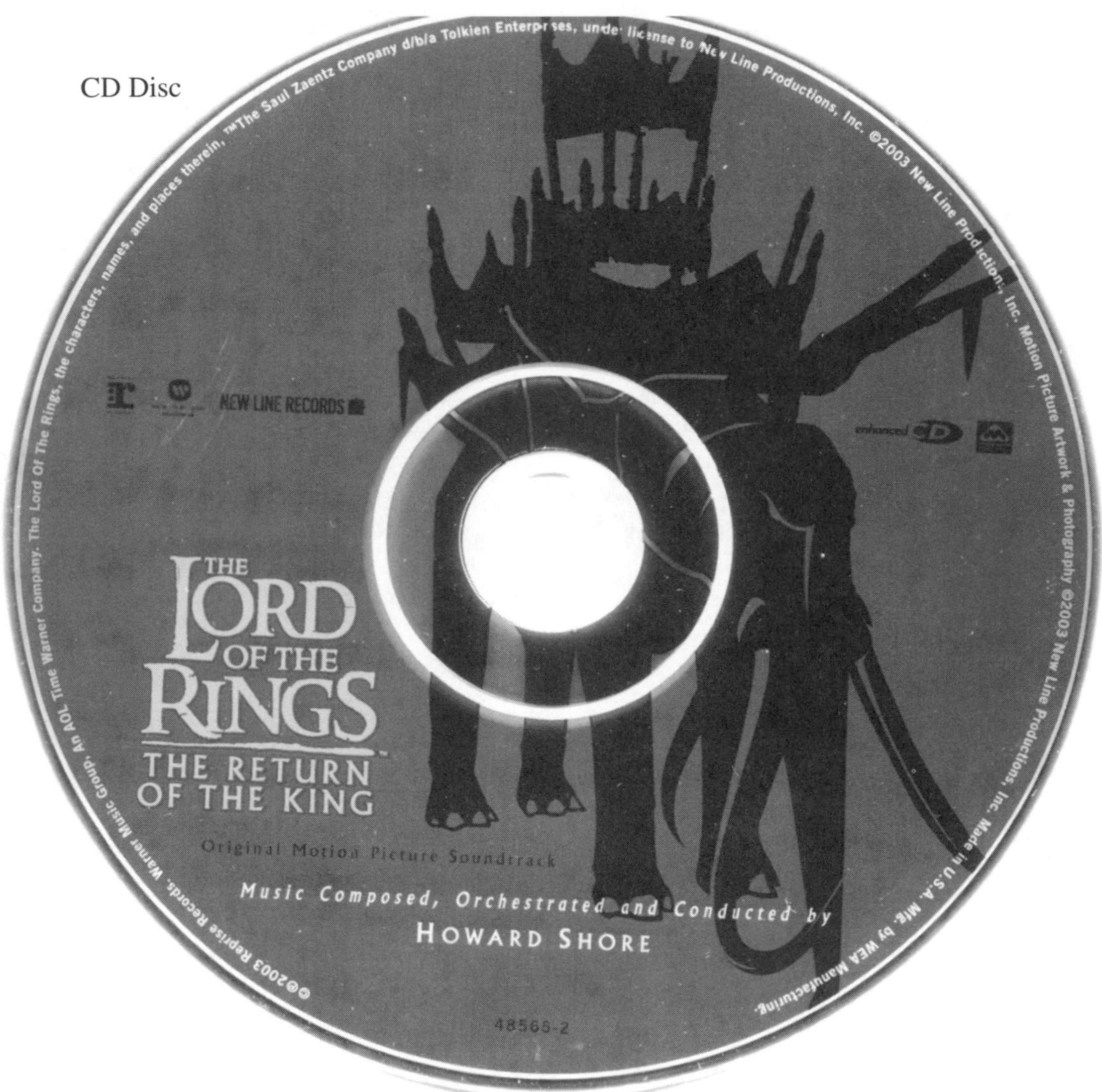

From Insert Booklet About CD

"HOWARD SHORE: AN INTROSPECTIVE"
DVD features:
• "Use Well The Days: A Behind the Scenes Portrait"; a glimpse
at Howard Shore's weeks in London creating the music for The Return Of The King by Elizabeth Cotnoir
• Photo gallery from the studio sessions of The Return Of The King
• Exclusive Supertrailer of The Lord Of The Rings™ Trilogy
• Photo gallery of film stills and text from The Return Of The King

USE WELL THE DAYS: A BEHIND-THE-SCENES PORTRAIT:
Director/Producer/Videographer: Elizabeth Cotnoir *Editor:* Nick Mougis *Sound Editor:* Jeff Stone
Technical Assistants: Lowell Pickett, Jim Bruening *Post Production Facility:* EvenTone Editorial, Tuxedo, New York / Bill Foley *Studio Manager*

(*Continued on Next Page*)

Exercise 103

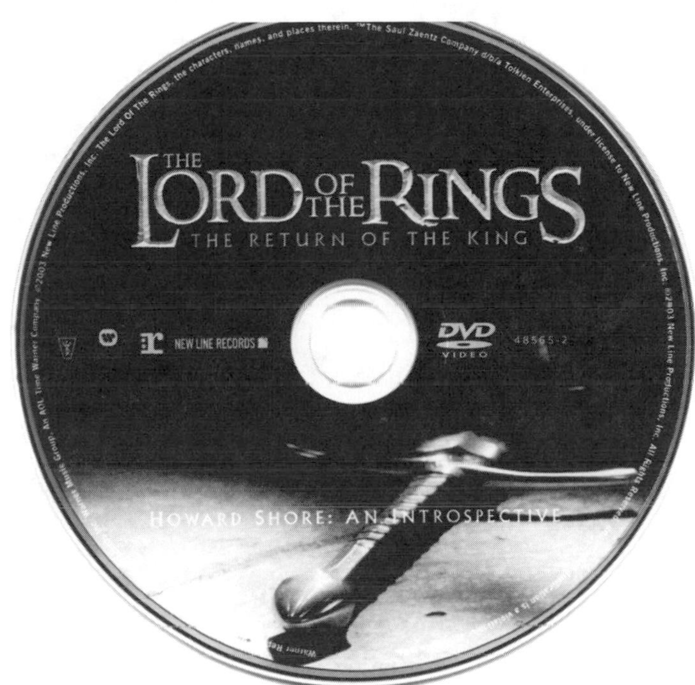

DVD Disc

Reprise Records, 3300 Warner Blvd., Burbank, CA 91505-4694. Warner Music Group, An AOL Time Warner Company. 75 Rockefeller Plaza, New York, NY 10019-6908. "The Lord of the Rings," the characters, names, and places therein, ™The Saul Zaentz Company d/b/a Tolkien Enterprises, under license to New Line Productions, Inc. All Rights Reserved. ©2003 New Line Productions, Inc. Motion Picture Artwork & Photography ©2003 New Line Productions, Inc. ©℗2003 Reprise Records for the U.S. and WEA International Inc. for the world outside the U.S. Made in U.S.A. All Rights Reserved. Unauthorized duplication is a violation of applicable laws. Made with Macromedia is a trademark of Macromedia, Inc. Certain computers may not be able to access the enhanced CD portion of this disc. Neither the manufacturer, distributor nor the developer make any representation or warranty, or assume any responsibility with respect to the enhanced CD portion of this disc.

www.lordoftherings.net AOL Keyword: Lord Of The Rings repriserecords.com lordoftherings-soundtrack.com

0 9362-48565-2 8

NEW LINE RECORDS enhanced CD DVD VIDEO 2.0 NTSC CC

Package Insert Details

NEW LINE CINEMA PRESENTS A WINGNUT FILMS PRODUCTION "THE LORD OF THE RINGS: THE RETURN OF THE KING" ELIJAH WOOD IAN McKELLEN LIV TYLER VIGGO MORTENSEN SEAN ASTIN CATE BLANCHETT JOHN RHYS-DAVIES BERNARD HILL CHRISTOPHER LEE BILLY BOYD DOMINIC MONAGHAN ORLANDO BLOOM HUGO WEAVING MIRANDA OTTO DAVID WENHAM BRAD DOURIF KARL URBAN JOHN NOBLE FEATURING ANDY SERKIS AS GOLLUM WITH IAN HOLM AND SEAN BEAN JOHN HUBBARD AND AMY MacLEAN VICTORIA BURROWS NGILA DICKSON RICHARD TAYLOR WETA LTD. NZ JIM RYGIEL HOWARD SHORE JAMIE SELKIRK GRANT MAJOR ANDREW LESNIE A.C.S. RICK PORRAS JAMIE SELKIRK MARK ORDESKY BOB WEINSTEIN HARVEY WEINSTEIN ROBERT SHAYE MICHAEL LYNNE BARRIE M. OSBORNE FRAN WALSH PETER JACKSON J.R.R. TOLKIEN FRAN WALSH & PHILIPPA BOYENS & PETER JACKSON PETER JACKSON

NEW LINE CINEMA

America Online Keyword: Lord of the Rings www.lordoftherings.net

(*Continued on Next Page*)

Exercise 103

Package Insert

Additional information:
In foldout leatherette container. Consists of a compact disc and an accompanying digital video disc. Includes a 28-page tipped-in booklet with color photographs and text; has a separate single-sheet package insert. CD has a running time of 72 minutes.
DVD information: Fine print on DVD reads: Warner Reprise Records, a division of Warner Bros. Records, Inc. Warner Music Group. An AOL TimeWarner Company. C2003 New Line Productions, Inc. *The Lord of the Rings*, the characters, names, and places therein, ™The Saul Zanetz Company d/b/a Tolkien Enterprise, under license to New Line Productions, Inc. ©2003 New Line Productions, Inc. All Rights Reserved. Unauthorized duplication is a violation of applicable laws.
Catalog number 48565-2.

Instructions: Prepare a catalog record for this item.

When cataloging this item, consider the following: Added entries; notes

***AACR2r* rules needed:** 1.1B1; 1.1B9; 1.1C1; 1.1E1; 1.1F1; 1.4C1; 1.4C3; 1.4D1; 1.4D4c; 1.4F6; 1.5B1; 1.5B4; 1.5C1; 1.5D1; 1.5E1d; 1.7A4; 1.7B11; 1.7B18; 1.7B19; 6.4D2; 6.5B1; 6.5B2; 6.5C2; 6.5C3; 6.5C8; 6.5D2; 6.5E1; 21.1A2; 21.29C; 21.30E1; 21.30H1; 21.30J1; 21.30J2; MARC 028

Exercise 104

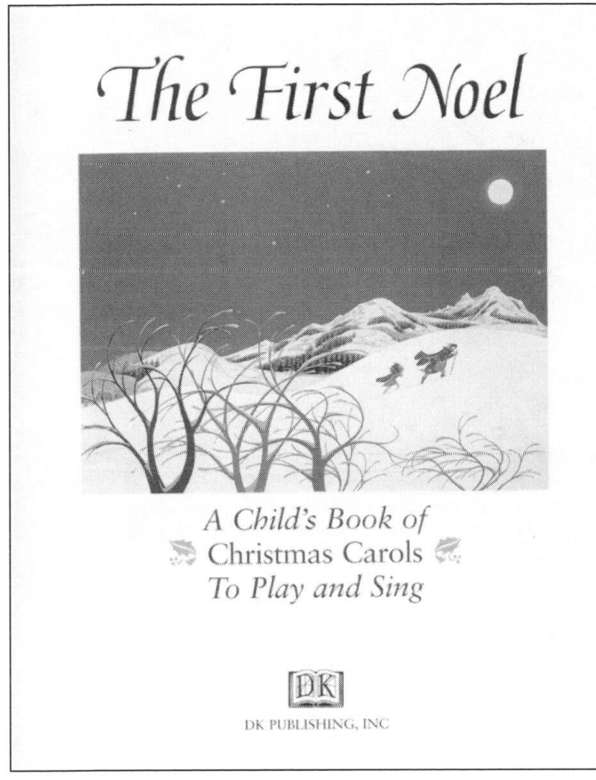

The First Noel

A Child's Book of
Christmas Carols
To Play and Sing

DK

DK PUBLISHING, INC

Title Page

CONTENTS

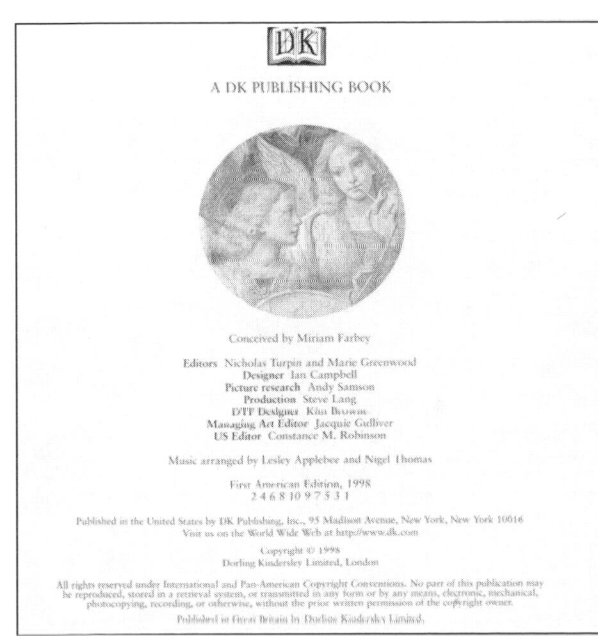

DK

A DK PUBLISHING BOOK

Conceived by Miriam Farbey

Editors Nicholas Turpin and Marie Greenwood
Designer Ian Campbell
Picture research Andy Samson
Production Steve Lang
DTP Designer Kim Browne
Managing Art Editor Jacquie Gulliver
US Editor Constance M. Robinson

Music arranged by Lesley Applebee and Nigel Thomas

First American Edition, 1998
2 4 6 8 10 9 7 5 3 1

Published in the United States by DK Publishing, Inc., 95 Madison Avenue, New York, New York 10016
Visit us on the World Wide Web at http://www.dk.com

Copyright © 1998
Dorling Kindersley Limited, London

All rights reserved under International and Pan-American Copyright Conventions. No part of this publication may be reproduced, stored in a retrieval system, or transmitted in any form or by any means, electronic, mechanical, photocopying, recording, or otherwise, without the prior written permission of the copyright owner.

Published in Great Britain by Dorling Kindersley Limited.

Title Page Verso

Additional information:
31 pages; colored illustrations; music; 29 cm.
ISBN: 0-7894-3483-0; LCCN: 98-23310
Music for the carol is given on one page with an illustration and the words given on the facing page.

Instructions: Prepare a catalog record for this item.

When cataloging this work, consider the following:

- How to do the physical description. Is there a general material designator (GMD)?

AACR2r **rules needed:** 1.1B1; 1.1E1; 1.2B1; 1.4C1; 1.4C4; 1.4D1; 1.4D2; 1.4F1; 1.5B1; 1.5C1; 1.5D1; 1.7B6; 1.7B9; 1.7B18; 5.5B1; 5.5C1; 5.5D1; 21.7B1; 21.29C; 24.1A; 24.5C1; MARC 010; MARC 020

Exercise 105

Back Cover—Portions

First Page—
Portions

Additional information: 6 pages; 31 cm.

Instructions: Prepare a catalog record for this item.

***AACR2r* rules needed:** 1.1B1; 1.1C1; 1.1F1; 1.3A; 1.4C1; 1.4C3; 1.4C5; 1.4D1; 1.4D4; 1.4D5; 1.4F6; 1.5B1; 1.5D1; 1.7B17; 1.7B19; 5.0B1; 5.1C1; 5.3B1; 5.5B1; 5.5B2; 5.5D1; 5.7B19; 21.1A2; 21.29B; 21.29C; 21.30B1; 21.30F1; 22.5A1; 24.1A; MARC 028

Exercise 106

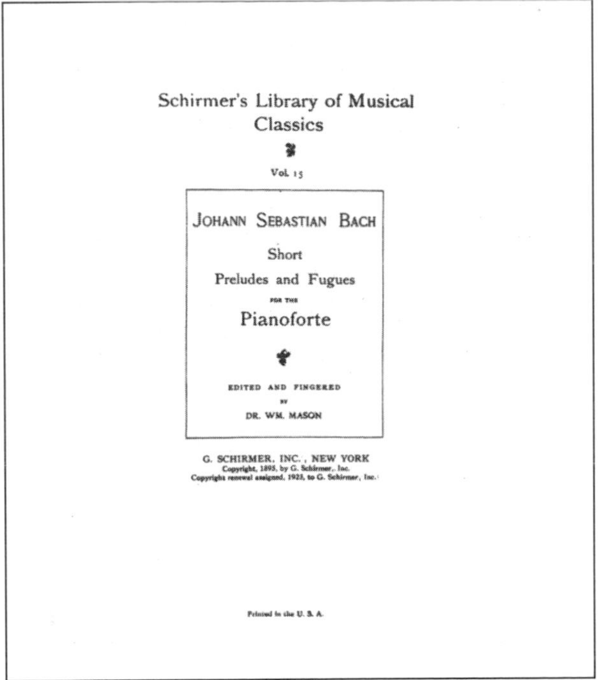

Schirmer's Library of Musical Classics

Vol. 15

JOHANN SEBASTIAN BACH

Short

Preludes and Fugues

FOR THE

Pianoforte

EDITED AND FINGERED

BY

DR. WM. MASON

G. SCHIRMER, INC., NEW YORK

Copyright, 1895, by G. Schirmer, Inc.

Copyright renewal assigned, 1923, to G. Schirmer, Inc.

Printed in the U. S. A.

Title Page

Preface—Portion

1. Twelve little Preludes for Beginners (page 3).

These pieces were probably jotted down by Bach while he was giving lessons, and were adapted to the immediate needs of individual pupils. Proofs for this assertion are afforded by Nos. 1, 4, 5, 8–11, which were written in the "Clavierbüchlein für W. F. Bach" by his father's own hand, and are exactly reproduced here. The others were in a volume in J. P. Kellner's handwriting. The date of the "Clavierbüchlein" is the approximate date of their composition (1720).

2. Six little Preludes for Beginners (page 14).

These are engraved after Forkel's old edition, published by C. F. Peters.

3. Little two-part Fugue (page 20).

This fugue, which, by the way, is also extant in the shape of a violin duet in a strange hand, appears in the present new edition with some not unessential emendations by J. P. Kellner's hand.

4. Fugue in C-major (page 22).

Reproduced after a single copy in Forkel's literary remains, no other exemplar being obtainable. It was probably written in Cöthen, shortly prior to 1723, as it exhibits the characteristics of the master's sublimest art-period.

5. Fugue in C-major (page 24).

After the autograph from the "Clavierbuchlein" above mentioned. This source approximately establishes the time of its composition. It appears to have been written as an exercise for the two weakest fingers, especially of the right hand.

6. Prelude and Fughetta, in D-minor (page 26).

7. Prelude and Fughetta, in E-minor (page 28).

For these two pieces autographs were at hand, and were followed implicitly. From their style we may conclude that they were written in Cöthen, before 1723.

8. Prelude and Fugue, in A-minor (page 33).

Of this piece only one copy could be found, in J. P. Kellner's hand, who, though himself a fine fugue-writer and a zealous admirer of Bach, was very often a careless copyist. The editor's task was, therefore, confined to the discovery and correction of slips of the pen. It is probable that this piece was written some years earlier than the two preceding.

F. K. GRIEPENKERL.

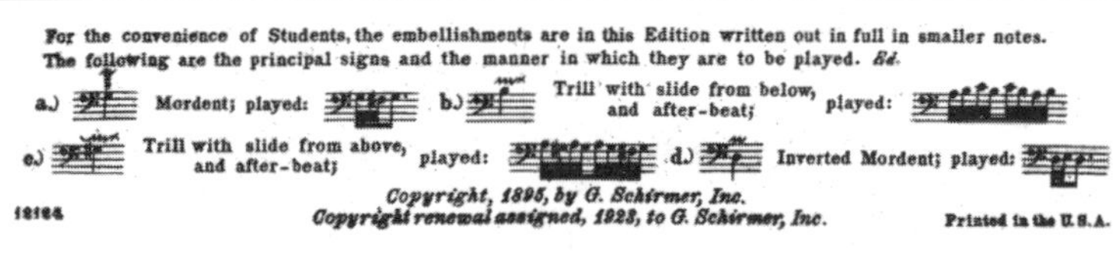

For the convenience of Students, the embellishments are in this Edition written out in full in smaller notes. The following are the principal signs and the manner in which they are to be played. *Ed.*

12124 *Copyright, 1895, by G. Schirmer, Inc.* *Copyright renewal assigned, 1923, to G. Schirmer, Inc.* Printed in the U.S.A.

Bottom of First Page of Music

CONTENTS.

SCHIRMER'S LIBRARY OF MUSICAL CLASSICS

Vol. 15

BACH

Short

Preludes and Fugues

For the Piano

(MASON)

$1.00

Cover

Additional information:
35 pages, 33 pages of music. 30 cm.; publisher number (as shown at bottom of first page): 12124; LCCN: 64-26515
Background information: Originally written for harpsichord in the early 1720s.

Instructions: Prepare a catalog record for this item.

***AACR2r* rules needed:** 1.1B1; 1.1C1; 1.1F1; 1.1F6; 1.1F7; 1.1G1; 1.4C1; 1.4D1; 1.4D2; 1.4D3; 1.4F6; 1.5B1; 1.7B4; 1.7B18; 1.7B19; 1.8B3; 1.8D1; 5.5B1; 5.5D1; 5.7B19; 5.8B2; 21.1A2; 21.30D; 22.5A1; 22.18A; MARC 028

Exercise 107

Box Cover

Additional information: LCCN 98-141104

Instructions: Prepare a catalog record for this item.

AACR2r **rules needed:** 1.1B1; 1.1C1; 1.1E1; 1.1F1; 1.1F6; 1.4C1; 1.4C3; 1.4D1; 1.4D4; 1.4D5; 1.4F6; 1.5B1; 1.5C1; 1.5D1; 1.7B10; 1.7B14; 1.7B17; 1.7B19; 1.8B1; 1.8D1; 10.5B1; 10.5C1; 10.5C2; 10.5D2; 21.0D1; 21.1A1; 21.8A1b; 21.24; 21.29B; 21.29C; 21.30C1; 21.30K2; 22.5A1; MARC 020

Back Box Cover

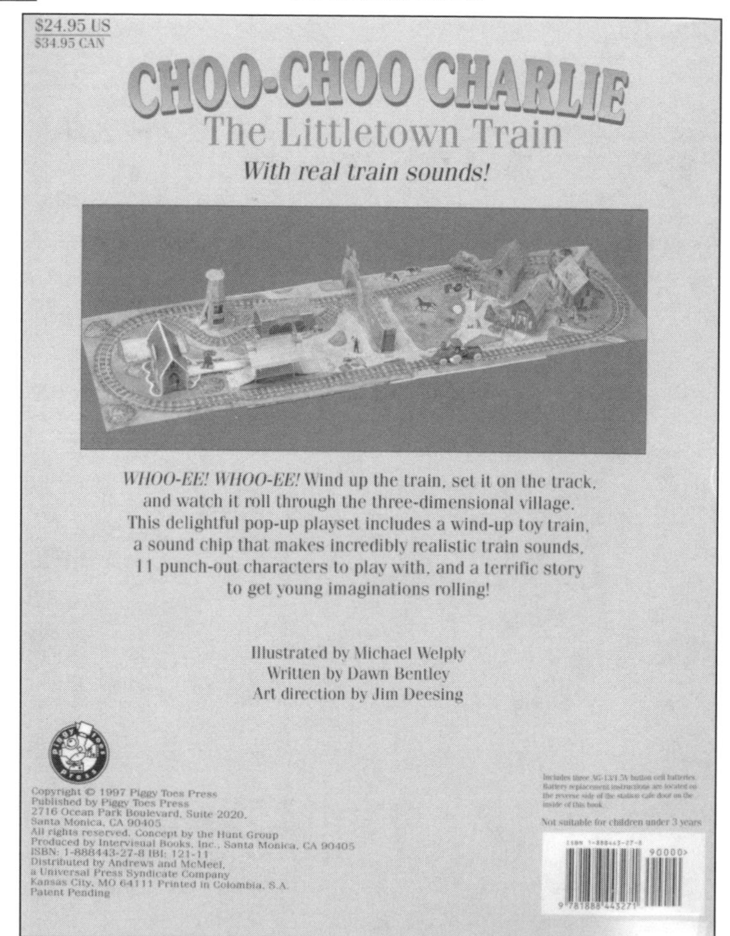

Exercise 108

Educators Marketing, Ltd.

"EDMARK"
P-100 A

EDMARK TWIN GEAR PUMP P-100

INSTRUCTOR GUIDE
P-100 A

The Edmark P-100 Twin Gear Pump should be used as the introductory pump for the Pump Set P-1000 lecture series.

The Edmark P-100 Twin Gear Pump may also be used to illustrate fluid flow characteristics for earth science or general science classes (see page 2). It may also be used to demonstrate a hydraulic motor (see page 5).

Preparation for Lecture

Using the diagram on page 6, make an ordinary transparency to use in the lecture.

Set up overhead projector and screen. Lay out the P-100 Twin Gear Pump transparency. Fill the Twin Gear Pump P-100 plastic unit with water to top of gears and add a pinch of fluid illuminator.

Lecture and Presentation of the Twin Gear Pump P-100

1. Place the Twin Gear Pump transparency on the overhead projector.
2. The upper gear is set up on the transparency to rotate clockwise. Point out that the rotation is an arbitrary selection as it can be rotated either direction.
3. Question the students on direction of fluid flow through the pump when the upper gear rotates clockwise.

   Note: There will be disagreement on the flow. It is suggested the instructor allow open debate until the students conclusively divide into two groups. (One group will believe the flow will be A to B. The others will believe the flow will be B to A.)

 -1-

Teacher's Directions

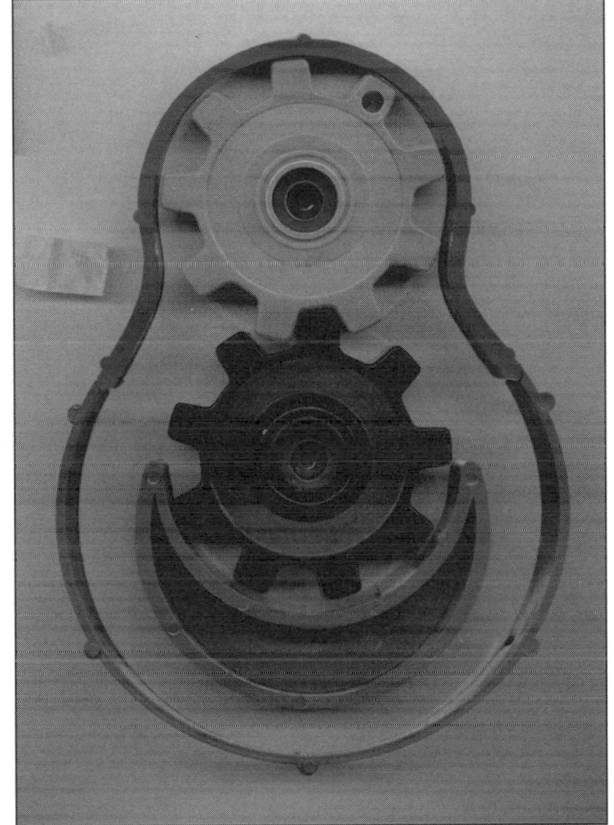

Additional information: This is a plastic model mounted on a transparent plastic board, 25 cm. x 20 cm. (10 x 8 inches). There is a six-page instructor's guide. This item is a part of a series.

Instructions: Prepare a catalog record for this item.

***AACR2r* rules needed:** 1.1B1; 1.1C1; 1.1E2; 1.4D1; 1.4D2; 1.4F6; 1.5B1; 1.5C1; 1.5D1; 1.5D2; 1.5E1(c); 1.7B14; 1.7B17; 10.5B1; 10.5C1; 10.5C2; 10.5D2; 10.5E1c; 10.5E2; 21.29B; 21.30E1

Exercise 109

Front

Back

Additional information:
In a sealed plastic case, 15 cm. wide, 97 mm. high; Etched on case: United States Minted Coin Set.

When cataloging this item, consider the following: Producer (what is SSCA?)

Instructions: Prepare a catalog record for this item.

***AACR2r* rules needed:** 1.1B1; 1.1C1; 1.4C6; 1.4D1; 1.4F6; 1.5B1; 1.5C1; 1.5D1; 1.5D2; 1.7B5; 1.7B3; 1.7B17; 10.0B1; 10.1B1; 10.5B1; 10.5B2; 10.5C1; 10.5D1; 10.5D2

Exercise 110

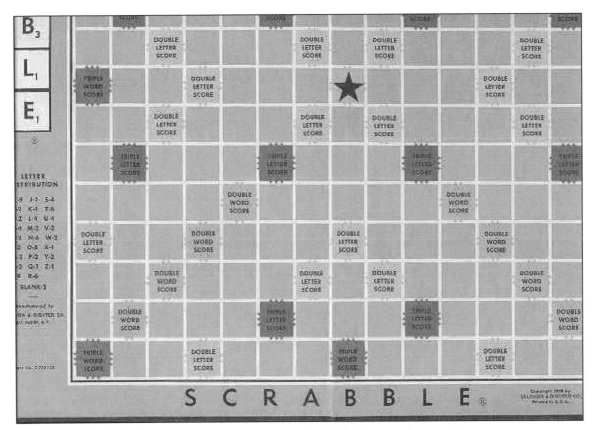

Scrabble Board—Portion

Scrabble Board Detail

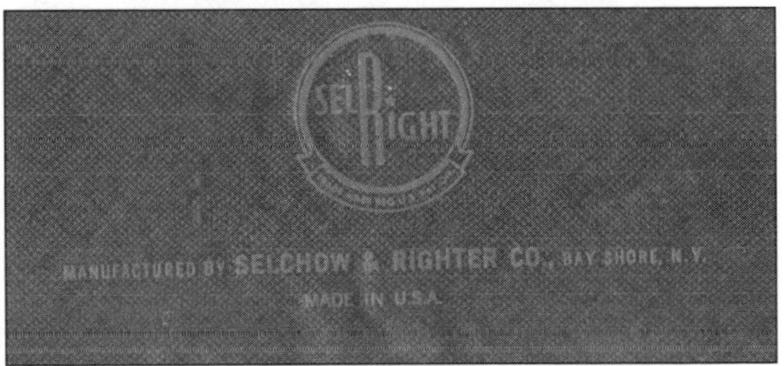

Box Lid Detail

Additional information: Scrabble is a game. Included is one board, 100 letter tiles, 1 letter bag, 4 individual letter racks. Board is 36 x 36 cm., contained in a box 37 x 19 x 4 cm. Summary: Players form words with the letters they have drawn and what is already on the board, hoping to use the higher-value letters and squares to finish first with the highest score.

Instructions: Prepare a catalog record for this item.

***AACR2r* rules needed:** 1.1B1; 1.1C1; 1.4C1; 1.4C3; 1.4D1; 1.4D2; 1.4F6; 1.5B1; 1.5C1; 1.5D1; 1.5D2; 10.5B1; 10.5B2; 10.5C2; 10.5D1; 10.5D2; 21.1C1; 21.30E1; 24.1A

Exercise 111

Cover

Back Cover

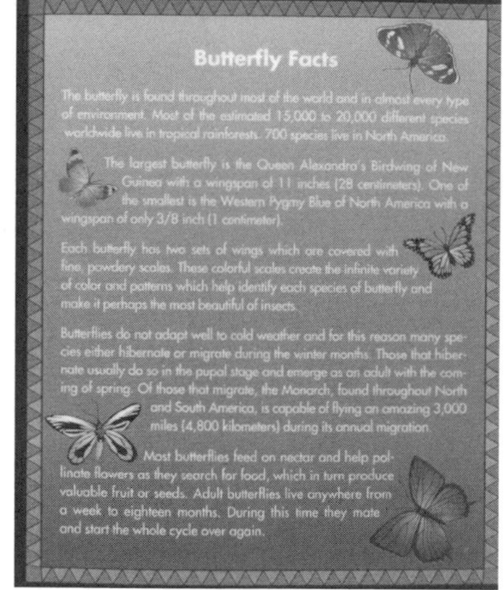

Inside the Game

Additional information:
Paper case is 148 mm. high, 145 mm. wide; opens to 294 mm. width. Color.

Instructions: Prepare a catalog record for this item.

***AACR2r* rules needed:** 1.1B1; 1.1C1; 1.1E6; 1.1F1; 1.4C1; 1.4C3; 1.4D1; 1.4D2; 1.4F6; 1.5B1; 1.5C1; 1.5D1; 1.7B14; 1.7B17; 1.7B18; 10.5B1; 10.5B2; 10.5C1; 10.5C2; 10.5D2; 21.1A1; 22.5A1; MARC 024

Exercise 112

Olivia Stuffed Doll

This is Olivia.
She is good at a lot of things.

© GUND, INC., EDISON, NJ 08817 USA
SURFACE WASHABLE / SURFACE LAVABLE
Remove all hang tags and their plastic fasteners before giving this toy to a child / Enlever toutes les étiquettes et leurs attaches en plastique avant de donner ce jouet à un enfant.

MADE IN CHINA / FABRIQUÉ EN CHINE
KEEP THIS TAG FOR REFERENCE
CONSERVEZ CES INFORMATIONS OU RECOPIEZ-LES
Come visit our website at www.gund.com
OLIVIA™ © 2002 Ian Falconer
Licensed by Silver Lining Productions Ltd

Hang Tag

Additional information:
The doll is approximately 7 1/2 inches in length; white, red, and black fabric

Instructions: Prepare a catalog record for this item.

***AACR2r* rules needed:** 1.1B1; 1.1C1; 1.1F1; 1.1F6; 1.1F8; 1.4C1; 1.4C3; 1.4D1; 1.4D2; 1.4F6; 1.5B1; 1.5C1; 1.5D1; 1.5E1(d); 1.7B3; 1.7B19; 10.0B1; 10.1B1; 10.1C1; 10.1F1; 10.4C1; 10.4D1; 10.4F1; 10.5B1; 10.5C1; 10.5C2; 10.5D1; 10.7B3; 10.7B10; 10.7B19

Exercise 113

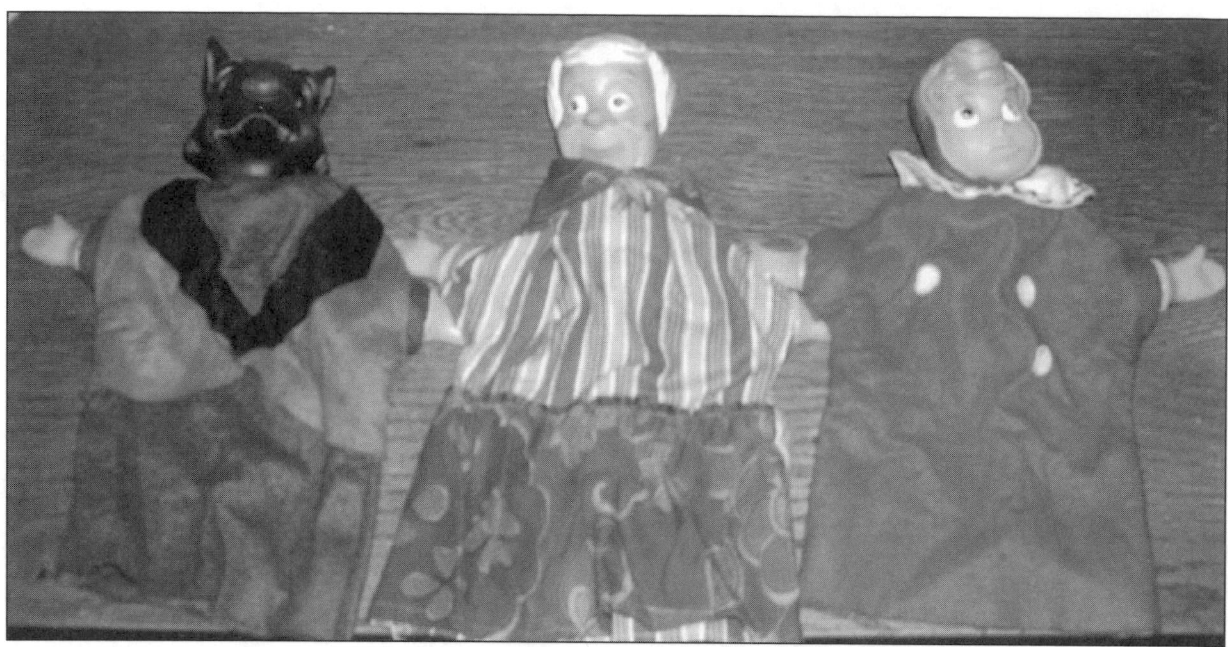

Puppets

Additional information:
There are three hand puppets. The characters are Red Riding Hood, Grandma, and the Wolf. They are each approximately 10 1/2 inches long. There is no manufacturing information available, but they were purchased in Paris, France, in 1967.

Instructions: Prepare a catalog record for this item.

When cataloging this item, consider the following:

- Title
- Publication information

AACR2r **Rules Needed:** 1.1B7; 1.1C1; 1.1F2; 1.4C6; 1.4D6; 1.4F7; 1.5B1; 1.5C1; 1.5D1; 1.7B3; 1.7B7; 10.1B1; 10.4C1; 10.4D1; 10.4G1; 10.5B1; 10.5B2; 10.5C1; 10.5C2; 10.5D1; 10.7B3; 10.7B7; 21.1C1

Exercise 114

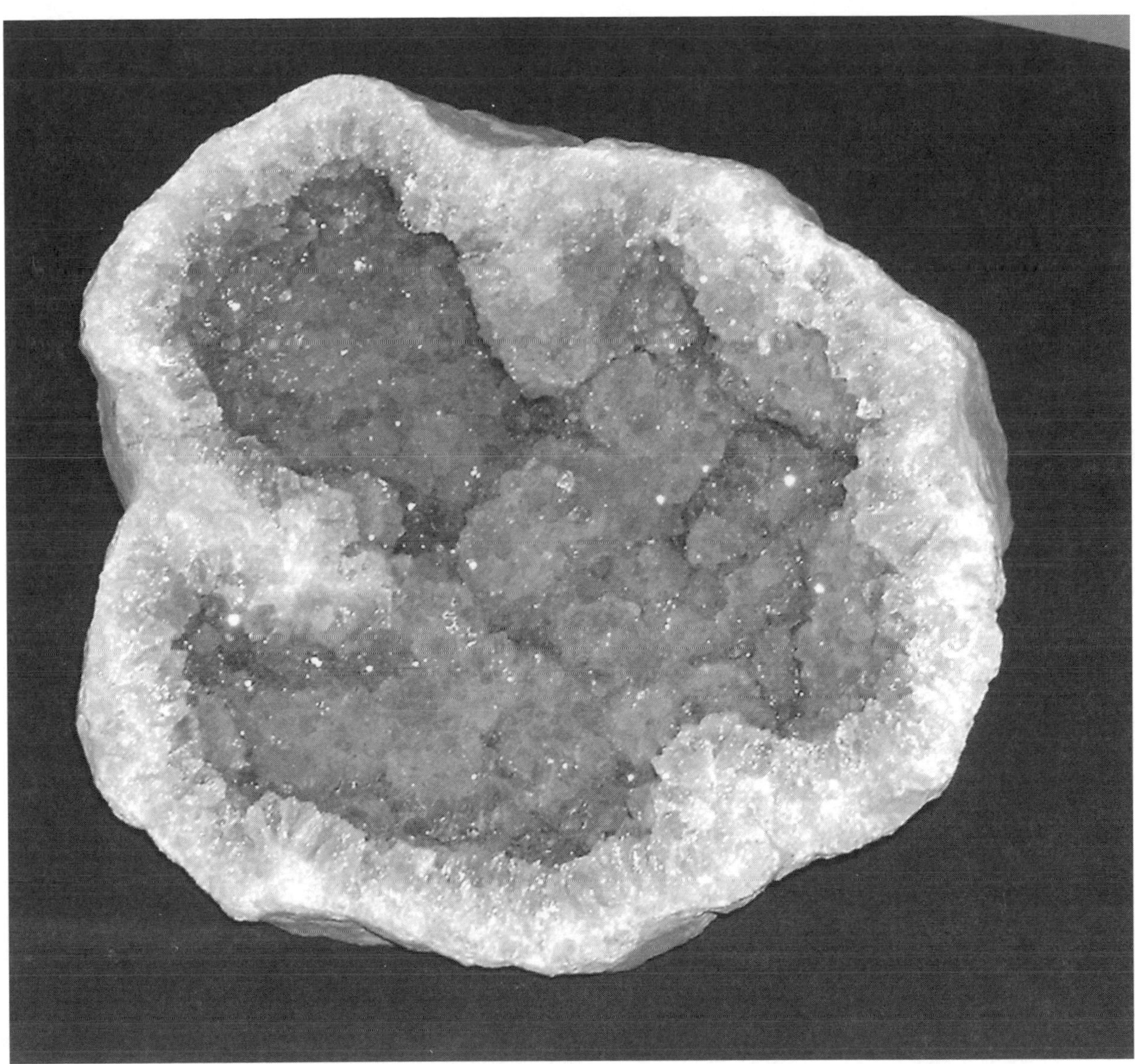

Additional information:
9 3/4 x 8 1/2 x 4 1/8 in.
Specimen collected at the Sheffler geode mine in the northeast corner of Missouri, about 13 miles southeast of Keokuk, Illinois. The "skin" is gray from the dolomite/shale that is still attached to the geode; inside it is white to bluish-gray, has the texture of coarse sand, and is lined with "smoky quartz" with some very small crystals of marcasite or pyrite.

Instructions: Prepare a catalog record for this item.

***AACR2r* rules needed:** 1.1B7; 1.1C1; 1.1F2; 1.4C8; 1.5B1; 1.5C1; 1.5D1; 1.7B3; 1.7B19; 10.1B1; 10.1C1; 10.5B1; 10.5C2; 10.5D1; 10.7B3; 10.7B10

Exercise 115

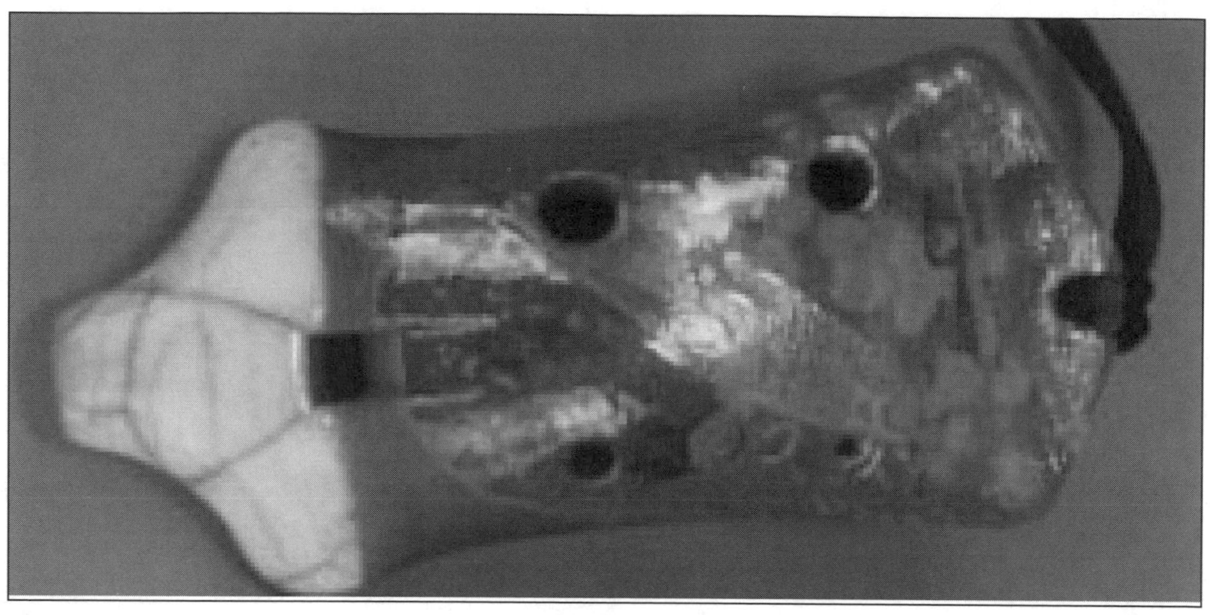

Ocarina

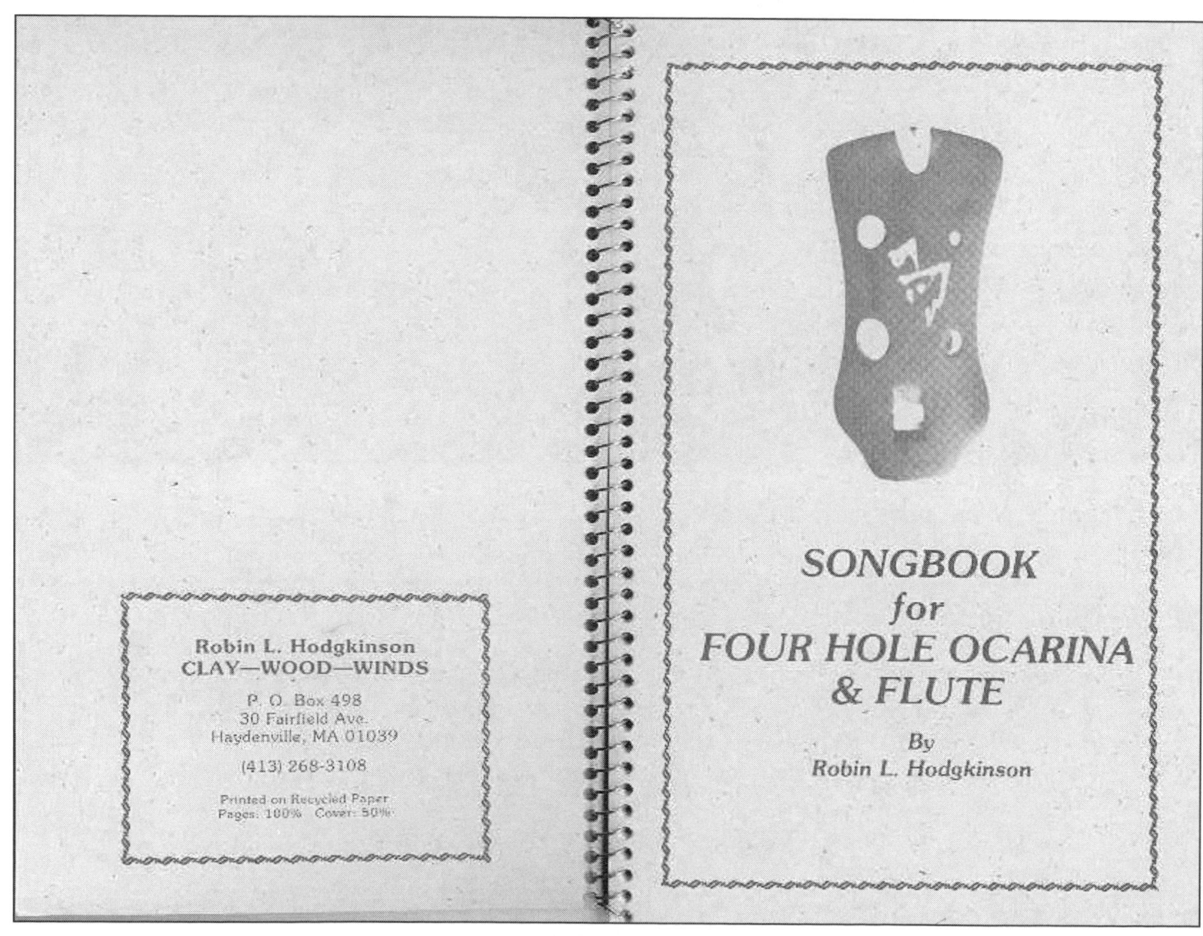

Accompanying Songbook Covers

(*Continued on Next Page*)

Exercise 115

Introduction:

This song-book was prepared for anyone who loves music, regardless of age, or whether they have any previous musical training. The songs contained in the book were chosen for their traditional popularity and familiarity. Each musical score is supplemented with the words to the song, fingering diagrams for the ocarina, and each note is assigned a name based on the familiar "do, re, mi,...," system. The text is intentionally simplified inorder not to frustrate or discourage even a child trying to play an instrument for the first time. The intent of the author in presenting this book is to provide a tool for musical self-expression. The book was conceived and designed to help the person with no musical training begin to play pleasing, familiar melodies in a very short time. Remember, the two most important qualities necessary when learning to play any musical instrument are patience and perseverance.

Ocarina

Brief History of the Ocarina:

The ocarina belongs to the ancient family of the musical instruments called "vessel flutes". Vessel flutes are made in a variety of shapes and sizes, but generally have a somewhat globular shape contrasted to the elongated open end tubular flute. Variations of the vessel flute have been played throughout history all over the world from the Maori of New Zealand to the imperial courts of China; from Central and South America to Africa; Europe and the United States. In Central and South America, clay whistle-ocarinas were made in the shapes of birds and other animals, or human forms, and even deities. These whistle-ocarinas were highly personalized musical instruments to the Indians of the Ulua Valley of Honduras. Every member of the tribe had a whistle call by which he or she could be recognized. Modern day versions of these ancient instruments were very popular in Europe in the late 1800's when entire ocarina bands were common. The name ocarina comes from Italy where the instrument was called "little goose", because its shape resembled a goose in flight.

Additional information:
This is a soprano ocarina, made out of clay. The dimensions are approximately 10 x 5 x 3 cm. It can be described as a raku-fired clay whistle flute.
The accompanying book has 40 pages, music, is 22 cm. high, and is spiral-bound. Includes basic instructions for playing a scale, reading the fingering charts in the music, a brief history of the ocarina, and 25 pages of folk songs. The ocarina was made by the author of accompanying song-book. Date of creation was sometime during the 1990s. It was acquired in 2000.

Instructions: Prepare a catalog record for this item.

When cataloging this item, consider the following: Title, physical description, notes general material designation.

***AACR2r* rules needed:** 1.1B7; 1.1C1; 1.4C1; 1.4D1; 1.5B1; 1.5C1; 1.5D1; 1.5E1(d); 1.7B9; 1.7B11; 1.7B17; 1.7B18; 10.0B1; 10.5B1; 10.5C1; 10.5C2; 10.5D1; 10.7B17; 21.1A2; 21.1C1a; 21.30G1; 21.30J1; 22.5A1

Exercise 116

Lantern Slide

Additional information:
Dimensions are 3 x 4 inches. There is no title given on the item. It was purchased at a garage sale in 1993.

Instructions: Prepare a catalog record for this item.

When cataloging this work, consider the following: How would you prepare the title statement for this item?

***AACR2r* rules needed:** 1.1B7; 1.4C1; 1.4C3; 1.4D3; 1.4D7; 1.4F7; 1.5B1; 1.5C1; 1.5D1; 1.7B; 1.7B20; 8.5B1; 8.5C2; 8.5D1; 8.5D5; 8.7B; 21.5; 21.29B; 21.29C; 21.30E1; 25.1A

Exercise 117

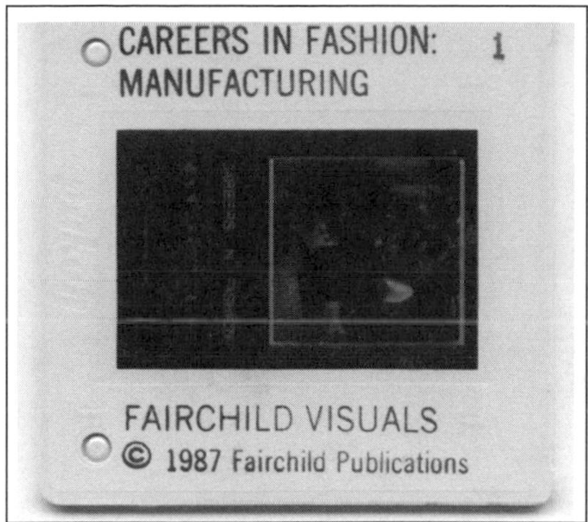

Slide One of Forty

Additional information:
40 colored slides (5 x 5 cm.) with tape and booklet. Booklet: 17 pages, 28 cm.; Glossary (pages 15-17). Booklet and slides in plastic notebook binder (29 cm.), slides in plastic sleeves.

Instructions: Prepare a catalog record for this item.

***AACR2r* rules needed:** 1.1B1; 1.1C1; 1.1E1; 1.1F6; 1.4C1; 1.4D1; 1.4D2; 1.5B1; 1.5C1; 1.5D1; 1.5E1(d); 1.6B1; 1.6G1; 1.7B10; 1.7B18; 1.8B1; 8.5B1; 8.5C2; 8.5D5; 8.5E; MARC 020

MODERN CAREERS IN FASHION

Set III

CAREERS IN FASHION

MANUFACTURING

FAIRCHILD VISUALS
NEW YORK

Booklet Cover

Copyright © 1987 by Fairchild Publications
Division of Capital Cities Media, Inc.

All Rights Reserved

0-87005-808-8

Printed in the United States of America

Booklet Cover Verso

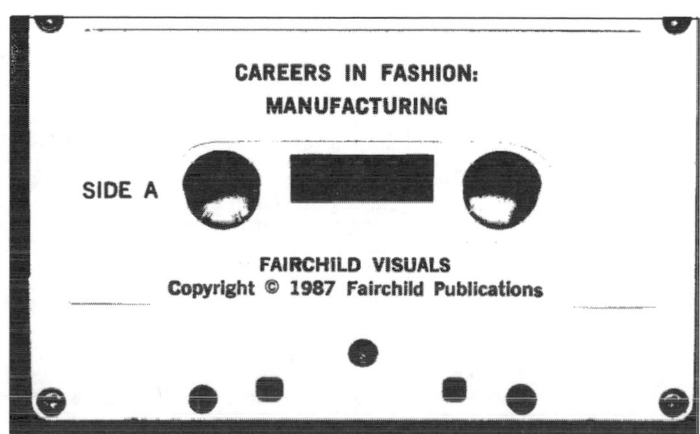

Accompanying Cassette

Exercise 118

Filmstrip #1 Container—Top

Cover of Teacher's Guide

CLOTHING
the visible self

Director, Creative and Editorial Services
Barbara Weiland

Production Coordinator
Marsha McCormick

Project Coordinators
Evelyn L. Brannon
Carolyn Rega

Writer
Mary Johnson

Title Page of Teacher's Guide

Approximate playing time of each filmstrip: 10 minutes
Approximate number of frames per filmstrip: 70

Library of Congress Catalog Card Number
75-736289
International Standard Book Number
Record: 0-88421-507-5
Cassette: 0-88421-508-3

First Edition

Copyright © 1976 by
Butterick Publishing
708 Third Avenue
New York, New York 10017
A Division of American Can Company

All rights reserved. No part of this audiovisual package, except conventional reproduction of student spirit masters, may be reproduced in any form or by any electronic or mechanical means, including information storage and retrieval systems, without permission in writing from the publisher, except by a reviewer who may quote brief passages in a review.

Printed in the U.S.A.

Title Page Verso

(*Continued on Next Page*)

Exercise 118

the visible self

Spirit Masters

an independent living program from Butterick Publishing

Title Page of Spirit Masters

Clothing:
the visible self
1. THE CLOTHES WE WEAR

Side A for Automatic Projectors

Copyright ℗ 1976 Butterick Publishing
Div. American Can Co. 161 Sixth Ave. New York, N.Y. 10013

Accompanying Cassette

Additional information:
Includes: 4 filmstrips, 4 cassette tapes, a teacher's guide (20 pages, 28 cm.), and 12 blackline spirit masters. Contained in a 37 x 32 cm. box.
Contents: 1. The clothes we wear. 2. Your clothing personality. 3. Your clothing collection. 4. Spending your clothing dollars.

Instructions: Prepare a catalog record for this item.

***AACR2r* rules needed:** 1.1B1; 1.1C1; 1.1E2; 1.1F1; 1.2B1; 1.4C1; 1.4F6; 1.5B1; 1.5B3; 1.5B4; 1.5C1; 1.5D2; 1.5E1(d); 1.7B6; 1.7B18; 1.8B1; 1.8B2; 1.8E1; 8.0B1; 21.30E1; 24.1A; MARC 020

Exercise 119

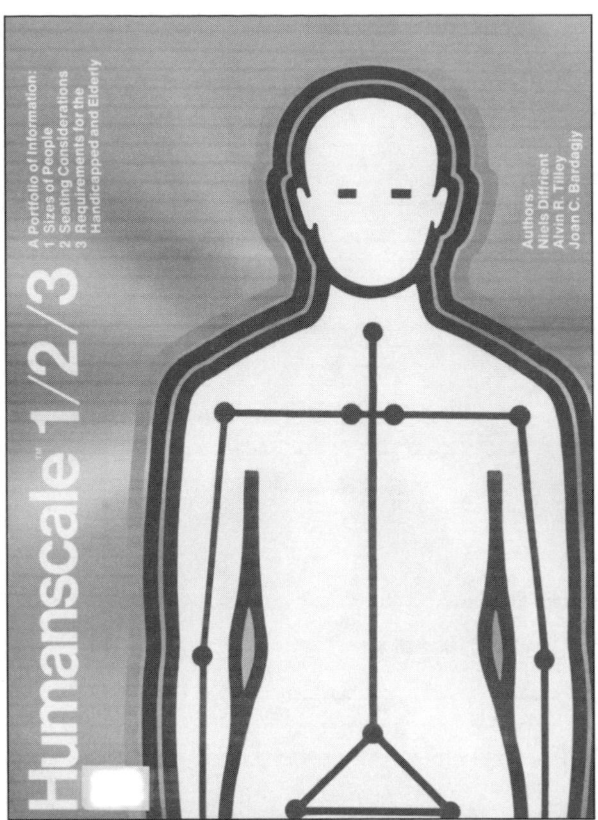

Manual Front Cover

Humanscale™ 1/2/3

Manual

Authors:
Niels Diffrient
Alvin R. Tilley
Joan C. Bardagjy

Designers:
Henry Dreyfuss Associates
888 Seventh Avenue
New York, New York 10019

Publishers:
The MIT Press
Massachusetts Institute of Technology
Cambridge, Massachusetts 02142

We wish to acknowledge the dedicated assistance of Janet Travell, M.D., who read all copy to ensure that our reference to medical or paramedical matters would be accurate and well-founded.

Copyright © 1974 by Henry Dreyfuss Associates

All rights reserved. No part of the manual or selectors may be reproduced in any form or by any means, electronic or mechanical, including photocopying, recording, or by any information storage and retrieval system, without permission in writing from the publisher.

Library of Congress catalog card number: 74-5041
ISBN: 0-262-54027-4

Printed in the United States of America

Manual Title Page

Manual Title Page Verso

A Portfolio of Information:
1 Sizes of People
2 Seating Considerations
3 Requirements for the
Handicapped and Elderly

Detail from Cover

(Continued on Next Page)

Exercise 119

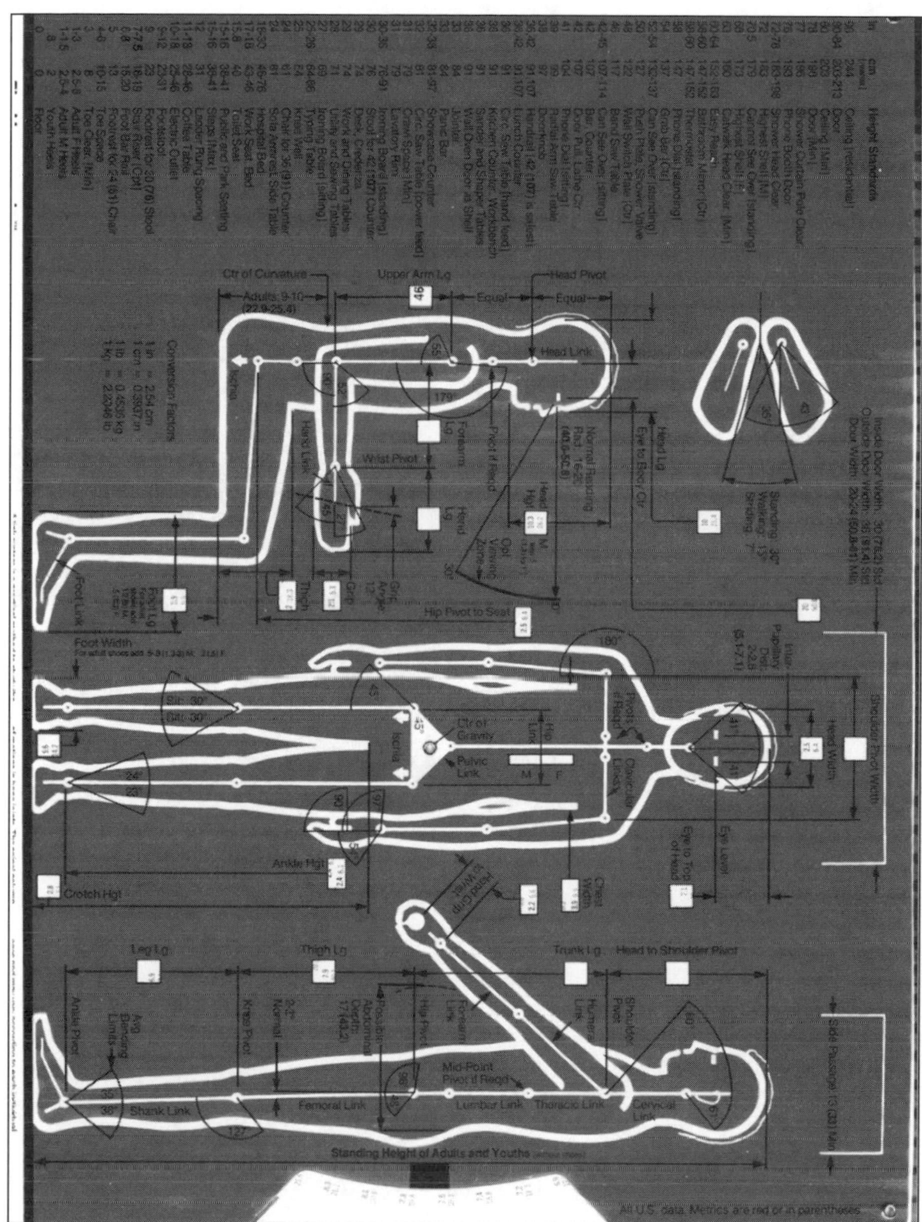

Sample Placard

Additional information:
3 double-sided scale placards with wheel; colored plastic; 22 cm. x 28 cm.; 1 manual (32 [1] pages, color and black and white illustrations, 22 cm. x 28 cm.) in plastic portfolio, 30 cm.; Bibliography (pages 32-[33])

Instructions: Prepare a catalog record for this item.

***AACR2r* rules needed:** 1.0E1 1.0H2; 1.1B1; 1.1C1; 1.1F1; 1.1F5; 1.4C1; 1.4C3; 1.4D1; 1.4F6; 1.5B1; 1.5B3; 1.7B18; 1.8B1; 8.5B1; 8.5B3; 8.5C1; 8.5C2; 8.5D1; 8.5E1; 10.5B1; 21.0D1; 21.4A1; 21.6B2; 21.29B; 21.30K2; 22.5A1; MARC 020

Exercise 120

Cover

Sample Print

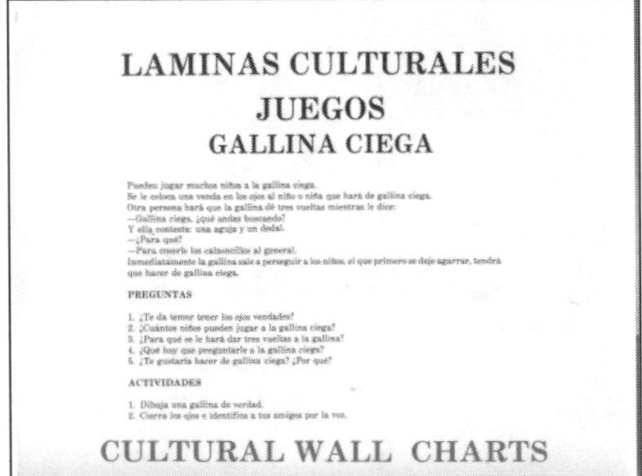

LAMINAS CULTURALES
JUEGOS
GALLINA CIEGA

Pueden jugar muchos niños a la gallina ciega.
Se le coloca una venda en los ojos al niño o niña que hará de gallina ciega.
Otra persona hará que la gallina dé tres vueltas mientras le dice:
—Gallina ciega, ¿qué andas buscando?
Y ella contesta: una aguja y un dedal.
—¿Para qué?
—Para coserle los calzoncillos al general.
Inmediatamente la gallina sale a perseguir a los niños, el que primero se deje agarrar, tendrá que hacer de gallina ciega.

PREGUNTAS

1. ¿Te da temor tener los ojos vendados?
2. ¿Cuántos niños pueden jugar a la gallina ciega?
3. ¿Para qué se le hará dar tres vueltas a la gallina?
4. ¿Qué hay que preguntarle a la gallina ciega?
5. ¿Te gustaría hacer de gallina ciega? ¿Por qué?

ACTIVIDADES

1. Dibuja una gallina de verdad.
2. Cierra los ojos e identifica a tus amigos por la voz.

CULTURAL WALL CHARTS

Sample Print Verso Top

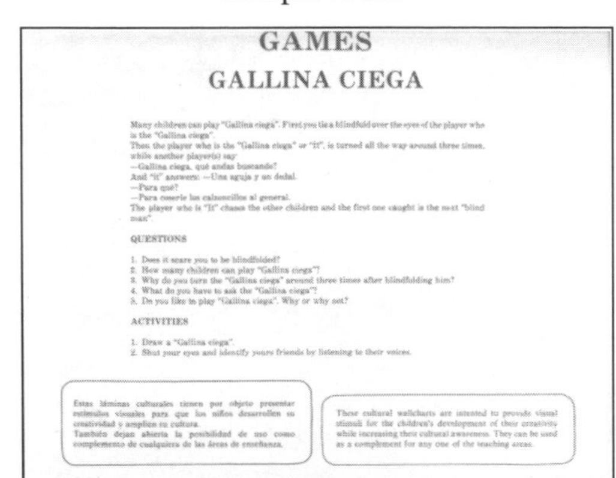

GAMES
GALLINA CIEGA

Many children can play "Gallina ciega". First you tie a blindfold over the eyes of the player who is the "Gallina ciega".
Then the player who is the "Gallina ciega" or "It", is turned all the way around three times, while another player(s) say:
—Gallina ciega, qué andas buscando?
And "It" answers: —Una aguja y un dedal.
—Para qué?
—Para coserle los calzoncillos al general.
The player who is "It" chases the other children and the first one caught is the next "blind man".

QUESTIONS

1. Does it scare you to be blindfolded?
2. How many children can play "Gallina ciega"?
3. Why do you turn the "Gallina ciega" around three times after blindfolding him?
4. What do you have to ask the "Gallina ciega"?
5. Do you like to play "Gallina ciega". Why or why not?

ACTIVITIES

1. Draw a "Gallina ciega".
2. Shut your eyes and identify youre friends by listening to their voices.

Estas láminas culturales tienen por objeto presentar estímulos visuales para que los niños desarrollen su creatividad y amplíen su cultura.
También dejan abierta la posibilidad de uso como complemento de cualquiera de las áreas de enseñanza.

These cultural wallcharts are intented to provide visual stimuli for the children's development of their creativity while increasing their cultural awareness. They can be used as a complement for any one of the teaching areas.

Sample Print Verso Bottom

Detail from Cover Verso

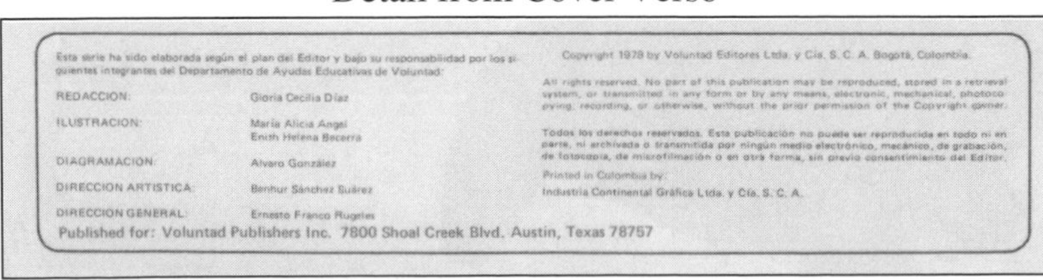

Esta serie ha sido elaborada según el plan del Editor y bajo su responsabilidad por los siguientes integrantes del Departamento de Ayudas Educativas de Voluntad:

REDACCION: Gloria Cecilia Díaz
ILUSTRACION: María Alicia Angel, Enith Helena Becerra
DIAGRAMACION: Alvaro González
DIRECCION ARTISTICA: Benhur Sánchez Suárez
DIRECCION GENERAL: Ernesto Franco Rugeles

Copyright 1979 by Voluntad Editores Ltda. y Cía. S. C. A. Bogotá, Colombia.

All rights reserved. No part of this publication may be reproduced, stored in a retrieval system, or transmitted in any form or by any means, electronic, mechanical, photocopying, recording, or otherwise, without the prior permission of the Copyright owner.

Todos los derechos reservados. Esta publicación no puede ser reproducida en todo ni en parte, ni archivada o transmitida por ningún medio electrónico, mecánico, de grabación, de fotocopia, de microfilmación o en otra forma, sin previo consentimiento del Editor.

Printed in Colombia by:
Industria Continental Gráfica Ltda. y Cía. S. C. A.

Published for: Voluntad Publishers Inc. 7800 Shoal Creek Blvd. Austin, Texas 78757

(*Continued on Next Page*)

Exercise 120

Las LAMINAS CULTURALES han sido diseñadas teniendo en cuenta la importancia de la imagen para la educación del niño. Por esta razón, se ha puesto un especial cuidado tanto en la calidad artística y pedagógica del dibujo como en su producción.

Las láminas han sido concebidas de tal manera que puedan utilizarse como ayuda para el desarrollo de los programas convencionales en el aula de clase o como motivadoras en actividades de enriquecimiento.

Su gran calidad artística hace que puedan utilizarse también como elemento decorativo en el aula.

Para un máximo aprovechamiento de las láminas se propone al maestro las siguientes sugerencias de manejo:

—**Motivar a los estudiantes antes de mostrar las láminas.** Hacer algunos comentarios sobre la importancia y el interés que tiene el tema que se va a desarrollar y para el cual va a utilizarse la lámina como ayuda.

—**Comunicarles el objetivo** que se espera de ellos después de que se haya examinado la lámina. Pueden formularse algunas preguntas a las cuales se van a dar respuesta con la ayuda de la lámina.

—**Llamar la atención de los estudiantes hacia la lámina.** Se trata de concentrar el interés variable de los niños durante el tiempo en que se les va a mostrar la lámina.

—**Mostrar la lámina de manera que sea visible a todo el grupo.** Deje un tiempo suficiente y en silencio para que los niños la observen.

—**Describir el motivo que se representa en la lámina.** Esto puede hacerlo fácilmente el maestro con las indicaciones que aparecen en la parte posterior de la lámina.

—**Formular preguntas a los estudiantes** para confirmar si han percibido lo más importante del motivo que se representa en la lámina.

—**Repetir**, de acuerdo con las respuestas, aquellos aspectos de la descripción que a juicio del maestro no hayan sido captados por los niños.

—**Motivar a los niños para que hagan preguntas, comentarios propios y actividades sobre la lámina.** Esta es una forma de incitar la creatividad y la gran inventiva de los niños que va a enriquecer sin duda el valor educativo de este material.

También se pueden utilizar las láminas murales de las distintas series en ejercicios combinatorios de clasificación.

Por ejemplo, el maestro le entrega a un niño la lámina cultural sobre la selva; el niño escoje el tipo de vivienda para esta región, entre la lámina de vivienda; también puede encontrar qué animales viven allí, o qué plantas. Y así entre muchas posibilidades buscar la motivación para la expresión oral y escrita del niño.

Otro punto de interés es la apreciación artística de la lámina, independiente del tema que trate. El niño puede desarrollar su habilidad manual teniendo el dibujo de la lámina como guía.

Las distintas posibilidades pedagógicas de las láminas culturales se amplían de acuerdo a la inventiva y necesidad del grupo y del maestro.

The CULTURAL CHARTS have been designed taking into account the importance of the visual image in the child's education. Special care has been given to both the artistic and instructional quality of each chart and to its elaboration.

The charts have been conceived in such a way that they may be used as an aid to the development of conventional programs in the classroom, or for motivating additional activities. They may also be used as decoration in the classroom, due to their artistic presentation.

So that the students may take full advantage of the charts. We suggest that the teacher try to:

—**Motivate the students** before showing the charts. Comment on the importance of the topic for which the chart will be used.

—**Inform them of the objective.** Tell them what is expected of them after they have looked at the chart. Questions for the students to answer with the help of the chart may be asked.

—**Call the students' attention to the chart.** Try to hold their interest during the time they are looking at the chart.

—**Display the chart so that everyone in the group can see it.** Allow enough time for the children to observe the chart silently.

—Describe what **the chart shows.** The instructions given on the back of the chart, make it easy for the teacher to do this.

—**Ask the students questions** to ensure that they have understood the most important aspects of the chart.

—**Repeat** those aspects which, as determined by their answers, have not been fully understood by the children.

—**Motivate the students to ask questions, make comments of their own, and suggest activities which utilize the charts.** This will stimulate their natural creative ability and imagination, and will undoubtedly enhace the educational value of this material.

These charts can also be used in various exercises for classification and matching. For instance, the teacher gives a child the cultural chart about the jungle and the child chooses the type of dwelling for this region from among the dwelling charts. He may also look for the kinds of animals that live there, and the kinds of plants which grow there. This activity in itself offers an excellent opportunity to observe the child's oral and written expression.

Another point of interest, aside from the variety of topics included in the charts, is their value as artistic material. By using the pictures on the charts as guides, the child may develop his abilities in arts and handicrafts. Furthermore the instructional possibilities of these charts are as unlimited as the imagination of the students and teacher.

Probablemente los juegos de esta serie han sido un poco olvidados. Pretendemos que el niño aprenda estos juegos que han sido el deleite de varias generaciones. Casi todos los juegos son de grupo lo cual dará más oportunidades al niño de comunicarse y compartir la alegría con sus amiguitos.

The games of this series have probably been almost forgotten. We hope that the child will learn to play these games which have been the joy of many past generations. Nearly all the games are played in group, which will give the child more opportunity to communicate and share his happiness with his friends.

Esta serie ha sido elaborada según el plan del Editor y bajo su responsabilidad por los siguientes integrantes del Departamento de Ayudas Educativas de Voluntad:

REDACCION: Gloria Cecilia Díaz
ILUSTRACION: María Alicia Angel, Enith Helena Becerra
DIAGRAMACION: Alvaro González
DIRECCION ARTISTICA: Benhur Sánchez Suárez
DIRECCION GENERAL: Ernesto Franco Rugeles

Printed in Colombia by:
Industria Continental Gráfica Ltda. y Cía. S. C. A.

Published for: Voluntad Publishers Inc. 7800 Shoal Creek Blvd. Austin, Texas 78757

Cover Verso

Additional information:
8 game prints, one title/guide print; 44 cm. high by 23 cm. wide; color; in plastic bag with handle

Instructions: Prepare a catalog record for this item.

***AACR2r* rules needed:** 1.1B1; 1.1C1; 1.1D1; 1.4C1; 1.4C2; 1.4D1; 1.4D2; 1.4F6; 1.5B1; 1.5C1; 1.5D1; 1.6B1; 1.6C1; 1.7B2; 1.7B17; 1.7B18; 8.0B1; 8.5B1; 8.5C2; 8.5D1; 21.1C1; 21.29B; 21.30E1; 21.30F1; 22.5A1; 22.5C1; 22.5C4; 24.1A; App D

Exercise 121

Cover

LIBRARY REFERENCE SKILLS

Teacher Guide

by
Carl B. Smith, Ph.D.
Elizabeth Batts
Mary Kathryn Dunn
Indiana University

ENCYCLOPAEDIA BRITANNICA
EDUCATIONAL CORPORATION

Teacher's Guide Title Page

Copyright © 1969 by Encyclopaedia Britannica Educational Corporation. All rights reserved. Printed in the United States of America. This work may not be transmitted by television or other devices or processes nor copied, recast, transformed, adapted or utilized in any manner, in whole or in part, without a license. For information regarding a license, write Encyclopaedia Britannica Educational Corporation, Chicago, Illinois.

Teacher's Guide Title Page Verso

Additional information:
Includes thirty-six transparencies, 26 x 22 cm. and a teacher's guide (64 pages, 23 cm.); in plastic container, 29 x 25 cm.

Instructions: Prepare a catalog record for this item.

***AACR2r* rules needed:** 1.0H2; 1.1B1; 1.1C1; 1.1E1; 1.1F1; 1.1F6; 1.4C1; 1.4C6; 1.4D1; 1.4D2; 1.4F6; 1.5B1; 1.5B3; 1.5C1; 1.5D1; 1.5D2; 8.5B1; 8.5C2; 8.5D1; 8.5D4; 8.5E1; 21.29B; 21.30A1; 22.5A1

(*Continued on Next Page*)

Exercise 121

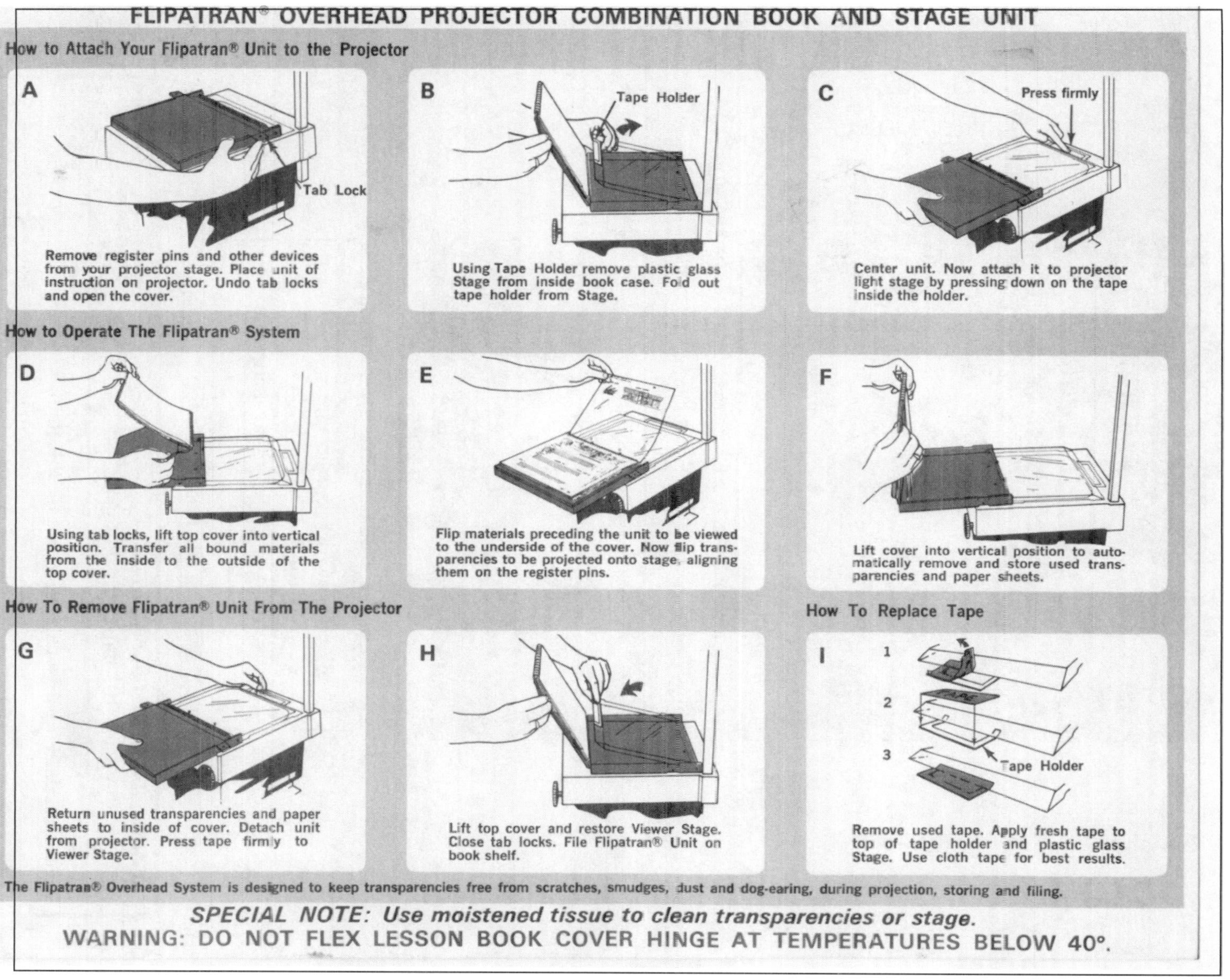

Directions for Using

Exercise 122

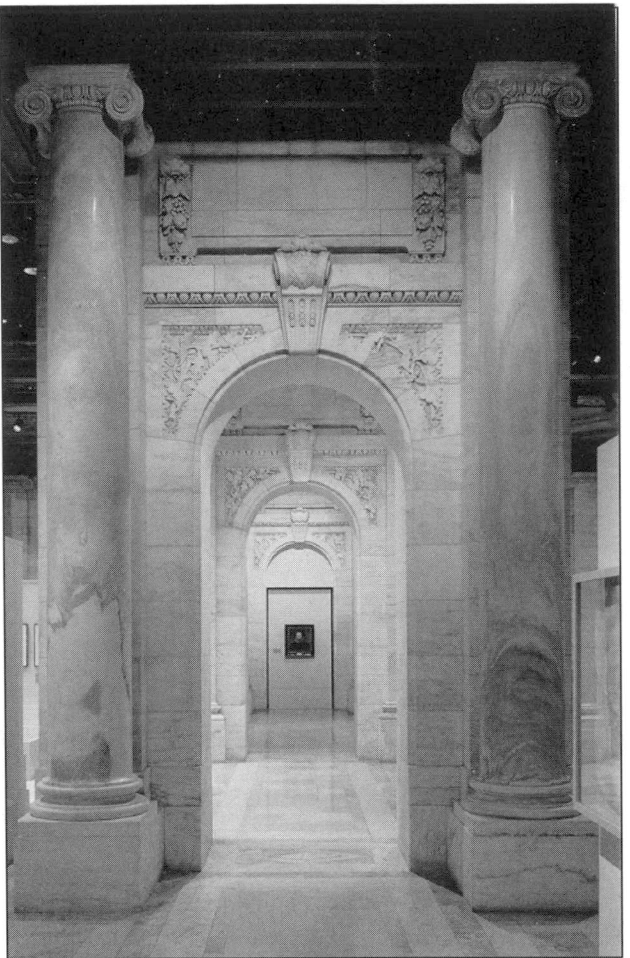

Front of Postcard

The New York Public Library Gottesman Exhibition Hall Photograph © Peter Aaron/ESTO

Detail—Back of Postcard

Additional information:
158 mm. high and 101 mm. wide. Postcard.

Instructions: Prepare a catalog record for this item.

***AACR2r* rules needed:** 1.1B1; 1.1C1; 1.1F1; 1.5B1; 1.5C1; 1.5D1; 8.5B1; 8.5C1g; 8.5C2; 8.5D1; 21.1A2; 22.5A1

Exercise 123

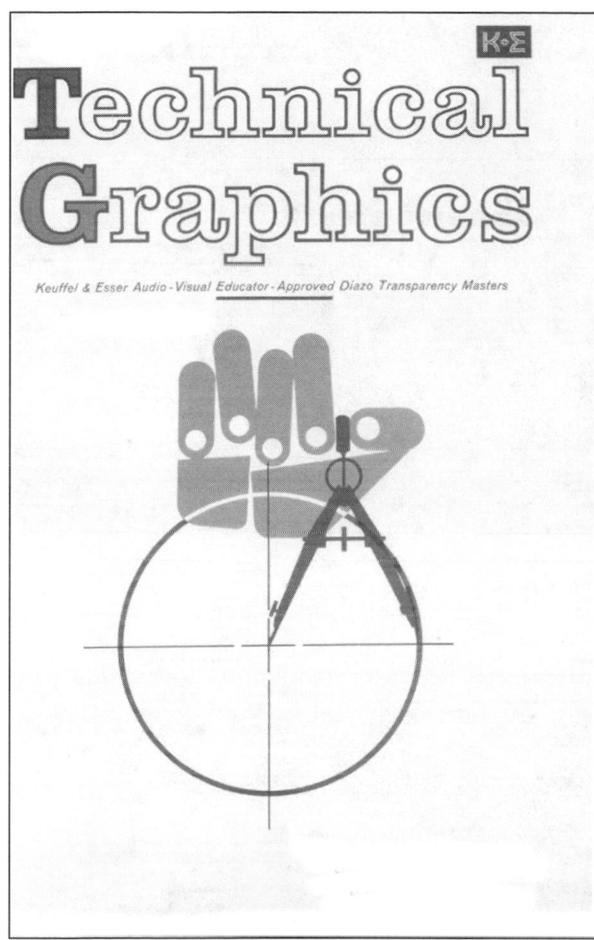

Cover

FOREWORD

Analysis of the wide variety of audiovisual media available for use in education points up the fact that the 10 x 10 inch overhead projector, with its exceptional flexibility of use and visual effectiveness, is outstanding as a visual communication device for the classroom teacher. Its ability to project accurate visual information to a large size under room light conditions makes the overhead projector an unusually versatile, true teaching tool. Any projector, however, including the overhead, is only as effective as the visual material it projects.

A problem facing the classroom teacher who uses the overhead projector has been the lack of effective visual material useable on this device. Professionally produced transparencies for the overhead are relatively expensive and limited in quantity and scope. Various reproduction processes on the market facilitate the local production of visuals, but these require creative ability on the part of the teacher to assure that the produced visuals are effective.

The Keuffel & Esser Company offers the Educator Approved Diazo Transparency Master Book as the solution to the classroom teacher's problem of obtaining high quality visual material for the overhead projector that is accurate, effective, and inexpensive. This book contains a wealth of carefully developed and tested visuals for the overhead projection medium. These visuals, expertly printed on K & E's famous Albanene* master paper, are designed for quick, easy reproduction onto Mercury™ diazo color projection film.

Completion of the Technical Graphics transparency series marks the availability of a basic "library" of K & E "Educator Approved" Diazo Transparency Master Books Publications. The previously published: Geometry, Physics, Chemistry, U.S. History and Biology have all met with an outstandingly favorable response from educators throughout the country; and are in constant use in our school systems' classrooms.

"Technical Graphics" joins this illustrious group as a primary contribution to the teaching of highly complex, visually oriented subject matter through the overhead projection technique.

In selecting its "Creative Consultant" for the Technical Graphics series, K & E was fortunate in finding Mr. W. R. Crosby. Mr. Crosby offers the most up-to-date experienced approach possible to the subject matter needs of today's drafting teacher.

Mr. Crosby combines his talents with the creative talent and artistic skills of Mr. Owen Finstad, the artist-visualizer of this project. Mr. Finstad's renown as a creator and visualizer of ultimate quality visual communication materials has been repeatedly acknowledged with his work on previous K & E transparency series.

K & E is proud to offer the educational field the results of this combination of talents and experience. We feel confident that this publication will make an outstanding contribution to visual communication in education.

Cover Verso

Additional information:
90 sets of Diazo transparency masters (8 1/2 x 11 in.); 474 pages; contained in a plastic notebook binder (30 cm. tall).

Instructions: Prepare a catalog record for this item.

***AACR2r* rules needed:** 1.1B1; 1.1C1; 1.1F1; 1.4F6; 1.5B1; 1.7B1; 1.7B6; 8.5B1; 8.5C2; 8.5C1j; 8.5D6; 21.0D1; 21.1A2; 21.29B; 21.30E1; 22.5A1; 24.1A; 24.5C1

Exercise 124

CD-ROM Disc 1 of 2

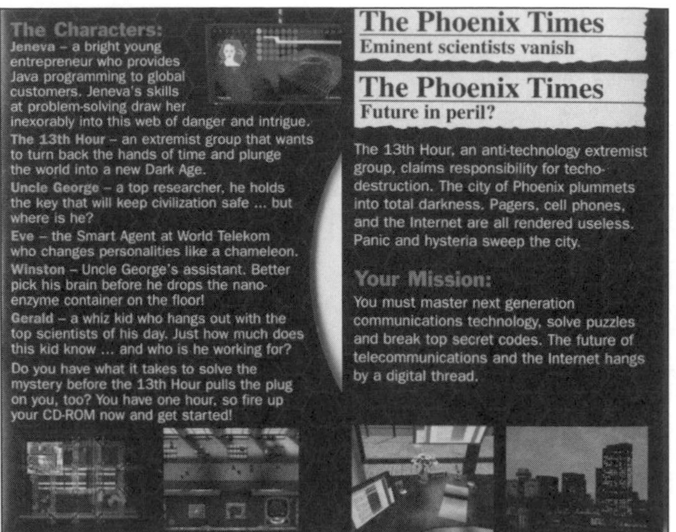

Inside Container

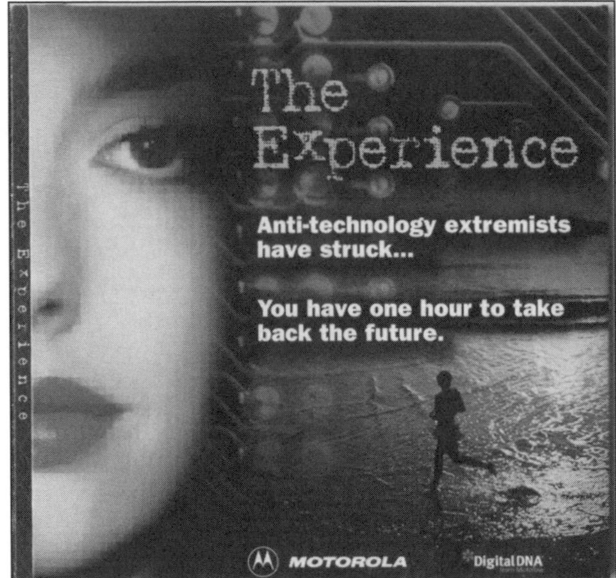

Front Cover

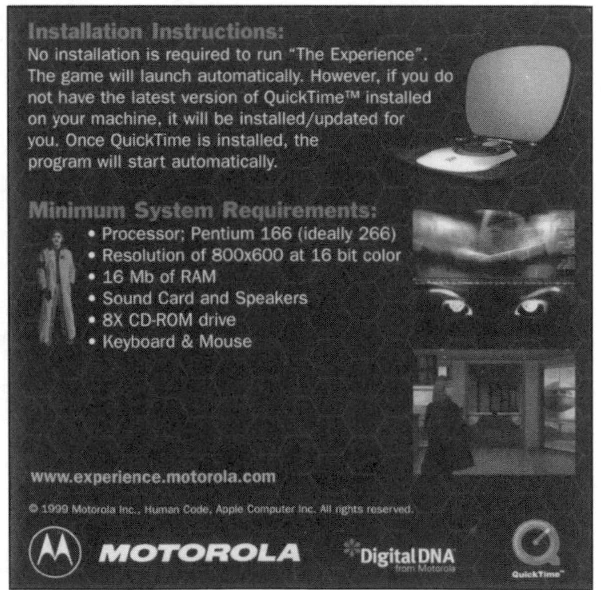

Back Cover

Instructions: Prepare a catalog record for this item.

***AACR2r* rules needed:** 1.1B1; 1.1C1; 1.1F1; 1.4D1; 1.4D2; 1.4F6; 1.5B1; 1.5C1; 1.5D1; 1.7B9; 1.7B10; 1.7B17; 1.7B18; 9.3B1; 9.5B1; 9.5C1; 9.5D1; 21.1C1a; 21.29C; 21.30E1; 24.1A

Exercise 125

Back Cover

Cover

Instructions: Prepare a catalog record for this item.

***AACR2r* rules needed:** 1.1B1; 1.1C1; 1.1E1; 1.2B1; 1.4C1; 1.4C3; 1.4D1; 1.5B1; 1.5D1; 1.7B1; 1.7B10; 1.7B17; 1.7B18; 6.5B1; 6.5D1; 6.7B1; 6.7B10; 6.7B17; 21.29B; 21.30E1

Exercise 126

Diskette Label

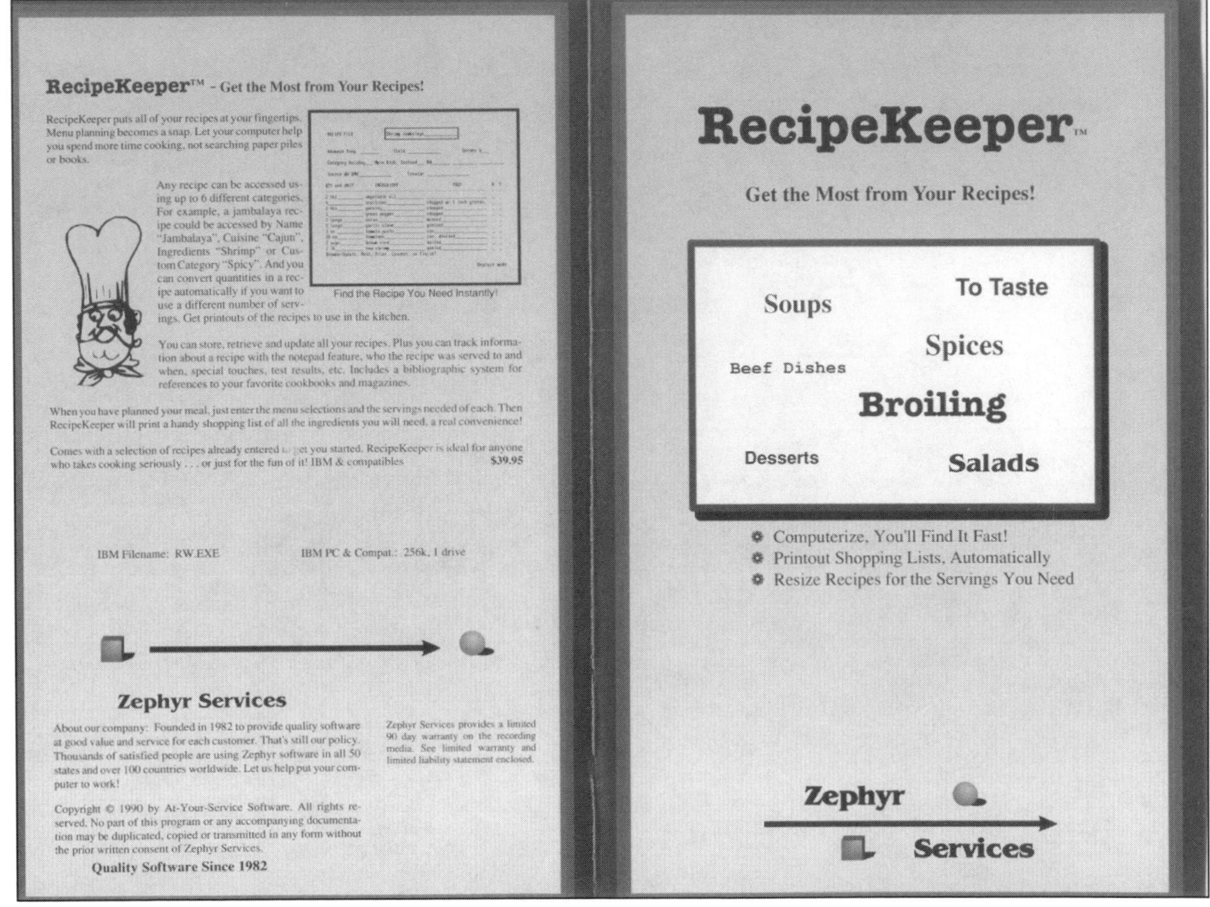

Cover

Additional information: A computer program on diskette with a 35-page guide (illustrated; 22 cm.)

Instructions: Prepare a catalog record for this item.

***AACR2r* rules needed:** 1.1B1; 1.1C1; 1.1F1; 1.4C1; 1.4C3; 1.4D1; 1.4F6; 1.5B1; 1.5D1; 1.5E1(e); 1.7B10; 1.7B17; 9.0B1; 9.5B1; 9.5D1; 9.5E1; 21.0B1; 21.1B2c

(*Continued on Next Page*)

Exercise 126

Welcome to Zephyr Services!

Thank you for choosing a Zephyr product. Basic information on starting and using the program is given here?plus some general tips on using your computer.

How To Start the Program

This information explains how to start the program on your computer. All programs have information provided on-screen for using the program after it is started. Some programs come with a manual; please review any manual for more details on program use.

Only the most straightforward steps to start the program are given here. If you are an experienced computer user you may wish to use other methods such as batch files, hard disk directories, system disks, etc. Your DOS manual explains more advanced computer usage.

General Information

You should first make a working copy of the original program diskette. Save the original diskette in a safe place as a backup in case your working copy becomes damaged.

Please follow the instructions in your computer manual for how to copy a diskette. Proceed carefully. (Some later versions of the IBM DOS are not totally compatible with earlier DOS versions when using the DISKCOPY command. Therefore, for the IBM you may need to format a blank diskette first then use the COPY command to copy all the files from the original diskette to the formatted diskette.)

NOTE: It is a violation of Federal law to make copies for use by anyone other than you the purchaser. The program and any documentation are copyrighted materials protected by U.S. Government and International Laws.

If you are using the program on a hard disk system, be sure to copy all files on the program diskette to the directory where the program is to be located. Also, be sure that the computer default drive is the one containing the program before you start to use the program. Your computer manual explains working with directories and drives.

Filename

In the instructions for starting the program, reference is made to the program filename. This is the filename for your computer type given on the reverse side of this sheet. Where filename is used in the instructions, substitute the actual filename for your program. For example, if the filename is FINANCER.EXE, then use FINANCER.EXE where the instructions show FILENAME.

IBM PC/XT/AT/PS2 & Compatibles

If the filename ends with .EXE

This type file is an executable file and is run directly from DOS. You should have the computer on and have the DOS prompt A> on the screen. (See below for how to get to A>)

Place the program disk in drive A: and close the door. Type and enter: FILENAME The program will load and start. Follow the instructions on the screen.

Getting To A>

If the computer is off, place the DOS system diskette in drive A: and turn on the computer. Answer any request for date and time. Then you will have A> on the screen.

If the computer is on, exit any program already running and return to DOS. If the DOS prompt is B> or C> then type and enter: A: to get to A>.

Commodore 64/128 Computers

Start with the computer, monitor and drive off. Turn on, in order, monitor, drive and computer. When READY appears on the screen, then insert the program disk into the drive and close door. Type and enter: LOAD"FILENAME",8 When screen reads READY, then type and enter: RUN The program will start. Follow instructions on screen.

Note that under some conditions you may see unexpected graphic symbols on the screen. If this occurs, press simultaneously the Commodore key and the Shift key. This will change the graphic symbols to normal characters. (The Commodore key is the one with the Commodore logo on it.)

APPLE IIe,IIc,IIgs and Compatibles

If the computer is off: Place the program disk in drive 1 and turn on the computer. The program will load and start. Follow the instructions on the screen.

If the computer is on: Finish use of any previously running program. Then press these three keys simultaneously: Open Apple, Ctrl and Reset. The program will load and start. Follow the instructions on screen.

Note that some early Apple computers will not automatically load and run a program. If this is true for your computer then use this method. With the DOS prompt on the screen and the program diskette in drive 1, type and enter: LOAD FILENAME When loading is complete type and enter: RUN Follow the instructions on screen. (See the note above about FILENAME.)

Also note that some programs may not run on some Apple II computers if they are not properly equipped to run ProDos programs. If this occurs please contact us for a possible DOS 3.3 version exchange.

Printing Program Output

Most programs have explicit menu options to send output to a printer. For explicit printing options just follow the information on screen. Some programs do not have explicit printing options but you can send information on the screen to the printer using the Print Screen Key (IBM computers) or Screen Dump Command (Apple computers).

IBM and Compatibles

To print what appears on the screen, press the Shift and Print Screen(PrtScr) keys at the same time. If the printer is on and ready, the screen information will printout.

For graphics information to print, (with a graphics capable printer), you must have first run the GRAPHICS.COM (or GRAPHICS.EXE) program at the DOS prompt (A> or C>) before running the program. GRAPHICS.COM is a program supplied on your DOS disk(s). Note that to print graphics information on the printer, the screen must be in the CGA graphics mode. You may need to set some EGA or VGA graphics cards to stay in the CGA mode if you want to print graphics. (The Dos GRAPHICS.COM program does not support EGA or VGA modes.)

Apple IIe/IIc/IIgs, C64 and Compatibles

These computers do not have built-in screen printing capabilities. You need to have an optional screen dump card installed to print screens. Most such cards require you to press certain key combinations and the screen will print-out. Follow the instructions for your hardware setup.

Printer Control Codes

Some programs request you to enter printer control codes. These are sets of three digit numbers that tell the printer what to do. For example if you want to have the printer print condensed (small) letters you might need the code 015 sent to the printer (you may need a different code for your printer). The code 018 may tell the computer to stop using the condensed letters.

Some printer commands may need two or even three codes sent. For example to skip over the paper perforation for Epson printers you use the codes 027 078 010. These codes are the decimal numbers that correspond to the ASCII codes used. Your printer manual may say the code is ESC N n for the skip over perforation command. These are the letter or symbol representations. You must use the decimal equivalents. Your computer operating manuals will normally have an ASCII character table giving the decimal numbers for each ASCII character.

For example the character A is code 065, the character a is 097 and the character 5 is 053. There are up to 256 ASCII characters (letters, numbers, symbols) depending on your computer type. Use these code numbers to translate your printer control codes (given in your printer manual) into three digit numbers to enter into the programs. If your printer does not have a feature called for by a program just use the code 000 which the printer will accept but ignore. Because there are hundreds of different printers, we are not able to supply all possible codes but explain the meaning of the code system so you can use the codes for your printer.

Registration Card

Please return the registration card so that we may provide you any news of program upgrades or other information on Zephyr products. Your comments on our programs are always welcome. Thank you for using Zephyr products!

Free Catalog If you did not receive a Zephyr catalog with this product, please write to request one.

Zephyr Services
1900 Murray Ave.
Pittsburgh, PA 15217

Limited 90-Day Warranty

The recording medium (diskette) is warranted to be free from material physical defects for 90 days from the date of purchase.

Should the diskette become defective during the warranty period, send your name and address and original diskette postpaid along with dated proof of purchase and a replacement disk will be sent to you free of charge.

Other Limitations

This warranty does not cover material that has been lost, stolen or damaged by accident or misuse. No other warranty, express or implied, including merchantability or fitness for a purpose is proved.

Zephyr Services will not be liable for special, incidental, consequential, or similar damages and in no event will its liability for any damages ever exceed the purchase price of this product.

Verso of Cover

W E L C O M E!

Welcome to The RecipeKeeper; soon, cooking will be more of a pleasure and less of a chore. The RecipeKeeper puts an end to recipe rubble, magazine mess, grocery guesswork, and dinner dullness!

You don't have to be a computer whiz to enjoy The RecipeKeeper. Simply complete the tutorial; you'll use these features in no time:

* Store, update, and retrieve recipes
* Convert recipes to usable quantities instantly
* Create customized cross references, using categories, ingredients, nutrition, etc.
* Generate a shopping list automatically
* Maintain bibliographic entries from your favorite cookbooks and magazines
* Track important recipe information with the notepad: who it was served to, special touches, reactions, test results, menus, guests, etc.
* Take printouts to the kitchen; no more messy cards

REQUIREMENTS

You need MS/PC-DOS (version 2.0 or higher), 192 KB of RAM (random access memory), and at least one floppy disk drive. An IBM compatible parallel printer is optional but required for printing.

MAKING COPIES OF The RecipeKeeper

It's OK to make copies of The RecipeKeeper for yourself as backups. It's not OK to make copies for other purposes, such as "lending" or "sharing" with a friend or relative. That type of duplication is against the law. Please read the next page for details

Created by:
At-Your-Service-Software

Published by:
Zephyr Services
1900 Murray Ave.
Pittsburgh, PA 15217

First Page of Guide

Exercise 127

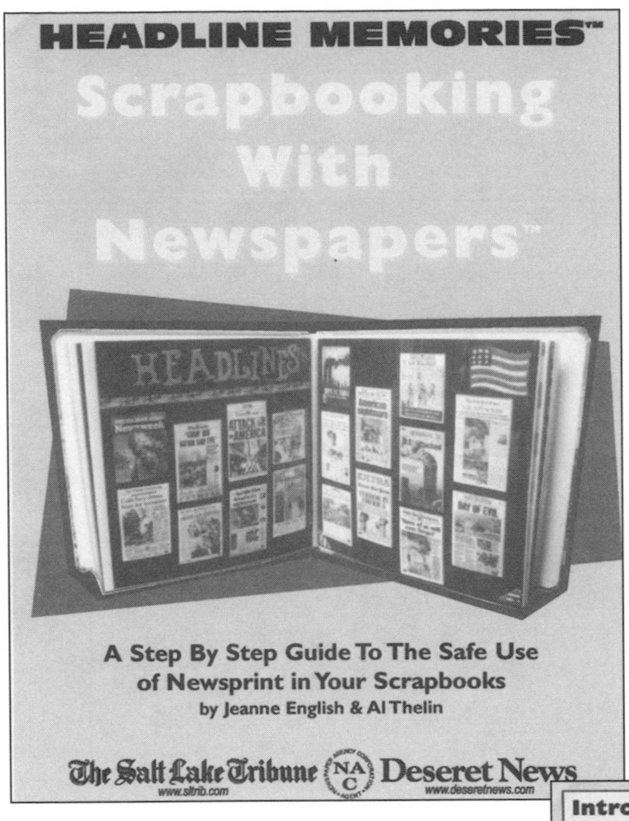

Top Level Web Page

Sample Internal Web Page

Introduction

Welcome to the world of scrapbooking with newspapers. Even though it's been done since the birth of the newspaper, it has never really been popular – UNTIL NOW!! In the past, scrapbookers have been trying to minimize the usage of original newsprint in scrapbooks. Why? Because of its acid and lignin content, both of which are harmful to photos and precious documents. BUT NOW, scrapping with newsprint is ALL THE RAGE. In can be done the easiest way possible with the HEADLINE MEMORIES™ newspaper scrapbook.

So start you newspaper scrapbook today! What is your interest or passion? Golf? Chocolate? Success Stories? Politics? Medical Discoveries? Sports Heroes? Great Events In History? A Favorite Comic Strip? Perennial Flowers? Imagine the fun you will have putting together an entire scrapbook full of news clippings that relate to your interest. Just think how much more savvy you will become in your area of interest. You may even become an expert!

Along with the fun and satisfaction you will derive, think of the treasures you will create for future generations. Someone in the future will have your same passion, and will consider your scrapbooks a goldmine!

The proper materials and methods are now available for safe newspaper scrapbooking. Headline Memories newspaper scrapbooks are made of quality acid-free paper and polypropylene sheet protectors that will help to preserve your clippings for a long, long time. The following step-by-step directions will help you with the simple process of newspaper scrapbooking.

Washing

Why do I want to wash my newspaper clippings? If the newspaper clipping is important to your heritage, washing can be one of

Scrapbooking can be easy as simply filing or quickly adhering your clippings in a Headline Memories scrapbook. (layout by Liz Whitesides)

the very best things you can do. Not only does it wash out the acid and give the paper a fresh start, but it also allows the fibers to expand and bond together to strengthen the paper. This is especially recommended for old newspapers that have been sitting around waiting to be preserved. Will the clippings turn to paper maché? No! Washing really works. Just follow these simple steps:

1. Cut and trim your newspaper clipping to a size that will fit in a 9" x 13" x 3" glass dish. It won't hurt to cut the clipping in sections to fit the dish because it will be put on a scrapbook page anyway.

Elaborate! with lots of special keepsakes and copied clippings. (layout by Debbie Anderson)

2. Pour distilled water, to a level of about one inch, into the dish.
3. Immerse the clipping in the water and let it soak for at least 20 minutes. If the water turns yellow, repeat the procedure.

Prepare a clean flat surface such as your kitchen counter top (it cannot be wood), and carefully lay the wet newspaper clipping flat. It will take about an hour to dry. If the temperature is around an even 70 degrees the article will dry flatter. A hot day will cause the edges to curl, but once you put it in your scrapbook, it will flatten again.

Any and all themes can be archived in your scrapbooks. (layout by Talia Hristou)

4. Optional: Spray with Archival Mist™ and Paper Bright™ (see below) to put a protective buffering on the clipping.

Arrange the clipping attractively on your scrapbook page.

Spraying

What if you need to preserve a whole page or section of the newspaper? The process of washing a whole page or section of a newspaper is difficult and impractical. Instead, use Archival Mist™ which is a spray especially made for deacidification and Paper Bright™ which absorbs UV light to prevent newspapers from fading and turning yellow. Both products are non-toxic, non-hazardous, non-flammable and odor free. For best results, use both products. The directions are on the consumer-friendly bottles.

1. Lay out tissue paper, so you have a clean surface.
2. Place the newspaper out flat on the tissue.
3. Use the Archival Mist product first.
4. Shake the container and pump its cap until firm.
5. Hold it about six inches away from the newspaper, and spray a light even application from left to right.
6. Repeat this process on the other side of the newspaper.
7. Next use Paper Bright and repeat steps 4 and 5, but spray only the front side of the newspaper.
8. It is important to let the newspaper dry thoroughly before you scrap-

Announcements make great scrapbook memories for your family. (layout by Paige Hill)

Additional information:
URL: http://www.headlinememories.com/Guide.html. This is a .pdf file. Publication information: Headline Memories, Wayne Matthews Corp., Safety Harbor, FL, 2001.

Instructions: Prepare a catalog record for this item.

***AACR2r* rules needed:** 1.1B1; 1.1C1; 1.1E1; 1.1F1; 1.1F4; 1.1F6; 1.3A; 1.4C1; 1.4C3; 1.4D1; 1.4F5; 1.7B; 1.7B3; 1.7B14; 1.7B17; 9.0B1; 9.1B1; 9.1B2; 9.1C1; 9.1E1; 9.1F1; 9.3B1; 9.4B2; 9.4D1; 9.7B1a; 9.7B1b; 9.7B1c; 9.7B3; 9.7B17; 9.7B22; 21.1A2; 21.6B1; 21.6B2; 21.30E1; 21.30F1; 22.5F1; 24.1A; MARC 856

Exercise 128

Reproduction of Portions of Webpage

Authority Tools for Audiovisual and Music Catalogers: An Annotated List of Useful Resources

Originally compiled by
Subcommittee on Authority Tools
Cataloging Policy Committee
OnLine Audiovisual Catalogers, Inc.
Robert Bratton, editor: 2003-
Content last revised: January 2, 2004

CONTENTS

INTRODUCTION

This list is designed to bring together, in one place, descriptions of information sources that are useful when developing authorized headings to support audiovisual and music catalog records. Work began on this project in 1999, and the list was first released in 2001.

Before we embarked on this project, we investigated what similar tools might already exist. After all, there is no point in reinventing the wheel! We did not find much. One valuable resource we did find was put together by the Working Group on Popular Music Sources, under the aegis of the Music Library Association Bibliographic Control Committee. Between 1991 and 1993, they compiled an annotated guide to resources used in cataloging various genres of popular music. Though it has not been updated, it is still very useful. It is available at http://www.music.indiana.edu/tech_s/mla/wgpms/wgpms.htm.

Our goal in putting together this list of resources is to highlight some of the tools that we find useful when creating authority records. We ask practitioners to contribute annotations, or short reviews, to explain

(Continued on Next Page)

Exercise 128

why they think a particular tool is useful for authority work. Each entry also includes a suggested way of citing the work in authority records.

We would like to take this opportunity to thank the many people who helped make this list possible. The OLAC Cataloging Policy Committee (CAPC) provided the forum for discussion about the list and electronic space for it on the OLAC website. CAPC appointed the Subcommittee on Authority Tools whose job it was to organize and compile the original list. Sue Neumeister deserves considerable appreciation for graciously providing the HTML mark-up. Of course there would be no list without the valuable contributions of titles and annotations given by AV catalogers. These folks deserve many thanks for their time and effort.

Subcommittee on Authority Tools

David Procházka, Co-Chair
Iris Wolley, Co-Chair
Robert Bratton
Ann Caldwell
Robert B. Freeborn

Additional information:
Web site: http://ublib.buffalo.edu/libraries/units/cts/olac/capc/authtools.html
Accessed May 4, 2004

Instructions: Prepare a catalog record for this item.

***AACR2r* rules needed:** 1.0A1; 1.1C1; 1.1B1; 1.1E1; 1.1F1; 1.1F6; 1.3A; 1.4B1; 1.4C6; 1.4D2; 1.4F8; 9.0B1; 9.1B2; 9.3B1; 9.4B2; 9.4C1; 9.4D1; 9.4F1; 9.7B1c; 9.7B3; 9.7B7; 9.7B17; 9.7B18; 9.7B22; 21.0D1; 21.1B1; 21.1B2a; 21.30D; 21.30J1; 22.5B1; 24.1A; 24.13A; 24.14

Exercise 129

Cover

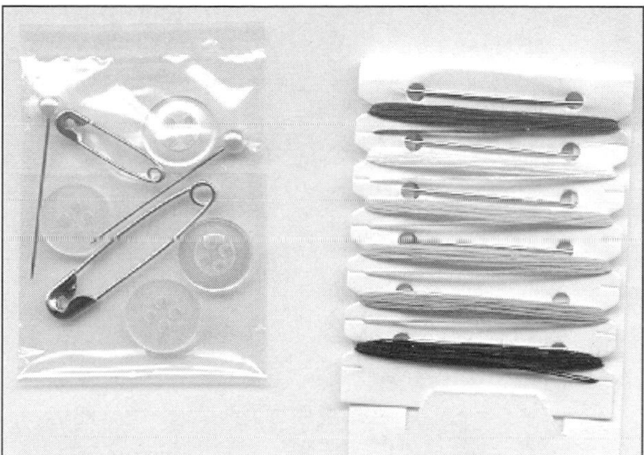

Contents

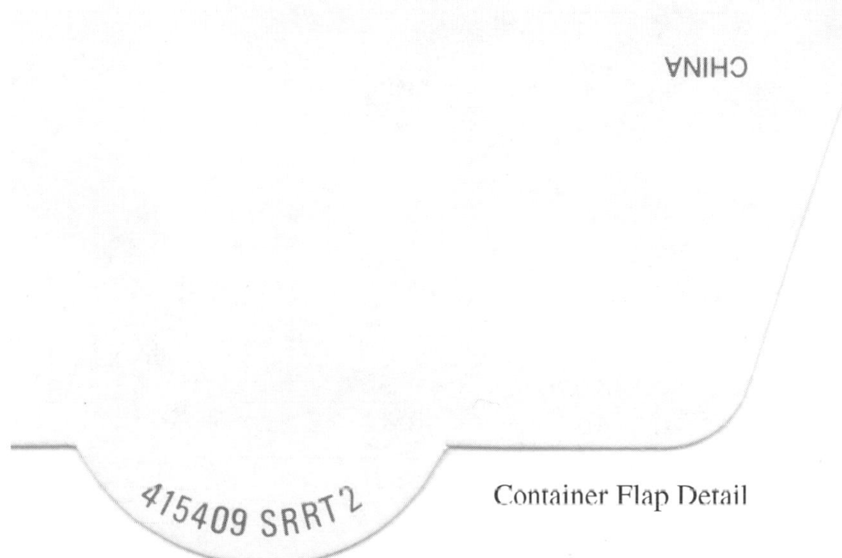

Container Flap Detail

Additional information:
In a paper container folded to 9 x 10 cm. Each thread skein has an attached needle. Acquired in the United States in 1998.

Instructions: Prepare a catalog record for this item.

***AACR2r* rules needed:** 1.1B1; 1.1F2; 1.4C6; 1.4D6; 1.4F7; 1.5B1; 1.5D1; 1.10C; 1.10C1; 1.10C2a; 10.5B1; 10.5C1; 10.5D2

Exercise 130

View of Front of Container

INSTRUCTIONS
ADJUSTABLE LIGHT REFLECTOR
PLACE SLIDE ON VIEWING PLATFORM, TURN DIAL TO FOCUS
SWING OUT TRAY FOR SLIDE STORAGE
NO.16063B
0 76666 16063 1
MADE IN CHINA
NO.16063B
0 76666 16063 1
Marketed by Wal-Mart Stores, Inc.
Bentonville, AR 72716
Shop at www.wal-mart.com
MADE IN CHINA

Back of Container & Detail

Additional information: Includes a microscope, forceps, dropper, two specimen tubes in a rack, and five specimen slides in a holder in container (30 x 18 cm.). Statement on package liner: For ages 5 and up.

Instructions: Prepare a catalog record for this item.

***AACR2r* rules needed:** 1.1B1; 1.1C1, List 2; 1.1C4; 1.1F2; 1.10C1; 1.10C2a; 1.1F2; 1.4D2; 1.4D3A; 1.4G1; 1.7B14; 1.7B17; 1.7B19; 10.10A; 21.1C; 24.1A; MARC 028

Exercise 131

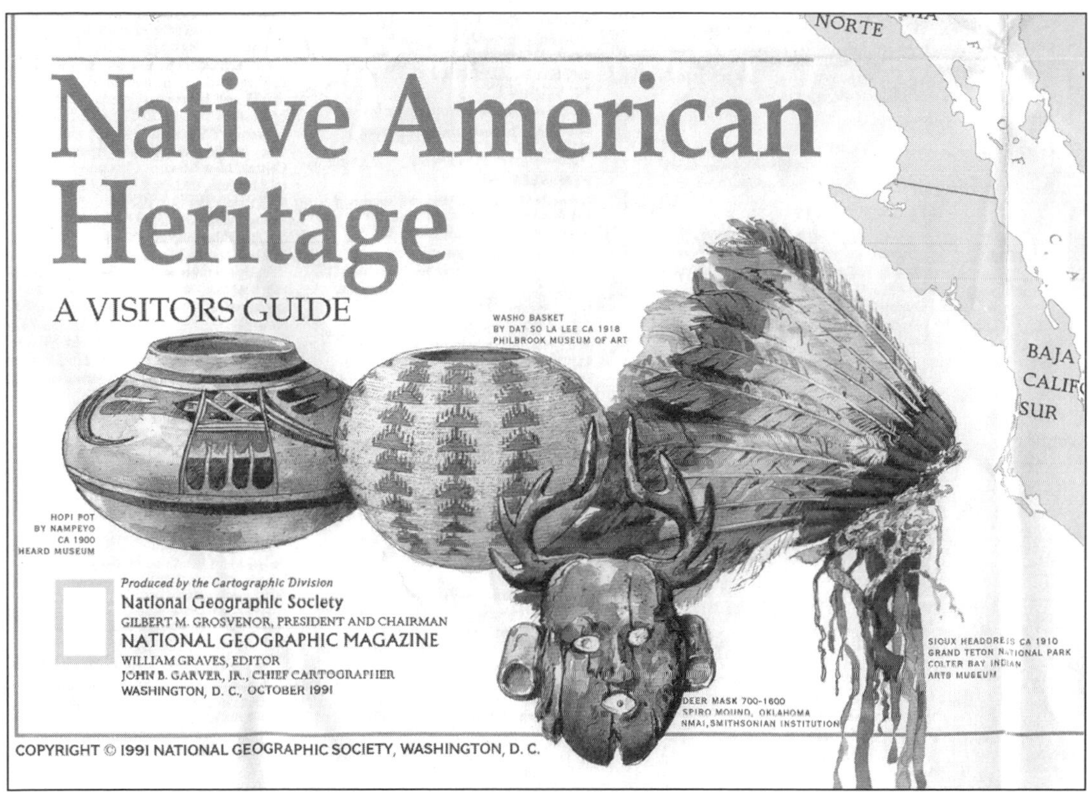

Detail from Front of Map

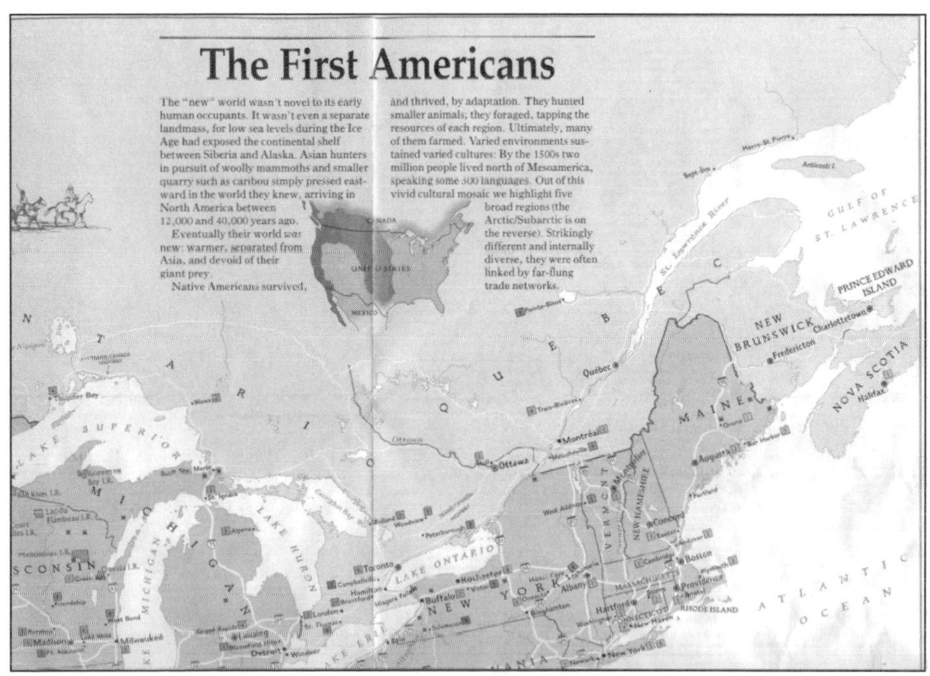

Top Right Quadrant of Map

(*Continued on Next Page*)

Exercise 131

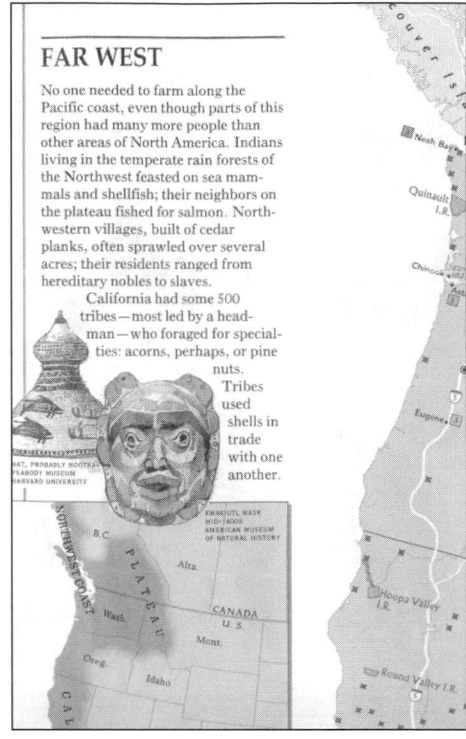

FAR WEST
No one needed to farm along the Pacific coast, even though parts of this region had many more people than other areas of North America. Indians living in the temperate rain forests of the Northwest feasted on sea mammals and shellfish; their neighbors on the plateau fished for salmon. Northwestern villages, built of cedar planks, often sprawled over several acres; their residents ranged from hereditary nobles to slaves.
California had some 500 tribes—most led by a headman—who foraged for specialties: acorns, perhaps, or pine nuts. Tribes used shells in trade with one another.
KWAKIUTL MASK MID-1800S AMERICAN MUSEUM OF NATURAL HISTORY
NORTHWEST COAST
PLATEAU
B.C.
Alta.
CANADA
U. S.
Wash.
Mont.
Oreg.
Idaho
Quinault I.R.
Eugene
Hoopa Valley I.R.
Round Valley I.R.

Inside Detail from Front of Map

Additional information:
50 x 71 cm., folded to 14 x 19 cm.; in color; insets include: "The First Americans," "Eastern Woodlands," "Great Plains," "Desert West," "Far West."
Scale: 1:7,747,000. 1 cm. = 77 km; 1 in. = 122 miles. Albers conical equal-area projection, standard parallels 29'30 and 45'30. LCCN: 98-680615

Instructions: Prepare a catalog record for this item.

When cataloging this item, consider the following: Physical description, scale, and projection information.

***AACR2r* rules needed:** 1.1B1; 1.1C1; 1.1E1; 1.1F1; 1.1F6; 1.3A; 1.4C1; 1.4C3; 1.4D1; 1.4F1; 1.5B1; 1.5C1; 1.5D1; 1.7B17; 1.7B18; 3.0B1; 3.3B1; 3.3B4; 3.5B1; 3.5C1; 3.5C5; 3.5D1; 21.1C1a; 21.29B; 21.30A1; 21.30E1; 22.5A1; 24.1A; 24.4C2; MARC 010

Supplement to the National Geographic, October 1991, Page 2A, Vol. 180 No. 4 - NATIVE AMERICAN HERITAGE

Map Detail

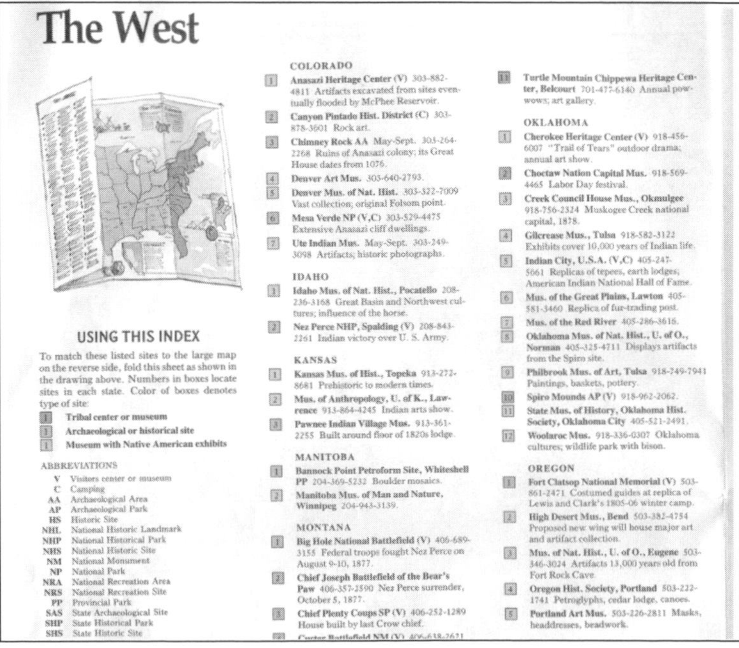

The West

USING THIS INDEX

To match these listed sites to the large map on the reverse side, fold this sheet as shown in the drawing above. Numbers in boxes locate sites in each state. Color of boxes denotes type of site:

- 1 **Tribal center or museum**
- 1 **Archaeological or historical site**
- 1 **Museum with Native American exhibits**

ABBREVIATIONS

- **V** Visitors center or museum
- **C** Camping
- **AA** Archaeological Area
- **AP** Archaeological Park
- **HS** Historic Site
- **NHL** National Historic Landmark
- **NHP** National Historical Park
- **NHS** National Historic Site
- **NM** National Monument
- **NP** National Park
- **NRA** National Recreation Area
- **NRS** National Recreation Site
- **PP** Provincial Park
- **SAS** State Archaeological Site
- **SHP** State Historical Park
- **SHS** State Historic Site

COLORADO

1. **Anasazi Heritage Center (V)** 303-882-4811 Artifacts excavated from sites eventually flooded by McPhee Reservoir.
2. **Canyon Pintado Hist. District (C)** 303-878-3601 Rock art.
3. **Chimney Rock AA** May-Sept. 303-264-2268 Ruins of Anasazi colony; its Great House dates from 1076.
4. **Denver Art Mus.** 303-640-2793.
5. **Denver Mus. of Nat. Hist.** 303-322-7009 Vast collection; original Folsom point.
6. **Mesa Verde NP (V,C)** 303-529-4475 Extensive Anasazi cliff dwellings.
7. **Ute Indian Mus.** May-Sept. 303-249-3098 Artifacts; historic photographs.

IDAHO

1. **Idaho Mus. of Nat. Hist., Pocatello** 208-236-3168 Great Basin and Northwest cultures; influence of the horse.
2. **Nez Perce NHP, Spalding (V)** 208-843-2261 Indian victory over U. S. Army.

KANSAS

1. **Kansas Mus. of Hist., Topeka** 913-272-8681 Prehistoric to modern times.
2. **Mus. of Anthropology, U. of K., Lawrence** 913-864-4245 Indian arts show.
3. **Pawnee Indian Village Mus.** 913-361-2255 Built around floor of 1820s lodge.

MANITOBA

1. **Bannock Point Petroform Site, Whiteshell PP** 204-369-5232 Boulder mosaics.
2. **Manitoba Mus. of Man and Nature, Winnipeg** 204-943-3139.

MONTANA

1. **Big Hole National Battlefield (V)** 406-689-3155 Federal troops fought Nez Perce on August 9-10, 1877.
2. **Chief Joseph Battlefield of the Bear's Paw** 406-357-2590 Nez Perce surrender, October 5, 1877.
3. **Chief Plenty Coups SP (V)** 406-252-1289 House built by last Crow chief.
4. **Custer Battlefield NM (V)** 406-638-2621

13. **Turtle Mountain Chippewa Heritage Center, Belcourt** 701-477-6140 Annual powwows; art gallery.

OKLAHOMA

1. **Cherokee Heritage Center (V)** 918-456-6007 "Trail of Tears" outdoor drama; annual art show.
2. **Choctaw Nation Capital Mus.** 918-569-4465 Labor Day festival.
3. **Creek Council House Mus., Okmulgee** 918-756-2324 Muskogee Creek national capital, 1878.
4. **Gilcrease Mus., Tulsa** 918-582-3122 Exhibits cover 10,000 years of Indian life.
5. **Indian City, U.S.A. (V,C)** 405-247-5661 Replicas of tepees, earth lodges; American Indian National Hall of Fame.
6. **Mus. of the Great Plains, Lawton** 405-581-3460 Replica of fur-trading post.
7. **Mus. of the Red River** 405-286-3616.
8. **Oklahoma Mus. of Nat. Hist., U. of O., Norman** 405-325-4711 Displays artifacts from the Spiro site.
9. **Philbrook Mus. of Art, Tulsa** 918-749-7941 Paintings, baskets, pottery.
10. **Spiro Mounds AP (V)** 918-962-2062.
11. **State Mus. of History, Oklahoma Hist. Society, Oklahoma City** 405-521-2491.
12. **Woolaroc Mus.** 918-336-0307 Oklahoma cultures; wildlife park with bison.

OREGON

1. **Fort Clatsop National Memorial (V)** 503-861-2471 Costumed guides at replica of Lewis and Clark's 1805-06 winter camp.
2. **High Desert Mus., Bend** 503-382-4754 Proposed new wing will house major art and artifact collection.
3. **Mus. of Nat. Hist., U. of O., Eugene** 503-346-3024 Artifacts 13,000 years old from Fort Rock Cave.
4. **Oregon Hist. Society, Portland** 503-222-1741 Petroglyphs, cedar lodge, canoes.
5. **Portland Art Mus.** 503-226-2811 Masks, headdresses, beadwork.

Detail from Verso of Map

Exercise 132

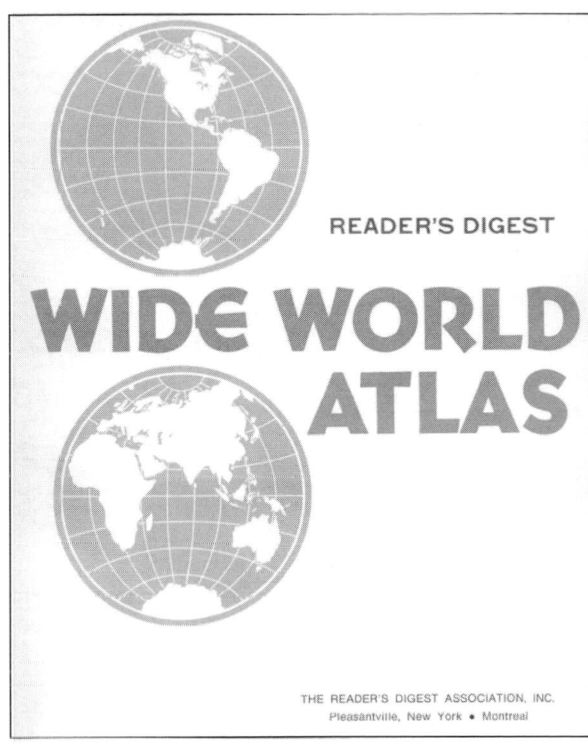

READER'S DIGEST

WIDE WORLD ATLAS

THE READER'S DIGEST ASSOCIATION, INC.
Pleasantville, New York • Montreal

Title Page

Wide World Atlas
Copyright © 1979 The Reader's Digest Association, Inc.
Copyright © 1979 *The Reader's Digest Association* (Canada) Ltd.
Copyright © 1979 Reader's Digest Association Far East Ltd.
Philippine Copyright 1979 Reader's Digest Association Far East Ltd.

Maps and other materials in this book were originally published and copyrighted as follows:
Pages 6 through 144 and pages 196 through 240 from *The International Atlas* © 1979, 1974, 1969 by Rand McNally & Company reedited for *The Rand McNally Concise Atlas of the Earth* © 1976 by Rand McNally & Company. Pages 146 through 151 and pages 190 through 195 from *Cosmopolitan World Atlas* © 1978, 1971, 1961 by Rand McNally & Company. Pages 152 through 167 from *Goode's World Atlas* © 1978, 1974 by Rand McNally & Company. Pages 168 through 189 © 1979, 1974 by Encyclopaedia Britannica.

Reproduction in any manner, in whole or in part, in English or in other languages, is prohibited. All rights reserved.
Library of Congress Catalog Card Number 78-65321

ISBN 0-89577-062-8

Printed for The Reader's Digest Association, Inc.
in the United States of America

2

Title Page Verso

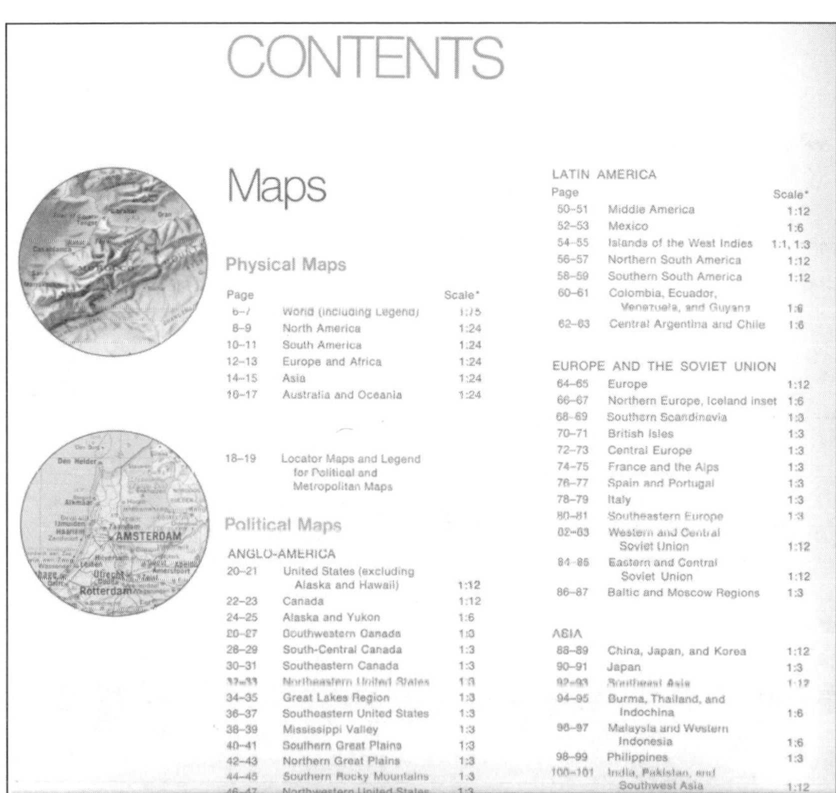

CONTENTS

Maps

Physical Maps

Political Maps

ANGLO-AMERICA

LATIN AMERICA

EUROPE AND THE SOVIET UNION

ASIA

(*Continued on Next Page*)

Exercise 132

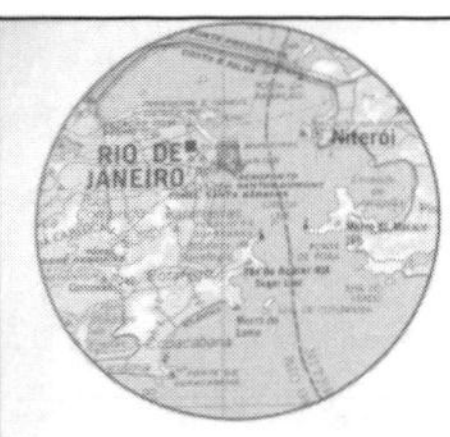

The World in Theme Maps

Metropolitan Maps**

The Earth and Space

Environmental Maps

World View

Ocean Floor Maps

* 1:75 or 1:75,000,000, meaning 1 centimeter on the map represents 750 kilometers on the ground (1 inch represents approximately 1,185 miles)

1:24 or 1:24,000,000, meaning 1 centimeter on the map represents 240 kilometers on the ground (1 inch represents approximately 380 miles)

1:12 or 1:12,000,000, meaning 1 centimeter on the map represents 120 kilometers on the ground (1 inch represents approximately 190 miles)

1:6 or 1:6,000,000, meaning 1 centimeter on the map represents 60 kilometers on the ground (1 inch represents approximately 95 miles)

1:3 or 1:3,000,000, meaning 1 centimeter on the map represents 30 kilometers on the ground (1 inch represents approximately 47 miles)

1:1 or 1:1,000,000, meaning 1 centimeter on the map represents 10 kilometers on the ground (1 inch represents approximately 16 miles)

** All Metropolitan Maps are at a scale of 1:300,000, meaning 1 centimeter on the map represents 3 kilometers on the ground (1 inch represents approximately 4.7 miles)

Tables and Index

Table of Contents—2nd page

Additional information:
240 pages; color illustrations; color maps; 39 cm.; "Reader's Digest joined Rand McNally … to produce this concise yet comprehensive edition of *The International Atlas.*"

Instructions: Prepare a catalog record for this item.

***AACR2r* rules needed:** 1.1B1; 1.1C1; 1.1F1; 1.3A; 1.4C1; 1.4C3; 1.4D1; 1.4D2; 1.4F6; 1.5B1; 1.5C1; 1.7B9; 1.7B18; 1.8B1; 3.0B1; 3.3B4; 3.5B3; 3.5C4; 3.5C5; 21.1C1; 21.29D; 21.30E1; 21.30J2; 24.1A; 24.5C1; App B.9; MARC 010; MARC 020

Exercise 133

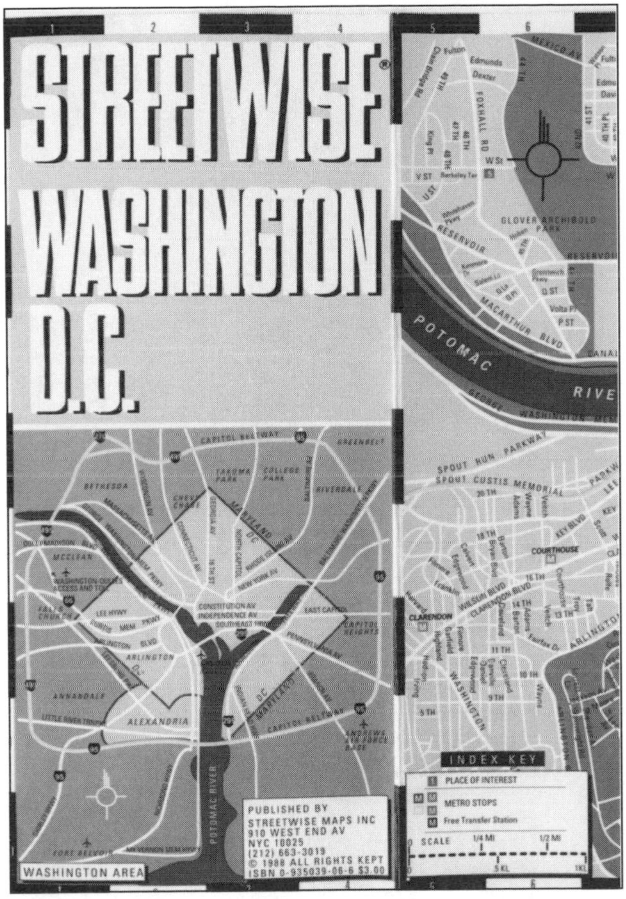

Portion of Front Panel

Additional information:
Foldout, plastic-coated, two-sided sheet; color; 22 cm. high and 50 cm. wide; folded dimension, 22 cm. and 10 cm.; scale 1/2 to 1 mile [ca. 1:40,000] Includes a street index, place index, list of parks and gardens, metrorail system map, and street map.

Instructions: Prepare a catalog record for this item.

***AACR2r* rules needed:** 1.1A2; 1.1B1; 1.1F1; 1.1F3; 1.3A; 1.4B4; 1.4C1; 1.4C4; 1.4D2; 1.4F6; 1.5B1; 1.5B3; 1.5C1; 1.5D1; 1.7B8; 1.7B18; 1.8B1; 3.0B2; 3.3B1; 3.3B4; 3.5B1; 3.5B2; 3.5C1; 3.5C2; 3.5C7; 3.5D1; 3.7B8; 3.7B18; 21.1B2; 21.30J2; 24.1A; MARC 020

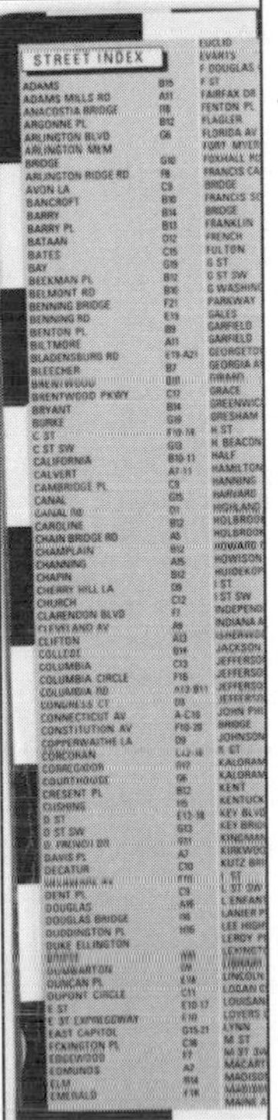

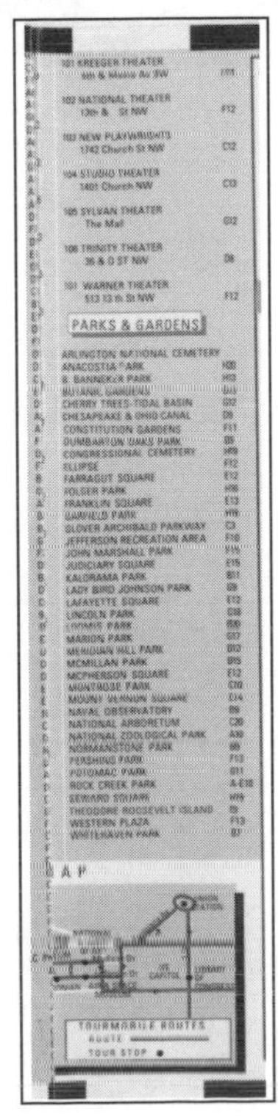

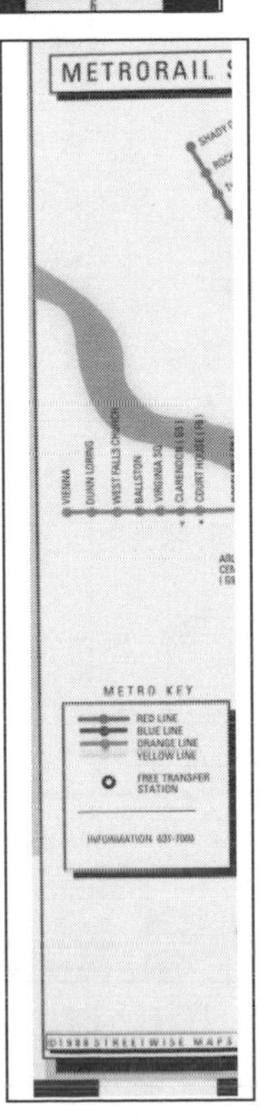

Portions of Verso

Exercise 134

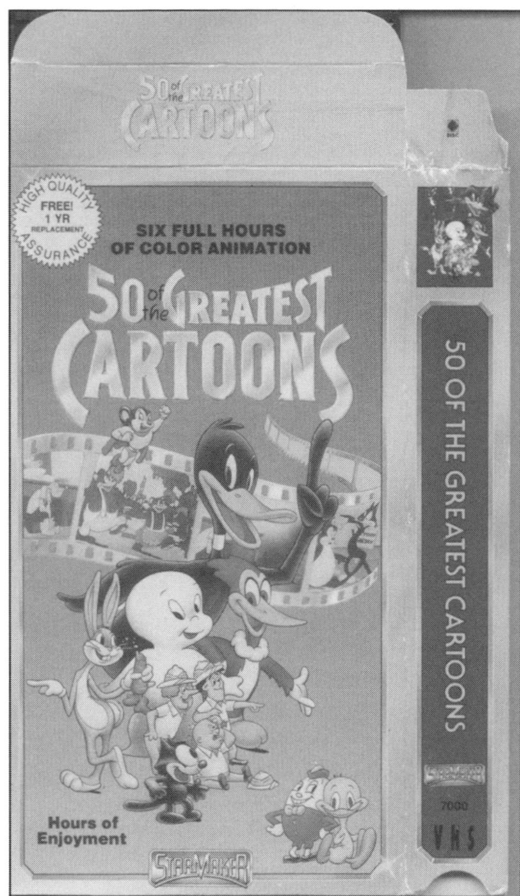

Case Front Cover

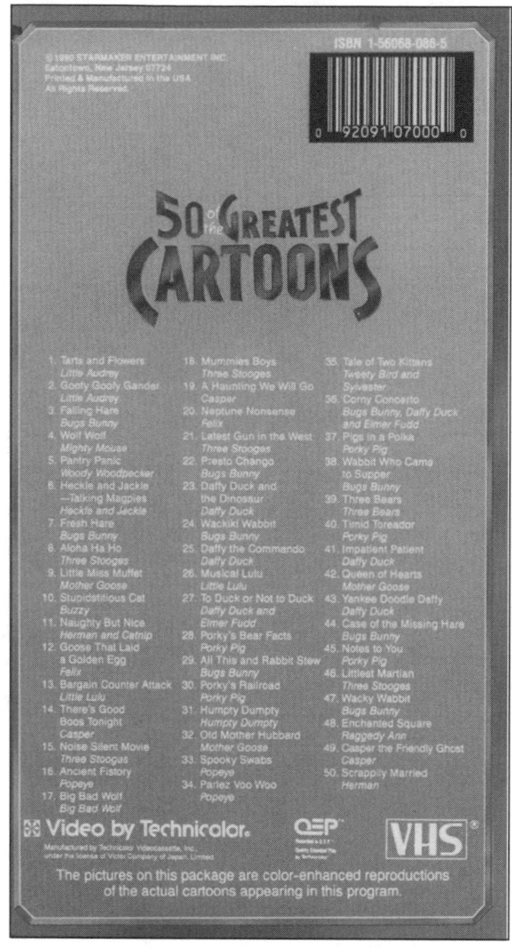

Case Back Cover (negative image)

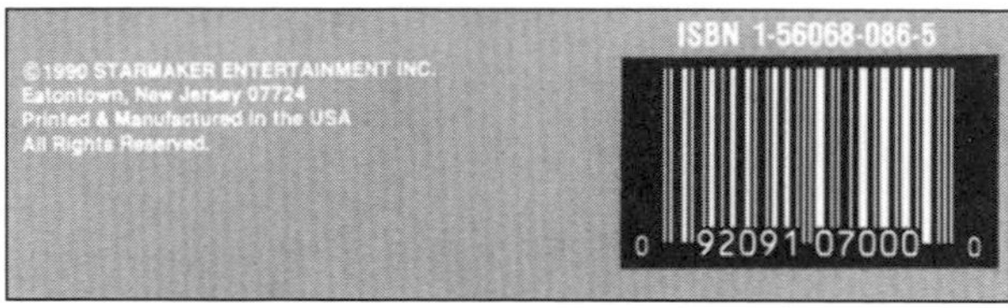

Detail from Case Back Cover (negative image)

Videocassette Label

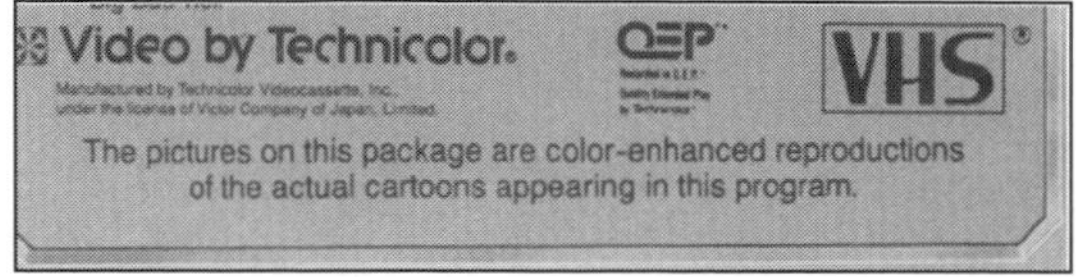

Detail from Case Back Cover

Instructions: Prepare a catalog record for this item.

***AACR2r* rules needed:** 1.1B1; 1.1C1; 1.4C1; 1.4C3; 1.4D1; 1.4D2; 1.4F1; 1.4F6; 1.5B1; 1.5B4; 1.5C1; 1.5D1; 1.7B1; 1.7B7; 1.7B10; 1.7B17; 1.7B18; 1.8B1; 7.0B1; 7.0B2; 7.5B2; 7.5C4; 7.7B1; 7.7B10c; 7.7B10f; 7.7B18; 21.1C1a; 21.1C1b; 21.1C1c; 21.7B1; MARC 020; MARC 028; MARC 655

Exercise 135

Case Cover

Les Bonnes

Genet's provocative play about two treacherous maid-servants who simultaneously love and hate their mistress. When they fail in their attempt to murder her, they manage to achieve the fate they have earned. Yet Genet sees humanity even in satanic urges and demands that we understand, rather than condemn, the fallen maids and their fallen mistress.

(**French**, 110 minutes, color)

French Literature on video includes works by:

Racine	Victor Hugo	Jean Genet
Molière	Balzac	Jean Giraudoux
Voltaire	Maupassant	Beckett
Marivaux	Flaubert	Nathalie Sarraute
Diderot	Simone de Beauvoir	

For more information on these and other programs, please call **800/257-5126** or **609/452-1128.**

NOTICE: This program is copyright under US and applicable international laws. It is a violation of copyright law to copy, duplicate, edit, or broadcast this program for any reason or by any means without prior written contract from FILMS FOR THE HUMANITIES & SCIENCES, INC. It is the policy of FILMS FOR THE HUMANITIES & SCIENCES, INC. to protect its copyright and prosecute copyright violators to the full extent of the law.

COPYRIGHT © 1991 FILMS FOR THE HUMANITIES & SCIENCES, INC • Box 2053 • Princeton, NJ 08543-2053

Case Back Cover

Videocassette Label

Jean Genet: *Les Bonnes*

FFH 996

FILMS FOR THE HUMANITIES & SCIENCES, INC

This videocassette is copyright under U.S. and applicable international law. It may not be broadcast, edited, or duplicated without the express written consent of Films for the Humanities, Inc.

Additional information:
Copyright 1991; sound, color; ISBN 0852616503; series: Glasgow introductory guides to French literature; vol. 42

Instructions: Prepare a catalog record for this item.

***AACR2r* rules needed:** 1.1B1; 1.1C1; 1.1F1; 1.1F6; 1.4C1; 1.4D1; 1.4D2; 1.4F6; 1.5B1; 1.5B4; 1.5C1; 1.7B2; 1.7B10; 1.7B17; 1.7B19; 7.0B1; 7.1C1; 7.5B1; 7.5B2; 7.5C3; 7.5C4; 7.5D3; 7.7B10f; 21.1A2; 21.30A1; 21.30F1; 22.5A1; MARC 028

Exercise 136

CONTEMPORARY AUTHORS:
HOW THE SERIES IS COMPILED AND EDITED.

Label on Videocassette Case

Contemporary Authors

How the series is compiled and edited

GALE RESEARCH CO.
DETROIT, MICHIGAN

running time: 11 minutes

Label on Videocassette

Additional information:
Copyright probably 1982; sound, color

Instructions: Prepare a catalog record for this item.

***AACR2r* rules needed:** 1.1B1; 1.1C1; 1.1E2; 1.4C1; 1.4C3; 1.4D2; 1.4F6; 1.5B1; 1.5B4; 1.5C1; 1.5D1; 7.0B1; 7.5B1; 7.5B2; 7.5C1; 7.5C3; 7.5C4; 7.5D1; 7.5D3; MARC 630

Exercise 137

MANAGING DIVERSITY
Diversity Leadership

FILMS FOR THE HUMANITIES & SCIENCES®

This videocassette is copyright under U.S. and applicable international law. It may not be broadcast, edited, or duplicated without the express written consent of Films for the Humanities & Sciences®.

FFH 6891

Videocassette Label

MANAGING Diversity

diversity leadership

Managing a diverse workforce, with its multicultural, gender, and handicap issues, requires special skills. This outstanding four-part series illustrates how to assess diversity within an organization, and how to use the information to develop a committed, productive workforce. Real-life case studies, dramatic vignettes, and advice from top executives highlight the skills needed to manage a workforce and tap its full potential. By examining the practices of actual companies and a fictitious organization, Simultech, we discover ways to create better working relationships within the organization. This is an excellent teaching tool for management staff of companies large and small, and for students who will one day use the skills to manage a diverse workforce.

This program shows the steps managers can take to provide leadership in establishing diversity initiatives within an organization. Managers from several companies discuss their employee training and awareness programs, and how these have benefited their organizations. Practices such as mentoring of employees by senior management staff are modeled. Such programs are shown to create a more open work environment where employee input is included in company policy-making decisions. (28 minutes, color)

The series *Managing Diversity* includes:
The Diversity Picture • Overcoming Barriers
Communication • Diversity Leadership

For information on other programs, please call
800/257-5126 or **609/275-1400.**

NOTICE: This program is copyright under US and applicable international laws. It is a violation of copyright law to copy, duplicate, edit, or broadcast this program for any reason or by any means without prior written contract from FILMS FOR THE HUMANITIES & SCIENCES®. It is the policy of FILMS FOR THE HUMANITIES & SCIENCES® to protect its copyright and prosecute copyright violators to the full extent of the law.

Package copyright © 1997 Films for the Humanities & Sciences® • Box 2053 • Princeton, NJ 08543-2053

1645691W

Case Back Cover

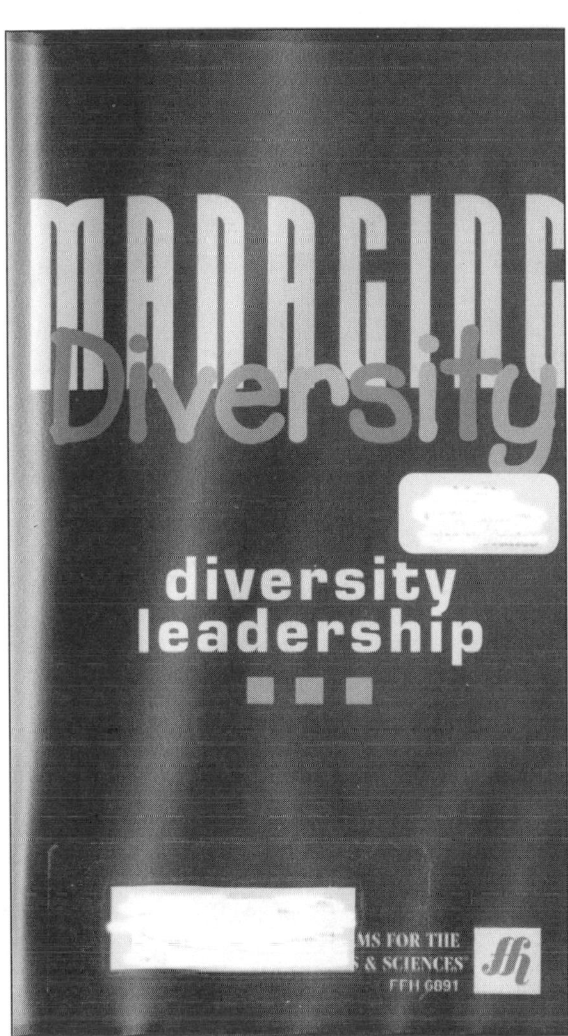

Videocassette Case Cover

Additional information:
A production of TV Ontario, the Ontario Educational Communications Authority: producers, Anne Dychtenberg, Kim Wilson; director, Christ Terry; 1997; sound, color, 28 minutes long.

Instructions: Prepare a catalog record for this item.

***AACR2r* rules needed:** 1.1B1; 1.1C1; 1.1F1; 1.1F6; 1.4F1; 1.5B1; 1.5B4; 1.5C1; 1.5D1; 1.6B1; 1.7B12; 1.7B17; 1.7B19; 7.0B1; 7.5B1; 7.5B2; 7.5C3; 7.5C4; 7.5D3; 21.4B1; 21.29B; 21.30A1; 21.30E1; 21.30F1; 22.5A1; 24.1A; MARC 028

Exercise 138

Empowering People with Disabilities Through Technology

FILMS FOR THE HUMANITIES & SCIENCES®

This videocassette is copyright under U.S. and applicable international law. It may not be broadcast, edited, or duplicated without the express written consent of Films for the Humanities & Sciences®.

FFH 8796

Videocassette Label

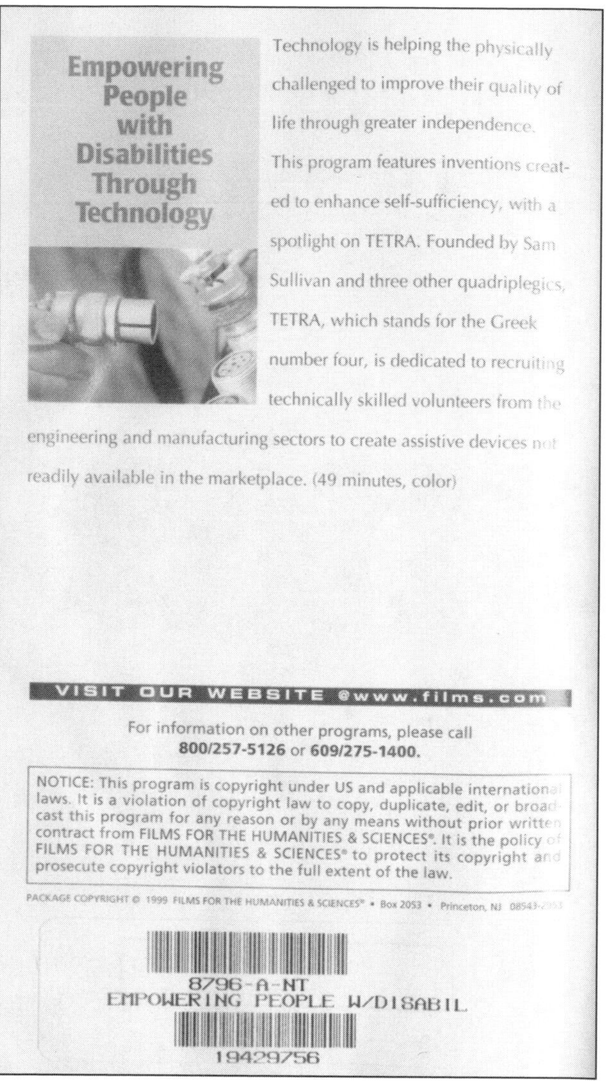

Empowering People with Disabilities Through Technology
Technology is helping the physically challenged to improve their quality of life through greater independence. This program features inventions created to enhance self-sufficiency, with a spotlight on TETRA. Founded by Sam Sullivan and three other quadriplegics, TETRA, which stands for the Greek number four, is dedicated to recruiting technically skilled volunteers from the engineering and manufacturing sectors to create assistive devices not readily available in the marketplace. (49 minutes, color)
VISIT OUR WEBSITE @www.films.com
For information on other programs, please call 800/257-5126 or 609/275-1400.
NOTICE: This program is copyright under US and applicable international laws. It is a violation of copyright law to copy, duplicate, edit, or broadcast this program for any reason or by any means without prior written contract from FILMS FOR THE HUMANITIES & SCIENCES®. It is the policy of FILMS FOR THE HUMANITIES & SCIENCES® to protect its copyright and prosecute copyright violators to the full extent of the law.
PACKAGE COPYRIGHT © 1999 FILMS FOR THE HUMANITIES & SCIENCES® • Box 2053 • Princeton, NJ
8796-A-NT
EMPOWERING PEOPLE W/DISABIL
19429756

Back Case Cover

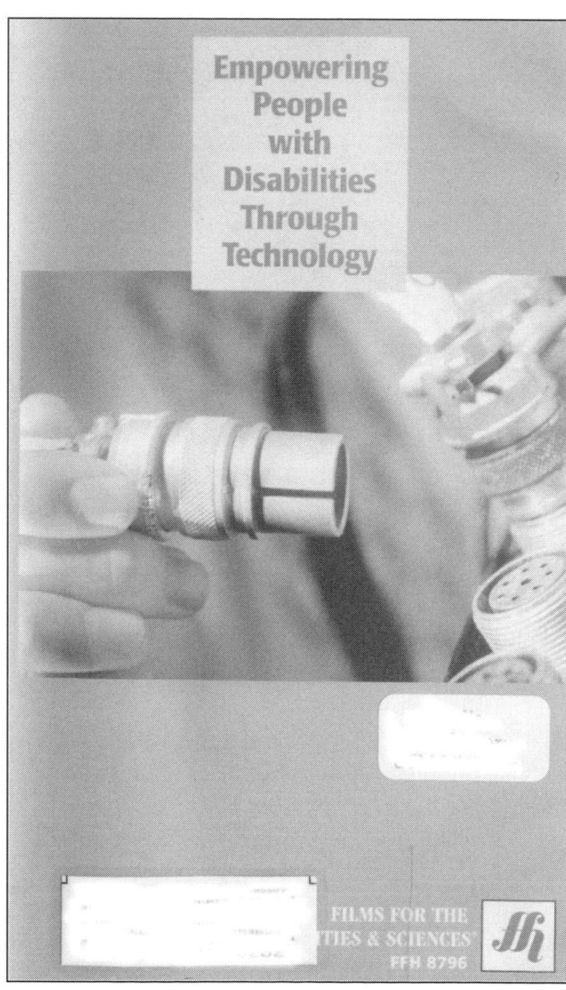

Videocassette Case Cover

Additional information:
A presentation of Films for the Humanities & Sciences; produced in association with the Discovery Channel and Workweek Television Productions, Inc. in 1999; sound, color

Instructions: Prepare a catalog record for this item.

***AACR2r* rules needed:** 1.1B1; 1.1C1; 1.1F1; 1.1F6; 1.4F1; 1.5B1; 1.5B4; 1.5C1; 1.7B19; 7.0B1; 7.5C3; 7.5C4; 21.29B; 21.30A1; 21.30E1; 24.1A; MARC 028

Exercise 139

FEMMES AUX
YEUX OUVERTS

TRT: 50:41

CALIFORNIA NEWSREEL
149 Ninth Street, No. 420
San Francisco, CA 94103
(415) 621-6196

Videocassette Label

Producer/Director: Anne-Laure Folly
52 minutes
Togo, 1994
in French with English Subtitles

A film about African women is a rarity, even more one made *by* an African woman. In **Femmes aux Yeux Ouverts (Women with Open Eyes)** award-winning Togolese filmmaker Anne-Laure Folly presents portraits of contemporary African women in four West African countries: Burkina Faso, Mali, Senegal and Benin.

We meet a woman active in the movement against female genital mutilation. She explains why in Africa it is easier to oppose this practice as a health issue than as a women's rights issues. We also join a health worker demonstrating condom use in a marketplace and explaining how diseases are sexually transmitted. Women are the traditional market traders in Africa. Successful businesswomen describe how they have set up an association to share expertise and provide mutual assistance.

Women with Open Eyes shows that women are organizing at the grassroots level to play a prominent role in Africa's current opening to democracy. It demonstrates why Africa's development is inextricably linked to the social and economic progress of its women.

California Newsreel
149 Ninth Street/ 420
San Francisco CA 94103
Telephone (415) 621-6196

Case Back Cover

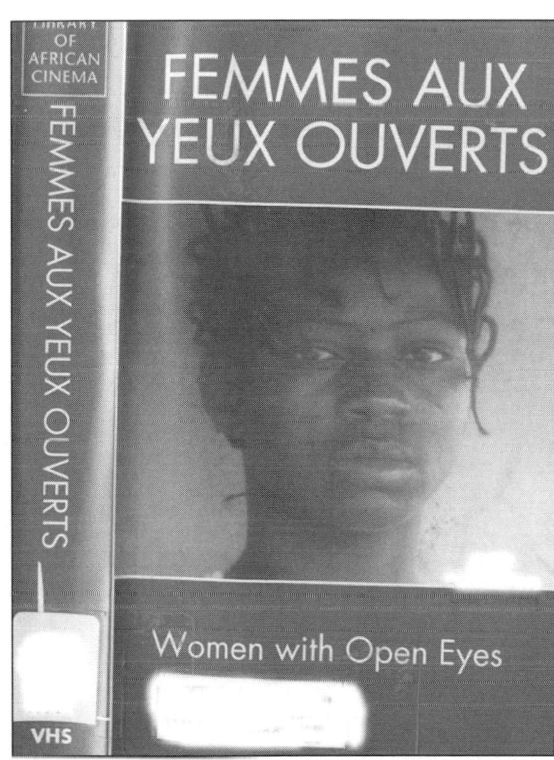

Videocassette Case Cover

Additional information:
Un film de Anne Laure Folly; sound, color; Montage, Sylvie Allombert; image, Jean-Louis Penez, Pap seck, Racine Arouna Keita; son, Richard Verthe [et al.]; musique, Ali Wade [et al.]; texts read by Djelika Diallo, Alimala Konate
Summary: The social condition and position of women in the West African countries of Burkina Faso, Mali, Senegal, and Benin are brought into focus with interviews of women active in the various political and social struggles of their countries.

Instructions: Prepare a catalog record for this item.

***AACR2r* rules needed:** 1.1B1; 1.1C1; 1.4C1; 1.4C3; 1.4D1; 1.4F1; 1.5B4; 1.5C1; 1.6B1; 1.7B2; 1.7B10; 1.7B17; 7.0B1; 7.5B2; 7.5C1; 7.5C3; 7.5C4; 7.5D3; 7.7B2; 7.7B10f; 21.29B; 21.29C; 21.30B1; 21.30E1; 22.5A1; 24.1A

Exercise 140

Green Medicines

FILMS FOR THE HUMANITIES & SCIENCES®

This videocassette is copyright under U.S. and applicable international law. It may not be broadcast, edited, or duplicated without the express written consent of Films for the Humanities & Sciences®.

FFH 5338

Videocassette Label

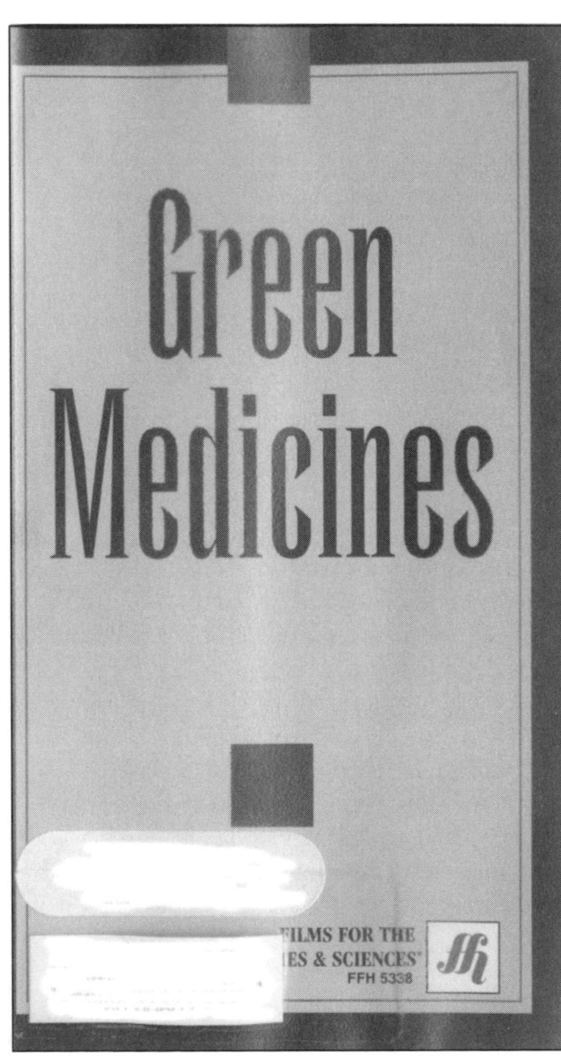

Videocassette Case Cover

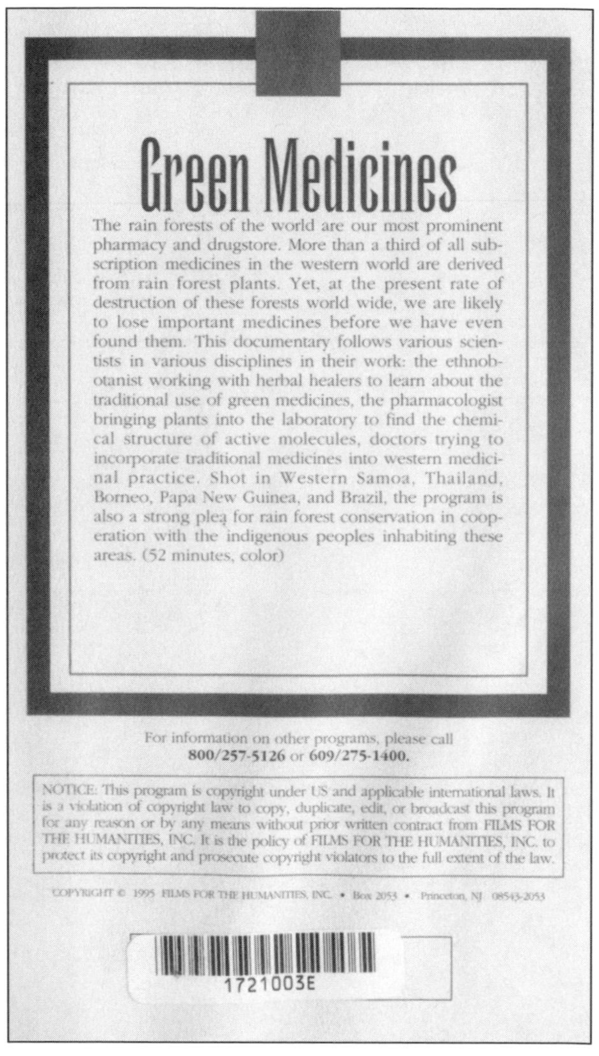

Green Medicines

The rain forests of the world are our most prominent pharmacy and drugstore. More than a third of all subscription medicines in the western world are derived from rain forest plants. Yet, at the present rate of destruction of these forests world wide, we are likely to lose important medicines before we have even found them. This documentary follows various scientists in various disciplines in their work: the ethnobotanist working with herbal healers to learn about the traditional use of green medicines, the pharmacologist bringing plants into the laboratory to find the chemical structure of active molecules, doctors trying to incorporate traditional medicines into western medicinal practice. Shot in Western Samoa, Thailand, Borneo, Papa New Guinea, and Brazil, the program is also a strong pleą for rain forest conservation in cooperation with the indigenous peoples inhabiting these areas. (52 minutes, color)

For information on other programs, please call **800/257-5126** or **609/275-1400.**

NOTICE: This program is copyright under US and applicable international laws. It is a violation of copyright law to copy, duplicate, edit, or broadcast this program for any reason or by any means without prior written contract from FILMS FOR THE HUMANITIES, INC. It is the policy of FILMS FOR THE HUMANITIES, INC. to protect its copyright and prosecute copyright violators to the full extent of the law.

COPYRIGHT © 1995 FILMS FOR THE HUMANITIES, INC. • Box 2053 • Princeton, NJ 08543-2053

1721003E

Case Back Cover

Additional information:
Gröna Mediciner: en växande tillgång (original title)
Scandinature Films presenterar en film prodcerad ar Scandinature Films för AB Borealis Sveriges Television. Scandinature Film.

Instructions: Prepare a catalog record for this item.

***AACR2r* rules needed:** 1.1B1; 1.1C1; 1.1F1; 1.4C1; 1.4C3; 1.4F6; 1.5B1; 1.5B4; 1.5C1; 1.5D1; 1.7B17; 1.7B19; 7.0B1; 7.5B1; 7.5B2; 7.5C1; 7.5C3; 7.5C4; 7.5D3; 21.4B1; 21.10A; 21.30G1; 21.30J1; 24.1A; MARC 028

Exercise 141

GUS GIORDANO PRESENTS

THE
JAZZ
DANCE
JIGSAW

A VIDEO DOCUMENTARY ON THE
FIRST AMERICAN

JAZZ DANCE WORLD CONGRESS

Director – Meg Amato

WARNING: This Jazz Dance Video is licensed only for unadvertised, private home or school use. All other rights are retained by the copyright owner. This videocassette may not be reproduced under penalty of law.

VHS – AMERICAN
VHS-PAL – EUROPE

Videocassette Label

Cover

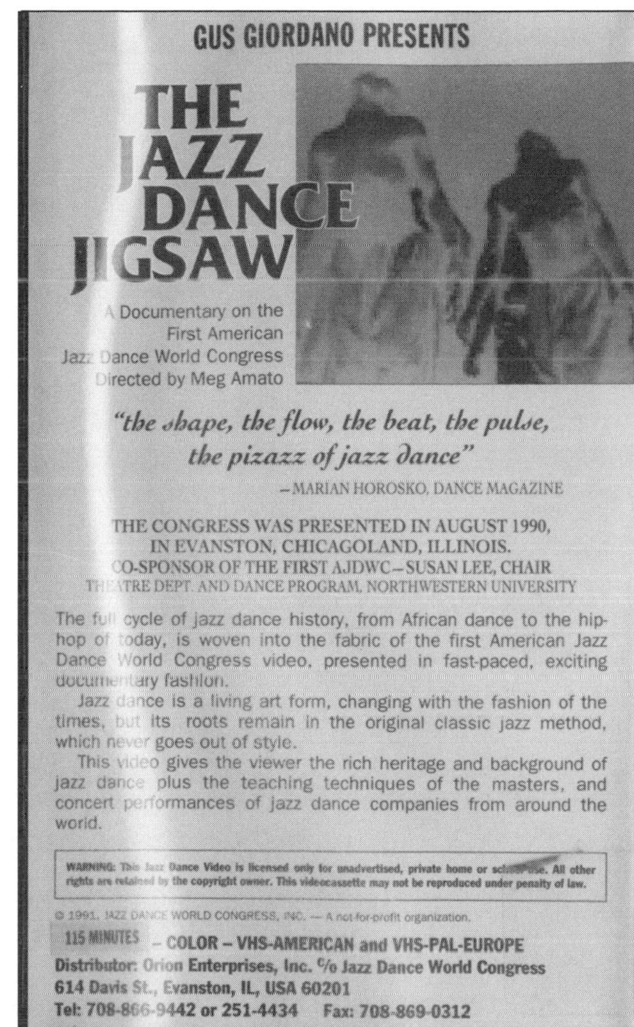

Back Cover

Additional information:
1991; sound, color

Instructions: Prepare a catalog record for this item.

***AACR2r* rules needed:** 1.1B1; 1.1C1; 1.1E1; 1.1E3; 1.1F1; 1.1F6; 1.4C1; 1.4C3; 1.4D1; 1.4D3; 1.4F6; 1.5B1; 1.5B4; 1.5C1; 1.5D1; 1.7B7; 1.7B10; 1.7B17; 7.0B1; 7.6B1; 7.7B1; 21.4A1; 21.29B; 21.29C; 21.30E1; 21.30F1; 22.5A1; 24.7B3

Exercise 142

© Ash•Quarry Productions

www.ashquarry.com
www.7dimensions.com.au

An exciting new series featuring leading international experts describing fresh challenges, innovative solutions and giving informed insights into the future of work.

COPYRIGHT WARNING
It is illegal to copy all or any part of this program

Videocassette Label

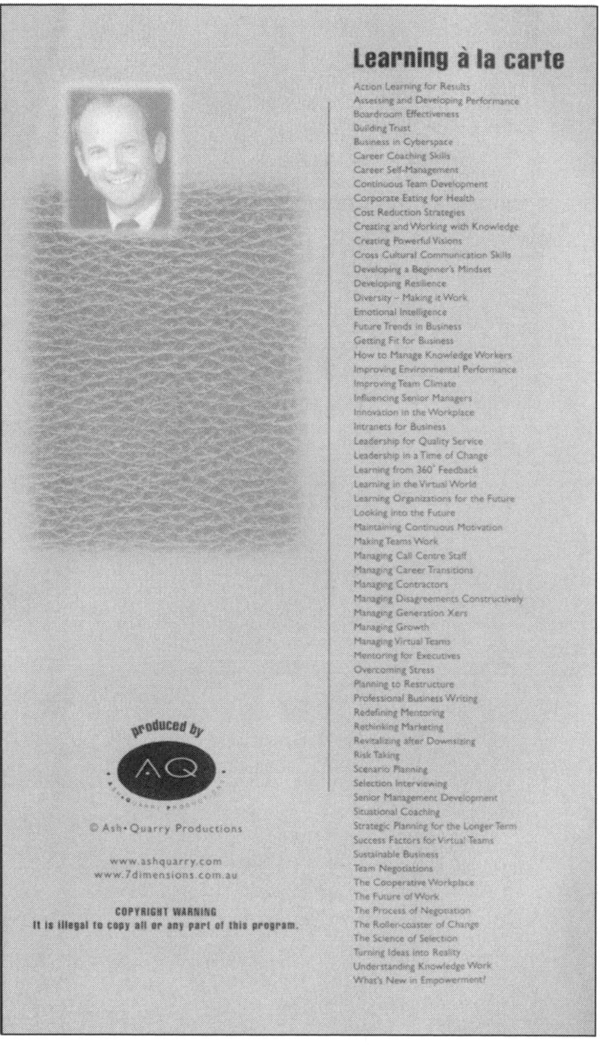

Learning à la carte
Action Learning for Results
Assessing and Developing Performance
Boardroom Effectiveness
Building Trust
Business in Cyberspace
Career Coaching Skills
Career Self-Management
Continuous Team Development
Corporate Eating for Health
Cost Reduction Strategies
Creating and Working with Knowledge
Creating Powerful Visions
Cross Cultural Communication Skills
Developing a Beginner's Mindset
Developing Resilience
Diversity – Making it Work
Emotional Intelligence
Future Trends in Business
Getting Fit for Business
How to Manage Knowledge Workers
Improving Environmental Performance
Improving Team Climate
Influencing Senior Managers
Innovation in the Workplace
Intranets for Business
Leadership for Quality Service
Leadership in a Time of Change
Learning from 360° Feedback
Learning in the Virtual World
Learning Organizations for the Future
Looking into the Future
Maintaining Continuous Motivation
Making Teams Work
Managing Call Centre Staff
Managing Career Transitions
Managing Contractors
Managing Disagreements Constructively
Managing Generation Xers
Managing Growth
Managing Virtual Teams
Mentoring for Executives
Overcoming Stress
Planning to Restructure
Professional Business Writing
Redefining Mentoring
Rethinking Marketing
Revitalizing after Downsizing
Risk Taking
Scenario Planning
Selection Interviewing
Senior Management Development
Situational Coaching
Strategic Planning for the Longer Term
Success Factors for Virtual Teams
Sustainable Business
Team Negotiations
The Cooperative Workplace
The Future of Work
The Process of Negotiation
The Roller-coaster of Change
The Science of Selection
Turning Ideas into Reality
Understanding Knowledge Work
What's New in Empowerment?
produced by
AQ
© Ash•Quarry Productions
www.ashquarry.com
www.7dimensions.com.au
COPYRIGHT WARNING
It is illegal to copy all or any part of this program.

Back Cover

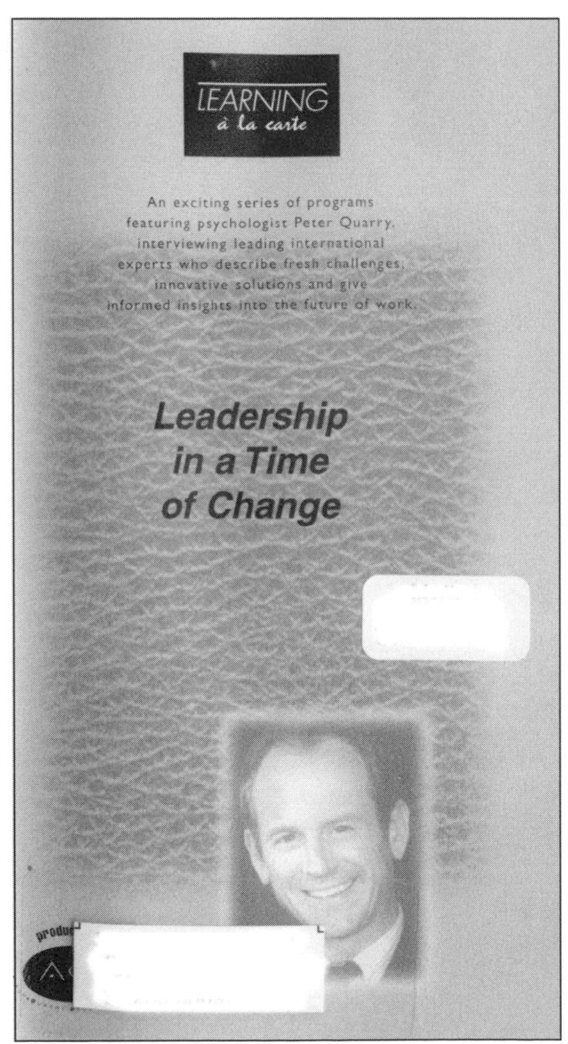

LEARNING
à la carte
An exciting series of programs featuring psychologist Peter Quarry, interviewing leading international experts who describe fresh challenges, innovative solutions and give informed insights into the future of work.
Leadership
in a Time
of Change

Cover

Additional information:
Title screen: Leadership in a time of change: Peter Quarry interviews Dennis Jaffe
Ash Quarry Productions; producer, Peter Quarry. 1999; 16 min., sound, color

Instructions: Prepare a catalog record for this item.

***AACR2r* rules needed:** 1.1B1; 1.1C1; 1.1E1; 1.1F1; 1.1F6; 1.4F1; 1.5B1; 1.5B4; 1.5C1; 1.5D1; 1.6B1; 1.7B12; 1.7B17; 1.7B19; 7.0B1; 7.5B1; 7.5B2; 7.5C3; 7.5C4; 7.5D3; 21.4B1; 21.6B1; 21.29B; 21.30A1; 21.30E1; 21.30F1; 22.5A1; 24.1A

Exercise 143

Cover

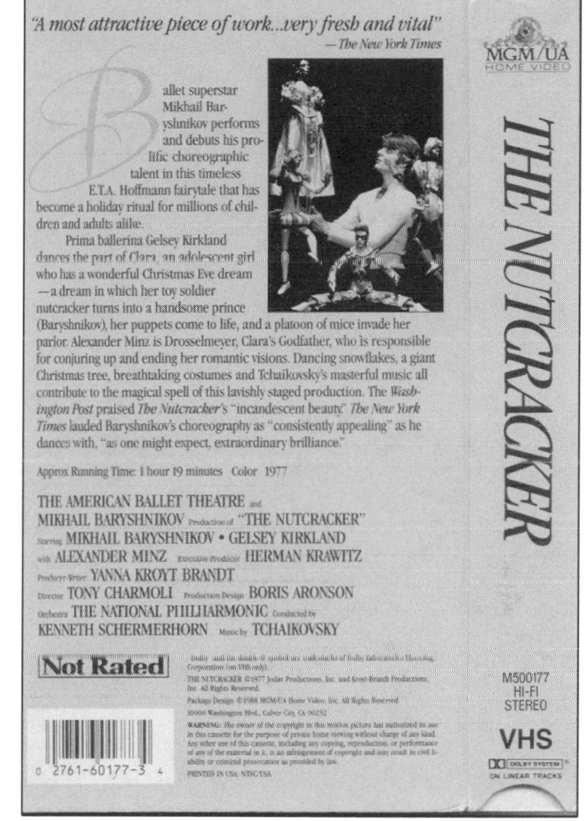

Back Cover

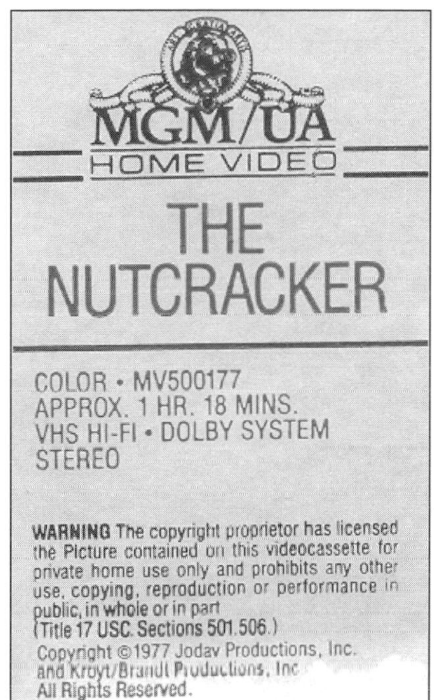

Videocassette Label

Instructions: Prepare a catalog record for this item.

***AACR2r* rules needed:** 1.1B1; 1.1C1; 1.1F2; 1.1F4; 1.1F6; 1.1F8; 1.4A2; 1.4C1; 1.4C3; 1.4D1; 1.4F1; 1.5A2; 1.5B1; 1.5B4a; 1.5C1; 1.5D1; 1.7B; 1.7B3; 1.7B6; 1.7B14; 1.7B17; 1.7B19; 7.0B1b; 7.1B1; 7.1F1; 7.4D1; 7.4F1; 7.4F2; 7.5B1; 7.5B2; 7.7B3; 7.7B6; 7.7B9; 7.7B10a; 7.7B10f; 7.5C1; 7.5C3; 7.5C4; 7.5D3; 7.7B6; 7.7B17; 7.7B19; 21.1A2; 21.6B2; 21.30A1; 21.30 E1; 21.30F1; 21.30G1; 22.5A1; 24.1A; 25.25A; 25.27A1; MARC 024; MARC 028

Exercise 144

Cathy Roe Productions

Tap Dictionary

Length: 59:39

Videocassette Label

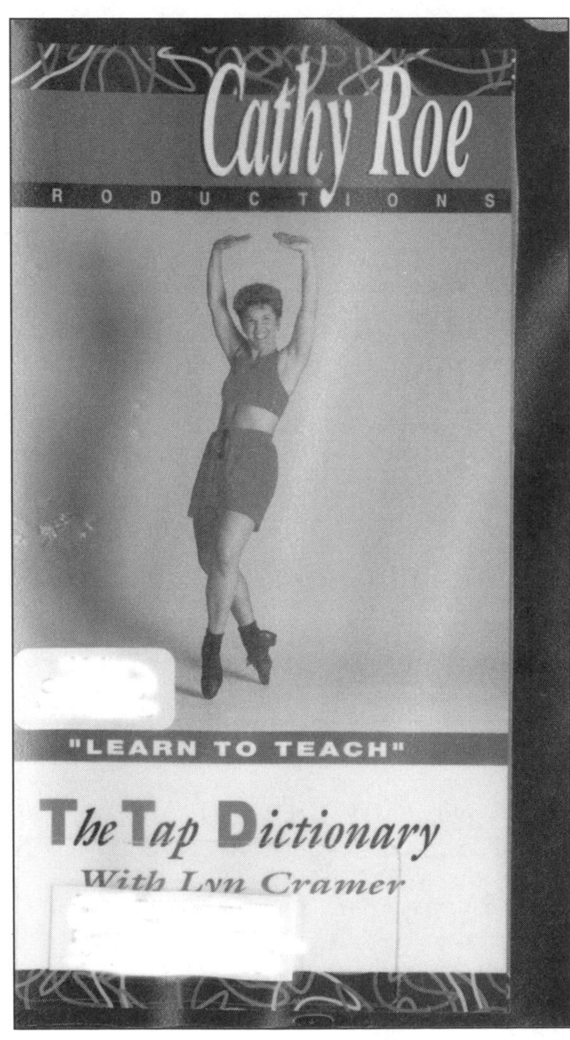

Cathy Roe
PRODUCTIONS
"LEARN TO TEACH"
The Tap Dictionary
With Lyn Cramer

Cover

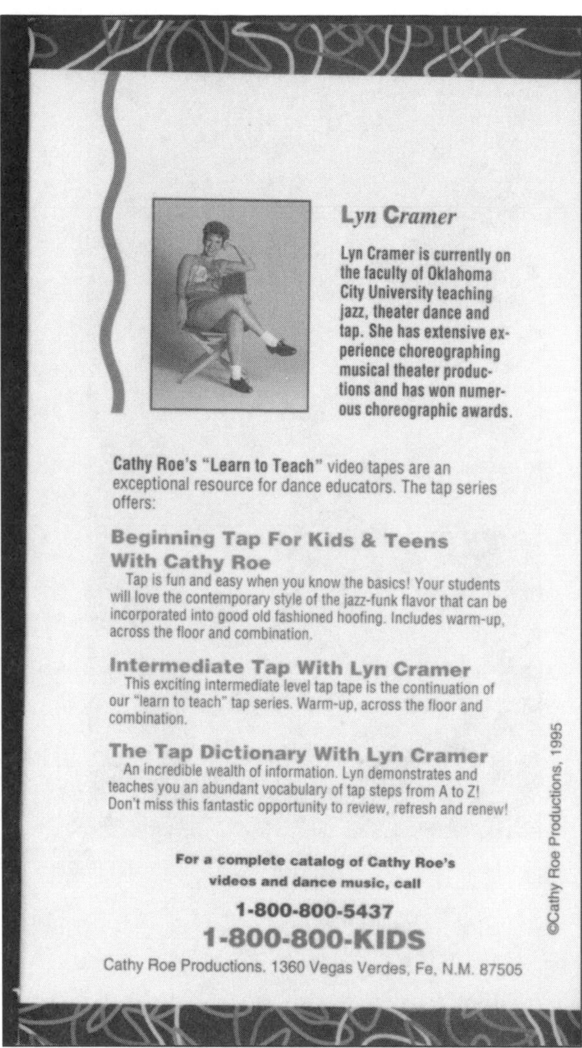

Lyn Cramer
Lyn Cramer is currently on the faculty of Oklahoma City University teaching jazz, theater dance and tap. She has extensive experience choreographing musical theater productions and has won numerous choreographic awards.
Cathy Roe's "Learn to Teach" video tapes are an exceptional resource for dance educators. The tap series offers:
Beginning Tap For Kids & Teens With Cathy Roe
Tap is fun and easy when you know the basics! Your students will love the contemporary style of the jazz-funk flavor that can be incorporated into good old fashioned hoofing. Includes warm-up, across the floor and combination.
Intermediate Tap With Lyn Cramer
This exciting intermediate level tap tape is the continuation of our "learn to teach" tap series. Warm-up, across the floor and combination.
The Tap Dictionary With Lyn Cramer
An incredible wealth of information. Lyn demonstrates and teaches you an abundant vocabulary of tap steps from A to Z! Don't miss this fantastic opportunity to review, refresh and renew!
For a complete catalog of Cathy Roe's videos and dance music, call
1-800-800-5437
1-800-800-KIDS
Cathy Roe Productions. 1360 Vegas Verdes, Fe, N.M. 87505
©Cathy Roe Productions, 1995

Back Cover

Additional information:
Produced by Cathy Roe Productions. Sound, color

Instructions: Prepare a catalog record for this item.

***AACR2r* rules needed:** 1.1B1; 1.1C1; 1.1F1; 1.4C1; 1.4C3; 1.4C4; 1.4D2; 1.4F6; 1.5B1; 1.5B4; 1.5C1; 1.6B1; 1.7A5; 1.7B17; 7.0B1; 7.5C3; 7.5C4; 7.7B3; 7.7B6; 7.7B10f; 7.7B14; 7.7B17; 21.1C1c; 21.30E1; 21.30F1; 21.30J2; 22.5A1

Exercise 145

Wake Up, America:
A Sleep Alert

FILMS FOR THE HUMANITIES & SCIENCES®

This videocassette is copyright under U.S. and applicable international law. It may not be broadcast, edited, or duplicated without the express written consent of Films for the Humanities, Inc.

FFH 5387

Videocassette Label

WAKE UP, AMERICA:
A Sleep Alert
Sleep disorders are a national problem, affecting millions and resulting in untold accidents. This program covers the functions of sleep and why some people need more sleep than others; circadian rhythm and events that can disrupt our sleep-wake cycles; the different kinds of sleep problems, including sleep apnea, insomnia, and narcolepsy; signs and symptoms of a sleep disorder and how stress, anxiety, and depression affect sleep patterns; the pros and cons of over-the-counter sleep medications; and the workings of a sleep lab. (24 minutes, color)
For information on these and other programs, please call
800/257-5126 or 609/275-1400.
NOTICE: This program is copyright under US and applicable international laws. It is a violation of copyright law to copy, duplicate, edit, or broadcast this program for any reason or by any means without prior written contract from FILMS FOR THE HUMANITIES, INC. It is the policy of FILMS FOR THE HUMANITIES, INC. to protect its copyright and prosecute copyright violators to the full extent of the law.
COPYRIGHT © 1995 FILMS FOR THE HUMANITIES, INC. • Box 2053 • Princeton, NJ
5387-A-NT
WAKE UP AMERICA A SLEEP ALE
19235044

Back Cover

Cover

Additional information:
Films for the Humanities & Sciences is located in Princeton, NJ. [Produced by] WKRC-TV and Medstar Communications; producer, Denise Cramsey; director, Sam Torre. Host, Kit Andrews. 1995. Sound, color, 24 min.

Instructions: Prepare a catalog record for this item.

***AACR2r* rules needed:** 1.1B1; 1.1C1; 1.1E1; 1.1F1; 1.1F6; 1.4F1; 1.5B1; 1.5B4; 1.5C1; 1.7B17; 1.7B19; 7.0B1; 7.5B1; 7.5B2; 7.5C3; 7.5C4; 7.5D3; 7.7B3; 7.7B10f; 7.7B17; 7.7B19; 21.29B; 21.30A1; 21.30E1; 21.30F1; 22.5A1;

Exercise 146

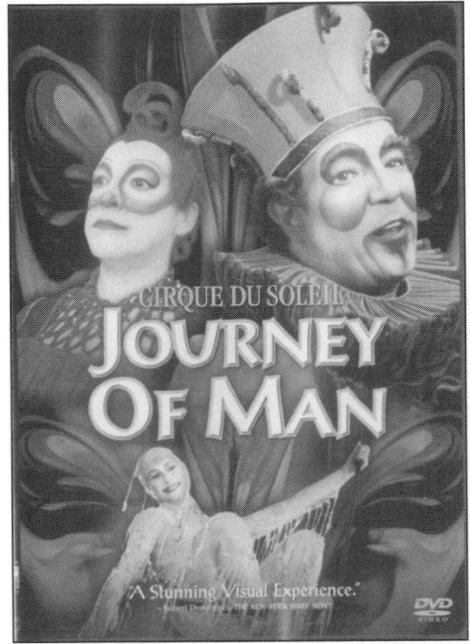

Front Cover

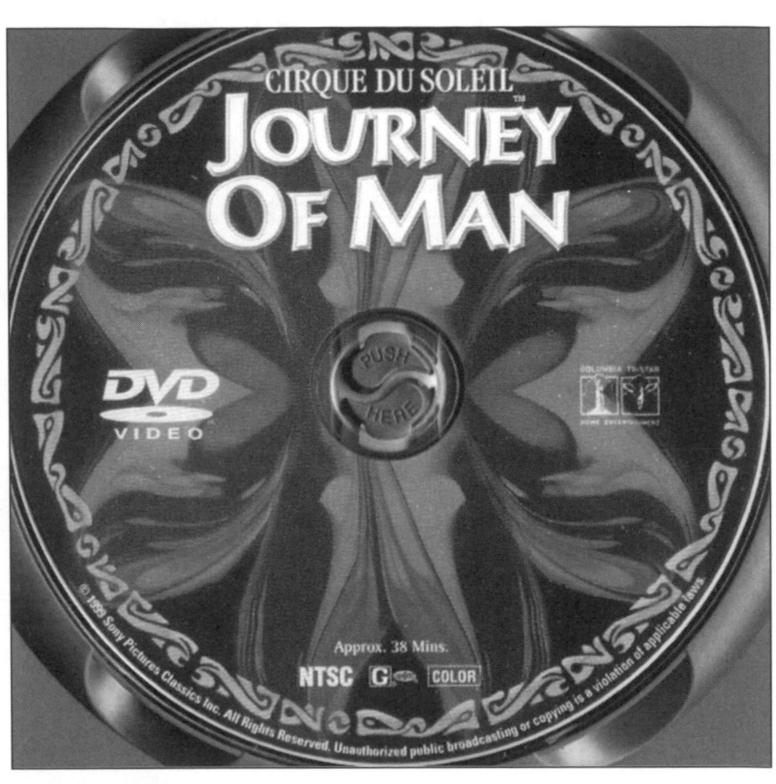

DVD Disc

Back Cover

Additional information: Published by Columbia TriStar Home Entertainment. Title on screen: Journey of Man. Narrated by Ian McKellan.

Instructions: Prepare a catalog record for this item.

***AACR2r* rules needed:** 1.1B1; 1.1C1; 1.1F1; 1.2B1; 1.2B3; 1.4C1; 1.4C3; 1.4F6; 1.5B1; 1.5B4; 1.5C1; 1.5D1; 1.5D2; 1.5E1(d); 1.6B1; 1.7B2; 1.7B10; 1.7B12; 1.7B17; 1.7B18; 1.8B1; 7.0B1; 7.5B1; 7.5B2; 7.5C1; 7.5C3; 7.5C4; 7.5D1; 7.5D4; 7.7B2; 21.1C1; 21.8A1b; 21.29B; 21.30E1; MARC 020

Exercise 147

Front Cover

Back Cover

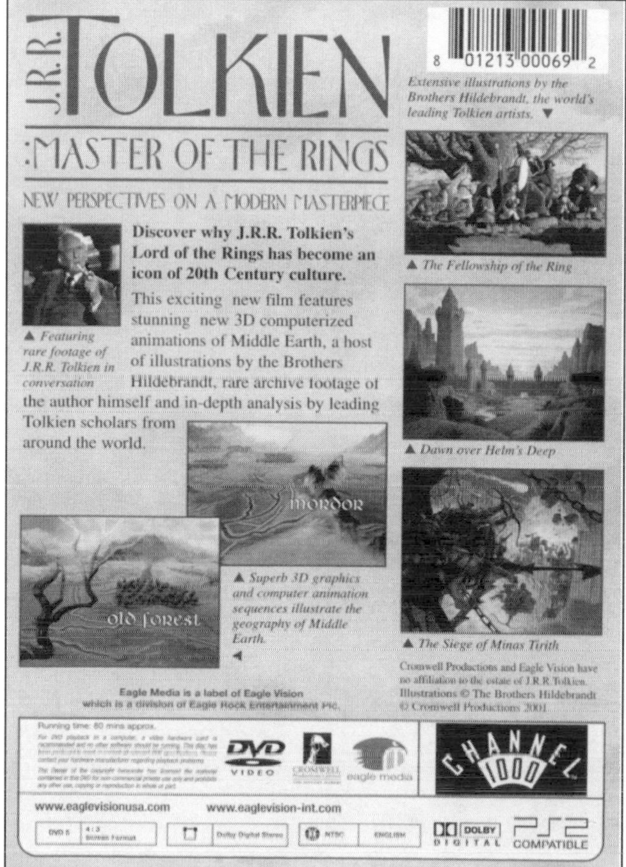

Instructions: Prepare a catalog record for this item.

***AACR2r* rules needed:** 1.1B1; 1.1C1; 1.1E1; 1.4D1; 1.4D2; 1.5B1; 1.5B2; 1.5B4; 1.5C1; 1.5D1; 1.7B17; 1.7B19; 7.0B1; 7.5B1; 7.5B2; 7.5C1; 7.5C2; 7.5C3; 7.5C4; 7.5C5; 7.5D4; 21.1C1; 21.30F1; 22.5A1; MARC 028

Exercise 148

Disc One

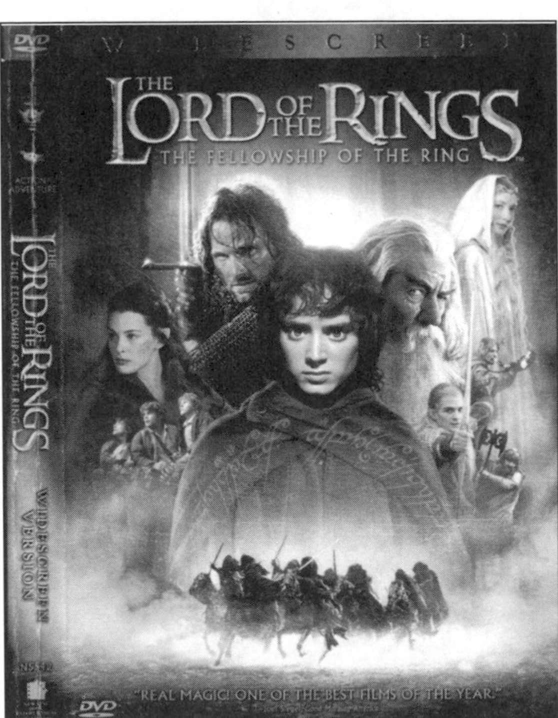

Front Case Cover

(*Continued on Next Page*)

Exercise 148

Case Back Cover—Portion

Back Cover Insert

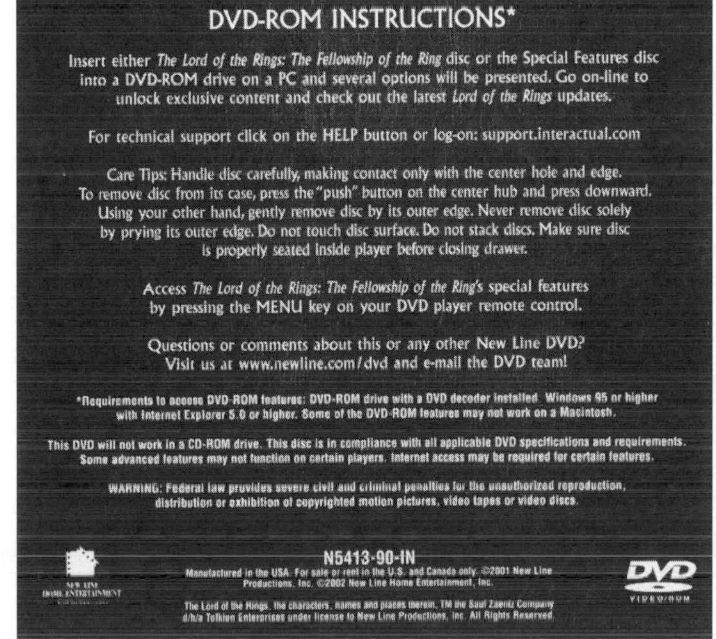

DVD-ROM INSTRUCTIONS*
Insert either The Lord of the Rings: The Fellowship of the Ring disc or the Special Features disc into a DVD-ROM drive on a PC and several options will be presented. Go on-line to unlock exclusive content and check out the latest Lord of the Rings updates.
For technical support click on the HELP button or log-on: support.interactual.com
Care Tips: Handle disc carefully, making contact only with the center hole and edge. To remove disc from its case, press the "push" button on the center hub and press downward. Using your other hand, gently remove disc by its outer edge. Never remove disc solely by prying its outer edge. Do not touch disc surface. Do not stack discs. Make sure disc is properly seated inside player before closing drawer.
Access The Lord of the Rings: The Fellowship of the Ring's special features by pressing the MENU key on your DVD player remote control.
Questions or comments about this or any other New Line DVD? Visit us at www.newline.com/dvd and e-mail the DVD team!
*Requirements to access DVD-ROM features: DVD-ROM drive with a DVD decoder installed. Windows 95 or higher with Internet Explorer 5.0 or higher. Some of the DVD-ROM features may not work on a Macintosh.
This DVD will not work in a CD-ROM drive. This disc is in compliance with all applicable DVD specifications and requirements. Some advanced features may not function on certain players. Internet access may be required for certain features.
WARNING: Federal law provides severe civil and criminal penalties for the unauthorized reproduction, distribution or exhibition of copyrighted motion pictures, video tapes or video discs.
N5413-90-IN
Manufactured in the USA. For sale or rent in the U.S. and Canada only. ©2001 New Line Productions, Inc. ©2002 New Line Home Entertainment, Inc.
The Lord of the Rings, the characters, names and places therein, TM the Saul Zaentz Company d/b/a Tolkien Enterprises under license to New Line Productions, Inc. All Rights Reserved.
DVD

(*Continued on Next Page*)

Exercise 148

*Requirements to Access DVD-ROM features: DVD-ROM drive with a DVD decoder installed, Windows 95 or higher with Internet Explorer 5.0 or higher. Some of the DVD-ROM features may not work on a Macintosh.

NEW LINE CINEMA PRESENTS A WINGNUT FILMS PRODUCTION "THE LORD OF THE RINGS: THE FELLOWSHIP OF THE RING" ELIJAH WOOD IAN McKELLEN LIV TYLER VIGGO MORTENSEN SEAN ASTIN CATE BLANCHETT JOHN RHYS-DAVIES BILLY BOYD DOMINIC MONAGHAN ORLANDO BLOOM CHRISTOPHER LEE HUGO WEAVING FEATURING SEAN BEAN AND IAN HOLM WITH ANDY SERKIS AS GOLLUM UK CASTING BY JOHN HUBBARD AND AMY MacLEAN COSTUME DESIGNERS NGILA DICKSON RICHARD TAYLOR SPECIAL MAKE-UP, CREATURE, MINIATURE AND DIGITAL EFFECTS BY WETA LTD. NZ VISUAL EFFECTS SUPERVISOR JIM RYGIEL MUSIC BY HOWARD SHORE FILM EDITOR JOHN GILBERT PRODUCTION DESIGNER GRANT MAJOR DIRECTOR OF PHOTOGRAPHY ANDREW LESNIE A.C.S. ASSOCIATE PRODUCER ELLEN M. SOMERS CO-PRODUCERS RICK PORRAS JAMIE SELKIRK EXECUTIVE PRODUCERS MARK ORDESKY BOB WEINSTEIN HARVEY WEINSTEIN EXECUTIVE PRODUCERS ROBERT SHAYE MICHAEL LYNNE PRODUCERS BARRIE M. OSBORNE PETER JACKSON FRAN WALSH TIM SANDERS BASED ON THE BOOK BY J.R.R. TOLKIEN SCREENPLAY BY FRAN WALSH & PHILIPPA BOYENS & PETER JACKSON DIRECTED BY PETER JACKSON

©2001 New Line Productions, Inc. ©2002 New Line Home Entertainment, Inc. The Lord of the Rings, the characters, names and places therein. TM The Saul Zaentz Company d/b/a Tolkien Enterprises under license to New Line Productions, Inc. All Rights Reserved.

Soundtrack Featuring "May It Be" and "Aniron" by Enya Available on Reprise Records

Widescreen Version: Presented in a "letterboxed" widescreen format preserving the 2.35:1 aspect ratio of its original theatrical exhibition. Enhanced for widescreen TVs. This DVD will not work in a CD-ROM drive. This disc is in compliance with all applicable DVD specifications and requirements. Some advanced features may not function on certain players. Internet access may be required for certain features. WARNING: Federal law provides severe civil and criminal penalties for the unauthorized reproduction, distribution or exhibition of copyrighted motion pictures, video tapes or video discs. Manufactured in the USA.

"Dolby" and the DD symbol are trademarks of Dolby Laboratories Licensing Corporation. For sale or rent in the U.S. and Canada only. InterActual, PCFriendly and the PCFriendly logo are either trademarks or registered trademarks of InterActual Technologies, Inc. LOGIC7 and the LOGIC7 logo are registered trademarks of Lexicon, Inc., A Harman International Company. Academy Awards® is a registered trademark and service mark of the Academy of Motion Picture Arts and Sciences. All Rights Reserved. Languages: English.

America Online Keyword: Lord of the Rings
www.lordoftherings.net www.newline.com

DVD VIDEO/ROM
InterActual PLAYER 2.0
LOGIC7
DOLBY DIGITAL
English: 5.1 Surround Sound
English: Stereo Surround Sound
PG-13 EPIC BATTLE SEQUENCES AND SOME SCARY IMAGES
SOUNDTRACK AVAILABLE ON
CC
Supplemental material not rated.
This disc supports parental lock.
NEW LINE HOME ENTERTAINMENT

Detail Back Case Cover

Additional information:
Includes a folded insert booklet of six pages (col. illus., 19 cm.)
Title and credits on case are the same as on the screen.
Fine print on discs reads: "©2001 New Line Productions, Inc. ©2002 New Line Home Entertainment, Inc. The Lord of the Rings, the characters, names and places therein. ™The Saul Zaentz Company d/b/a Tolkien Enterprises under license to New Line Productions, Inc. All Rights Reserved. N5542."

Instructions: Prepare a catalog record for this item. Tell what the various symbols on the back of the case cover mean.

***AACR2r* rules needed:** 1.1B1; 1.1B2; 1.1B9; 1.1C1; 1.4C1; 1.4C6; 1.4D1; 1.4F6; 1.5C1; 1.5D1; 1.5E1(d); 1.7B2; 1.7B10; 1.7B11; 1.7B14; 7.0B1; 7.0B2; 7.1F1; 7.2B1; 7.5C3; 7.5C4; 7.5D4; 7.7B10a; 7.7B10f; 7.7B18; 7.5E1; 21.1C1; 21.29B; 21.29C; 21.30A1; 21.30C1; 21.30D1; 21.30E1; 21.30G1; 22.5A1; 24.1A; 25.1A; 25.6A1; MARC 028

Exercise 149

Disc One of Three

Box Cover

Program Guide Disc Cover

(*Continued on Next Page*)

Exercise 149

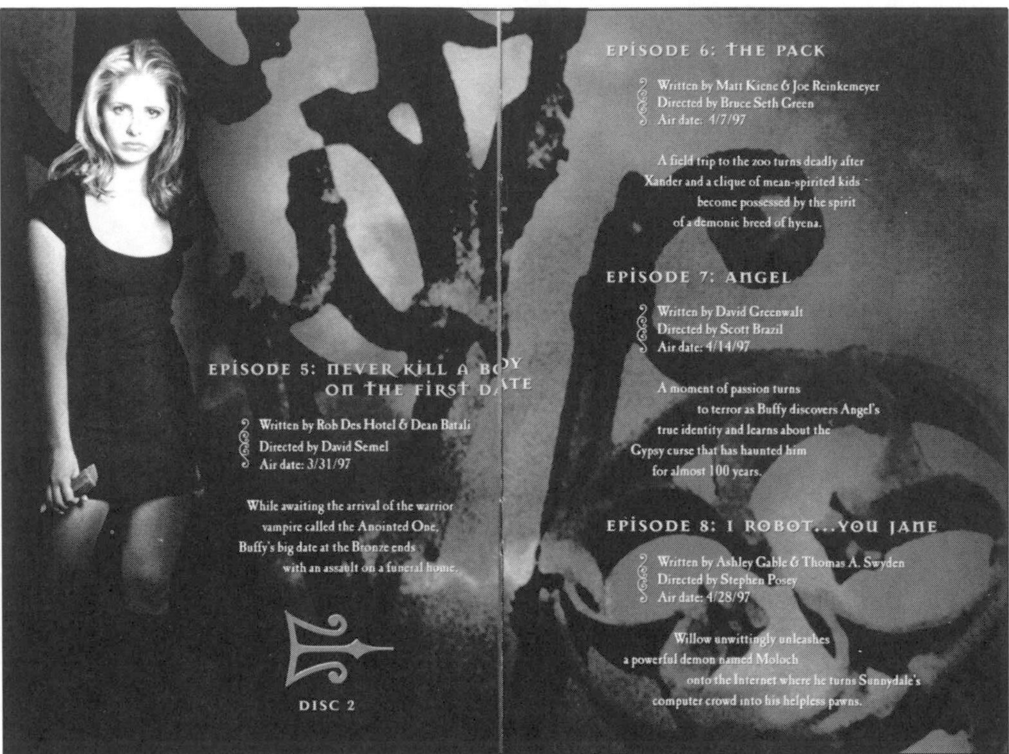

Program Guide—Discs Two and Three

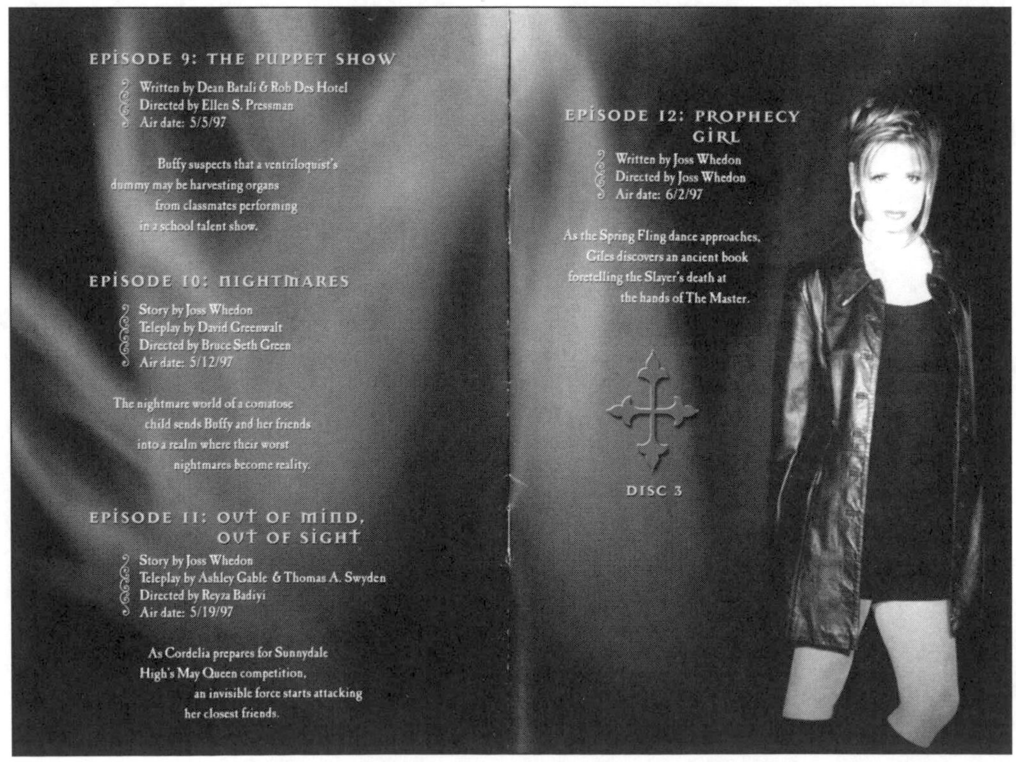

(*Continued on Next Page*)

Exercise 149

Package Insert—Portion

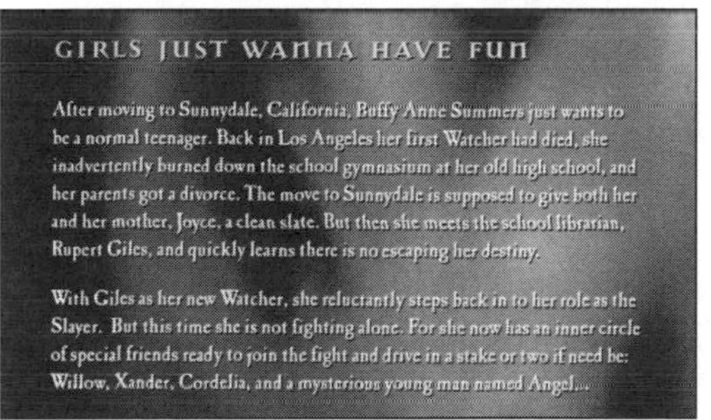

Summary from Program Booklet

Package Insert Detail

Additional information: The following was obtained by viewing the program on the DVD. Regular cast members in opening credits: Sarah Michelle Gellar, Nicholas Brendon, Alyson Hanigan, Charisma Carpenter, and Anthony Stewart Head as Giles. Recurring guest stars: Mark Metcalf, David Boreanaz, Kristine Sutherland; created by Joss Whedon. Ending credits: Executive Producer, Joss Whedon; Unit Production Manager/Co-producer, Joseph M. Ellis; Director of Photography, Michael Gershman; Production Designer, Steve Hardie; Edited by Geoffrey Rowland; Costume Designer, Susanna Puisto; Special Makeup Effects created by John Vulich, Optic Nerve Studios.

Copyright ©1997 by Twentieth Century Fox Film Corporation; [Produced by] Mutant Enemy, Inc., Kuzui Enterprises, [and] Sandollar Television.

DVD set published by Twentieth Century Fox Home Entertainment, ©2001. 600 minutes; DVD-ROM system requirements: a DVD-ROM drive on a PC with Windows 95 or higher is necessary to operate the enhanced features of Disc 1. Some of Disc 1's enhanced features will not work on a Macintosh. Disk 1 will not work in a CD-ROM drive.

Instructions: Prepare a catalog record for this item.

When cataloging this item, consider the following:

- How cast and crew are treated
- System requirements
- Subject headings

***AACR2r* rules needed:** 1.1B1; 1.1C1; 1.1E1; 1.1F1; 1.1F4; 1.1F6; 1.4C6; 1.4D1; 1.4D2; 1.4D3; 1.4D4; 1.4E1; 1.4F6; 1.5B1; 1.5B3; 1.5B4; 1.5C1; 1.5D1; 1.5D2; 1.5E1(d); 1.7B3; 1.7B10; 1.7B17; 1.7B18; 1.8B3; 7.5B1; 7.5B2; 7.5C3; 7.5C4; 7.5D4; 7.5E1; 7.7B6; 7.7B9; 7.7B11; 7.7B17; 7.7B18; 7.7B19; 21.1C; 21.29B; 21.29C; 21.30F1; 24.4B1; MARC 028

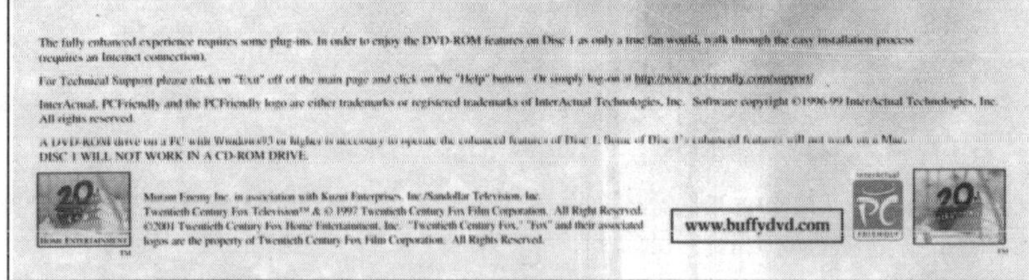

Program Guide Book Page Detail (negative image)

Exercise 150

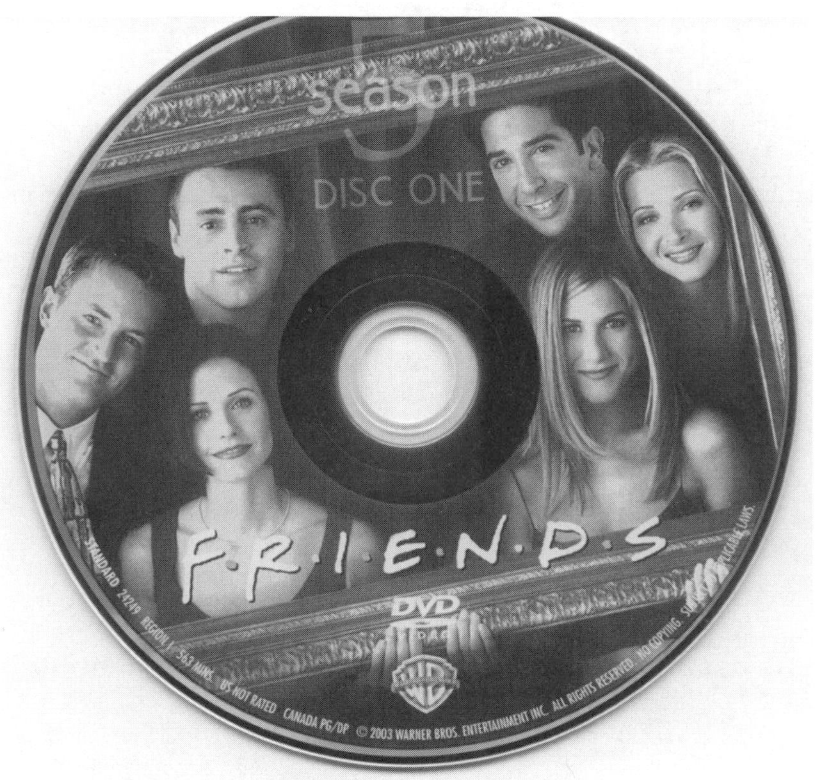

Disc One of Four

Container Bottom Flap

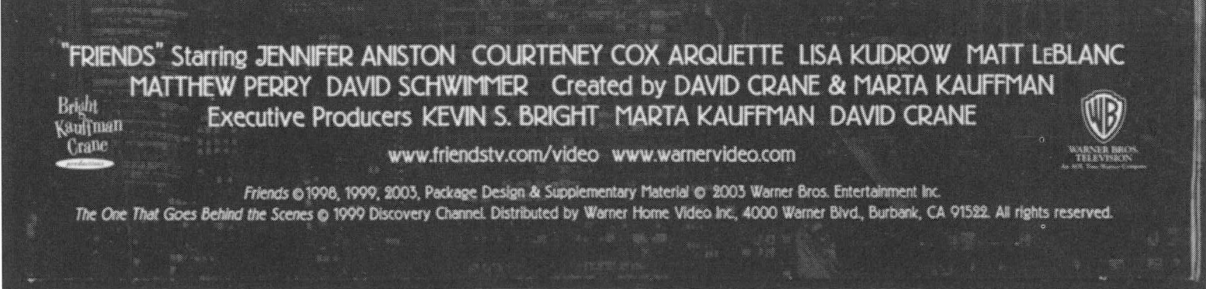

Cover of Inside Container Detail

(*Continued on Next Page*)

Exercise 150

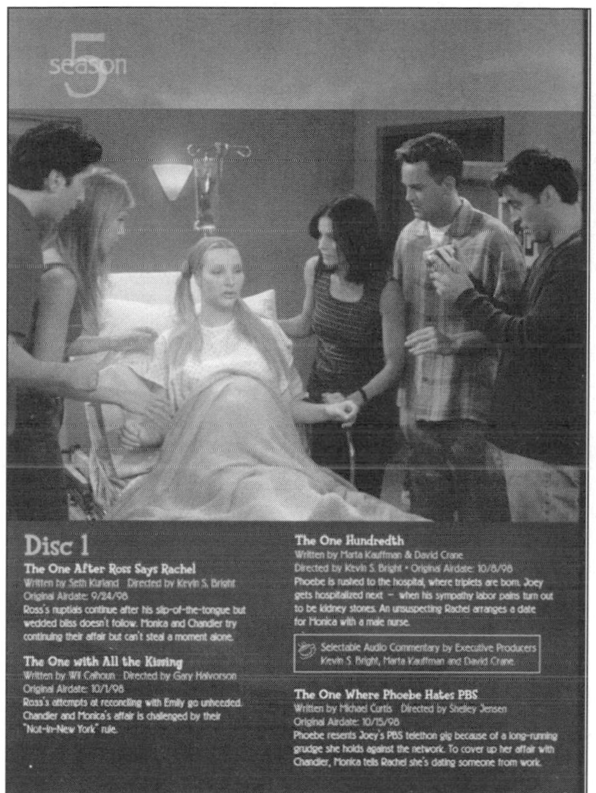

season 5

Disc 1

The One After Ross Says Rachel
Written by Seth Kurland Directed by Kevin S. Bright
Original Airdate: 9/24/98
Ross's nuptials continue after his slip-of-the-tongue but wedded bliss doesn't follow. Monica and Chandler try continuing their affair but can't steal a moment alone.

The One with All the Kissing
Written by Wil Calhoun Directed by Gary Halvorson
Original Airdate: 10/1/98
Ross's attempts at reconciling with Emily go unheeded. Chandler and Monica's affair is challenged by their "Not-in-New York" rule.

The One Hundredth
Written by Marta Kauffman & David Crane
Directed by Kevin S. Bright • Original Airdate: 10/8/98
Phoebe is rushed to the hospital, where triplets are born. Joey gets hospitalized next – when his sympathy labor pains turn out to be kidney stones. An unsuspecting Rachel arranges a date for Monica with a male nurse.

Selectable Audio Commentary by Executive Producers Kevin S. Bright, Marta Kauffman and David Crane.

The One Where Phoebe Hates PBS
Written by Michael Curtis Directed by Shelley Jensen
Original Airdate: 10/15/98
Phoebe resents Joey's PBS telethon gig because of a long-running grudge she holds against the network. To cover up her affair with Chandler, Monica tells Rachel she's dating someone from work.

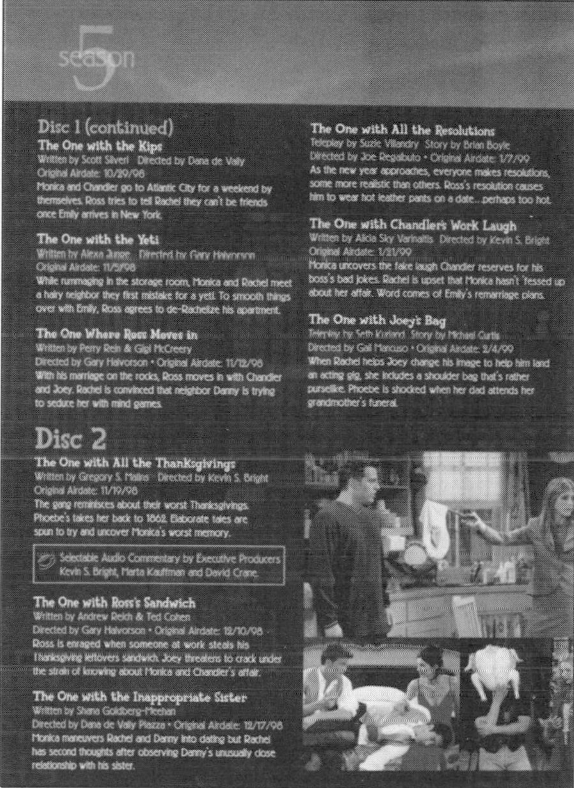

season 5

Disc 1 (continued)

The One with the Kips
Written by Scott Silveri Directed by Dana de Vally
Original Airdate: 10/29/98
Monica and Chandler go to Atlantic City for a weekend by themselves. Ross tries to tell Rachel they can't be friends once Emily arrives in New York.

The One with the Yeti
Written by Alexa Junge Directed by Gary Halvorson
Original Airdate: 11/5/98
While rummaging in the storage room, Monica and Rachel meet a hairy neighbor they first mistake for a yeti. To smooth things over with Emily, Ross agrees to de-Rachelize his apartment.

The One Where Ross Moves In
Written by Perry Rein & Gigi McCreery
Directed by Gary Halvorson • Original Airdate: 11/12/98
With his marriage on the rocks, Ross moves in with Chandler and Joey. Rachel is convinced that neighbor Danny is trying to seduce her with mind games.

Disc 2

The One with All the Thanksgivings
Written by Gregory S. Malins Directed by Kevin S. Bright
Original Airdate: 11/19/98
The gang reminisces about their worst Thanksgivings. Phoebe's takes her back to 1862. Elaborate tales are spun to try and uncover Monica's worst memory.

Selectable Audio Commentary by Executive Producers Kevin S. Bright, Marta Kauffman and David Crane.

The One with Ross's Sandwich
Written by Andrew Reich & Ted Cohen
Directed by Gary Halvorson • Original Airdate: 12/10/98
Ross is enraged when someone at work steals his Thanksgiving leftovers sandwich. Joey threatens to crack under the strain of knowing about Monica and Chandler's affair.

The One with the Inappropriate Sister
Written by Shana Goldberg-Meehan
Directed by Dana de Vally Piazza • Original Airdate: 12/17/98
Monica maneuvers Rachel and Danny into dating but Rachel has second thoughts after observing Danny's unusually close relationship with his sister.

The One with All the Resolutions
Teleplay by Suzie Villandry Story by Brian Boyle
Directed by Joe Regalbuto • Original Airdate: 1/7/99
As the new year approaches, everyone makes resolutions, some more realistic than others. Ross's resolution causes him to wear hot leather pants on a date...perhaps too hot.

The One with Chandler's Work Laugh
Written by Alicia Sky Varinaitis Directed by Kevin S. Bright
Original Airdate: 1/21/99
Monica uncovers the fake laugh Chandler reserves for his boss's bad jokes. Rachel is upset that Monica hasn't 'fessed up about her affair. Word comes of Emily's remarriage plans.

The One with Joey's Bag
Teleplay by Seth Kurland Story by Michael Curtis
Directed by Gail Mancuso • Original Airdate: 2/4/99
When Rachel helps Joey change his image to help him land an acting gig, she includes a shoulder bag that's rather purselike. Phoebe is shocked when her dad attends her grandmother's funeral.

Contents and Credits

season 5

Disc 3

The One Where Everybody Finds Out
Written by Alexa Junge Directed by Michael Lembeck
Original Airdate: 2/11/99
When Phoebe finds out about the Monica/Chandler affair, she tests Chandler via flirtation. Ugly Naked Guy's apartment goes up for rent and Ross wants it.

Selectable Audio Commentary by Executive Producers Kevin S. Bright, Marta Kauffman and David Crane.

The One with the Girl Who Hits Joey
Written by Adam Chase Directed by Kevin S. Bright
Original Airdate: 2/18/99
When Joey starts dating Katie, he finds she packs a painful punch. Ross has trouble making friends with his new neighbors.

The One with the Cop
Teleplay by Gigi McCreery & Perry Rein
Story by Alicia Sky Varinaitis Directed by Andrew Tsao
Original Airdate: 2/25/99
Phoebe finds a police badge inside the Central Perk sofa. Rather than return it, she decides to embark on a "good-deeds" campaign. Joey is unnerved by his romantic dream about Monica.

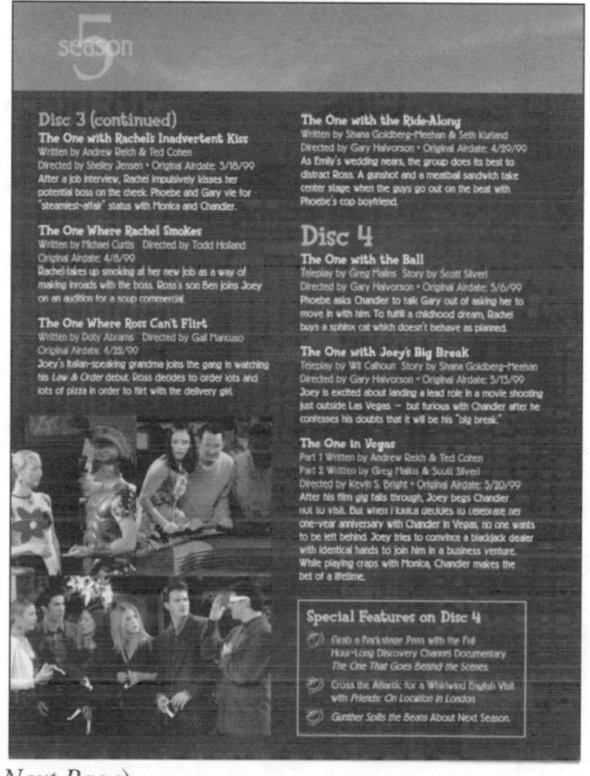

season 5

Disc 3 (continued)

The One with Rachel's Inadvertent Kiss
Written by Andrew Reich & Ted Cohen
Directed by Shelley Jensen • Original Airdate: 3/18/99
After a job interview, Rachel impulsively kisses her potential boss on the cheek. Phoebe and Gary vie for "steamiest-affair" status with Monica and Chandler.

The One Where Rachel Smokes
Written by Michael Curtis Directed by Todd Holland
Original Airdate: 4/8/99
Rachel takes up smoking at her new job as a way of making inroads with the boss. Ross's son Ben joins Joey on an audition for a soup commercial.

The One Where Ross Can't Flirt
Written by Doty Abrams Directed by Gail Mancuso
Original Airdate: 4/22/99
Joey's Italian-speaking grandma joins the gang in watching his *Law & Order* debut. Ross decides to order lots and lots of pizza in order to flirt with the delivery girl.

The One with the Ride-Along
Written by Shana Goldberg-Meehan & Seth Kurland
Directed by Gary Halvorson • Original Airdate: 4/29/99
As Emily's wedding nears, the group does its best to distract Ross. A gunshot and a meatball sandwich take center stage when the guys go out on the beat with Phoebe's cop boyfriend.

Disc 4

The One with the Ball
Teleplay by Greg Malins Story by Scott Silveri
Directed by Gary Halvorson • Original Airdate: 5/6/99
Phoebe asks Chandler to talk Gary out of asking her to move in with him. To fulfill a childhood dream, Rachel buys a sphinx cat which doesn't behave as planned.

The One with Joey's Big Break
Teleplay by Wil Calhoun Story by Shana Goldberg-Meehan
Directed by Gary Halvorson • Original Airdate: 5/13/99
Joey is excited about landing a lead role in a movie shooting just outside Las Vegas – but furious with Chandler after he confesses his doubts that it will be his "big break."

The One in Vegas
Part 1 Written by Andrew Reich & Ted Cohen
Part 2 Written by Greg Malins & Scott Silveri
Directed by Kevin S. Bright • Original Airdate: 5/20/99
After his film gig falls through, Joey begs Chandler not to visit. But when Monica decides to celebrate her one-year anniversary with Chandler in Vegas, no one wants to be left behind. Joey tries to convince a blackjack dealer with identical hands to join him in a business venture. While playing craps with Monica, Chandler makes the bet of a lifetime.

Special Features on Disc 4

- Grab a Backstage Pass with the Full Hour-Long Discovery Channel Documentary *The One That Goes Behind the Scenes.*
- Cross the Atlantic for a Whirlwind English Visit with *Friends: On Location in London.*
- *Gunther Spills the Beans* About Next Season.

(*Continued on Next Page*)

Exercise 150

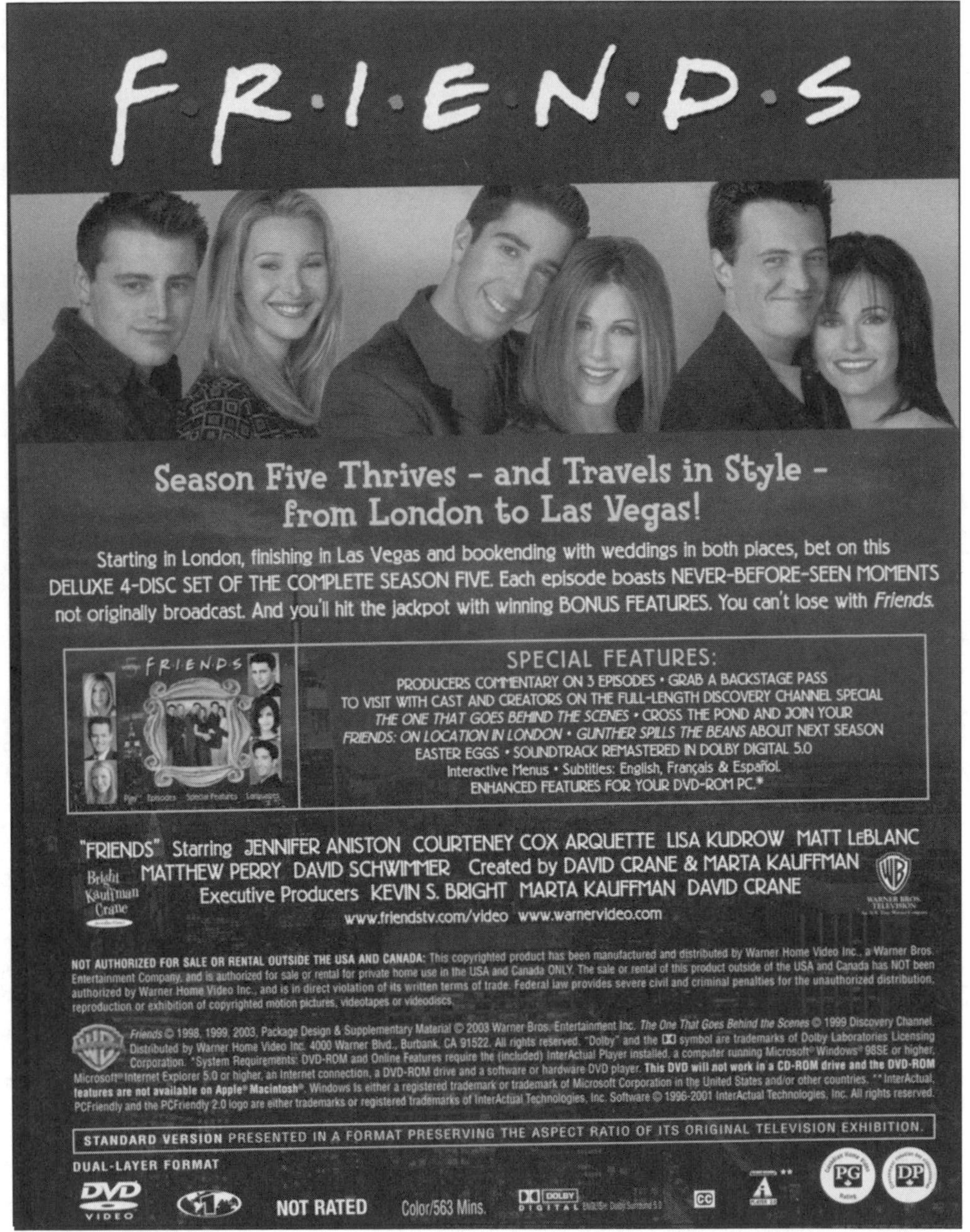

Container Back Cover

Additional information: On-screen information is the same as that found on the container. Discs housed in a folded container that can be removed from a slipcover box.

Instructions: Prepare a catalog record for this item.

***AACR2r* rules needed:** 1.0H2; 1.1B1; 1.1C3; 1.1E1; 1.1F1; 1.1F2; 1.4C1; 1.4C3; 1.4D1; 1.4D2; 1.4D5; 1.4E1; 1.4F6; 1.5B1; 1.5B3; 1.5B4; 1.5C1; 1.5D1; 1.7B3; 1.7B6; 1.7B7; 1.7B17; 1.7B18; 1.8B1; 7.5B1; 7.5B2; 7.5C3; 7.5C4; 7.5D4; 7.7B6; 7.7B7; 7.7B10f; 7.7B10j; 7.7B17; 7.7B18; 7.7B19; MARC 020; MARC 024; MARC 028

Appendix A

Selected Genre Terms (Used in MARC Field 655—Form and Genre Terms)

January 2004

Use MARC field 655 for terms indicating "the genre, form, and/or physical characteristics of the materials being described." Essentially, *this is the term that indicates what the item* ***is***, as opposed to what the item is about. Subfield "a" contains the term and ends in a period. We may now give the source information with a numeral in the second indicator position if our source has its own indicator value. If it does not, the second indicator will always be a "7," and we will put the alphabetic code for the source subfield "2." For example:

655 _0 ***Fantasy drama*** *[An lcsh term; set the second indicator at 0 (zero).]*
655 _1 ***Humorous plays*** *[An lcshac term; set the second indicator at 1 (one).]*
655 _7 ***Movie novels. ≠2 gsafd*** *[or]* ***655 _7 ≠a Movie novels ≠2 gsafd*** *[2nd indicator set to 7 (seven)]*
655 _7 ***Fantasy radio programs. ≠2 sears*** *[or]* ***655 _7 ≠a Fantasy radio programs. ≠2 sears*** *[2nd indicator set to 7 (seven)]*

Use MARC field 650 for those same terms when they indicate the topical subject content of the materials—what they are ***about.*** For example, a periodical featuring articles about techniques and legalities of creating novels based on movies might have the following subject heading:

650 _0 Movie novels ≠v Periodicals *[or] 650 _0* ***≠a Movie novels ≠v Periodicals***

The following list is based on a full listing of genre terms in the 2nd edition of ***Guidelines on Subject Access to <u>Individual Works</u> of Fiction, Drama, Etc.,*** for which the MARC source code is "gsafd." * Alternative forms for "gsafd" terms have been added for purposes of comparison. Most of these terms have been standardized in current English usage and can be found in other published lists of terms. Be aware, however, that guidelines for the *application* of the terms sometimes vary from one list to another. The Library of Congress assigns source codes for many lists. The source code from any applicable list may be used in subfield 2. This handout includes the most commonly used: *lcsh*[†], *lcshac*[†], and *sears*[‡]. ***[Note: Terms from lcshac are given here in bold type as an aid to children's catalogers. However, italic and bold type are not used in bibliographic records.]***

Adventure fiction[1] *gsafd, sears*
Adventure films *gsafd, lcsh, sears*
Adventure games *lcsh*
Adventure radio programs *gsafd, sears*
Adventure stories[1] *lcsh*
Adventure television programs *gsafd, sears*
Allegories *gsafd, lcsh, sears*
Alternative histories (Fiction) *gsafd, sears*
Animated films *gsafd, lcsh, sears*
Animated television programs *gsafd, lcsh, sears*
Arthurian romances *gsafd,* ***lcshac****, lcsh, sears*
Autobiographical fiction *gsafd, lcsh, sears*
Bible fiction *gsafd, sears*
Bible films *gsafd, lcsh, sears*

Bible plays *gsafd, lcsh, sears*
Bildungsroman *lcsh*
Bildungsromans[2] *gsafd, sears*
Biographical drama *lcsh*
Biographical fiction *gsafd, lcsh, sears*
Biographical films *gsafd, lcsh, sears*
Biographical radio programs *gsafd, sears*
Biographical television programs *gsafd, lcsh, sears*
Black humor (Literature) *gsafd, lcsh, sears*
Caricatures and cartoons *lcsh*

Cartoons and caricatures *sears*
Cartoons and comics *lcshac*
Christian drama *lcsh*
Christian fiction[3] *gsafd, lcsh,sears*
Christian films *lcsh*
Christian poetry *lcsh*
Christmas drama[4] *lcsh*
Christmas plays[4] *lcsh*
[*Christmas poetry*[5]]
Christmas stories[6] *lcsh*
Comedies *gsafd, sears*
Comedy films *gsafd, lcsh, sears*
Comedy programs *lcsh*
Comedy radio programs[7] *gsafd, sears*
Comedy television programs[8] *gsafd, sears*
Comic books, strips, etc.[9] *gsafd, lcsh, sears*
Detective and mystery comic books, strips, etc. *lcsh*
Detective and mystery films *lcsh*
Detective and mystery plays *lcsh*
Detective and mystery stories[10] *lcsh*
Detective and mystery television programs *lcsh*
Didactic drama *gsafd, lcsh, sears*
Didactic fiction *gsafd, lcsh, sears*
Didactic literature *lcsh*
Didactic poetry *gsafd, lcsh, sears*
Domestic fiction *lcsh*
Dystopias *gsafd, lcsh, sears*
Elegiac poetry *gsafd, lcsh, sears*
Epic fiction *gsafd, sears*
Epic films *gsafd, lcsh, sears*
Epic literature *lcsh, sears*
Epic poetry *gsafd, lcsh, sears*
Epistolary fiction *gsafd, lcsh, sears*
Epistolary poetry *gsafd, lcsh, sears*
Erotic comic books, strips, etc. *gsafd, lcsh*
Erotic drama *lcsh*
Erotic fiction *gsafd, sears*
Erotic films *gsafd, sears*
Erotic literature *lcsh, sears*
Erotic poetry *gsafd, lcsh sears*
Erotic stories *lcsh*
Fables *gsafd, lcsh, sears*
Fairy plays *lcsh*
Fairy poetry *lcsh*
Fairy tales *gsafd, lcsh, sears*
Fantasy comedies (Motion pictures) *lcsh*
Fantasy comic books, strips, etc. *lcsh*
Fantasy drama *lcsh*
Fantasy fiction gsafd, *lcsh, sears*
Fantasy films *lcsh, sears*
Fantasy literature *lcsh*
Fantasy poetry *lcsh, sears*
Fantasy radio programs *sears*
Fantasy television programs *lcsh, sears*
Farces *gsafd, lcsh, sears*
Feature films *gsafd, lcsh*
Feature stories *lcsh*
Film noir *gsafd, lcsh, sears*
Folklore *gsafd, lcsh,* ***lcshac****, sears*
Gangster films *gsafd, lcsh, sears*
Ghost plays *lcsh*
Ghost stories[11] *gsafd, lcsh, sears*
Gothic fiction *gsafd*
Gothic literature *lcsh*
Gothic novels *sears*
Gothic revival (Literature) *lcsh*
Historical drama *gsafd, lcsh, sears*
Historical fiction *gsafd, lcsh, sears*
Historical films *gsafd, lcsh*
Historical poetry *gsafd, lcsh, sears*
Horror comic books, strips, etc. *lcsh*
Horror fiction[12] *gsafd, sears*
Horror films *gsafd, lcsh, sears*
Horror plays *gsafd, lcsh, sears*
Horror radio programs *gsafd, lcsh, sears*
Horror stories *lcshac*
Horror tales *lcsh*
Horror television programs *gsafd, lcsh, sears*
Humorous fiction *gsafd, sears*
Humorous plays *lcshac*
Humorous poetry *gsafd, lcsh, sears*
Humorous stories *lcsh*
Imaginary voyages *sears*
Legal drama *gsafd*
Legal drama (Films) *gsafd, sears*
Legal drama (Radio programs) *gsafd, sears*
Legal drama (Television programs) *gsafd, sears*
Legal stories *gsafd, lcsh, sears*
Legends *gsafd, lcsh, sears*
Love poetry[13] *gsafd, lcsh, sears*

Love stories[14] *gsafd, lcsh, sears*
Medical drama (Films) *gsafd, sears*
Medical drama (Radio programs) *gsafd, sears*
Medical drama (Television programs) *gsafd, sears*
Medical novels *gsafd, sears*
Melodrama *gsafd, lcsh, sears*
Melodramatic fiction *gsafd*
Moralities *gsafd, lcsh*
Morality plays *sears*
Motion picture plays *gsafd, lcsh, sears*
Motion picture serials *gsafd, lcsh, sears*
Movie novels *gsafd, sears*
Musical fiction *lcsh*
Musical films *gsafd, lcsh, sears*
Mysteries and miracle plays *gsafd, lcsh, sears*
Mystery and detective plays ***lcshac****, sears*
Mystery and detective stories ***lcshac***
Mystery and detective stories, films, etc. *lcsh*
Mystery and detective television programs ***lcshac***
Mystery comic books, strips, etc. *gsafd, sears*
Mystery fiction[15,16] *gsafd, sears*
Mystery films *gsafd, sears*
Mystery plays *gsafd*
Mystery radio programs *gsafd, sears*
Mystery television programs[17] *gsafd, sears*
Narrative poetry *gsafd, lcsh, sears*
Noir fiction *gsafd*
Occult fiction *gsafd, lcsh, sears*
Parables *gsafd, lcsh, sears*
Passion plays *gsafd, sears*
Passion-plays *lcsh*
Pastoral drama *gsafd, lcsh, sears*
Pastoral fiction *gsafd, lcsh, sears*
Pastoral literature *lcsh*
Pastoral poetry *gsafd, lcsh, sears*
Picaresque literature *gsafd, lcsh, sears*
Political fiction *gsafd, lcsh*
Political plays *lcsh*
Political poetry *lcsh*
Political satire *lcsh*
Psychological fiction *gsafd*
Radio and television novels *gsafd, sears*
Radio comedies *lcsh*
Radio plays *gsafd, lcsh, sears*
Radio programs *sears*
Radio programs, Musical *lcsh*
Radio scripts *gsafd, lcsh, sears*
Radio serials *gsafd, lcsh, sears*
Regency fiction *gsafd*
Regency novels *sears*
Road fiction *gsafd*
Road films *lcsh*
Robinsonades *gsafd, lcsh, sears*
Romances *gsafd, lcsh, sears*
Romans à clef *gsafd, lcsh, sears*
Romantic suspense fiction *gsafd*
Romantic suspense novels *sears*
Satire *gsafd, lcsh, sears*
Science comic books, strips, etc. *gsafd*
Science fiction *gsafd, lcsh, sears*
Science fiction comic books, strips, etc. *sears*
Science fiction films *lcsh, sears*
Science fiction plays *lcsh, sears*
Science fiction poetry *lcsh, sears*
Science fiction radio programs *lcsh, sears*
Science fiction television programs *lcsh, sears*
Science films *gsafd, lcsh*
Science plays *gsafd*
Science poetry *gsafd*
Science radio programs *gsafd*
Science television programs *gsafd, lcsh*
Sea poetry *sears*
Sea stories *gsafd lcsh, sears*
Short films *gsafd, lcsh, sears*
Short stories *gsafd,* ***lcshac****, lcsh, sears*
Silent films *gsafd, lcsh, sears*
Spy films *gsafd, lcsh, sears*
Spy radio programs *gsafd, sears*
Spy stories *gsafd,* ***lcshac****, lcsh, sears*
Spy television programs *gsafd, lcsh, sears*
Stream of consciousness fiction *lcsh*
Superhero comic books, strips, etc. *gsafd, sears*
Superhero films *gsafd, sears*
Superhero radio programs *gsafd, sears*
Superhero television programs *gsafd, sears*
Superman films *lcsh, sears*
Suspense fiction *gsafd, lcsh*
Suspense films *gsafd*
Suspense radio programs *gsafd*
Suspense television programs *gsafd*
Tall tales *gsafd, lcsh, sears*
Television movies *gsafd, sears*
Television plays *gsafd, lcsh, sears*
Television scripts *gsafd, lcsh, sears*
Television serials *gsafd, lcsh, sears*
Tragedies *gsafd, sears*
Utopian fiction *gsafd, sears*
Variety films *gsafd*
Variety shows *gsafd*
Variety shows (Radio programs) *gsafd, sears*

Variety shows (Television programs) *gsafd, lcsh, sears*
Voyages, Imaginary[18] *gsafd, lcsh*
War films *gsafd, lcsh, sears*
War poetry[19] *lcsh, sears*
War radio programs *gsafd, sears*
War stories[20] *gsafd, lcsh, sears*
War television programs *gsafd, sears*
Western comic books, strips, etc. *gsafd, lcsh, sears*
Western films *gsafd, lcsh, sears*
Western radio programs *gsafd, lcsh*
Western stories[21] *gsafd, lcsh, sears*
Western television programs *lcsh*
Westerns (Radio programs) *sears*
Westerns (Television programs) *sears*

Similar terms used as topical subject matter with a form subdivision (650, subfields **a** and **v**), **and alternate forms filed under other letters of the alphabet:**

1 Adventure and adventurers—Fiction ***lcshac****, sears*
2 Coming of age—Fiction (***lcshac*****: 650av**)
3 Christian life—Fiction (***lcshac*****: 650av**)
4 Christmas—Drama (*sears:* 650av)
5 Christmas—Poetry (*lcsh, sears:* 650av)
6 Christmas—Fiction (***lcshac****, sears*: 650av)
7 Radio comedies *lcsh*
8 Television comedies *lcsh*
9 Cartoons and comics ***lcshac***
10 Mystery and detective stories ***lcshac***
11 Ghosts—Fiction (***lcshac*****: 650av**)
12 Horror—Fiction (***lcshac*****: 650av**)
13 Love—Poetry (***lcshac*****: 650av**)
14 Love—Fiction (***lcshac*****: 650av**)
15 Detective and mystery stories, [films, etc.] *lcsh*
16 Mystery and detective stories ***lcshac***
17 Mystery and detective television programs ***lcshac***
18 Imaginary voyages *sears*
19 War—Poetry (***lcshac*****: 650av**)
20 War—Fiction (***lcshac*****: 650av**)
21 West (U.S.)—Fiction (***lcshac*****: 650av**)

---

* *2nd ed., American Library Association, 2000*
† *22nd ed., Library of Congress, 1999*
‡ *17th ed., H. W. Wilson, 2000*

Appendix B

MARC Records for Selected Exercises

Includes records for the following exercises: Includes records for the following exercises: 1, 2, 3, 10, 16, 19, 21, 22, 25, 28, 30, 33, 36, 38, 39, 41, 47, 50, 53, 57, 60, 62, 63, 66, 68, 71, 75, 76, 77, 78,.79, 85, 86, 90, 94, 98, 100, 104, 107, 110, 112, 117, 121, 124, 127, 129, 132, 137, 146, 150

Exercise 1

Leader 00781cam 2200217 4500
008 700428s1970 nyua j 000 1 eng
010 a 72099008
040 a DLC ‡c DLC ‡d DLC ‡d TxGeoBT
042 a lcac
050 00 a PZ7 .A7475 ‡b Ju
082 00 a [Fic] ‡2 21
100 1 a Aruego, José.
245 10 a **Juan and the Asuangs** : ‡b a tale of Philippine ghosts and spirits / ‡c by Jose Aruego.
260 a New York : ‡b Charles Scribner's Sons, ‡c c1970.
300 a [32] p. : ‡b col. ill. ; ‡c 27 cm.
520 a A young Filipino boy makes the best of a bad situation in order to rescue his village's dogs and chickens from the terrible Asuangs, or jungle spirits.
655 0 a Ghost stories.
650 1 a Ghosts ‡v Fiction
650 1 a Philippines ‡v Fiction.

Exercise 2

Leader 00918cam 2200265 a 4500
008 000210s2001 mnua b b 001 0 eng
010 a 00023056
020 a 0736806628
040 a DLC ‡c DLC ‡d DLC ‡d TxGeoBT
042 a pcc ‡a lcac
050 00 a BM695.H3 ‡b S27 2001
082 00 a 394.267 ‡2 22
100 1 a Schaefer, Lola M., ‡d 1950-
245 10 a **Hanukkah** / ‡c by Lola M. Schaefer.
260 a Mankato, Minn. : ‡b Pebble Books, ‡c c2001.
300 a 24 p. : ‡b col. ill. ; ‡c 18 cm.
440 0 a Holidays and celebrations
500 a Includes index and resource lists: Words to know, Read more, and Internet sites.
520 a Presents, in simple text and photographs, the history of the Jewish Hanukkah holiday, and how it is celebrated.
521 0 a For use with early readers.
650 0 a Hanukkah ‡v Juvenile literature.
650 1 a Hanukkah.
650 1 a Holidays.

Exercise 3

Leader 01161cam 2200289 a 4500
008 990730s1999 nyua j b 001 0beng
010 a 98050208 /AC
020 a 0395633672
040 a DLC ‡c DLC ‡d DLC ‡d TxGeoBT
043 a n-us—-
050 00 a GV697.Z26 ‡b F74 1999
082 04 a 796/.092/4 a B ‡2 22
100 1 a Freedman, Russell.
245 10 a **Babe Didrikson Zaharias** : ‡b the making of a champion / ‡c by Russell Freedman.
260 a New York : ‡b Clarion Books, ‡c c1999.
300 a 192 p. : ‡b ill. ; ‡c 27 cm.
504 a Includes bibliographical references (p. 179-183) and index.
520 a A biography of Babe Didrikson, who broke records in golf, track and field, and other sports at a time when there were few opportunities for female athletes.
600 10 a Zaharias, Babe Didrikson, ‡d 1911-1956 ‡v Juvenile literature.
650 0 a Athletes ‡z United States ‡v Biography ‡v Juvenile literature.
650 0 a Women athletes ‡z United States ‡v Biography ‡v Juvenile literature.
600 11 a Zaharias, Babe Didrikson, ‡d 1911-1956.
650 1 a Athletes.
650 1 a Golfers.
650 1 a Women ‡v Biography.

Exercise 10

Leader 01027cam 2200289 a 4500
008 980407s1998 nyu g b 001 0beng
010 a 98019996
020 a 0553106031
020 a 0553380664 (pbk.)
040 a DLC ‡c DLC ‡d TxGeoBT
043 a n-us—-
050 00 a E840.8.J62 ‡b R63 1998
082 00 a 328.73/092 ‡a B ‡2 22
100 1 a Rogers, Mary Beth.
245 10 a **Barbara Jordan** : ‡b American hero / ‡c by Mary Beth Rogers.
260 a New York : ‡b Bantam Books, ‡c 1998.
300 a xviii, 414 p. : ‡b ill. ; ‡c 24 cm.
504 a Includes bibliographical references and index.
600 10 a Jordan, Barbara, d 1936- ‡v Juvenile literature.
610 10 a United States. ‡b Congress. ‡b House ‡v Biography ‡v Juvenile literature.
650 0 a African American women legislators ‡v Biography ‡v Juvenile literature.
600 11 a Jordan, Barbara, ‡d 1936-
650 1 a African Americans ‡v Biography.
650 1 a African American women ‡v Biography.
650 1 a Legislators ‡v Biography.
650 1 a Women ‡v Biography

Exercise 16

Leader 00692cam 2200217 a 4500
008 950622s1996 nyua g b 001 0 eng
010 a 95032588
020 a 038797993X (hardcover : alk. paper)
040 a DLC ‡c DLC ‡d DLC ‡d TxGeoBT
050 00 a QA241 ‡b .C6897 1996
082 00 a 512/.7 ‡2 20
100 1 a Conway, John Horton.
245 14 a **The book of numbers** / ‡c John H. Conway, Richard K. Guy.
260 a New York : ‡b Copernicus, ‡c c1996.
300 a ix, 310 p. : ‡b ill. (some col.) ; ‡c 24 cm.
504 a Includes bibliographical references and index.
520 a Guides readers at different levels of mathematical sophistication in understanding the origins, patterns, and interrelationships of numbers.
650 0 a Number theory ‡v Popular works.
650 1 a Numbers.
700 1 a Guy, Richard K.

Exercise 19

Leader 01013cam 2200301 a 4500
008 010815s2001 nyua g 000 0 eng
010 a 2001047367
020 a 0486418065 (pbk.)
040 a DLC ‡c DLC ‡d DLC ‡d TxGeoBT
042 a pcc
043 a a-cc—-
050 00 a TT870 ‡b .S666 2001
082 04 a 736/.982 ‡2 22
100 1 a Soong, Maying.
240 10 a Art of Chinese paper folding for young and old
245 10 a **Chinese paper folding for beginners** / ‡c Maying Soong.
260 a Mineola, NY : ‡b Dover Publications, ‡c 2001.
300 a xii, 132 p. : ‡b ill. ; ‡c 22 cm.
500 a Originally published: New York : Harcourt, Brace, 1948 as The art of Chinese paper folding for young and old.
650 0 a Paper work.
650 0 a Paper toys.
650 0 a Origami.
650 0 a Paper toy making ‡z China.
650 1 a Origami.
650 1 a Paper toys.
856 42 3 Publisher description: ‡u http://www.loc.gov/catdir/description/dover031/2001047367.html

Exercise 21

Leader 01358cam 2200313 a 4500
008 921119s1993 nyua j f 000 0 eng
010 a 92041736
020 a 0670849944
040 a DLC ‡c DLC ‡d DLC ‡d TxGeoBT
041 0 a engspa
042 a lcac
050 00 a PC4445 ‡b .L48 1993
082 00 a 468.2/421 ‡2 22
245 00 a **Let's speak Spanish** : ‡b a first book of words / ‡c edited by Katherine Farris ; illustrated by Linda Hendry.
260 a New York : ‡b Viking, ‡c 1993.
300 a 48 p. : ‡b col. ill. ; ‡c 32 cm.
546 a English and Spanish.
500 a Adapted from The Kids Can Press French & English word book. First published in Canada: 1991; translated by Arshes Anasal.
520 a Labeled pictures in Spanish and English introduce vocabulary for everyday scenes in the home, school, and neighborhood, as well as essential concepts such as colors, numbers and opposites.
650 0 a Spanish language ‡x Vocabulary ‡v Juvenile literature.
650 0 a Spanish language ‡x Textbooks for foreign speakers ‡x English ‡v Juvenile literature.
650 1 a Spanish language ‡x Vocabulary.
650 1 a Picture dictionaries, Spanish.
650 1 a Picture dictionaries.
655 1 a Spanish language materials ‡x Bilingual.
700 1 a Farris, Katherine, ‡e ed.
700 1 a Hendry, Linda, ‡e ill.

Exercise 22

Leader 01137cam 2200277 a 4500
008 900711s1991 mnua c 000 0 eng
010 a 90043744
020 a 0895656264
040 a DLC ‡c DLC ‡d DLC ‡d TxGeoBT
042 a lcac
050 00 a QE861 ‡b .R47 1990
082 00 a 567.9 ‡2 22
100 1 a Riehecky, Janet, ‡d 1953-
245 10 a **Dinosaur relatives** / ‡c by Janet Riehecky ; illustrated by Diana Magnuson.
260 a Mankato, MN : ‡b Child's World, ‡c c1991.
300 a 32 p. : ‡b ill. (some col.) ; ‡c 26 cm.
490 1 a Dinosaur books
520 a Describes reptiles besides dinosaurs that were alive during the same time, including creatures that lived in the sea or that flew through the skies.
650 0 a Reptiles, Fossil ‡v Juvenile literature.
650 1 a Reptiles, Fossil.
700 1 a Magnuson, Diana, ‡e ill.
710 2 a Child's World (Firm)
800 1 a Riehecky, Janet, ‡d1953- ‡t Dinosaur books.

Exercise 25

Leader 00871cam 2200277 a 4500
008 000309s2000 nyua g b 000 0deng
010 a 00029584
020 a 078686513X
040 a DLC ‡c DLC ‡d DLC ‡d TxGeoBT
050 00 a HQ 1206 ‡b .S663 2000
082 00 a 305.4 ‡2 21
082 04 a 155.3'33 ‡2 22
100 1 a Snyderman, Nancy L.
245 10 a **Necessary journeys** : ‡b letting ourselves learn from life / ‡c Nancy L. Snyderman and Peg Streep.
250 a 1st ed.
260 a New York : ‡b Hyperion, ‡c c2000.
300 a 248 p.; ‡c 20 cm.
504 a Includes bibliographical references (p. 241-248)
650 0 a Women ‡x Psychology.
650 0 a Women ‡x Conduct of life.
650 0 a Self-actualization (Psychology)
650 0 a Women ‡v Life skills guides.
600 10 a Snyderman, Nancy L.
700 1 a Streep, Peg.

Exercise 28

Leader 01049cam 2200265 a 4500
008 990730s2000 nyu e 000 f eng
010 a 99069500
020 a 0345437934 (pbk.)
040 a DLC ‡c DLC ‡d TxGeoBT
050 00 a PS 3573 .O6414 ‡b I55 1999
082 00 a 813/.54 ‡2 21
082 04 a [Fic] ‡2 22
100 1 a Woods, Paula L.
245 10 a **Inner city blues** : ‡b a Charlotte Justice novel / ‡c Paula L. Woods.
250 a 1st Ballantine Books ed.
260 a New York : ‡b One World : ‡b Ballantine Pub. Group, ‡© 2000, ©1999.
300 a 316 p. ; ‡c 21 cm.
520 a African-American homicide detective Charlotte Justice defuses a violent confrontation, saving Dr. Lance Mitchell from a potential eating by Los Angeles' finest - but that only opens up a more ominous picture.
655 0 a Detective and mystery stories.
650 0 a African Americans ‡z Los Angeles ‡v Fiction.
650 0 a African American women ‡z Los Angeles ‡v Fiction.
650 0 a Women detectives ‡z Los Angeles ‡v Fiction.
650 0 a Women ‡v Fiction.

Exercise 30

Leader 01069cam 2200289 a 4500
008 871105s1988 nyua b 000 0 eng
010 a 87033268
020 a 0812059360
040 a DLC ‡c DLC ‡d DLC ‡d TxGeoBT
050 00 a RJ 131 ‡b .P365 1988
082 00 a 612.6 ‡2 22
100 1 a Pearse, Patricia.
245 10 a **See how you grow** : ‡b a lift-the-flap body book / ‡c Patricia Pearse ; with illustrations by Edwina Riddell.
250 a 1st ed. for the U.S., Philippines, & Canada.
260 a Hauppauge, N.Y. : ‡b Barron's Educational Series, ‡c 1988.
300 a [32] p. : ‡b col. ill. ; ‡c 29 cm.
440 2 a A lift-the-flap body book
500 a Edition statement from colophon.
500 a "conceived, edited and produced by Frances Lincoln Limited, ... London, England"—T.p. verso.
500 a "5 9870 9876"—T.p. verso.
650 0 a Child development ‡v Juvenile literature.
650 1 a Child development.
700 1 a Riddell, Edwina, ‡e ill.
710 2 a Frances Lincoln Limited.

Exercise 33

Leader 01417cam 2200373 a 4500
008 900918s1991 scuac g b 001 0ceng d
010 a 90048424
020 a 0878440798
020 a 0878441026 (pbk.)
040 a DLC ‡c TxGeoBT ‡d TxGeoBT
043 a n-us-sc
050 4 a CT 3260 ‡b .B62 1991
082 00 a 920.72/09757 ‡2 22
100 1 a Bodie, Idella.
082 10 a **South Carolina women** / ‡c Idella Bodie.
250 a Rev. ed.
260 a Orangeburg, S.C. : ‡b Sandlapper Pub., ‡c c1991.
300 a x, 178 p. : ‡b ill. ; ‡c 27 cm.
504 a Includes bibliographical references (p. 163-172), an index, and a glossary.
520 a Lively profiles of current and past notable women of the Palmetto state, 51 leaders in a variety of areas, White and Black, old and young from Colonial times through the 20th century. Includes additional lists of women outstanding in their fields, and honored in public forums.
600 11 a Monigault, Judith Giton.
600 11 a Pinckney, Eliza Lucas.
600 11 a Geiger, Emily.
600 11 a Grimké, Sarah.
600 11 a Grimké, Angelina.
600 11 a Evans, Matilda Arabella.

650 0 a Women ‡z South Carolina ‡v Biography.
650 0 a Leadership.
651 0 a South Carolina ‡v Biography.
650 1 a Women z South Carolina ‡v Biography.
651 1 a South Carolina ‡x History.
650 1 a Leadership.

Exercise 36

Leader 01223cam 2200253 a 4500
008 991215s2000 maua g 000 0deng
010 a 99087248
020 a 1580623174
040 a DLC ‡c DLC ‡d DLC ‡d TxGeoBT
050 00 a CS 16 ‡b .I4 2000
082 00 a 929/.1/072/073 ‡2 22
245 00 a **In search of our ancestors** : ‡b 101 inspiring stories of serendipity and connection in rediscovering our family history / ‡c [compiled by] Megan Smolenyak.
246 30 a 101 inspiring stories of serendipity and connection in rediscovering our family history
246 30 a One hundred and one inspiring stories of serendipity and connection in rediscovering our family history
260 a Holbrook, Mass. : ‡b Adams Media Corp., ‡c c2000.
300 a x, 241 p. : ‡b ill. ; ‡ c22 cm.
500 a A companion book to the PBS television series ancestors.
520 a A compilation of true stories of luck, kindnesses, and serendipity encountered by persons researching their family histories.
650 0 a Genealogy ‡v Anecdotes.
651 0 a United States ‡x Genealogy ‡v Anecdotes.
650 1 a Genealogy.
700 1 a Smolenyak, Megan, ‡e comp..
730 0 a Ancestors (Television program)

Exercise 38

Leader 01051cam 2200301 a 4500
008 000809s1999 nyu 000 1 eng
010 a 00504559
020 a 0671041177
040 a DLC ‡c DLC ‡d TxGeoBT
050 00 a PS 3557 .O35927 ‡b I48 1999
082 00 a 813/.54 ‡2 22
100 1 a Golden, Christopher.
245 10 a **Immortal** : ‡b a Buffy, the vampire slayer novel / ‡c by Christopher Golden & Nancy Holder.
246 3 a Buffy the vampire slayer : immortal
250 a [1st Pocket Books hardcover].
260 a New York : ‡b Pocket Books, ‡c 1999.
300 a 309 p. ; ‡c 22 cm.
490 1 a Buffy, the vampire slayer
520 a Based on characters from the television series Buffy the vampire slayer.
650 0 a Buffy the Vampire Slayer (Fictitious character) ‡v Fiction.

650 0 a Teenage girls ‡v Fiction.
650 0 a Vampires ‡v Fiction.
655 7 a Horror tales. ‡2 gsafd
655 1 a Horror stories.
700 1 a Holder, Nancy.
830 0 a Buffy, the vampire slayer (Series)

Exercise 39

Leader 01056cam 2200265 a 4500
008 001101s2001 nyua j 000 0 eng
010 a 00053512
020 a 0060294833
020 a 0060294841 (lib. bdg.)
040 a DLC ‡c DLC ‡d DLC ‡d TxGeoBT
042 a pcc ‡a lcac
050 00 a BJ1631 ‡b .S445 2001
082 00 a 170/.44 ‡ 21
100 1 a Sheindlin, Judy, ‡d 1942-
245 10 a **Judge Judy Sheindlin's you can't judge a book by its cover** : ‡b cool rules for school / ‡c illustrated by Bob Tore.
246 30 a You can't judge a book by its cover
250 a 1st ed.
260 a New York :b ‡cliff Street Books, ‡c c2001.
300 a 1 v. (unpaged) : ‡b ill. ; ‡c 24 cm.
520 a Examines the deeper meaning behind popular sayings such as "Never put off to tomorrow what you can do today" and "You can't judge a book by its cover," and applies these rules of thumb to familiar school situations.
650 0 a Conduct of life ‡v Juvenile literature.
650 1 a Conduct of life.
700 1 a Tore, Bob, ‡e ill.

Exercise 41

Leader 00710nam 2200241 i 4500
008 791016s1981 wiua 001 0 eng
020 a 0824930010
040 a TxGeoBT ‡c TxGeoBT
050 4 a TX 757 ‡b .S68 1981
082 04 a 641.5/3 ‡2 22
100 1 a Turner, June.
245 10 a **Soup, salad, sandwich cookbook** / ‡c by June Turner and Naomi Arbit.
246 3 a Ideals soup, salad, sandwich cookbook
260 a Milwaukee, Wis. : ‡b Ideals Pub. Corp., ‡c c1981.
300 a 224 p. : ‡b ill. (some col.) ; ‡c 29 cm.
500 a Includes index.
650 0 a Cookery.
650 1 a Cookery.
650 1 a Quick and easy cookery.
700 1 a Arbit, Naomi.
730 0 a Ideals.

Exercise 47

Leader 00932cam 2200205 a 4500
008 030611s2003 ohua f b 001 0 eng
010 a 2003013199
020 a 1586830899 (pbk.)
040 a DLC ‡c DLC ‡d TxGeoBT
042 a pcc
050 00 a PN6710 ‡b .G68 2003
082 00 a 741.5/09 ‡2 21
100 1 a Gorman, Michele.
245 10 a **Getting graphic!** : ‡b using graphic novels to promote literacy with preteens and teens / ‡c Michele Gorman ; with a foreword by Jeff Smith.
260 a Worthington, Ohio : ‡b Linworth, ‡ c c2003.
260 a xii, 100 p. : ‡b ill. ; ‡c 28 cm.
504 a Includes bibliographical references (p. 91-92) and index.
520 a Discusses comic books and graphic novels, their role in libraries, school media centers and classrooms, and suggests appropriate selection, uses and approaches to promoting graphic works for young people.
650 0 a Graphic novels ‡x History and criticism.

Exercise 50

Leader 01271cam 22002895a 4500
008 020802r20022001maub 001 1 eng
020 a 2002524228
020 a 0618260242
020 a 0618260250 (pbk.)
040 a DLC ‡c DLC ‡d DLC ‡d TxGeoBT
050 00 a PR 6039 .O32 ‡b L6 2002
082 00 a 823/.912 ‡2 22
100 1 a Tolkien, J. R. R. ‡q (John Ronald Reuel), ‡d 1892-1973.
245 14 a **The lord of the rings** / ‡c by J.R.R. Tolkien.
260 a Boston : ‡b Houghton Mifflin, ‡c [2002?], c1994.
300 a xviii, 1137 p. : ‡b ill., maps ; ‡c 21 cm.
500 a First published: Great Britain : HarperCollins Publishers, 1994.
500 a Includes indexes and "Note on the Text" revised 1994 from 1987 ed.
505 0 a The fellowship of the ring — The two towers — The return of the king.
520 a Bilbo Baggins, a hobbit, gives his young cousin Frodo the ring he had found years earlier. It is the One Ring, which rules all the other Rings of Power, and Sauron, the Dark Lord, searches for it to complete his dominion as Frodo and his friends undertake its destruction in the Cracks of Doom.
650 0 a Baggins, Frodo (Fictitious character) ‡v Fiction.
650 0 a Middle Earth (Imaginary place) ‡v Fiction.
650 0 a Fantasy fiction, English.
655 0 a Fantasy fiction
852 42 3 Reading group guide
‡u http://www.houghtonmifflinbooks.com/readers_guides/lotr/lotr_rg.shtml ‡z Valid as of Nov. 21, 2002
852 42 3 Publisher description ‡u http://www.loc.gov/catdir/description/hm022/2002524228.html

Exercise 53

Leader 00764cam 2200265 a 4500
008 990216s1976 nyu c 000 1 eng
010 a 74003586
020 a 0064408388 (pbk.)
040 a DLC ‡c DLC ‡d TxGeoBT
042 a lcac
050 00 a PZ7.R6155 ‡b Esp
082 00 a [Fic] ‡2 21
100 1 a Rodgers, Mary, ‡d 1931-
240 10 a Billion for Boris
245 10 a **ESP TV** / ‡c Mary Rodgers.
250 a 1st Harper Trophy ed.
260 a New York : ‡b HarperTrophy, ‡c 1976.
300 a 216 p. ; ‡c 20 cm.
500 a Previously published: A billion for Boris. 1974.
500 a "An Ursula Nordstrom book."
500 a "A Freaky Friday book"—Cover.
650 1 a Television ‡v Fiction.
650 1 a Mothers ‡v Fiction.

Exercise 57

Leader 01148cam 2200289 a 4500
008 990309s1999 nyua c 000 1 eng
010 a 99014752
020 a 0789447673
040 a DLC ‡c DLC ‡d TxGeoBT
042 a lcac
050 00 a PZ 7 .G3264 ‡b Li 1999
082 00 a [Fic] ‡2 21
100 1 a Gerver, Jane E.
245 10 a **Little women** / ‡c Louisa May Alcott ; adapted by Jane Gerver ; illustrated by Chris Molan.
250 a 1st American ed.
260 a New York : ‡b DK Pub., ‡c 1999.
300 a 64 p. : ‡b col. ill. ; c ‡26 cm.
440 0 a Eyewitness classics
520 a Chronicles the joys and sorrows of the four March sisters as they grow into young women in 19th-century New England, during the Civil War. Uses photography and narrative illustration throughout the text to explain the historical background of the story.
521 a "A retelling for young readers"—T.p. verso.
650 1 a Family life ‡z New England ‡v Fiction.
650 1 a Sisters ‡v Fiction.
650 1 a New England ‡v Fiction.
700 1 a Alcott, Louisa May, ‡d 1832-1888. ‡t Little women.
700 1 a Molan, Chris, ‡e ill.

Exercise 60

Leader 00899pam 2200265 a 4500
008 871014t19891988onc 000 1 eng
010 a 87047795
020 a 0553276999
040 a DLC ‡c DLC ‡d DLC ‡d TxGeoBT
050 00 a PS 3563 .A464 ‡b G72 1988
082 00 a 813/.54 ‡2 22
100 1 a Mandino, Og.
245 14 a **The greatest salesman in the world**. ‡n **Part II**, ‡p **the end of the story** : ‡b featuring the ten vows of success / ‡c Og Mandino.
246 30 a End of the story
250 a 1st ed.
260 a New York : ‡b Bantam Books, ‡c 1989, c1988.
300 a 134 p. ; ‡c 18 cm.
500 a Sequel to: The greatest salesman in the world.
600 00 a Jesus Christ x Nativity ‡v Fiction.
655 0 a Christmas stories.
740 42 a The ten vows of success.

Exercise 62

Leader 00964cam 2200253 a 4500
008 920928s1993 nyu gd 000 f eng
010 a 92037034 //r932
020 a 0385470401
040 a DLC ‡c TxGeoBT ‡d TxGeoBT
050 00 a PS 3523 .A446 ‡b R545 1993
082 00 a 813/.52 ‡2 22
100 1 a L'Amour, Louis, ‡d 1908-
240 10 a Hopalong Cassidy and the riders of High Rock
245 14 a **The riders of High Rock** : ‡b a Hopalong Cassidy novel / ‡c Louis L'Amour
250 a Large print ed.
260 a New York : ‡b Bantam Books, ‡c 1993.
300 a 338 p. ; ‡c 24 cm.
500 a "Previously published as Hopalong Cassidy and the riders of High Rock by Louis L'Amour (writing as Tex Burns)"—T.p. verso.
650 0 a Cassidy, Hopalong (Fictitious character) ‡v Fiction.
655 0 a Western stories.
650 1 a Cassidy, Hopalong (Fictitious character) ‡v Fiction.
651 1 a West (U.S.) ‡v Fiction.

Exercise 63

Leader 01002cam 2200277 a 4500
008 900522s1991 maua j 000 0 eng
010 a 90004838
020 a 0395505976 (reinforced cover)
020 a 0395974968 (pbk.)
040 a DLC ‡c DLC ‡d DLC ‡d TxGeoBT

042 a lcac
050 00 a PZ8.2.B14 ‡b Ae 1991
082 00 a 398.24/52 ‡2 22
100 1 a Bader, Barbara.
245 10 a **Aesop & company** : ‡b with scenes from his legendary life / ‡c prepared by Barbara Bader ; pictures by Arthur Geisert.
246 3 a Aesop and company
260 a Boston : ‡b Houghton Mifflin, ‡c c1991.
300 a 64 p. : ‡b col. ill. ; ‡c 26 cm.
520 a A collection of concise stories told by the Greek slave, Aesop. Includes facts and legends about his life and commentary on the timeless appeal of his fables.
630 00 a Aesop's fables ‡v Adaptations.
650 1 a Folklore.
655 1 a Fables.
700 1 a Geisert, Arthur, ‡e ill.
730 0 a Aesop's fables.

Exercise 66

Leader 01426cam 2200349 a 4500
008 810318s1981 nyua b 000 p eng
010 a 81004823
020 a 0805002855 (hard cover)
020 a 0805003177 (pbk.)
040 a DLC ‡c DLC ‡d DLC ‡d TxGeoBT
041 1 a engspa
042 a lcac
050 00 a PQ 6267 .E4 ‡b N87
082 00 a 398/.8/0946 ‡2 19
082 04 a 398.8/098 ‡2 22
245 00 a **Tortillitas para mamá and other nursery rhymes** : ‡b Spanish and English / ‡c selected and translated by Margot C. Griego ... [et al.] ; illustrated by Barbara Cooney.
260 a New York : ‡b H. Holt, ‡c c1981.
300 a [32] p. : ‡b col. ill. ; ‡c 22 cm.
520 a A collection of nursery rhymes, each in both English and Spanish, collected from the Spanish community in the Americas, many with instructions for accompanying finger plays or other activities.
655 0 a Nursery rhymes, Spanish ‡x Translations into English.
655 0 a Nursery rhymes, Spanish American ‡x Translations into English.
655 0 a Nursery rhymes, Spanish.
655 0 a Nursery rhymes, Spanish American.
655 1 a Nursery rhymes.
655 1 a Spanish American poetry.
655 1 a Spanish language materials ‡x Bilingual.
650 1 a Finger play.
650 1 a Griego, Margot C.
700 1 a Cooney, Barbara, ‡d 1917- ‡e ill.

Exercise 68

Leader 01048cam 22002411a 4500
008 720420s1964 nyu g 000 d eng
010 a 63017001 //r83
040 a DLC ‡c DLC ‡d TxGeoBT
041 1 a eng ‡h ger
050 04 a PT 2607 .U493 ‡b P53
082 00 a 832/.914 ‡2 22
100 1 a Dürrenmatt, Friedrich.
240 10 a Physiker. ‡l English
245 14 a **The physicists** / ‡c by Friedrich Dürrenmatt ; translated from the German by James Kirkup.
260 a New York : ‡b Grove Press, ‡c c1964.
300 a 94 p. ; ‡c 21 cm.
500 a Original German version: Zurich, Switzerland : Verlags AG "Die Arche," c1962.
520 a In this two-act comedy, Dürrenmatt addresses the broad themes of a person's responsibility is in a world in which the individual appears to have less and less influence, and what a scientist's responsibility is for the uses to which individual research is put.
650 0 a Physicists ‡v Drama.
650 0 a German drama ‡v Translations into English.
700 1 a Kirkup, James, ‡e tr.

Exercise 71

Leader 01075cam 2200265 a 4500
008 860625t1986uuuunyuaf c 000 0 eng d
010 a 86016673
020 a 0517603578
040 a DLC ‡c DLC ‡d TxGeoBT
042 a lcac
050 00 a PZ8.3 ‡b .M85 1986c
082 04 a 398.8 ‡2 22
130 0 a Mother Goose.
245 14 a **The Jessie Willcox Smith Mother Goose** : ‡b a careful and full selection of the rhymes ... / ‡c by Jessie Willcox Smith ; foreword by Corey Nash.
246 30 a Mother Goose
260 a New York : b Derrydale Books : ‡b Distributed by Outlet Book Co., ‡c 1991, c1986.
300 a 173 p., [22] p. of plates : ‡b ill. (some col.) ; ‡c 23 x 27 cm.
520 a An illustrated collection of over 600 Mother Goose nursery rhymes including both the well-known and the less familiar rhymes.
500 a Remainder of title: with numerous illustrations in full color and black and white.
655 0 a Nursery rhymes.
655 0 a Children's poetry.
655 1 a Nursery rhymes.
700 1 a Smith, Jessie Willcox, ‡e comp.

Exercise 75

Leader 00963cam 2200265 a 4500
008 990319s2000 ilua g be 001 0deng
010 a 99062063
020 a 0716601001 (set)
040 a DLC ‡c DLC ‡d DLC ‡d TxGeoBT
050 00 a AE 5 ‡b .W55 2000
082 00 a 031 ‡2 22
245 04 a **The World Book encyclopedia**.
246 34 i Cover title: ‡a World Book millennium 2000
250 a 2000 ed.
260 a Chicago : ‡b World Book, ‡c c2000.
300 a 22 v. : ‡b ill. (some col.), maps ; ‡c 26 cm.
500 a Vol. 22: Research guide and index.
504 a Includes bibliographical references and index.
520 a General-interest encyclopedia.
655 0 a Encyclopedias and dictionaries.
655 1 a Encyclopedias and dictionaries.
710 2 a World Book, Inc.

Exercise 76

Leader 01019cam 2200265 a 4500
008 991001s2002 nyuab b b 001 0 eng
010 a 99049779
020 a 068815431X (trade)
020 a 0688154328
040 a DLC ‡c DLC ‡d DLC ‡d TxGeoBT
042 a pcc a lcac
050 00 a GT 2430 ‡b .L35 2002
082 00 a 394.2 ‡2 21
100 1 a Lankford, Mary D.
245 10 a **Birthdays around the world** / ‡c by Mary D. Lankford ; illustrated by Karen Dugan.
250 a 1st ed.
260 a New York : ‡b HarperCollins, ‡c c2002.
300 a 32 p. : ‡b col. ill., col. map ; ‡c 21 x 26 cm.
504 a Includes bibliographical references (p. 31) and index.
520 a Describes the way birthdays have been celebrated in the past and the customs used to mark these special occasions in such countries as Finland, Malaysia, Mexico, New Zealand and others.
650 0 a Birthdays ‡v Cross-cultural studies ‡v Juvenile literature.
650 1 a Birthdays.
700 1 a Dugan, Karen, ‡e ill.

Exercise 77

Leader 01414ntm 2200277 a 4500
008 040421s1999 f 001 0deng d
050 4 a Z 674.82 ‡b T47 H39 1999
082 04 a 021.6'42 ‡2 22

100 1 a Haynes, Dorothy Elizabeth, ‡d 1945-
245 14 a **The Texas Library Connection network** : ‡h [manuscript] : ‡b usage by school library media specialists related to the Stages of concern / ‡c by Dorothy Elizabeth Haynes.
246 3 a TLC network : ‡h [manuscript]
260 c 1999.
300 a xii, 133 leaves ; ‡c 28 cm.
500 a "August 1999"
504 a Includes bibliographical references (p. 127-131)
520 a "The TLC is a statewide network serving school library media centers with a bibliographic database of member library holdings and access to selected commercial indexing and full-text databases. [This study sought] to ascertain the impact of selected factors on the use of TLC and on the concerns of library media specialists about using TLC."—Abstract.
610 10 a Texas Library Connection ‡x Research.
630 00 a Stages of concern questionnaire ‡x Research.
630 00 a Concerns-based adoption model ‡x Research.
650 0 a Library catalogs ‡x Research.
650 0 a Catalogs, Union ‡x Research.
650 0 a Interlibrary loans ‡x Research.

Exercise 78

Leader 01405cam 22002894a 4500
008 020612s2002 nyua g 000 0 eng
010 a 2002075811
020 a 0743241908
040 a DLC ‡c DLC ‡d DLC
042 a pcc
043 a n-us—- ‡a n-us-ny
050 00 a HV 6432 ‡b .W46 2002
082 00 a 973.931 ‡2 21
110 2 a CBS News.
245 10 a **What we saw** / ‡c CBS News ; with an introduction by Dan Rather.
260 a New York : ‡b Simon & Schuster, ‡c c2002.
300 a 143 p. : ‡b ill. ; ‡c 24 cm. + ‡e 1 digital video disc (sd., col. ; 4 3/4 in.) in book.
538 a System requirements: Digital videodisc player.
520 a The DVD contains news footage of the airplane attacks on the World Trade Center in New York City on the morning of Sept. 11, 2001, and surrounding events, as recorded on camera by the staff of CBS News (Columbia Broadcasting System). Samples and related materials are available at: http://www.cbsnews.com/stories/2002/08/29/september11/main520241.shtml.
650 0 a September 11 Terrorist attacks, 2001 ‡v Personal narratives.
650 0 a September 11 Terrorist attacks, 2001 ‡x Press coverage.
700 1 a Rather, Dan.
710 2 a CBS News.
856 42 i Related web site:
‡u http://www.cbsnews.com/stories/2002/08/29/september11/main520241.shtml

Exercise 79

Leader 01093cam 2200289 a 4500
008 980403s1999 nyu g b 000 0 eng
010 a 98018306
020 a 019510921X (cloth : alk. paper)

020 a 0195109228 (pbk. : alk. paper)
040 a DLC ‡c DLC ‡d DLC ‡d TxGeoBT
043 a e-uk—-
050 00 a PR 3506 .H94 ‡b A6 1999
082 00 a 824/.5 ‡2 21
100 1 a Haywood, Eliza Fowler, ‡d 1693?-1756.
240 10 a Female spectator. ‡k Selections. ‡f 1999
245 10 a **Selections from the female spectator** / ‡c by Eliza Haywood ; edited by Patricia Meyer Spacks.
260 a New York : ‡b Oxford University Press, ‡c 1999.
300 a xxii, 313 p. ; ‡c 22 cm.
490 0 a Women writers in English 1350-1850
504 a Bibliography: p. xxi-xxii.
500 a The female spectator was originally published in London during 1744-1746.
650 0 a Women ‡x Literary collections.
650 0 a Women ‡z Great Britain ‡x Conduct of life ‡x History ‡y 18th century ‡x Sources.
650 0 a Early British periodicals.
700 1 a Spacks, Patricia Ann Meyer, ‡e ed.

Exercise 85

Leader 01140cam 2200241 a 4500
008 800909q1934uuuuenka g 000 1 eng
010 a 36010905
040 a DLC ‡c DLC ‡d DLC ‡TxGeo BT
050 00 a PZ 3 .A93 ‡b P11
082 04 a 823/.7 ‡2 22
100 1 a Austen, Jane, ‡d 1775-1817.
245 10 a **Persuasion**.
260 a New York : ‡b E.P. Dutton, ‡c [1934?]
300 a v, 219 p. : ‡b col. ill. ; ‡c 19 cm.
490 0 a Works of Jane Austen
500 a Includes frontispiece and some plates (unnumbered); illustrated by Maximilien Vox.
520 a Sir Walter Elliot, a widower, lives extravagantly - and in debt - in Kellynch Hall on his estate. The eldest of his three daughters, Elizabeth, has been the mistress of the home since her mother's death, and shares his vanity and class consciousness. When she strikes up a friendship with Mrs. Clay, the daughter of the family lawyer, her sister Anne distrusts Mrs. Clay's motives.
650 0 a Class consciousness ‡v Fiction.
650 0 a Pride and vanity ‡v Fiction.
650 0 a Social classes ‡z England ‡y 19th century ‡v Fiction.
700 1 a Vox, Maximilien, ‡e ill.

Exercise 86

Leader 01373cam 2200289 a 4500
008 771102s1978 nyu g 000 0 eng
010 a 75031193
020 a 0824021444
040 a DLC ‡c DLC ‡d DLC ‡d TxGeoBT
050 00 a PR4525.D2 ‡b A6 1978
082 00 a 822/.7 ‡2 22

100 1 a Darley, George, ‡d 1795-1846.
240 10 a Errors of ecstasie
245 14 a **The errors of ecstasie** : ‡b [and] Sylvia ; Nepenthe / ‡c George Darley ; with an introduction for the Garland edition by Donald H. Reiman.
260 a New York : ‡b Garland, ‡c 1978.
300 a 391 p. in various pagings (43, vii, 217, 69) ; ‡c 21 cm.
490 1 a Romantic context : poetry
440 2 a A Garland series. ‡p Significant minor poetry, 1789-1830
500 a Facsimile reprint of the 1822 ed. of The errors of ecstasie, printed for G. and W. B. Whittaker, London; the 1827 ed. of Sylvia, published for J. Taylor and sold by J.A. Hessey, London; and the 1835 ed. of Nepenthe, published by the author, London.
500 a "Printed in photo-facsimile in 128 volumes; selected and arranged by Donald H. Reiman, the Carl H. Pforzheimer Library"—Series t.p.
700 12 a Darley, George, ‡d 1795-1846. ‡t Sylvia ‡f 1978.
700 12 a Darley, George, ‡d 1795-1846. ‡t Nepenthe ‡f 1978.
740 02 a Sylvia.
740 02 a Nepenthe.
830 0 a Romantic context. ‡p Poetry.

Exercise 90

Leader 01460cam 2200349 a 4500
008 040304s2002 flua d 000 c eng
010 a 2004297236
020 a 1593140126
040 a MLN ‡c MLN ‡d DLC ‡d TxGeoBT
042 a lccopycat
050 4 a PN 6727 .W26 ‡b K56 1997
082 04 a 741.5 ‡a 813'.6 ‡2 22
100 1 a Waid, Mark.
245 10 a **Ruse** : ‡b **enter the detective** / ‡c Mark Waid, writer.
246 30 a Enter the detective
250 a Traveler ed.
260 a Oldsmar, Fla. : ‡b CrossGeneration Comics, ‡c c2002.
300 a 1 v. (various pagings) : ‡b col. ill. ; ‡c 21 cm.
440 0 a Ruse ; ‡v 1
500 a "Originally published in single magazine form as Ruse, vol. 1, issues #1-#6"—Cover, p.2.
508 a Butch Guice, penciler ; Mike Perkins, inker ; Laura Martin, colorist. Chapter 6: Jeff Johnson, penciler ; Paul Neary, inker ; Jason Lambert, colorist ; Dave Lanphear, letterer. Cover art by Butch Guice & Laura Martin.
520 a Detective Simon Archard and his assistant Emma Bishop begin to suspect that Partington's newest resident, a mysterious baroness, may be responsible for a rash of serial killings.
650 0 a Murder ‡v Fiction.
650 0 a Police ‡v Fiction.
655 0 a Detective and mystery stories.
655 0 a Comic books, strips, etc.
655 0 a Graphic novels.
655 1 a Mystery and detective stories.
700 1 a Guice, Butch.
700 1 a Perkins, Mike.
700 1 a DePuy, Laura, ‡e ill.

Exercise 94

Leader 01361nim 2200277 a 4500
007 ss lunjlcmunnd
008 811116s1999 nyunnn g p eng d
020 a 0898458854
028 03 a CO 1713 ‡b Harper Audio
050 a TxGeoBT ‡c TxGeoBT
050 4 a PS 3509 ‡b .L43 O55 1983
082 04 a 821/.912 ‡2 22
100 1 a Eliot, T. S. ‡q (Thomas Stearns), ‡d 1888-1965.
245 10 a **Old Possum's book of practical cats ‡h** [sound recording] / ‡c T.S. Eliot ; performed by Sir John Gielgud and Irene Worth.
246 30 a Book of practical cats ‡h [sound recording]
260 a New York : ‡b HarperCollins : ‡b Caedmon Audio, ‡c 1999.
300 a 1 sound cassette (36 min.) ; ‡c in container 19 cm.
500 a "Unabridged poems"—Cover.
505 0 a side 1. The naming of cats — The old gumbie cat — Growltiger's last stand — The rum tum tugger — The song of the jellicles — Mungojerrie and Rumpelteazer — Old Deuteronomy. Side 2: Of the aweful battle of the Pekes and the Pollicles — Mr. Mistoffelees — McCavity : the mystery cat — Gus : the theatre cat — Bustopher Jones : the cat about town — Skimbleshanks : the railway cat — The addressing of cats.
650 0 a Cats ‡v Poetry.
700 1 a Gielgud, John, ‡c Sir.
700 1 a Worth, Irene.
710 2 a Caedmon Audio.
710 2 a HarperCollins Publishers Inc.

Exercise 98

Leader 01835njm 2200373 a 4500
007 sdlbmmennmplne
008 970606q19501972mx crn g spa d
028 02 a DM 859 ‡b Musart
040 a TxGeoBT ‡c TxGeoBT
050 4 a M 2065 ‡b .N38
082 04 a 782.28 ‡2 22
110 2 a Coro de Madrigalistas.
245 10 a **Navidad** ‡h [sound recording] / ‡c Coro de Madrigalistas ; director, Luis Sandi.
260 a [Mexico] : ‡b Musart ; ‡a Hialeah, Fla. :b Records Distributors of America : ‡b Distributed by Musical Records Co., ‡c [196-?]
300 a 1 sound disc : ‡b analog, 33 1/3 rpm ; ‡c 12 in.
546 a Sung in Spanish.
511 0 a Luis Sandi, director and musical arranger.
520 a Mexican unaccompanied mixed voice madrigal choir sings traditional Christmas carols.
505 0 a 1. Blanca Navidad / Irvin[g] Berlin — ¿Qué haces pastorcito? — Adeste fideles — En los brazos de la luna / Letelier — Canto de posadas / arr. Luis Sandi — Puer natus in Bethlehem / Davis — 2. Noche de paz / Gruber — Villancico — Aleluya — Campana navideña / J. Piorpont [i.e., Pierpont] — Ave María / Schubert ; arr. L.G. Moncada — Verbum caro.
655 0 a Carols.
655 0 a Christmas music.

650 0 a Choruses (Mixed voices), Unaccompanied.
655 1 a Carols.
655 1 a Christmas music.
650 1 a Choruses (Mixed voices), Unaccompanied.
655 1 a Spanish language materials.
700 1 a Sandi, Luis.
700 12 a Berlin, Irving, ‡d 1888. ‡t White Christmas ‡l Spanish.
700 1 a Letelier Llona, Alfonso, ‡d 1912-
700 12 a Gruber, Franz Xaver, ‡d 1787-1863. ‡t Stille Nacht, heilige Nacht ‡l Spanish.
700 12 a Pierpont, James, ‡d 1822-1893. ‡t Jingle bells, ‡e arr. ‡l Spanish.
700 12 a Schubert, Franz, ‡d 1797-1828. ‡t Ellens Gesang ‡b D. 839, ‡e arr. ‡l Spanish.

Exercise 100

Leader 01064nim 2200277 a 4500
007 sd fungnnmmned
008 960403s19991997mdunnn g f eng d
020 a 0788746375
028 02 a C1212 ‡b Recorded Books
040 a TxGeoBT ‡c TxGeoBT
050 4 a PS 3503 .R167 ‡b S66
082 04 a 813'.54 ‡a [Fic] ‡2 22
100 1 a Bradbury, Ray.
245 10 a **Something wicked this way comes ‡h** [sound recording] / ‡c by Ray Bradbury ; an unabridged performance by Paul Hecht.
260 a Prince Frederick, MD : ‡b Recorded Books, ‡c p1999, c1997.
300 a 7 computer optical discs (8 hrs.) : ‡b sd. ; ‡c 4 3/4 in.
500 a "Recorded Books presents Unabridged books on CD"—Container liner.
520 a When a seductive stranger and his mysterious carnival arrives in town, terrifying things begin to happen as two boys discover its secret.
651 0 a West (U.S.) ‡v Juvenile fiction.
655 0 a Horror tales ‡v Juvenile literature.
655 0 a Fantasy fiction.
651 1 a West (U.S.) ‡v Fiction.
655 1 a Horror stories.
655 1 a Fantasy.
700 1 a Hecht, Paul.
710 2 a Recorded Books, LLC.

Exercise 104

Leader 01610ncm 2200325 a 4500
008 981023s1998 nyucra g eng d
010 a 98023310
020 a 0789434830
040 a DLC ‡c TxGeoBT ‡d TxGeoBT
050 00 a M2193 ‡b .F53 1998
082 04 a 782.28/1723 ‡2 22
245 04 a **The first Noel** : ‡b a child's book of Christmas carols to play and sing / ‡c conceived by Miriam Farbey ; editors, Nicholas Turpin and Marie Greenwood ; music arranged by Lesley Applebee and Nigel Thomas.

250 a 1st American ed.
260 a New York : ‡b DK Pub., ‡c 1998.
300 a 1 score (31 p.) : ‡b col. ill. ; ‡c 29 cm.
500 a Credits on t.p. verso.
500 a "Illustrated with festive paintings"—Cover.
505 0 a O come, all ye faithful — We three kings of Orient are — Hark! the herald angels sing — Good King Wenceslas — Away in a manger — The holly and the ivy — O little town of Bethlehem — The first Noel— Song of the crib — Silent night — It came upon the midnight clear — I saw three ships — We wish you a merry Christmas.
520 a Presents the words and music for 13 classic Christmas carols, arranged for piano and guitar; each complemented by a holiday illustration.
655 0 a Carols, English ‡v Juvenile literature.
655 0 a Christmas music ‡v Juvenile literature.
650 0 a Christmas in art ‡v Juvenile literature.
655 1 a Carols.
655 1 a Christmas music.
650 1 a Christmas in art.
700 1 a Farbey, Miriam.
700 1 a Turpin, Nicholas, ‡e ed.
700 1 a Greenwood, Marie, ‡e ed.
700 1 a Applebee, Lesley.
700 1 a Thomas, Nigel.

Exercise 107

Leader 01289cam 2200277 a 4500
008 980420s1997 caua b 000 1 eng d
010 a 98141104
020 a 1888443278
050 a DLC ‡c DLC ‡d DLC ‡d TxGeoBT
042 a lcac
050 00 a PZ7.W46848 ‡b Ch 1997
082 00 a [E] ‡2 22
100 1 a Welply, Michaël.
245 10 a **Choo-choo Charlie, the Littletown train ‡h** [toy] : ‡b a pop-up play village... / ‡c [illustrated by Michael Welply ; written by Dawn Bentley ; art direction by Jim Deesing].
260 a Santa Monica, CA : ‡b Piggy Toes Press ; ‡a Kansas City, MO : ‡b Distributed by Andrews and McMeel, ‡c c1997.
300 a 1 plastic train : ‡b col. ; ‡c 4 in. + ‡e in box printed with simple story line on facing sides when folded out (29 cm.)
500 a Title from container.
521 a For children over 3 years of age.
520 a The simple story is told through a three-dimensional village pop-up play set with a wind-up toy train with real train sounds and 11 punch-out characters.
655 0 a Toy and movable books ‡v Specimens.
650 0 a Railroads ‡x Trains ‡v Fiction.
650 1 a Railroads ‡x Trains ‡v Fiction.
650 1 a City and town life ‡v Fiction.
655 1 a Sound effects books.
655 1 a Toy and movable books.
700 1 a Bentley, Dawn.

Exercise 110

Leader 00871nrm 2200217 a 4500
008 000000s1948 nyunnn g gneng d
040 a TxGeoBT ‡c TxGeoBT
050 4 a GV 1507 .S3 ‡b S
082 04 a 793.734 ‡2 22
245 00 a **Scrabble** ‡h [game] / ‡c Selchow & Righter Co.
260 a Bay Shore, N.Y. : ‡b Selchow & Righter, ‡c c1948.
300 a 1 game (1 board, 100 letter tiles, letter bag, 4 individual letter racks) : ‡b col. ; ‡c board 36 x 36 cm. ; in box 37 x 19 x 4 cm.
520 a Players form words with the letters they have drawn and what is already on the board, hoping to use the higher-value letters and squares to finish first with the highest score.
650 0 a English language ‡v Vocabulary.
650 0 a Word games.
650 1 a Recreations.
650 1 a Word games.
650 1 a Games.
710 2 a Selchow & Righter Co.

Exercise 112

Leader 00925nrm 2200253 a 4500
008 040421s2002 njunnn a wneng d
024 1 a 02399751013 ‡2 Gund, Inc.
040 a TxGeoBT ‡c TxGeoBT
050 4 a PZ 7 .F1865 ‡b O1 2002
082 04 a 688.7'22 ‡2 22
245 00 a **Olivia [doll]** ‡h [toy] / ‡c Ian Falconer ; licensed by Silver Lining Productions Ltd.
260 a Edison, NJ : ‡b Gund, ‡c c2002.
300 a 1 doll : ‡b white, red, and black fabric ; ‡c 7 1/2 in. + ‡e 1 name tag with other information.
500 a Title from tag.
500 a "This is Olivia. She is good at a lot of things."
520 a Designed by the author of the Olivia books, with a washable surface.
500 a "Made in China. Keep this tag for reference."
650 1 a Pigs.
655 1 a Toys.
650 1 a Olivia (Fictitious character)
700 1 a Falconer, Ian, ‡d 1959-
856 42 2 www.gund.com

Exercise 117

Leader 01205ngm 2200325 a 4500
007 gs cubfje
008 900112s1987 nyunnn d sneng d
020 a 0870058088
040 a TxGeoBT ‡c TxGeoBT
050 4 a HD 9940 .U4 ‡b C37 1987
082 04 a 687' .023 ‡2 22

245 00 a **Careers in fashion ‡h** [slide] : ‡b manufacturing.
246 3 a Careers in fashion manufacturing ‡h [slide]
246 30 a Manufacturing ‡h [slide]
260 a New York : ‡b Fairchild Visuals, ‡c c1987.
300 a 40 slides : ‡b col. ;‡c 5 x 5 cm + ‡e 1 sound cassette + 1 booklet (17 p. ; 28 cm.) in binder (29 cm.)
490 1 a Modern careers in fashion ; ‡v set 3
538 a Requires standard slide projector and cassette player.
500 a Includes a glossary.
520 a Discusses the manufacturing aspects of the clothing and fashion industry.
650 0 a Fashion ‡x Vocational guidance.
650 0 a Manufacturing ‡x Vocational guidance.
650 0 a Clothing industry ‡x Vocational guidance.
650 1 a Manufacturing industry ‡x Vocational guidance.
650 1 a Fashion industry ‡x Vocational guidance.
650 1 a Clothing industry ‡x Vocational guidance.
710 2 a Fairchild Books and Visuals.

Exercise 121

Leader 01034ngm 2200265 a 4500
006 gnnn fn
007 gt cu vc
008 980330s1969 ilunnn f tneng d
040 a TxGeoBT ‡c TxGeoBT
050 4 a Z 711 ‡b .L53 1969
082 04 a 028.7'028 ‡2 22
245 00 a **Library reference skills ‡h** [transparency].
260 a Chicago : ‡b Encyclopaedia Britannica Educational Corp., ‡c c1969.
300 a 36 overhead transparencies : ‡b col. ; ‡c 26 x 22 cm. + ‡e 1 teacher's guide ; in plastic container 29 x 25 cm.
538 a Requires overhead projector.
508 a Teacher guide by Carl B. Smith, Elizabeth Batts, Mary Kathryn Dunn
650 0 a Library orientation ‡v Audio-visual aids.
610 20 a Flipatran (TM) ‡v Audio-visual aids.
650 0 a Reference services (Libraries) ‡x Study and teaching ‡v Audio-visual aids.
700 1 a Smith, Carl B.
700 1 a Batts, Elizabeth.
700 1 a Dunn, Mary Kathryn.
710 2 a Encyclopaedia Britannica Educational Corp.

Exercise 124

Leader 01473nmm 2200277 a 4500
008 20040210124005.4
007 co cga mucuu
008 780725s1999 xxu d m eng d
040 a TxGeoBT ‡c TxGeoBT
050 4 a GV 1469.2 ‡b .E97 1999
082 04 a 607/.385 ‡2 22

245 04 a **The experience** ‡h [electronic resource] : ‡b [game] / ‡c Motorola ; Digital DNA ; Human Code ; Apple Computer.
256 a Computer programs and files.
260 a [United States] : ‡b Motorola, ‡c c1999.
300 a 2 computer optical discs : ‡b sd., col. ill. ; ‡c 4 3/4 in.
538 a System requirements: Pentium 1 or higher with 16 MB of RAM; sound cards and speakers; 8X CD-ROM drive; keyboard and mouse; QuickTime (included)
500 a Title from CD-ROM disc surface.
500 a "Anti-technology extremists have struck... You have one hour to take back the future"
520 a Simulation game; enables a person to explore communications without use of pagers, cell phones, or the Internet. Explores the potentials of personal networks that allow such technology applications as video calls, high speed data transfers, and engaging in many kinds of financial transaction using various communications devices.
650 1 a Technology ‡x Study and teaching.
650 1 a Technology ‡v Computer assisted instruction.
655 0 a Computer games.
710 2 a Motorola, Inc.
710 2 a Apple Computer, Inc.
856 41 i Game also available online at:
u http://www.experience.motorola.com/

Exercise 127

Leader 01520nmm 2200301 a 4500
007 cr cn —–mnuan
008 030105s2001 flu g j eng d
040 a TxGeoBT ‡c TxGeoBT
050 4 a Z 701.3 .N48 ‡b S37 2001
082 04 a 676/.286/0288 ‡b 22
100 1 a English, Jeanne.
245 10 a **Scrapbooking with newspapers ‡h** [electronic resource] : ‡b a step by step guide to the safe use of newsprint in your scrapbooks / ‡c by Jeanne English & Al Thelin ; The Salt Lake Tribune ; NAC - Newspaper Agency Corporation Agent ; Deseret News
256 a Computer data.
260 a Safety Harbor, FL : ‡b Headline Memories, Wayne Matthews Corp., ‡c 2001.
300 a 4 p. : ‡b col. ill. ; ‡c 28 cm. (printed version)
538 a World Wide Web site.
500 a Title from web site: http://www.headlinememories.com/pdfs/Guide.pdf.
500 a Download the printable file from <http://www.headlinememories.com/pdfs/Guide.pdf> or http://www.headlinememories.com/guide.html
538 a World Wide Web site.
500 a "Date web site last modified: Wednesday, October 09, 2002 7:57:01 PM GMT"— "Page info".
650 0 a Scrapbooks ‡v Handbooks, manuals, etc.
700 1 a Thelin, Al.
710 2 a Headline Memories.
710 2 a Wayne Matthews Corporation.
856 40 u http://www.headlinememories.com/pdfs/Guide.html

Exercise 129

Leader 00705nom 2200229 a 4500
007 onnn bn-ou-ou
008 020217s1990 ch nnn g bneng d
040 a TxGeoBT ‡c TxGeoBT
050 4 a TT 715 ‡b .S49
082 04 a 646/.6 ‡2 22
245 00 a **Sewing kit** ‡h [kit].
260 a China : ‡b [s.n., ‡c 199?]
300 a 1 sewing kit ; ‡c in container folded to 9 x 10 cm.
500 a "415409 SRRT2"—On edge of flap.
505 0 a Contents: 6 colors of thread, each with attached needle, on card; 4 buttons, 2 hat pins, 2 safety pins
520 a Clothes mending kit.
650 0 a Sewing.
655 7 a Sewing equipment and supplies. ‡2 gmgpc

Exercise 132

Leader 01376cem 2200301 a 4500
007 ad canzn
008 800414s1979 nyu e 1 eng
010 a 78065321
020 a 0895770628
040 a DLC ‡c DLC ‡d DLC ‡d TxGeoBT
050 00 a G 1021 ‡b .R54 1979
082 00 a 912 ‡2 22
110 2 a Reader's Digest Association.
245 1 a **Wide world atlas ‡h** [cartographic material].
246 30 a Reader's Digest wide world atlas
260 a Pleasantville, N.Y. : ‡b Reader's Digest Association, ‡c c1979.
300 a 240 p. : ‡b col. ill., col. maps ; ‡c 39 cm.
500 a "Reader's Digest joined Rand McNally ... to produce this concise yet comprehensive edition of The International Atlas."
500 a Pages 6-144, 196-240 from The international atlas c1979 by Rand McNally; pages 146-151, 190-195 from Cosmopolitan world atlas c1978 by Rand McNally ; pages 152-167 from Goode's World atlas c1978 by Rand McNally ; pages 168-189 c1979 by Encyclopaedia Britannica.
500 a Includes index.
650 0 a Atlases.
710 2 a Rand McNally and Company.
710 2 a Encyclopaedia Britannica, Inc.
710 22 a Rand McNally and Company. ‡t International atlas. ‡f 1979.
710 22 a Rand McNally and Company. ‡t Cosmopolitan world atlas. ‡f 1978.
710 22 a Rand McNally and Company. ‡t Goode's world atlas. ‡f 1978.

Exercise 137

Leader 00827ngm 2200229 a 4500
007 vf cbahou

008 960403s1997 nju028 f vleng d
028 02 a FFH 6891 ‡b Films for the Humanities & Sciences
040 a TxGeoBT ‡c TxGeoBT
050 4 a RA 971.35 ‡b .D58 1997
082 04 a 331.11/43 ‡2 22
245 00 a **Diversity leadership** ‡h [videorecording] / ‡c Films for the Humanities & Sciences.
260 a Princeton, NJ : ‡b Films for the Humanities & Sciences, ‡c 1997.
300 a 1 videocassette (28 min.) : ‡b sd., col. ; ‡c 1/2 in.
440 0 a Managing diversity
538 a VHS.
500 a Title from cassette label.
650 0 a Diversity in the workplace ‡z United States.
650 0 a Pluralism (Social sciences) ‡z United States ‡x Personnel management.
700 1 a Hunt, Portia L.

Exercise 146

Leader 01634ngm 2200421 a 4500
007 vd cvaizz
008 011101s2001 cau038 g vleng d
020 a 0767873890
024 1 a 043396070691
040 a unk ‡c unk ‡d TxGeoBT
050 4 a GV 1821 .C578 ‡b J68 2001
082 04 a 791.34 ‡2 22
110 2 a Cirque du Soleil.
245 10 a **Journey of man ‡h** [videorecording] / ‡c Sony Pictures Classics presents Cirque du Soleil ; produced by Peter Wagg and André Picard ; written by Steve Roberts & Peter Wagg ; directed by Keith Melton.
246 33 a Cirque du Soleil journey of man ‡h [videorecording]
260 a [Burbank, Calif.] : ‡b Columbia TriStar Home Entertainment, ‡c c2001.
300 a 1 videodisc (38 min.) : ‡b sd., col. ; ‡c 4 3/4 in.
538 a DVD.
546 a Closed-captioned.
500 a At head of title: Cirque Du Soleil.
511 1 a Narrated by Ian McKellen.
508 a Director of photography, Reed Smoot ; editor, Harry B. Miller, III ; music, Benoit Jutras ; production designer, John Zachary ; 3-D & visual effects supervisor, Peter Anderson.
650 0 a Circus.
650 0 a Acrobats.
650 0 a Acrobatics.
655 7 a Performance art.
655 7 a Video recordings for the hearing impaired.
700 1 a Wagg, Peter.
700 1 a Picard, André, ‡d 1944-
700 1 a Roberts, Steve, ‡d 1941-
700 1 a Melton, Keith.
700 1 a McKellen, Ian.
700 1 a Smoot, Reed.
700 1 a Miller, Harry B., ‡c III., ‡e ed.
700 1 a Jutras, Benoit.

Exercise 150

Leader 01925ngm 2200421 a 4500
007 vd cvaizu
008 011123t20031999cau563 g vleng d
020 a 0790776154
024 1 a 08592424924 ‡2 Warner Home Entertainment
028 43 a 24249 ‡b Warner Home Video
040 a TxGeoBT ‡c TxGeoBT
050 4 a PN 1992.77 .F76 ‡b F75 2003
082 04 a 791.45'6164 ‡2 22
245 00 a **Friends**. ‡p **Season 5 ‡h** [videorecording] / ‡c directed by James Burrows ; executive producers Kevin S. Bright, Marta Kauffman, David Crane.
250 a Standard version.
260 a Burbank, Calif. : ‡b Warner Brothers, ‡c 2003, c1999.
300 a 4 digital video discs (563 min.) : ‡b sd., col. ; ‡c 3/4 in.
538 a System requirements: DVD player, sound and video cards.
546 a Closed captioned; English produced with Dolby surround sound.
500 a Title from Disc one.
500 a Edited, with new music, additional audio, visual and other cinematographic material for the DVD production of the original 1999 television series.
511 1 a Jennifer Anniston, Courteney Cox Arquette, Lisa Kudrow, Matt LeBlanc, Matthew Perry, David Schwimmer.
508 a Created by David Crane and Marta Kauffman
520 a The six friends start their year together in London and finish in Las Vegas, with weddings in both places. Includes scenes not included in the original broadcasts, and other bonus features.
655 7 a Situation comedy ‡v Television series. ‡2 migfg
700 1 a Anniston, Jennifer.
700 1 a Arquette, Courteney Cox.
700 1 a Kudrow, Lisa.
700 1 a LeBlanc, Matt.
700 1 a Perry, Matthew, ‡d 1969-
700 1 a Schwimmer, David, ‡d 1966-
700 1 a Burrows, James, ‡d 1940-
700 1 a Bright, Kevin S.
700 1 a Kauffman, Marta, ‡d 1956-
700 1 a Crane, David, d 1957-
710 2 a Warner Brothers Entertainment, Inc.

Title Index

Number in parentheses refers to the exercise.

Index to Exercises in Numerical Order

Index to Types of Material

MUSIC (PRINTED)

The First Noel
The Rainbow Connection
Short Preludes and Fugues

THREE-DIMENSIONAL MATERIALS & REALIA

107 Choo-Choo Charlie *[toy]*
108 Edmark Twin Gear Pump *[model+]*
109 Shell Case Penny Collection
110 Scrabble
111 Travel Triazzle *[puzzle]*
112 Olivia *[doll]*
113 Little Red Riding Hood Puppets
114 Geode *[realia]*
115 Ocarina *[3D]*

VISUAL MATERIALS

116 Battle Scene *[slide]*
117 Careers in Fashion. Manufacturing *[slides+]*
118 Clothing. The Visible Self *[filmstrips+]*
119 Humanscale *[placards]*
120 Juegos = Games *[study prints]*
121 Library Reference Skills *[transparencies]*
122 New York Public Library *[postcard]*
123 Technical Graphics *[transparency master]*

ELECTRONIC RESOURCES

124 The Experience [CD-ROM]
125 The World's Greatest Speeches [CD-RM]
126 Recipe Keeper [diskette]
127 Scrapbooking with Newspapers [remote]
128 Authority Tools ... for Catalogers [remote]

MIXED MATERIAL—KITS

129 Sewing Kit
130 12 Piece Lab Kit

CARTOGRAPHIC MATERIALS

131 Native American Heritage *[map]*
132 Wide World Atlas
133 Washington D.C. *[map]*

VIDEO RECORDINGS

134 50 of the Greatest Cartoons [vc]
135 Les Bonnes [vc]
136 Contemporary Authors: How the … [vc]
137 Diversity Leadership [vc]
138 Empowering People with Disabilities [vc]
139 Femmes aux yeus ouverts [vc]
140 Green Medicine [vc]
141 Jazz Dance Jigsaw [vc]
142 Leadership in a Time of Change [vc]
143 The Nutcracker [vc]
144 The Tap Dictionary [vc]
145 Wake Up, America [vc]
146 Journey of Man [DVD]
147 J.R.R. Tolkien, Master of the Rings [DVD]
148 Lord of the Rings. The Fellowship.. [DVD]
149 Buffy the Vampire Slayer. 1st Season [DVD]
150 Friends [DVD]

Index to Rules, by Title

Index to Rules, by Number

Numbers in parentheses refer to the exercises.

About the Authors

ELIZABETH HAYNES is Assistant Professor of Library and Information Science at the University of Southern Mississippi, Hattiesburg.

JOANNA F. FOUNTAIN is an independent cataloging consultant and adjunct faculty member in the School of Information at the University of Texas, Austin, and the School Library Media Program at McDaniel College.